Praise for

BEAST

T0049557

"One of the best music books of the year."   —Best Classic Bands

"...Kushins has done Zeppelin scholarship a service with his new biography...[He] points out subtle musical details which should enhance the understanding and appreciation of the Zeppelin catalog for any fan."   —*The Houston Press*

"[C. M. Kushins] covers all the bases in delineating the life of his subject and makes a convincing case for his iconic status...[He] brooks no dissent about his subject as the greatest rock drummer ever."
      —*Kirkus*

"A well-written, lively, and balanced biography."   —*Library Journal*

"C. M. Kushins gives us a wild, behind-the-scenes look at one of the greatest rock bands ever, and brings John 'Bonzo' Bonham back to life in this well-written rock classic."
      —Peter Leonard, bestselling author of
      Voices of the Dead and *Raylan Goes to Detroit*

BEAST

Also by C. M. Kushins

Nothing's Bad Luck: The Lives of Warren Zevon

BEAST

John Bonham and the Rise of Led Zeppelin

C. M. KUSHINS

hachette
BOOKS

NEW YORK

Hachette Books
Hachette Book Group
1290 Avenue of the Americas
New York, NY 10104
HachetteBooks.com
Twitter.com/HachetteBooks
Instagram.com/HachetteBooks

First Trade Paperback Edition: December 2022

Published by Hachette Books, an imprint of Perseus Books, LLC, a subsidiary of Hachette Book Group, Inc. The Hachette Books name and logo is a trademark of the Hachette Book Group.

The Hachette Speakers Bureau provides a wide range of authors for speaking events.

To find out more, go to www.hachettespeakersbureau.com or call (866) 376-6591.

The publisher is not responsible for websites (or their content) that are not owned by the publisher.

Print book interior design by Linda Mark.

Library of Congress Cataloging-in-Publication Data has been applied for.

ISBNs: 978-0-306-84668-7 (hardcover); 978-0-306-84667-0 (ebook);
      978-0-306-84669-4 (trade paperback)

Printed in the United States of America

LSC-C

Printing 1, 2022

For all those who never stop hearing the sound of the drums.

The days and nights went by like flashes of white and black lightning.

One midnight a lion came and stood in front of him,
proudly shaking its mane. Its voice was like a man's . . .

"Who are you?"

"Yourself—the hungry lion inside your heart and loins that at
night prowls around the sheepfolds, the kingdoms of this world,
and weighs whether or not to jump in and eat."

—NIKOS KAZANTZAKIS, *The Last Temptation of Christ*

From the midst of that radiance, the usual sound of Reality,
reverberating like a thousand thunders simultaneously sounding,
will come. That is the natural sound of thine own real self.
Be not daunted thereby, nor terrified, nor awed.

—The Tibetan Book of the Dead

CONTENTS

PART THREE
INFERNO, 1975–1980
The Loneliness of the Long-Distance Drummer

PART FOUR
ASH, 1980
Bungelosenstrasse: "The Street Without Drums"

FOREWORD

"**O**K, Dave . . . you ready?"

Andrea's thick Italian accent hung in the air of the cold, cavernous warehouse as I nervously took one last hit off my joint, nodded yes, and waited for the sharp, electric buzz of his home-made tattoo gun (fashioned from a salvaged doorbell machine) to fill the room. This was no sanctioned, licensed tattoo parlor, mind you. It was an abandoned post office in downtown Amsterdam by the name of "Van Hall" that a group of punks had squatted in in the mid-'80s, currently serving as a home base for my band Scream during my first European tour at the tender age of eighteen. Not the most sterile set-ting for such a surgical procedure, but like most fledgling rock 'n' rollers, I had longed to be branded for years. Within seconds, the burn of the needle sent chills down my spine as it sank into the soft flesh of my right shoulder, but I remained still, focusing on the searing pain while Andrea's hand gracefully traced the intricate pattern that I had carefully chosen to be my very first tattoo: the John Bonham "three circles" logo.

It's no coincidence that I chose this iconic design. As I stood in-specting Andrea's work in the dirty mirror beside us, I reflected upon the fact that this wasn't the first indelible impression John Bonham had made on my life. His drumming had penetrated much deeper than just a few millimeters beneath my skin from the first time I heard "When the Levee Breaks" at the age of twelve, eventually burrowing into my soul and transforming everything I knew (or thought I knew) about the drums. From that day forward, music was no longer just sound residing between the grooves of a record; it was a form of sublime human expression. The weight and echo of Bonham's thunderous drums seemed more like a force of nature than an instrument, rolling in hurricane-force waves through my speakers as I listened in awe, never having imagined that a human could create something so mystical. My mind had been opened, and so began a lifetime of trying to translate what I considered to be a language of its own, spending hours upon hours playing along to every Led Zeppelin album, studying each recording like an ancient text, hoping that I might someday channel his feel, anticipate his instinct, and find that sound.

It wasn't long before I realized that this was totally impossible. Beyond his humbling, superhuman abilities, I soon discovered that there are some things in life that just cannot be replicated or fully understood. Like a fingerprint or strand of DNA, sometimes there is only one. This is most true in the case of John Henry Bonham, and herein lie the mystery and indefinable concept of his "feel."

Every musician plays differently, we know, but there must be something intangible that differentiates the music written on a chart from what is created by one drummer to the next. Is it the way that each mind interprets a pattern? The internal clock that is defined by one's physical and emotional construct? The way they see the space between the notes? I have watched many producers try to explain and manufacture "feel," but I am convinced that overintellectualizing it is futile. It is something divine that only the universe can create, like a heartbeat or a star. A solitary design within every musician that is only their own. I liken "feel" to the cadence of poetry, sometimes comforting, other times unsettling, but always a gift from one soul to another. A romance between the giver and receiver that serves as the punctuation of one's truth.

To me, the test of a great drummer comes from this short five-second exercise. Close your eyes, hit play, and if you can name them in that time, then they have achieved their "sound." That I equate to greatness, no matter how proficient. A sonic signature. Their drummer DNA; their fingerprint. And there is no better example of this than the grace and fury that Bonham captured on Led Zeppelin's eight studio (and four live) albums, recordings that changed the course of drumming history forever.

From the seductive swing of "Since I've Been Loving You" and "I'm Gonna Crawl," to the charging funk of "Trampled Under Foot" and "The Wanton Song," to the hypnotic pulse of "Kashmir" and "In the Light," Bonham's sound is entirely his own, showing a range of emotion and dynamic that not only dwarfs every drummer who has ever lived but also reveals a deep sense of empathy for the listener. This is heart and soul laid bare for all to hear, a resounding series of confessions from a man who didn't need a microphone or pen to describe himself, just a drum kit and two sticks (which he would sometimes forgo, using only his bare hands). With every seismic kick and snare, he was transcribing a sort of melodic EKG, giving us a glimpse into what made him tick. *His* DNA. In so doing, he was offering the listeners a chance to open themselves up to their own raw emotions— lust, fury, pain. That's where the empathy came in.

I believe that the connection between a musician's heart and hands can serve as a direct window into his soul, and if that window is opened, their true voice can be revealed. Over the years I have discovered that one can learn more about a person with instruments on than off, finding an intimacy and intuition that can be attributed only to uninhibited musical communication, something Zeppelin clearly had an abundance of. It's rare, but when found it can eclipse most other connections in life. A language learned by ear. Fortunately, the world was witness to this every time Jimmy Page, John Paul Jones, Robert Plant, and John Bonham played a song together.

Volumes have been dedicated to Bonham's power and precision, but to be honest I have never been one for technical introspection. Never mind how a part was played. I would rather know why. What drives a musician to do what they do the way that they do it? Could it be every day that led to that moment? Every word they ever said? Every person they ever loved, feeling they ever felt?

Chad Kushins's *Beast* is a deep and entertaining dive into the life of John Bonham, one that walks with him up to and through his days with Led Zeppelin. To read *Beast* is to add another dimension to John Bonham, shedding further light on what inspired him to play those iconic beats, and serves as a worthy companion piece to his recorded work, which is the greatest story of all. And as we continue on our ongoing quest to translate his language, to decode the magic of his feel, let's allow his music to serve as the celebration of the man behind the myth, the greatest drummer of all time. After all, there can be only one.

It has been thirty-four years since that night in Amsterdam when I received my first tattoo, and every time I look in the mirror I am reminded of its meaning. Over time, tattoos inevitably fade as the ink begins to blur and bleed. The shallow puncture of a needle can brand only so deep; it's the heart that is marked forever. And we can all thank John Bonham for that. So, let's begin.

"We've done four already, but now we're steady, and then they went . . . 1 . . . 2 . . . 3 . . . 4 . . . "

—*Dave Grohl, 2021*

PROLOGUE

A FINAL, RADIANT HOUR

Sunday, July 17, 1977
The Kingdome
Seattle, Washington
10:20 p.m.

Two and a half hours into the show, under dozens of hot lights—their multitude of colors burning their beams down upon the four men—thousands of twinkling dots in the vast darkness formed a swaying ocean of incandescence like a sea full of stars. The cigarette lighters among the sixty-two thousand in attendance had been flickering since the music started—since fans first heard the sound of the drums rumbling and watched the pyrotechnics light up the stage. The thunder and the lightning.

The lithe blond front man took to the center of the stage, brushing his damp, curled locks behind his ear with a flick of the wrist. He moved it with a flourish of his left hand before stepping to the microphone. The calls of the thousands resounded in the arena's echo as an all-encompassing deafening pulse. He was visibly weary. Weary from the previous thirteen songs he'd already performed, from the thirty-nine shows this leg of the tour around America had included, from a lingering limp—the memento of the automobile accident that should have killed him.

"This next piece features a man who needs very little introduction," announced Robert Plant. "The man who played tambourine on 'Battle of Evermore'—*John Henry Bonham! Over the top!*"

The final word repeated electronically through the arena's PA system, screeching into a falsetto alarm—"*TOP-OP-OP!*"

John Bonham had long believed that a band's drummer should be featured front and center on the stage, symbolically leading the other musicians as the ensemble's engine, while also amplifying the sound of the drums even louder for the crowd. During any given performance by Led Zeppelin, there would come a point in every set list when John would have the opportunity for as long, brash, and kinetic a solo as he desired—the closest thing to becoming the visible nucleus he'd always envisioned. And he used that opportunity for all it was worth: over the course of the band's nine-year existence, John's time in the spotlight had evolved from ten minutes to the better part of an hour.

Bandmates Plant, bassist John Paul Jones, and leader in both guitar and overall creative direction Jimmy Page didn't mind backing down for so long a hiatus; it would mean a good twenty minutes backstage to sit down, catch their breath, grab a cigarette, or knock back a few swigs before again being on public display. But first, Page would lead into John's solo with two scorching rounds of "Out on the Tiles," the spotlight revealing Page's own presence behind Plant in unison with the first explosion of the guitarist's 1959 Gibson Les Paul Standard, a warm, brown contrast to the blaring sight of his "poppy" white-dragon jumpsuit—the "heroin suit."

From there, John was on his own.

Tonight would be no different. As he launched into what would be a twenty-four-minute rendition of his famed solo, "Moby Dick," John was unaware that it would be one of the last times American audiences would have the chance to see him in all his brazen glory. And while there were always detractors who shunned John's legendary marathon solos, accusing both him and the entire band of self-indulgence, most would stand in awe of the human firework dominating their senses. That had always been the point of the song, John's own concoction that not only displayed his own abilities and virtuosity, but also demonstrated for fans, critics, and scores of jealous fellow drummers just how innovative his technique could be.

He had been working on the extended solo for years, cribbing a few licks from Art Blakey and moves from Gene Krupa, while adding his own signature rapid-fire paradiddles into a shotgun speed, making for an almost trancelike spectacle once he really got rolling: forsaking a traditional linear pattern for his own layered style, working his booted feet into double-kicks for a brash filler that was more like controlled chaos. As John smashed clockwise in lightning circles around the kit's toms, he added a foot ostinato faster and faster, bringing Pat's piece to a climax like a flow of power. Halfway through, John would throw the sticks and take to the toms with his hands, leaving his body drenched in sweat and his hands smeared with blood.

When John fell in love, it was fun to entertain the soon-to-be Mrs. Bonham with the one-man show, so much to her amusement that John had originally named the track for her. When Led Zeppelin took off, he'd played "Pat's Delight" at every show. Jimmy loved it, too. By the time the mysterious guitarist-cum-producer opted to add the song to the group's second album, John had renamed it to match young son Jason's own innocent observation. Indeed, the thunderous solo was, as the child had claimed, as big as Melville's mythic whale. "Moby Dick" became a near-instantaneous drumming classic.

By Led Zeppelin's 1977 tour of North America, John had refined it into a massive performance piece, integrating electronic elements and extended portions and allowing the modernized tension lugs of his recently acquired stainless-steel Ludwig to get even louder. Hearing the new sound before heading out on tour, the band had renamed the song once again: "Over the Top."

The title was more than appropriate for the song; it spoke volumes about John's style—and the band itself. The group's notorious penchant for hard partying and even harder living was slowly catching up with them all. This tour, their eleventh across the United States, had seemed doomed from the start: *the grounding of their beloved Boeing 707,* The Starship . . . *the latest album not selling as well as the others, much to everyone's chagrin . . . the riots in Cincinnati and Tampa . . . Jimmy's "food poisoning" and the canceled shows . . .*

It seemed as though the only thing right this time around was the money, always the money. Their manager saw to that—all six feet and three hundred pounds of him—and anything that could even be attributed to a dollar sign he strictly monitored with the help of his notorious henchmen.

But the worst of the tour—Led Zeppelin's final one—was yet to come. In only a few days, Robert Plant would be called on the road and notified that his five-year-old son was dead—and John would be arrested in America for the first time, facing criminal action for letting his rage get the best of him. *At one time,* he thought, *this country had loved us.*

As John played his solo, none of that existed: not the sins of the past or the crimes yet to be committed. For tonight, there was only the music—the playing, the rising storm that had brought John to America from the quiet English village where he was known simply as the affable carpenter with a love of cars and designer suits.

Tonight, there was only this—the final, radiant hour when the music and its power could still keep a beast at bay.

PART ONE

KINDLING

1948–1968

The Flight of the Rocket

Chapter One

MAY 1948–DECEMBER 1965

I t was as if by predetermination that John Henry Bonham III was born to work with his hands.

Every element of his being spoke of hard labor. Twenty-six hours of it to push him out, and only then for his heart to immediately stop beating. The on-duty doctor had already left for the day, driving nurses into a frenzy to find a fill-in. When one was finally found, the infant was revived. And so, on May 31, 1948, John Bonham was born and died and was born again in Redditch, Worcestershire, in the Midlands of England. He had been born with what was considered an extremely enlarged and bruised cranium. The day nurse told the child's parents, John Henry II (Jack or "Jacko" to his closest mates) and Joan Isobel, that their son's survival had been a miracle—a ten-pound, four-ounce miracle.

Despite the numeral, while John was named for his father, he was not named for his grandfather. Eschewing chronology, the young parents took as a namesake the newborn's great-great-great-grandfather. The first John Bonham had died in 1871; Jacko Bonham was born in 1918, exactly two hundred years after the first Bonham—Thomas, of Oxfordshire—appeared in Midlands records. Jacko was also the youngest of three sons, all born and raised in Worcestershire. Their father, Albert, had been one of eight. Indeed, the roots of the Bonham family bloodline were as permeated into the Midlands soil as the blood-red clay sediment of the nearby River Arrow, the oft-flooded vein of the greater River Avon.

The Bonhams' hometown of Redditch held much in the way of superstitions but was largely unaccustomed to such miracles. History's first mention of the town harked back to the Middle Ages, forever linking the land with the spread of the Black Plague. Centuries before, the Romans had cut a road through the region, using the path as the main thoroughfare across the occupied city of Alcester. During the modern era, the ancient road had long since become known as Iknield Street, the Roman path swallowed up by sections of the A38 M5 motorway. Beginning at Bourton-on-the-Water and ending at Rotherham, where once essential salts had been carted by caravans, now trucks hauled freight. Likewise, the Roman city of Alcester had eventually been rechristened as Derby—then, finally, Birmingham.

Located only ten miles south of Birmingham and southeast of Kidderminster, the industrial town lay in the very center of the Black Country—those areas north and west of Birmingham so named for the dense soot and smog that would billow from the endless sea of factory chimneys, casting an ever-present dark pall in the sky. As early as 1830, the Black Country's 130 square miles of lush countryside had already been transformed into a landscape defined by mines, foundries, and factories—a consequence of sitting upon the thickest coal seam in the country.

Although the glory days of the Black Country's mining industry had passed by the time John Henry III was born, laborers were still proudly hewing coal out of the land's rich earth. Iron and steel were worked intensively in local factories for decades, until glassmaking eventually took over as the region's greatest export. To many, the blood and sweat decanted within the Black Country had funded the wealth and luxury of the British Empire: the anchors and chains of the RMS *Titanic* had been forged in the fires of the nearby town of Netherton, while the ship's famed glass and stemware were molded in nearby Stourbridge. At the same time, Redditch had blossomed as the center for needle making and fishhooks. By the birth of the third John Henry Bonham, the production of such gear had become the very lifeblood of the town he called home. It had been through the town's laborious roots that Redditch remained prosperous during some of its most economically harrowing years following World War II. In 1939 Redditch found itself the temporary home of "the Erie Hammer," a four-hundred-ton piece of state-of-the-art machinery constructed across the Atlantic Ocean in America and shipped to the Midlands piece by piece. Newspapers had deemed the monolithic construction, used by the Allies to quickly manufacture the pistons of England's aero engines, "the largest hammer in the world"—one whose size and power could rival even that of Mjolnir, the chosen weapon of the Norse god of thunder, and whose abilities had helped slay the Axis armies.

Indeed, nearly a decade before the birth of John Henry Bonham III, Redditch had already been home to a hammer of the gods.

✳ ✳ ✳

THE BONHAMS LIVED IN A SMALL THREE-BEDROOM SEMIDETACHED house in Hunt End, a village district just on the outskirts of town and about twenty miles from the larger city of Brum, as locals lovingly referred to Birmingham. Jacko was a carpenter by trade and owned and operated the family's construction firm, J. H. Bonham & Son, a long-standing company stable enough for the family to remain relatively comfortable throughout much of John's youth—a rarity among the primarily blue-collar community. However, all members of the Bonham family pitched in—Joan (née Sargent) worked as the manager of a small local newspaper shop, while both John and younger brother Michael (Mick) worked alongside their father as soon as they'd both reached their teens.

"As kids, we went to the building sites, because of our granddad's firm, which dad and our uncle Ernie ran," brother Mick Bonham recalled years later in his posthumously published memoir. "They

seemed like mega-playgrounds, and me and John were always mess-
ing around there." There would be many more such playgrounds for
the Bonham boys to enjoy throughout their youth. With the end of
the Second World War, the Black Country's landscape was forever
changed—Redditch included. Although the war had been won, its
aftereffects could be felt by hundreds of families. The rationing of
foodstuffs, such as meat and dairy, continued throughout Britain until
1954, when the Bonham boys were already in grade school.

During John and Mick's earliest years, many of the cities and
towns throughout the Black Country still bore the scars from six years
of warfare: as a major manufacturer of munitions, the Black Country's
industrial nucleus had been a prime target for German bombs. Although Redditch had been fortunate in retaining most of its inherent
natural beauty, many of its sister communities were punctuated by
the sight of blasted houses and the shells of abandoned buildings. It
was an everyday occurrence for children playing in the streets to find
the tail ends of used bombs and shards of jagged, burned shrapnel.

※ ※ ※

THE BONHAM BROTHERS WERE SENT TO THE NEARBY WILTON HOUSE
Private School on Worcester Road, complete with high expectations
of its students and a strictly enforced uniform that Mick recalled "was
brown, white, and blue stripes with a cap to match." Two years Mick's
senior, John began his formal schooling in 1953, all the experience primarily consisting of "three classrooms with three lady teachers and
a matronly headmistress who," Mick later claimed, "luckily for us,
didn't believe in slapping young children if they were naughty.

"We used to have to walk past another school at the bottom of our
road, called St. Stephen's," Mick remembered, adding that the boys'
daily route always led them through the center of town before winding up at their home at the end of Easemore Road. "We went to the
posh school, and they were slumming it. Of course, the kids would
shout out, 'Got your pajamas on?' Our John would say to me, 'Come

on, kid, let's have a bit of this'—and there'd be ten more of them! . . .
We had to run the gauntlet every night."

It was generally understood that no matter the sticky situation,
the Bonham brothers stuck together. "We had our fair share of fights,"
Mick later explained. "But all brothers do. One minute you love each
other, and the next minute you are knocking the hell out of each
other. . . . When we worked on the building sites, we often had fisti-
cuffs, and he sacked me more times than he sacked anybody else.

"When we were at school together, John might have been kicking
the hell out of me, but as soon as somebody else came near me, the
two of us would have a go back. He'd stick up for me every time."
Mick and John took to calling this new phase of neighborhood bully-
ing the "start of the Hard Fights"—and it seemed it would never end.

※ ※ ※

IN 1960, JOHN WAS SENT TO LODGE FARM COUNTY SECONDARY
School, beginning four years of intensive studies under Headmaster
Gordon Antiss, a particularly strict disciplinarian, "a tall, lean man
who ruled by the cane"—once telling young John that he "would
probably not even make a good dustman." The younger Mick, on
the other hand, was enrolled in the nearby Ridgeway School. It was
both a luxury and a necessity for the brothers to attend such prestigious private schools, as the new decade also saw a noticeable rise
in the Black Country's population and an overcrowding within the
school districts. Only a few months before John graduated in 1964,
Redditch had been officially declared a "new town" by the British
government's New Towns Act of 1946, a law that sought to relocate the families of poor or bombed-out housing following the war.
The New Towns mandate caused Redditch's population to increase
dramatically during the Bonham brothers' adolescence, rising from
thirty-two thousand to around seventy-seven thousand throughout
the towns of the Black Country. Nearby housing developments such
as Church Hill, Matchborough, Winyates, Lodge Park, and Woodrow

were created to accommodate a large overspill from the industrially expanding Birmingham. Redditch had been envisioned as a flagship town and was constructed using new methods of urban planning: all the main roads were banked to reduce noise to the new housing estates, and the whole town of Redditch was landscaped. It only helped that nationally, the economy was on an upswing and wages for skilled labor increased. A rush by the British to be socially upwardly mobile left a void for unskilled workers that was filled by successive governments with immigrant labor from around the Commonwealth. With these workers populating the steel mills and factories—and automotive plants, as well—the towns and cities of the Black Country soon ranked among the country's most multicultural areas. For the first time in its history, the Black Country became host to families from the Caribbean, India, and Pakistan—creating a true melting pot and affirming Birmingham's status as the most populated city in the United Kingdom outside of London.

Under the new law, the Bonham family prospered; luckily for Jacko, the influx of new families necessitated the construction of new homes. Atypical of the times and especially within their own community, this meant that the Bonham boys enjoyed a comfortable existence, complete with their private school tuition and three holidays a year. Young John Bonham was brought up with the expectation that he would one day enter the family construction business, settling down to "a proper job" that would guarantee the type of stability that eluded so many others in their region, but had blessed the Bonhams.

John, however, was already thinking quite differently, later recalling, "I was determined to be a drummer as soon as I left school. I was so keen, I would have played for nothing. In fact, I did for a long time. But my parents stuck by me."

✳ ✳ ✳

JOHN'S LIFELONG OBSESSION WITH PERCUSSION BEGAN AT THE AGE of five. He had started drumming on a bath-salts container, tying thin strands of wire across the barrel to filter in the salts from the bottom;

he also began beating out rhythms on tin coffee cans using kitchen utensils, instinctively replicating snare-drum-like sounds. In this, his earliest search for a satisfactory sound, John trolled around the kitchen playing all the pots and pans and driving his parents crazy. By his tenth birthday, however, Joan broke down and bought him a real snare drum—a new toy that he banged to pieces over time. Five years later, his dad followed suit and bought John his first proper kit. "It was almost prehistoric," John later recalled. "Most of it was rust."

As Mick later remembered, John's first real tutelage came from a family friend. Jacko Bonham kept the family caravan, or trailer, and boat, the *Isobel*, at the nearby riverside town of Stourport-on-Severn. It was there that they met Charlie Atkins, a "lovely" man who rented his own caravan next to the Bonham family's during holidays and summer weekends. Atkins was the leader of a Birmingham-based dance band that specialized in tango, waltz, and fox-trot, the kind, as Mick recalled, "where the band use Brylcreem and the drummer uses brushes." During those visits, however, Atkins was always available to talk music with the Bonham boys and took a keen interest in young John's obsession with the drums. "It may not sound exciting now," Mick later admitted, "but to John, this was the business, and he would sit and listen to Charlie talk about *paradiddles* and other such drumming terminology until the cows came home. It was after one of these meetings that Charlie gave John his own set of brushes, which was fine by me because there was no way they would hurt as much as sticks."

As a gift, Atkins also gave John a white pearl snare drum to add to his small collection; the boy had already used his saved pocket money to acquire a snare drum, bass drum, and floor tom. When John was eleven years old, Atkins had enough confidence in his young pupil to invite him to play his first gig, sitting in with the dance band at the Caravan Club's Members Dance. "This, I believe, was the turning point for John Bonham," noted Mick, "and I don't think that from this point onwards, anyone or anything was ever going to stop him from being a drummer."

By the time he was fourteen, John was already playing with local bands and in school events. Despite his rambunctious reputation, he even provided the sound effects for a school Christmas pageant, playing his beloved drum kit on the side of the stage.

Although John showed genuine aptitude and enthusiasm for his father's carpentry lessons, the boy's natural talent on drums had already diverted his attention toward a future in music. That year, when pupils were asked what they wanted upon middle school graduation, only John had a ready answer: "I want to be a drummer."

※ ※ ※

MUSIC WAS EVER PRESENT IN THE BONHAM HOUSEHOLD, ALTHOUGH the soundtrack remained limited. John and his younger brother sought solace in the changing sounds of the radio waves, which always brought the latest chart toppers into their home. As the airwaves grew more diversified, so popular music in Britain became as much of a melting pot as Birmingham itself. Longtime pop staples like Nat King Cole, Doris Day, and Frankie Lane were soon brushed aside, as Little Richard, Bill Haley, and Elvis Presley made their way to the forefront. Within Birmingham, the "Brum scene" also saw new acts emerge, younger musicians inspired by what they were hearing on their radios; local acts like Lonnie Donegan, Adam Faith, Cliff Richard, and Marty Wilde soon took hold of the local fan base.

Young John Bonham's own taste in music was decidedly eclectic, thanks to both the melting pot of UK radio and the personal preferences of his parents. John's musical influences soon stretched to Edmundo Ross and His Band—one of the first mainstream successes in Latin American music—whose drumming riffs and heavy percussion inspired John's own technical experimentation. "We would sit in front of the 'wireless' every Saturday and listen to Edmundo's show," remembered Mick, "which was a rare treat, seeing that there were only three choices of music at home: Jacko's Lena Horne albums, Mum's Frank Sinatra records, and *Children's Favourites* for us kids.

Nevertheless, it was all making way for a new era of sound drifting over from America, namely, rock 'n' roll."

At the time, the music most widely accepted adhered to the typical social norms of 1950s Britain—strict and "buttoned-up." All that began to change, however, with the emergence of Elvis Presley, whose early releases during the summer of 1954 directly led to new blends of black soul and blues music coupled with the "white" sounds of country and honky-tonk. America called it rock 'n' roll—and Elvis's international appeal was soon followed by the likes of fellow rockers Jerry Lee Lewis, Little Richard, and Buddy Holly. The first rock 'n' roll infiltrator into Birmingham arrived in February 1957, in the form of thirty-two-year-old Bill Haley, whose singles "Rock Around the Clock" and "Shake, Rattle and Roll" became instant sensations and inaugurated the coming shifts in America's music scene. When Haley and his band performed at the Birmingham Odeon that winter, local teenagers looped around the building to get tickets.

But of all the early rock 'n' roll songs that seemed to really perk John's critical ear, it was drummer Sandy Nelson's 1959 percussion-laden instrumental "Teen Beat." Like the guitar-driven Duane Eddy hit "Rebel-Rouser" the year before, Nelson's instrumental sleeper hit had struck a chord with teenagers who wanted to get up and dance, sending the tune to number four on the UK singles chart. John was "mesmerized" by the song, sitting three days straight at his drum kit until he could perfectly replicate the song's distinctive percussion patterns. When he'd mastered it, his ambition became "like kick-starting a Harley-Davidson," according to Mick, who added that before long John claimed that "he was going to form a band."

Even without a group of his own or formal training, John instinctively gravitated toward any musical genre that posed a challenge to his natural abilities and any preconceived notions of drumming that he'd heard before. He was particularly obsessed with the jazz techniques of Gene Krupa and Buddy Rich and the showmanship that both men brought to the instrument, demonstrating the spectacle that a drum virtuoso could harness in truly acting as a musical group's driving force.

"Gene Krupa was God," brother Mick recalled, adding that it was watching the 1956 biopic *The Benny Goodman Story* that started John's love of jazz drumming—particularly a scene featuring Krupa playing tom-toms on his theme tune, "Sing, Sing, Sing." John was also enamored with a scene in the 1946 film *Beat the Band*, wherein Krupa played with sticks on boiler-room steam pipes. "John had decided that this was the drummer he wanted to emulate," said Mick, "and he spent hours listening to and learning Krupa's technique."

In later years, John's youngest sibling, Deborah, would too remember her brother's affection for the two jazz greats, whose music had become a staple in the Bonham household. "John got his influence from Gene Krupa and Buddy Rich, because my mum and dad used to play those bands all the time," Deborah later claimed. "They loved the Tommy Dorsey band and Glenn Miller and Harry James and Frank Sinatra. . . . And that's what John used to play to, in the shed, till the neighbors would come 'round and start banging on the door to my mum: 'Tell him to turn it down!'"

Still in his teens, John could be seen mimicking Krupa's signature posture over his kit, leaning over his drums as he played. Like Krupa, John wanted to get subtle sounds and controlled reverberations out of his kit, as opposed to merely bashing them. It was a lifelong exploration that would often confound fellow musicians and create a misguided notion that it was John's forcefulness that was the source of his power. When the Bonham family attended a Harry James concert twenty miles away at Birmingham Town Hall, young John was impressed by James's drummer, Sonny Payne. Witnessing Payne perform one of his signature stunt moves—bouncing sticks off the skins and catching them behind his back—it stood as real-life proof that a band's drummer wasn't just a backing member of the rhythm section; with the right stage presence, the drummer could be a fellow soloist— he could be the star attraction.

Another such performer who helped shaped John's views on showmanship was flamboyant rock 'n' roller Screaming Lord Sutch. At the time, the bizarre entertainer—born David Edward Sutch in Hampstead, London, in 1940—was slowly leading the way in "shock rock," making headlines throughout the United Kingdom with his horror movie–inspired stage show. Popping out of a black coffin dressed as Jack the Ripper, Sutch dangled macabre props, such as daggers and skulls, in front of his audience while belting out rock 'n' roll lyrics with all the high-octane wildness of Little Richard. Sutch garnered further scandal with his highly publicized attempts to become a member of Parliament via his self-created Monster Raving Loony Party, demonstrating how a carefully crafted persona could only add to a performer's offstage image and mystique.

John was fascinated, to say the least. Desperate to see the shock rocker live and, hopefully, hustle his way backstage for an autograph, he'd pedaled his bicycle forty-eight miles round-trip to see Sutch's show by himself. During a family holiday in Brighton on the South Coast of England later that year, John and Mick were also able to attend a concert of local rock 'n' roll hero Joe Brown, whose 1960 single "The Darktown Strutters' Ball" had been a fast hit. The Bonham brothers witnessed as Brown and the Bruvvers launched into their cover of the Spotniks' "Havah Nagila." During the song, Brown swung his guitar around and played his blazing solo behind his head.

It was after returning from that trip that John Bonham made his first attempt to assemble his own rock 'n' roll band. "John returned to school and made friends with another aspiring young musician called John Hill, who played guitar," claimed Mick Bonham. "Together, they decided to form a band, but before they got started, they would spend many a night setting up the drum kit, leaning the guitar against it and standing back staring at their mock stage setup—moving it every now and then for better effect. . . . The name of the band would be the 'Avengers,' but they unfortunately never got a gig."

✳ ✳ ✳

ASIDE FROM PREDOMINANTLY LEARNING TO PLAY HANDS-ON, JOHN eventually sought the advice of a local drummer who was widely considered one of the best throughout the Midlands. In 1962 he knocked on Garry Allcock's door without thinking twice, sure that both his seriousness about the drums and a shared passion for fast cars would forgive the spur-of-the-moment intrusion. Luckily for John, it did.

"The front doorbell rang, and there's this lad standing on the doorstep saying, 'Are you Garry Allcock? Do you play drums? Do you work at Austin? My name's John Bonham. I'm a drummer and I'm potty about cars,'" Allcock remembered. "He just turned up at the house and asked to come in."

Another Redditch-born musician, Allcock was recently married and was completing an engineering apprenticeship at the Austin Motor Company. He had started playing drums in 1951 and was very much into big bands and jazz. "I had been playing with orchestras for some years," Allcock recalled. "John was working on a building site at the time—he was obviously much younger than me, but someone had told him there was a drummer living up at Astwood Bank that he should have a chat with."

Allcock's own technique was solidly based on traditionally jazz drumming, the fundamentals of which John was just beginning to meld with the rock 'n' roll stylings he studied on the radio. "To be honest, I never thought John was very good, although he was a quick learner," said Allcock. "Being brought up on Count Basie and Stan Kenton, I was into big-band drumming. For me, all the beat-group stuff was comparatively easy. . . . Half the time, we were talking about cars. I could see why he sought me out, because I was a drummer doing a car-design apprenticeship."

Much to the chagrin of Allcock's young wife, he and John would set up twin kits in the front living room of the older drummer's home. Hanging out with Allcock also inspired John's interest in listening to other rock 'n' roll bands. Although he was by no means a purist, jazz had provided him with enough inspiration to begin playing with the sounds of a traditional kit, soon integrating jazz technique and flourishes into more modern, primal rock 'n' roll.

During the course of a friendship that would last for decades, Allcock observed that young John wasn't really interested in the jazz-oriented syncopated style of playing that he preferred, but he admirably studied the rules in order to successfully break them. As he had expressed early on in his conversations with Allcock, John already believed that the drummer was placed front and center for a reason: to steal the show. Within the next year, that philosophy would pay off. He was soon in demand among bands needing last-minute fill-ins. John's goal, however, was never simply to take part in a jam session; from the very beginning, he meant to bring his notorious competitive edge to the stage.

⁂ ⁂ ⁂

"THERE'S A LOT OF HONEST WORK OUT THERE, JOHN," JACKO OFTEN reminded his oldest son. "You can make a decent living if you really want to."

For all his jamming, practicing, and self-discipline at his kit, John was yet to find a steady means of turning music into an honest living. With John having recently graduated, the family pressure had begun to mount. Buying himself time and staving off the constant nagging from his parents, John fell back on the dependability of his father's construction company. For years, keeping one foot in his carpentry apprenticeship would continue to provide his only steady source of income.

But working within the family business didn't give John a pass to come and go as he pleased; Jacko Bonham was sure to keep both his sons in line during their periodic stints as laborers. Soon, John had to grow accustomed to a daily routine that found him getting up at seven in order to report for duty at one of his father's many construction sites, then getting home by dusk with just enough time to wash up and head back out to play with various local rock 'n' roll bands throughout the night. Most nights, John wouldn't return home until dawn, leaving him only one to two hours of sleep before having to rise again for Jacko's next backbreaking assignment. "I went to work for my father in the building trade, but drumming was the only thing I was any good at, and I stuck at it," John later told a reporter. "So gradually, it was more music and less building, but I always worked hard all the time."

At the same time that the harsh physical labor of the construction trade built up his strength and endurance, his forays into the Brum club scene made him a known face among scores of reputable local musicians. Garry Allcock may have been the earliest friend to double as a mentor, but it wasn't long after that he made the acquaintance of another drummer, Bill Harvey, at the local youth club in 1963. According to Mick Bonham, the Redditch Youth Club was the best place for young musicians like John to network and score tryouts, as it was the only local venue that consistently welcomed new acts, like Bill Harvey's Blue Star Trio, to the venue.

"The group comprised of Terry Beale and Mick Ellis, a pair of guitarists and singers who had played together after splitting with the Nighthawks," Mick later explained. "Someone suggested they might sound better if they had a drummer, so enter Bill Harvey."

※ ※ ※

AT TWENTY-THREE, HARVEY HAD EIGHT YEARS ON JOHN, BUT HE had already established himself as one of the hottest drummers in Redditch, as well as being a founding member of the popular Blue Star Trio—a small rock ensemble that had already won over its fair share of devoted teens throughout the Black Country. "John was a bit younger than me," Harvey later noted. "I was over twenty and not supposed to be at the youth club anymore, but I went because it was a place to play. They used to have a different band on every Wednesday night, and quite often Roy Wood and Bev Bevan would play there."

Harvey recalled that it was during his stint managing another Redditch-based band that often rehearsed at a club called the Cellar on nearby Queen Street that he first crossed paths with fifteen-year-old John Bonham. "John appeared there one night. He was a tiny lad, although he blossomed out later. I guess we were sort of wary of each other, but we struck up a relationship. I had been playing for some years, and John was very pushy, even then."

But it was at a Blue Star Trio gig that John was finally given his opportunity to show the band what he could do on drums. Just before showtime, Harvey got into a heated argument with the Trio's dual guitarists, Beale and Ellis. "They were a bit lazy about helping to load the equipment," Harvey clarified, "and I said, 'Sod it, if that's your attitude.' I had the van, and I had to load and unload the gear every night. I just got fed up and blew my top."

Having witnessed the altercation, John was quickly asked to sit in once Harvey refused to take the stage. "When I went along to the club, I was sick in my stomach to see John playing my gig," he later remembered. "But he said, 'Come on, let's do a solo together—I'm only sitting in for you.' So, we both got up on the same kit. I played the two tom-toms, and John played the snare drum."

The crowd loved it. Based on the audience response, John immediately suggested they make their duo a regular act, to which Harvey enthusiastically agreed. Rehearsing every Wednesday afternoon for weeks, the two quickly saw the fruits of their woodshedding together pay off: in addition to the Blue Star Trio's straightforward rock shows, John and Harvey racked up a number of their own side gigs. "[John] would pull me up out of the audience," Harvey said, "or the other way around, and we'd do this great drum routine together. Everybody used to say, 'How did they do that?' They didn't realize we had rehearsed it for hours. And it seemed like we were rivals, playing against each other. . . . [The audience] never realized we were the best of mates."

Not yet sixteen, John was beginning to earn his first legion of fans, as well as his first acknowledgment in the press; when an announcement of the Blue Star Trio's residency at the Redditch Youth Club ran in the local press on July 16, 1963, John was pictured as a full-fledged member of the group—clean-shaven and decked out in a blazer and tie.

Maybe there was a future in music for John after all, Jacko and Joan Bonham mused, expressing their newfound faith in him with a symbolic gift—a brand-new sparkling red Trixon drum set.

✳ ✳ ✳

"WHEN I WAS SIXTEEN, I WENT FULL-TIME INTO MUSIC FOR A WHILE," John later remembered, "and we'd have an attempt to make a success of a professional group. [But] then you'd have to go back to work to make some money to live. You'd go on the road, and then there'd be no more gigs and no more money, and you were back to where you started. . . . You had to do that to survive and play, locally."

While his parents were now supportive of John's drumming career, he continued to line his pockets from the daily rigors of "bricking" for Jacko and his crew. He was only a year out of school, after all, and aspirations for rock superstardom came with no guarantees. Simultaneously, John continued his stints with both the Blue Star Trio and Harvey and continued to practice new techniques and styles. "[John] was very adaptable," Bill Harvey noted. "On top of that, he was self-taught, which made a heck of a difference because you could pick things up—you didn't have to rehearse too much. The one thing that marked him out at that stage was his kick-drum technique, which absolutely flabbergasted all of us, the way he could do these triplets with the bass drum. I asked him once how he did it, and he said, 'Oh, no, I'm not gonna tell ya, but I'll tell ya what I have done: I've took the leather strap off the bass-drum pedal, and I've put a bike chain on instead.' And of course, all the bass-drum pedals now are chain driven. To my mind, he was the first one that ever did it."

Like Garry Allcock before him, Harvey's influence on John's playing extended beyond mere hands-on tips. Whereas Allcock had shared his affection for big-band players with John, Bill Harvey introduced the younger drummer to the styles of his favorite jazz players—Joe Morello of the Dave Brubeck Quartet being at the top of the list.

"Joe did this finger-tapping thing where he wet his thumb and rubbed it on the snare drum to produce a lion's roar," Harvey recalled. "He'd imitate a bow and arrow, and also did this African rhythm by finger-tapping that was absolutely fabulous."

Morello was also well known among jazz aficionados for his unusual time signatures on a number of Brubeck's crossover hits, including "Take Five" and "It's a Raggy Waltz." Additionally, he had developed a unique finger-control technique, which enabled him to play high-speed triplets with one stick on the snare drum while summoning a diverse array of different sounds. It was this signature technique—the triplet—that would prove the greatest impact on John Bonham's own heavy rock 'n' roll sound.

Bill Harvey also taught John one of Morello's tricks for hitting the drum with his hands and fingers without injuring himself. Ever determined, John spent days at his Trixon kit without taking a break, slowly mastering the intricate fingering and rhythms with his bare hands. When Harvey visited a few days later, John answered the door with his fingers wrapped in Elastoplast bandages. "I said, 'John, what have you done?'" Harvey remembered. "He'd cut his hands by hitting the edge of the cymbals." John was soon known for solos so energetic, his hands would be streaked with blood by the end.

✳ ✳ ✳

JOHN ALSO ENJOYED BRITISH BANDS OF THE TIME, SUCH AS THE Hollies, Johnny Kidd & the Pirates, and the Graham Bond Organisation, but it was American rhythm and blues (R&B) that was most fascinating to him at the time. "It was just that feel, that sound," he claimed. "I said to myself, 'I'll get that sound.'" It was the start of his quest for the big, open drum tone, which led him to go for large drums, free of the dampers and mufflers that roadies, soundmen, and recording engineers liked to inflict on drum kits in their efforts to control the sound. As far as his approach to playing, John later summed it up by saying: "I think feeling is a lot more important than technique. . . . If you play technically, you sound like everyone else—it's originality that counts. I yell out like a bear when I'm playing to give my playing a boost.

"I like it to be like a thunderstorm."

✳ ✳ ✳

BETWEEN THE NIGHTS OF CONSTANT GIGGING AND ALL FORMS OF personal study in his rare downtime, John was beginning to meld the influences of the diverse music around him and the practices of other drummers into both his playing and his unique kit customizations. Bill Harvey remembered a strange positioning that John adopted on his snare drum, keeping it lower to the floor than almost any other player—in addition to the homemade effects he insisted made his sound stand apart. "We used to argue about this," Harvey later laughed. "I had always been told to keep the snare drum as high as possible. John said, 'Why? I like it down in me lap.' I tried to explain this meant the drum strokes had further to travel. If the drum was higher, it made the rim shots easier. . . . 'Oh, bullshit,' he'd say."

Harvey once inquired into John's astounding ability to create the triplets, only to be playfully shunned as if he'd asked the secret to a magic trick. "'How did you do that bass-drum triplet, John?'" Harvey remembered asking. "'Ah,' said John, 'you've gotta have the technique,' and just laughed. He wouldn't give away the secret, not even as a trade-off. Maybe he guessed the future of rock drumming lay in foot power, rather than finger control. . . . His feel for rock music was unbelievable."

Instead of divulging his trade secrets, John instead agreed to fill in for Harvey at a few pickup gigs, as he was now able to play nearly any style or genre thrown his way—so much so that he viewed each genre as a new challenge. "I went out with him a couple of nights to see a band, and the first thing he'd say to me was, 'That drummer is crap,'" Harvey recalled. "When they came off for a break, he'd go straight up to the bandleader and say, 'Your drummer's not much good, is he? Let me have a go, and I'll show you.' He'd get on the drums, and everyone would be amazed. So, the poor chap would get the sack, and John would take his job."

Along with his growing reputation among the Midlands was a new nickname to match—one that would stick for the rest of his life. If a Birmingham band needed a hot drummer at the last minute—or if a new challenger to the title of best percussionist on the Brum scene inquired as to who to look out for—they were told to look for "Bonzo."

❋ ❋ ❋

FOLLOWING HIS STINTS WITH THE BLUE STAR TRIO AND THE TWO-man drum act he'd crafted with Bill Harvey, John began what would be common practice in his early years: hopping from band to band in the hopes of landing steady, lucrative—and challenging—work. By mid-1963, he was sitting in with Terry Webb & the Spiders—a band whose singer wore a gold-lamé jacket, while the rest of the band wore purple jackets with velvet lapels in the popular "teddy-boy" style, complete with bootlace ties and slicked hair. In an attempt to fit in, John agreed to don the purple jacket for shows. Besides, the gigs that Terry Webb racked up around the Brum scene only added to John's exposure on the circuit, eventually landing his first experience opening for bona fide headliners—Brian Poole and the Tremeloes.

The Tremeloes were widely known as the band chosen over the Beatles for an exclusive deal with Decca Records, and many banked on their staying power in the world of rock 'n' roll. During 1963 alone, they scored consecutive hit singles for the Decca label, including their cover of the Isley Brothers' smash "Twist and Shout" and a cover of the Contours' hit "Do You Love Me." Such an opportunity didn't come without its own pressure. "They rehearsed a lot," remembered Mick, "intent that no one cock up the set, and there was a lot of exciting talk about it being their big break, but when the night was upon them, they set off for the gig in purple jackets and with frayed nerves. . . . Everyone except for John, that is."

As was his habit at the time, John was the last member of the Spiders to arrive for the big gig opening for the Tremeloes, finding that drummer Dave Munden was only moments away from replacing him onstage. With only seconds to spare, John swung on his cursed purple jacket and sat at his kit, launching into the first number without missing a beat.

Only a few months later, John's diligence earned him a recording debut playing and singing backup vocals on a track for another local outfit, the Senators, known among Midlands teens for their ongoing residency at the Navigation Inn in nearby Coventry. John, never one to swear allegiance to one band at this point, had already jammed with the Senators a few times, and when the group scored an opportunity to lay down a track for an upcoming compilation album put out by the influential magazine *Brum Beat*, Terry Beale—formerly of the Blue Star Trio—insisted "Bonzo" be their drummer. The Senators' original bassist, Bill Ford, later said, "At this stage in 1963, the Senators still had an unreliable drummer and were let down by him on a number of occasions. . . . Our drummer let us down again one night when we had a double gig. [Lead singer Terry Beale] played drums on the first set at the first gig at Perry Hall, Bromsgrove. During the break, he shot off in his car to fetch his 'mate' who he said could play the drums. He came back twenty minutes later with this lad named John Bonham. We started the second half, and it was as if someone had stuck rocket fuel in our drinks! We went down a storm, and John joined us as our drummer there and then."

The core lineup of the Senators at that time also included Trevor McGowan on lead guitar and Graham Dennis on rhythm guitar—along with Beale, who knew John from their time in the Blue Star Trio. For the initial recording of "She's a Mod," the group gathered at historic Hollick & Taylor Studios. Built nearly a century before, the ornate Victorian building at 16 Grosvenor Road had been converted into a state-of-the-art recording mecca in 1945, drawing bands and solo artists from all over the Midlands. Second only to Abbey Road, it was soon recognized as the oldest functioning studio in the United Kingdom, and, at 947 square feet, it was also the Midlands' largest recording space.

"With this final lineup, we played regularly at many of the Birmingham venues and pubs—Ma Regan's places—the Ritz, the Plaza, and the Cavern, the West End Ballroom and the Moat House Club, just to mention a few," Ford reminisced. "We had a big following there as well—regularly playing Redditch Youth Club, Alcester Trades and Labour Club, and other pubs and clubs in the Worcestershire area."

The "Ma Regan Circuit," as it was lovingly called, was legendary among local musicians and teens alike. The string of clubs took its name from the woman who owned numerous music venues throughout the Midlands, which she ran with her husband, and also worked as the various clubs' booking agent. In the early 1960s, all the local bands aspired to play at her venues, and if your group made the cut to play one, you were almost certainly guaranteed gigs at the other spots, making for very lucrative work.

✳ ✳ ✳

STILL BAND-HOPPING, JOHN FOUND HIS NEXT ONGOING STINT WITH the Nicky James Movement, another of the Brum scene's well-known pop acts. James—born Michael Clifford Nicholls—had started the Birmingham-based ensemble following his departure from Denny and the Diplomats. During John's time with Nicky James, he and the founding singer became close, often working thick as thieves in order just to make it in time to gigs together. One night, James was home preparing for a show at Adelphi Ballroom in West Bromwich when his phone rang at the last minute.

"Nicky, you've got to help me," John's voice pleaded from the receiver.

"Why?" James replied.

"Because my dad won't let me have my drums."

"Why?"

"Because I've pronged the van again." James already knew John had made a habit of crashing Jacko's van—and now it was one too many times.

"You idiot," James said.

John huffed on the other end. "Don't call me an idiot or I'll smack you."

"Bless him, he used to smack me regular, and we would end up scrapping on the floor," James later recalled. "Then, we would burst out laughing and go and do the gig. And you know what? It was always a better gig. I promise you it was a fun thing. Anyway, John said, 'Me dad's locked the drums in the garden shed.' 'Can't you get the key?' I asked. 'No, because if I go into the house, he'll know what I'm up to and hide the keys, or keep them in his pocket.' So, we devised a little plan. We had this black and maroon Bedford van with side-loading doors, so I pulled up outside the alleyway that led to the garden and met John 'round the corner."

John jumped out from behind a tree, and he and James ran toward the shed. After climbing up the wall nearest the shed, James lifted the roof for John to climb inside and pass the singer the drum kit, one piece at a time, out the window. James remembered, "John was yelling, 'Quick! Grab this,' and started passing the gear to me. . . . We went running down the alley, banging against the fence and wall, and as we were piling everything into the van, we heard a cry of 'Call the police!' So, we shot off down the road roaring with laughter at what had happened. When we arrived at the gig, John began to unpack his kit, only to find he'd left most of it behind."

Among the pieces, all John had been able to smuggle out of Jacko's shed were the snare drum and stand, a bass drum, and a pedal, but no cymbals or hi-hat—and, worst of all, no drumsticks. With no other drummer around to borrow from, James jokingly suggested John play the gig using only his hands. "I'd seen him do it a couple of times before and had asked him if it hurt," James remembered. "'No,' he'd replied. 'Actually, when I do this, it goes down like a storm.' Well, this night he'd have to prove it—and that is when he started bashing his drum kit with his hands. He played the whole gig just using his hands and fingers, and it was the most exciting gig we ever played. The crowd absolutely loved him. . . . There are drummers of outstanding ability out there, but John was the first, the man who did it for everyone. . . . John was one of those drummers. He set a standard, like Gene Krupa did."

As the year came to a close, John again sought steady work elsewhere. When the members of Nicky James's band broke up the following year, its roster went their separate ways to join up with other successful acts: Roy Wood and Bev Bevan with the Move and, later, the Electric Light Orchestra (ELO), while Mike Pinder became the keyboardist for the Moody Blues.

Bevan later recalled, "My first recollection of John was him coming to see me when I was with Denny Laine and the Diplomats back in 1963, and Carl Wayne and the Vikings in 1964, just before we started the Move. I was older than him, and I can remember him coming along to watch me play. I was the loudest drummer in the area at the time, and if John learned one thing from me, it was that drums are meant for hitting, as opposed to being tickled. . . . I think he used to take a few ideas, until he overtook me and became the best rock drummer of all time." John and Bevan would remain the best of friends, far outlasting their joint stints with Nicky James.

More determined than ever, John approached the middle of the decade still hoping he would somehow find his way into a rock 'n' roll band with the same kind of staying power.

Chapter Two

JANUARY 1966–SEPTEMBER 1968

Nearly every night of 1966 was spent onstage, one way or another.
For months, John continued to get up at the crack of dawn
in order to report to Jacko's construction site by 7:30. Although
he was the boss's son, John was expected to act as just another of his
father's crew, being allowed only a ten-minute tea break, a half-hour
lunch, and, on rare occasion, a second cup of tea brought out to the
men in a bucket. At 5:30 he'd promptly rush off home to clean up and
load up his kit for that night's gig.

"John would find this all very hard," remembered Mick Bonham,
"because he spent most of the day with his head in the clouds thinking about being in a band. This didn't impress the foreman, who gave
John a lot of grief while he worked for Jacko."

Combining the few pounds from each gig with his construction
salary, John was able to make just enough for cigarettes, beer, and—on
the occasions Jacko still let him borrow it—gas for the van. But John's
financial plight was far from unique. During the 1960s, Birmingham
was chock-full of rock 'n' roll hopefuls, all itching to get out of the
Midlands—or, at least, the factories that surrounded them. Where
fame failed, the assembly line beckoned.

"Birmingham was a different place back then," explained Trevor Burton, later the rhythm guitarist for the Move. "It was a very industrial city, and we were pretty tough people. You were factory fodder. . . . [Music] was a way out of going into a factory. I was making fifteen pounds a week, and that was twice as much as my dad was making in a factory."

Out of that desperation came a very distinct homegrown form of rock 'n' roll, more angsty than London and hipper than Liverpool—despite the worldwide attention that shipbuilding port town garnered thanks to the Beatles. Pound for pound, more bands came out of the Brum scene than any other place in England, and the Brummies knew it. "In the Midlands, a lot of people couldn't climb out of it because all we had there were pubs," remembered Bill Bonham, of no relation to John but the star keyboardist for the Midlands-based band Obs-Tweedle. "The musicianship was incredible. We were a really tight little society. But you still had to go down to London and pay to play or play for nothing. It was very hard to get people to come up [from London] and listen to you."

Local trumpeter and producer Jim Simpson was already a veteran of the Birmingham scene long before meeting John Bonham in 1966. "People don't remember what came out of this place," said Simpson. "Maybe they could scoot down to London too quickly. We were always told that London knew best, so quite a few bands went down there and made very cheesy records, [and] Birmingham hasn't proved the most elegant place to live. . . . But the fact is, we produced a lot of really great players and bands—more than our fair share. The bands we had were tough and rough, and they didn't aim at the charts as neatly as those silly *Liverpudlians* with fringy haircuts and stupid collars on their jackets."

✳ ✳ ✳

Now seventeen years old, John Bonham was talented enough to never be out of work for very long. By the winter of 1965, his worst problem—aside from finding a singular steady gig—was figuring out how to transport his ever-evolving drum kit from Redditch to Birmingham for his many nightly gigs. After an appropriate amount of pleading, John had finally persuaded Jacko to let him use one of his three construction vans for carting around his numerous bandmates and their gear—while a neighborhood friend, Eddie Conoly, offered to act as John's part-time roadie, driving him to and from every show, regardless of the band. That arrangement was short-lived, however, after it dawned on John that he could pocket Eddie's roadie share if he lugged the gear himself, as well as manning the drums. It was also a surefire way for him to remain invaluable to each of the individual bands—lugging their gear, supplying them with cigarettes, and, finally, attracting his loyal Brum following to the shows.

❊ ❊ ❊

WITH ALL THE MANY BANDS IN BIRMINGHAM FIGHTING FOR STAGE time among the Brum scene—particularly on the Ma Regan Circuit—there was an ever-present culture of competition among the young musicians. In those days, everyone wanted to be scouted by a manager or record-label representative who might be in the audience. John's natural abilities and instinctive flairs for showmanship and competition didn't always make him the most popular with other musicians—the jealousy was too thick. His fellow drummers, however, soon recognized that John was creating his own style and, in effect, a new approach to the drums themselves.

At the same time, John's reputation as one of Birmingham's star drummers was matched only by his love of mischief. "He used to leave his drum stool outside the front door of his house," Bill Harvey later remembered. "There was a concrete plinth above the door with ivy growing up the side, and he hid the stool behind the ivy so he could climb out the window, down the drainpipe, and onto the stool to sneak out at night. And then he'd go back the same way. He told me that in confidence one night and said, 'For God's sake, don't tell my dad.'"

Harvey recalled one night when he stopped by to see John sitting in with the Birmingham-based band the Locomotive. "John got absolutely paralytic that night," Harvey said. "He used to go and do a solo to start the evening—just like Buddy Rich used to do. John would get up there, go wild, and come off as sober as a judge." John, it appeared, would be sober by the end of the gig.

"In Locomotive, we called John 'Bonnie,' though we may have called him 'Bonzo,' as well," recalled Jim Simpson, who helped form the Locomotive in 1965 but later assumed the role of manager once the group abandoned jazz and R&B in favor of the more psychedelic "prog" rock. "He could have walked in to any band in the world and felt comfortable. . . . I had to sack him two or three times. We all loved him, but he was utterly outrageous—or maybe just boisterous. We got banned from several places because of him. He took his shirt off and stood on his drum kit at Frank Freeman's School of Dancing in Kidderminster. Frank said to me, 'You were very good tonight, Jim, but we're never going to book you again with that drummer.'"

On the nights Jacko would allow it, John would borrow the family's Ford Zephyr convertible and vanish with friends and bandmates, often Bill Harvey. That summer John first lost his license for drinking and driving, despite the lax laws for such behavior at that time. Although nearly everyone in the local music scene drank to excess, the foundations were being laid for John's increasing dependence on alcohol. "John could outdrink me—and I could down a pint in under four seconds," Mick Bonham later remembered.

John had been working for his father off and on for years, but with mounting stage gigs the hours at the sites were slowly beginning to wear him down. For both more money and a set schedule that would allow for a proper night's sleep, he began to scour local retail shops for steady part-time sales work. Surprisingly, he was hired as an assistant at a well-known high-end tailor shop called George Osbourne & Son. Not necessarily known for his sense of fashion, John had nonetheless begun to notice the flashy clothes many musicians were now donning as part of their all-encompassing stage personae—the cultural influence of swinging London finally making its way into the Midlands.

"Fancy suits and ties were cast aside in favor of bright clothes and a more flamboyant look," Mick Bonham clarified. "Loud clothes to match loud music. . . . The Rolling Stones and the Who were now belting out a kind of music that kicked off a whole new ball game. Indeed, John had been so impressed when he saw the Who's drummer, a young Keith Moon, for the first time on TV, that he began to experiment with fashion."

Moon was already recognized as the drummer who had transformed orderly "beat group" drumming into a one-man spectacle—both for his wild, high-energy solos and for the offstage antics that had made him infamous within the music industry. As a stylist, however, he was soon outmatched by the Graham Bond Organisation's Ginger Baker, who quickly assumed Moon's mantle as the top-rated rock percussionist. At twenty-six, Baker had already earned a reputation as the wildest drummer around—and the most experimental when it came to live performance. By utilizing a rare blend of solid technical control and forceful stage presence, Baker was never overshadowed by his bandmates, Bond and bassist Jack Bruce. "That's the way I want to be," he would explain, "an equal member of the band, not someone just keeping the beat for the forward musicians." Impressed by Moon's persona and Baker's skill, John was already determined to assume the mantle next.

Not long after watching the Who's first television performances, John began to play with fashion styles that would likewise complement his outward stage presence. To the amusement of his friends and family, his clothing experiments weren't limited to the stage; he was often seen around town running errands in the most flamboyant clothes that his new position at George Osbourne & Son tailors could provide. Before long, John started getting as equally creative in customizing his wardrobe as he had with his drum kits. One early experiment found John dyeing a secondhand white milkman's jacket bright yellow and its patch pockets blood red; another foray into fashion saw Joan Bonham sewing her son a long frock coat made from a dark-green curtain material, laden with lime flowers all over it—a vision of John's own design. But John's pièce de résistance, as brother Mick would lovingly refer to it later, was a suede Levi's-style jacket with a black leather collar—that John later dyed green. "He'd go out wearing this thing, and nobody had seen anything like it," Mick later recalled. "People stared, but he was completely oblivious. . . . When you saw an eighteen-year-old coming down the street wearing a mauve milk-man's jacket, or a frock coat made out of bright-green curtain mate-rial, it caused quite a stir."

Needing cash more than modular clothing, John once offered to sell a jacket to Mick for five pounds. Soon after the transaction, how-ever, Mick was surprised to run into drummer Bev Bevan at a party wearing an identical orange suede jacket. It quickly dawned on Mick that his big brother had stolen the jacket back and resold it to Bevan—in exchange for the opportunity to fill in for his group, the Move.

For his day job at George Osbourne & Son, John toned down his flamboyance, opting instead for the more acceptable—though no less spiffy—suit and tie, which he could now afford with the tailor's employee discount. As Mick later remembered, "He settled in well, and the job allowed him to wear the smart suits of the day, which he loved. . . . He'd spend hours in front of the mirror making sure the Windsor knot was just right, his trouser creases would cut paper, and it was on with the cuff links and off to work on the bus."

❋ ❋ ❋

ON THE RARE NIGHTS THAT HE WASN'T BOOKED FOR A GIG, JOHN would still venture downtown and offer his services as a drummer for hire to any band that might be in need. As the streets surround-ing the Ma Regan venues were often lined with the vans loaded with musicians and their gear, John would usually strike gold and wind up onstage. While out in Kidderminster with Eddie Conoly on such a night, John happened upon a cute, petite blonde named Patricia "Pat" Phillips. Like John and Eddie, Pat was out on the town with her sister Beryl, checking out the Old Hill Plaza club scene. She and Beryl often went out with their two other sisters, Sheila and Margaret.

From the moment John asked her to dance, the two were inseparable. As Mick later recalled, "He met Pat when he was sixteen, and his love for her didn't diminish at all, through all their years together. . . . Pat went with him everywhere."

They had been together only a few months when Pat discovered she was pregnant. Despite his youth—he'd only just turned seventeen—John wanted to make an honest woman out of the girl he had already decided he wanted to marry. He broke the news to his friends twenty-four hours before the wedding itself in typical John fashion: showing up at the local pub, the Bulls Head, wearing a suit. As one of John's friends, fellow drummer Mac Poole, later said, "Everyone else was dressed in tie-dyed T-shirts and jeans. 'Why are you wearing a suit, John?' 'Oh, I'm practicing for tomorrow. I'm getting married.'"

With no time for a proper stag party, John instead bought the rounds for those already seated at the bar. "He lined up all these drinks and got absolutely out of his brain," Poole remembered. "He jumped on to my kit and pepper-potted the drums. . . . He absolutely whacked it, which I thought was quite funny—even though it was my kit."

John and Pat opted for a small civil ceremony, keeping the marriage quiet for the time being and downplaying the pregnancy that had dictated the quick decision. When they wed the following day, February 19, 1966, only a select few friends, as well as Pat's sisters and John's brother, Mick, were in attendance.

Although a happily married man, John was still living with his parents and brother when his son, Jason, was born on July 15, 1966. For all those months, Pat had continued to live with her own parents and three sisters in Dudley, all of whom helped her during the pregnancy, while John was able to visit only when the attainable bus fare from Hunt End permitted. However, once Jason was born, John was forced to make good on a promise he had made to his young wife early in their marriage: he would forsake his music career and buckle down to a proper job, unless that "big break" he had always dreamed of finally hit. "It's just a matter of time," he told her. "I'm going to make it if you have faith in me. Don't give up on me."

But John later admitted, "I swore to Pat that I'd give up drumming when we got married, but every night I'd come home and just sit down at the drums. . . . I'd be miserable if I didn't."

With no savings to speak of, the new family of three first set up camp at Pat's parents' house on the Priory Estate. When that situation grew cramped with Pat's sisters still at home, the trio took up Jacko Bonham's offer to allow them use of his fifteen-foot trailer, parked behind the family's home. "Our dad had sold the previous caravan and bought a big touring van, which was parked at the back of Mum's shop," Mick Bonham said. "There was also a storeroom attached to the shop, which we decorated and turned into a lounge. So, Pat and John could sleep in the van and live in the storeroom. It was quite a big caravan, and it was fitted out and stocked from the shop."

Not wanting to raise his new family in a trailer, John also made a deal with his father to own one of the business's work-in-progress homes outright. At the time, Jacko's company was finishing up work on a pair of homes not far from the shop and, in exchange for labor, agreed to give one to John and Pat once the long-term project was completed. Once again waking up at the crack of dawn, John now spent the bulk of his days laying the new floorboards. But the agreement with Jacko was short-lived; one morning, John had been so antsy to finish the day's work, he'd forgotten to mark the water pipes before hammering nails into the floor, puncturing the pipes and causing a downpour upon the plumbers hired to install the house's water supply. As Mick recalled, "He did a disappearing act and went back to playing drums after that."

John's and Pat's parents supported them with loans, only agreed to now that a baby was part of the mix. It wasn't long before fights between the couple began, as any substantial cash flow was still being spent on ale and new drums. "Of course, he and Pattie were always rowing, 'How can we pay the bills?'" remembered Mac Poole.

❋ ❋ ❋

JOHN'S DEPENDENCY ON THREE JOBS HAD WHITTLED DOWN TO TWO—his continuing work at the tailor shop and the nightly rounds of gigging on the drums. With the exception of sleeping, for the first year of his marriage to Pat, John was almost never home. At the beginning of 1966, John had already been spending his nights sitting in with Terry Webb and the Spiders, as well as fellow Birmingham-based groups Pat Wayne and the Beachcombers, Steve Brett and the Mavericks, and Danny King and the Mayfair Set. But as the year closed, his promise to Pat had won out, and the nightly excursions into town to play for crumbs were coming to an end.

He'd first started filling in with Pat Wayne's group, the Beach-combers, during the middle of the previous year. Originally formed as a skiffle band in 1957, the band had been the brainchild of Birmingham's Patrick Curley, later known by his stage name, Pat Wayne. Over the next few years, Wayne's band morphed into the Rockin' Jaymen and then, finally, the Beachcombers, just before welcoming John on board as their regular drummer. He joined the group with high hopes, as the Beachcombers' cover of Chuck Berry's "Roll Over Beethoven" had been recorded at the legendary Abbey Road Studios in London and released just prior to the Beatles' hit version. But alas, they never achieved Fab Four fame. The Mavericks, on the other hand, had already signed with Columbia Records and had even recorded a few tracks at Hollick & Taylor Studios before onboarding him. Nonetheless, neither band gained mainstream success.

In 1966 John tried his luck with one more semistable Birmingham band, A Way of Life. As he had already promised Pat to be on the lookout for steady, ongoing work, John agreed to take on A Way of Life only as a full-fledged member—no more fill-ins and no more part-time status. The gamble paid off, and John's stint with A Way of Life proved to be his longest-standing tenure with a local band up to that point.

A Way of Life was the labor-of-love project of Birmingham brothers Chris and Reggie Jones, with Chris acting as the group's lead singer and Reggie on lead guitar. For all intents and purposes, the band had much going for it by the time John joined them. The Move's Ace Kef-ford was the Jones brothers' cousin, and guitarist Mike Hopkins had previously played with the popular Denny Laine and the Diplomats. With that track record and successful musical contacts, John sought out the Joneses as soon as he heard they needed a drummer.

"We were holding auditions on a Sunday afternoon at the Cedar Club in Birmingham, and we had about twenty drummers audition," Reggie Jones later reminisced. "John came along and said, 'What gigs we got then?' and I thought, 'Blimey, he's cocky, you know—what gigs we got?—even before he'd had his audition!' I said, 'Well, you seem pretty confident.' Anyway, he got the job, and we did a gig that same night at the Cedar Club."

According to Jones, he and John nearly came to blows on the very first night playing together—leading to the first of John's many firings from the band. Desperate to keep the steady work that A Way of Life seemed to represent, John swallowed his pride and woke Jones up at his home the following morning. "We were getting the gear out of the van [and] ready to rehearse," Jones said, "and who should be watch-ing us—wearing what I used to call his 'Harold Wilson' pinstripe suit, carrying a little suitcase—but John. I felt sorry for him, so I said, 'Look, if you're gonna be in my band, what I say goes.' He said, 'Okay,' he was back in the band, and he rehearsed with us that afternoon."

John's tenure in A Way of Life also heralded the beginning of a lifelong friendship with bass player Dave Pegg, who would always look back fondly on his time playing with John. "It was short-lived: our first gig was on September 17, 1967, at the Crown and Cushion at Perry Barr, and our last was the 23rd of October at the Queen's Head. . . . We didn't do much original material. We'd do cover ver-sions of Vanilla Fudge, and we did some Hendrix things. We played everywhere you could play on the Midlands circuit."

The group's most infamous gig occurred at the Top Spot, a popular club in Ross-on-Wye. The venue was home to a notorious "traffic light" system next to the stage—a defaulted green light that would burn red if a band's sound level got too high. Once red, the electricity was programmed to automatically cut out. "It was a kind of decibel meter," remembered Pegg. "John hit the bass drum, and it immediately went to red. He cut the power off. . . . No one else could actually do that to get that bass drum sound. It was the loudest drum kit in the world."

Playing with John was soon becoming a liability to any band brave enough to take him on as a drummer. "We did the Tyburn House one night," Reggie Jones recalled, "and the gaffer [manager] was really moaning. The gaffers always moaned, but the audience never did. I got sick of it, and I shouted down the mic, 'Do you think we're playing too loud?' And they shouted 'No! No!' John got annoyed and threw his cymbal. It hit the wall and stuck in the brick."

"If you were in a band with Bonham, you knew you'd never get booked back again," added Dave Pegg. "We only did about twenty gigs around Birmingham. Often, we only did the first half of the evening because it was so loud the promoters would say, 'If you can't turn it down, you can't do the second half.' That happened at 50 percent of the gigs, mainly because of John. This was in the days when we had a 100-watt PA system [for vocals] and nothing [else] miked up, and a 50-watt guitar amp."

Around the same time, John befriended another fellow Birmingham musician named Tony Iommi, a left-handed guitarist who was John's age. Like John, Iommi started as a drummer, but when his parents banned the brash sounds from his house, he took up the guitar and was soon jamming with a number of local bands. "[John]'d last about five minutes in this band because he was too loud, and they'd fire him," Iommi laughed. "Then, he'd sneak back in with another band, and before long, they would get rid of him for the same reason. He had this drum case with all the names of the bands he'd been with on it, and they were all crossed out. And the names would get smaller and smaller so that he could get them all on."

For a while, John lived a transient existence out of necessity, alternating between crashing with his friends after late-night gigs and returning home to his family. "John lived at our house on and off for about two years and was one of the family, becoming very close to my father," Chris Jones recalled. "John had a suitcase of clothes he used to carry around to different gigs, but one day he lost it. Dad spoke with him and gave him a wad of cash to get some more. Dad and John were very close, and when Dad died, John took the news very badly."

"He actually lived at my mum's house for a while," Reggie Jones added. "We used to go out drinking in Warstock and Kings Heath. I remember when he tried to grow a moustache . . . [and] he had thickened his mustache up with mascara. He was standing at the bar chatting to some girls saying, 'Looks pretty good, doesn't it?' and all of a sudden, from the heat of the lights and sweat from playing, his mustache started to run down his face. He didn't know what it was, but the rest of the band had a good laugh about it."

※ ※ ※

Playing with A Way of Life also led to John's biggest break yet: opening for the Kinks at the Plaza in nearby Handsworth. Thanks to strong word of mouth, the group also booked more better-paying jobs around the Midlands, both inspiring John to improve his drum kit and affording him enough money to do so. At the time, British kits like Premier were the most affordable, making them the most popular among local bands. But as the 1960s wore on, many drummers—and rock 'n' roll drummers in particular—had started using the more fashionable American kits, starting when Beatles drummer Ringo Starr swapped out his own Premier kit for a Ludwig in 1963. During his time with A Way of Life, John almost exclusively used the same kit as his old friend Mac Poole—a Ludwig Super Classic. "His was green sparkle, and mine was silver sparkle," Poole smiled. "He used to treat his kit abysmally. It was because his dad had paid for it. It was the old story—when you're spoiled, you don't look after it."

John's Ludwig kit was of the Super Classic line, featuring a twenty-two-by-fourteen-inch bass drum, thirteen-by-nine-inch and sixteen-by-sixteen-inch tom-toms, and a powerful fourteen-by-five-inch Supraphonic 400 metal-shell snare. Ludwig's signature three-ply shells, which came in both mahogany or poplar, looked particularly glamorous onstage, and Ludwig's "Remo" heads were generally considered more durable than the more common Everplay Extra heads manufactured by Premier. As a foreign import, Ludwig kits also came with a substantially higher price tag, making them all the more coveted by young rock drummers throughout Britain. "It sounded absolutely huge," recalled Dave Pegg. "It wasn't a huge kit, but it was phenomenally loud."

Although Mac Poole didn't bash the kit nearly as hard as John, both agreed that the Ludwig kit was more aligned with the louder, harder rock style that John fancied. "He was no technician, but he always wanted to be one of the loudest drummers in the West," Poole added. "He was determined not to be drowned out by guitarists, which I could understand. He even lined his bass drum with silver paper [tinfoil] to make it louder."

But he didn't stop there. Like many other drummers, John was convinced the more reflective the interior, the less sound would be absorbed by the bass drum itself.

"He would have some strange ideas," remembered Chris Jones. "This one gig he turned up with fur all 'round his drums, boasting to us that they were unique and no one would have drums like these. Problem was, it turned out to be his mother's genuine mink coat, which was her pride and joy."

Sometimes, John's customizations were merely for dramatic effect, as Reggie Jones recalled. "We played a Flower Power party in a marquee in Balsall Heath with the Move. That's when John took these big plastic flowers and covered his whole kit in them. The audience couldn't believe it, this big powerful sound coming from behind a mass of flowers."

If John was to outshine a band's lead guitarist, this would prove crucial, as the next generation of guitar amplifiers were powerful enough to drown out the drummer. But John already had it in mind to neither dominate the guitarist nor allow the guitarist to overpower him; rather, John's vision was to make the drums a secondary lead, circumventing the preconceived notion that the drum was just another part of the rhythm section, a mere timekeeper. His philosophy soon set him apart from his fellow rock drummers and was more akin to the examples in showmanship and persona set by his childhood heroes, Gene Krupa and Buddy Rich. But the new school of hard-rock bands, particularly Cream and the Jimi Hendrix Experience, catered to the dominance of a lead guitarist, a practice exemplified in their stage shows, where audiences would see rows and rows of multiple speakers onstage and demand louder rock.

In A Way of Life, lead guitarist Chris Jones and bassist Dave Pegg were left with little option but to give the people what they wanted, and so both players now utilized their own four-by-twelve Marshall cabinet, equipped with a 50-watt amp, at shows. In an attempt to match their rock 'n' roll compatriots, both musicians truly wanted at least four cabinets onstage—an investment that proved too costly for a still localized act like A Way of Life. "We didn't have any money," recalled Pegg. "John said, 'Oh, I'll make 'em. Just bring your cabinet over to my caravan.'"

John soon demonstrated to Pegg that his time working with Jacko's construction crew had provided carpentry skills that could, surprisingly, benefit their band—aside from charging the needed lumber to Jacko's business account. "I took the cabinet over, and [John] took it apart. The next time I went over, he had built another six of these four-by-twelve cabinets out of incredibly high-quality wood—I think it was marine ply. . . . He built them in about a week—they were fantastic! He also had a mate who was an upholsterer, and he covered the cabinets in real orange leather, and we had lime-green speaker cloths. It made you sick to look at them. It was quite a psychedelic experience."

Pegg added, "Of course, we had no speakers to put in them."

John and Pegg had become close during their time in A Way of Life and often hung out at the local pub or even running the band's errands together—with Pegg driving, of course, as John's driver's license was still suspended. As Reggie Jones recalled, John "traveled on the bus because he drove like a maniac. Whenever he borrowed his dad's van, he would do hand-brake skids on the gravel."

John and Pegg often teamed up to collect A Way of Life's pay from a promoter's or agent's office. On one specific occasion, they refused to pay up, claiming John had played too loud. "I remember John and me [Pegg] going to collect the money after the tour from the agents in Wake Green Road. These were the people who ran Mother's at the time, and we got nothing. . . . [They] told Bonzo that he was unrecordable and should just go back to hod carrying for a living. The problem was that he was just too loud, and the equipment he'd got could not cope with the bass-drum input level on his mixing desk."

According to Pegg, the manager of Mother's, a local promoter named Johnny Haynes, also owned a nearby studio, but he also refused to record John during A Way of Life's demo sessions for the same reason. "I was with Bonzo when he was banned from Zella Studios. Johnny couldn't record Bonzo—the kit was too loud. It was the days before you had stuff to cut down signals, and as a result it overloaded the tape recorder." During their confrontation, Haynes claimed that John was "unrecordable" and would prove to be "uncontrollable" for any producer or engineer who attempted to work with him. As Pegg added, "Bonzo dined out on that story many times."

❋ ❋ ❋

For all its promise, the final lineup of A Way of Life, featuring John Bonham, lasted a mere five weeks. Although the band's popularity on the Brum scene never dwindled, previous predictions regarding the sheer level of their volume sadly rang true. "We broke up because nobody would book us, as we were too loud," remembered Dave Pegg. "Bands used to carry their own PA [system], but only for their vocals; you never amplified the guitars or drums through it. Bonzo only hit his bass drum once, and it immediately went to red, turning the power off. This was before we'd played a number." With half their gigs canceled or shut down midshow, the Jones brothers opted to call it quits.

Throughout his tenure with A Way of Life, John attempted his own form of adult prioritizing by keeping one foot in and out of the band, never forgetting the two additional mouths he had to feed. After the first few gigs yielded harsh criticism for his brash playing, he never made it a secret that he continued to seek occasional side work with other local bands. "John was known for going from band to band," brother Mick later recalled. "As soon as he got a better offer, he was gone. You could turn up expecting to see him at a gig, and he wouldn't be there. He'd be off playing somewhere else with another band [and] was always hoping the band would build up a following [and] be asked back."

When he first foresaw A Way of Life's dismal future, he made the difficult decision to swallow his pride and take up a second job. His time as an assistant tailor was long since over, and while Jacko Bonham had no problem letting his son and family live out back in the caravan, he kept to his word after the plumbing incident that John would never again be his full-time employee. Out of options, John unhappily yielded to the classic purgatorial fate of most young men throughout the Midlands—he punched in at a factory, first on a wire-cordage assembly line and then finally at the local Associated Electrical Industries (AEI) factory located right in Birmingham.

Whether he wanted to admit it or not, John had been fortunate to land the latter position. It paid well enough to keep his young family afloat and had come to him as a favor from an old friend who also worked for AEI, Birmingham local Matthew Maloney. "Matthew was one of the lucky few that had a van and had been a roadie for his brother Stefan's band when he met up with John," Mick Bonham noted. Soon, Maloney's experience as a part-time roadie would lead to John's returning the favor of employment, hiring the younger driver to help lug gear for various gigs—a job Maloney would keep off and on for years. It was during that time when John started to pick up a few gigs with a local blues outfit slowly inching its way toward a devoted fan base around the Midlands. The group, calling themselves the Crawling King Snakes, had taken both their name and their snarling blues-driven set list from a John Lee Hooker classic. Although the group was composed of competent players, it was their lithe, seductive blond lead singer from nearby Kidderminster who attracted the most attention among the Ma Regan Circuit. Word of mouth had spread of the young man's flamboyant hippie fashions and androgynous stage presence, even among fellow Birmingham bands.

"All the musicians got to know each other," recalled Mick Bonham, "and that's how John and Robert Plant met."

＊ ＊ ＊

JOHN HAD FIRST SEEN THE CRAWLING KING SNAKES FEATURING seventeen-year-old Robert Plant when they performed a twenty-minute slot at Old Hill Plaza. He appreciated Plant's unique fashion sense and modern blues approach and had waited until after the concert to pay him the compliment. To Plant's amusement, John also mentioned that the group's drummer was "hopeless" and that he, John Bonham, would make a much better fit. "John came up to me [Plant] at the gig and said, 'You're only half as good a singer as I am a drummer,' with his typical understatement."

Sensing a cheeky arrogance that matched his own, Plant took an immediate liking to his new mate.

Robert Anthony Plant was only three months younger than Bonham, born on August 20, 1948, in West Bromwich, Staffordshire. Against the wishes of his greatly disapproving parents—his father, a civil engineer, hoped to see Robert settle down as an accountant—Plant had dropped out of school the year before he met Bonham in order to focus on music. That decision, along with the length of his hair, forced sixteen-year-old Robert to leave home and take up an itinerant existence, largely living on the couches and bedroom floors of friends.

"[John] was really flash, a little whiz kid, and so was I," Plant remembered. "Because of our outgoing, gregarious natures, we terrorized other musicians if we didn't think they were any good. . . .

I think the whole thing about Bonzo and I was that we were always trying to prove something."

Plant soon proved himself an expert on American blues music, something that John appreciated since he'd mostly favored jazz and R&B. Plant had discovered his own love of the blues upon first hearing Robert Johnson at the age of fifteen—although he never lost his childhood love of Elvis Presley.

Like John, Plant frequently band-hopped, always in the hopes of landing a steady gig that could catapult him to Elvis-level superstardom, yet still allow him creative freedom. By the time he joined up with the Crawling King Snakes, Plant had already been in numerous bands throughout the Midlands—the Delta Blues Band at the Seven Stars in Stourbridge, the New Memphis Bluesbreakers, the Brum Beats, and the Sounds of Blue. Afterward, he sang and played guitar with another blues-rock outfit, Black Snake Moan, and then with a group calling themselves the Banned. Plant finally joined up with the Crawling King Snakes toward the end of 1965.

In John Bonham, Plant had found a new partner in crime, as well as another bedroom floor to occasionally inhabit. "I'd been fast asleep late one night when John had brought Robert back to our house in Hunt End," Mick Bonham later remembered. "My bedroom door was open when Robert came upstairs to use the toilet and by mistake came into my bedroom. I awoke to see a silhouette of what I thought was Jesus. With the long hair, he looked just like the pictures I'd seen at Sunday school."

The two proved to be an iconic pair. Plant noted, "John was very colorful to be around. We were both proud owners of unbelievably huge egos. I was going to be the greatest singer in the area where I lived, and he was definitely going to be the best drummer. . . . The two of us in the same room often made it impossible for anybody else to get in because of our egos and our personalities and our aggressive natures. It was very hard for anybody else to stomach."

＊ ＊ ＊

WITH A WIFE AND CHILD AT HOME, JOHN DIDN'T HAVE THE LUXURY of staying with any one band merely due to friendship or onstage chemistry, and the Crawling King Snakes quickly proved to be a less than profitable use of his time. In mid-1966 John briefly sidled back up with a rekindled A Way of Life, while Plant found himself in yet another band, a Motown-Tamla cover band called the Tennessee Teens. A few months later, the band changed their name to Listen and recorded a single, "You'd Better Run," but Plant quit soon after and opted to cut a few crooner-type songs on his own. When that endeavor tanked, Plant finally decided to start a band of his own, one in which he could both front and act as chief creative visionary and one that would embrace his growing love of the West Coast country-rock in the United States. In January 1967, he christened his new group the Band of Joy—but he still needed a good drummer.

When Plant was finally able to coerce John to join up with the Band of Joy during the middle of that year, the group had already been through two incarnations. With John now on board, the band was quickly able to solidify a string of steady gigs at two prestigious clubs in London: the Middle Earth and the Marquee. The pay was better than either John or Plant had ever received, and the very idea that London was embracing their hippie-influenced progressive blues was a promising sign that the collaboration was heading in the right direction.

"Nowadays, everybody communicates with everybody else in other bands, but you never did that much then," said Tony Iommi. "There was always this thing between bands from London and from Birmingham, from the Midlands. London musicians always . . . looked down on people from the Midlands, and we in turn looked at Londoners as being snobby. There was a lot of competition because of that, with bands trying to outdo each other."

With that ideology well in place, the Band of Joy's recurring success on the London scene made both John and Plant hopeful that their latest project would be the one to really take off.

"Audiences found Robert was being a bit too experimental," recalled Bev Bevan. "With Denny Laine and Carl Wayne, our bands were just playing the hits and what people wanted to hear. We'd play a lot of Beatles stuff, and the audience really loved that. . . . But Robert and the Band of Joy were doing stuff that was much heavier. It was quite bluesy, but they weren't playing Top 40 stuff, and they didn't always go down that well with audiences."

※ ※ ※

UNLIKE THE PREVIOUS HALF-DOZEN BANDS HE'D PLAYED WITH, Robert Plant was fully invested in Band of Joy. This time around, it was his brainchild, and aside from the creative control he sought for his set list and overall performance design, it marked the first real financial investment he'd made in a band. Much like John, Plant now acquiesced to the routine of a day job, laying asphalt on the streets for six shillings an hour, keeping a cash flow coming in to buy the band a gear van of its own as well as to support himself and his live-in girlfriend, Maureen. This time, the hard work was beginning to pay off, as the group's flamboyant Moby Grape and Love covers, sprinkled with a few of Plant's own original compositions, jived well enough with London teens to bring the band a respectable sixty pounds per gig. One original they performed was John and Robert's first collaboration, "Memory Lane."

In the end, too much competition with other local bands eventually led to fewer gigs. Plant and John were both fueling much of their creative energy into the band, conflicting with their family responsibilities, and both musicians needed steadier work. Even two gigs per week couldn't legitimize the long hours and gas money required for the trips to London and back. The group disbanded in May 1968, but John and Robert agreed to keep in touch.

Without a musical outlet, John was immediately frustrated and bored at work. Begrudgingly, he prepared to sell off his drum equipment when word reached him that a visiting act from the States wanted him to audition—Tim Rose, a folk crooner whose previous tours of the

United Kingdom had drawn critical praise and substantial fanfare. Initially, Rose started playing guitar alongside John Phillips and Scott McKenzie in the Journeymen, then joined up with Cass Elliot and James Hendricks to form the Big Three. Recently, Rose had scored a few singles on the *Billboard* chart, including a modest hit titled "Morning Dew."

Now preparing for his most recent English tour, Rose knew immediately that John was the type of dynamic drummer who could make his stage act transcend his studio albums. "I had been using a very fine drummer by the name of Aynsley Dunbar, who had learnt his trade with the Mojos, Jeff Beck, and John Mayall's Bluesbreakers, when I [previously] toured the UK," Rose later remembered. "Aynsley was unavailable for the 1968 tour, but I remembered seeing a drummer playing with the Band of Joy and thinking, 'I want him.' I eventually found John and offered him the job, paying about forty pounds a week."

❊ ❊ ❊

LOOKING FOR ANY EXCUSE NOT TO GIVE UP HIS DRUMMING FULL-time, it was an easy sell to John—especially when he learned that old friend Dave Pegg had also signed on to Rose's band. "We backed [Rose] on the first gigs he did in Britain," said Pegg, who alternated on bass with local player Steve Dolan. "We played with him at two Air Force bases in Oxfordshire, including the American base at Upper Heyford. I lived in Birmingham, and John lived in Redditch. He had got his license back, and so we rented a van to drive to the gigs [together]."

Mick Bonham later added, "I remember John thinking it was the break he had been waiting for because, back then, one pound would get you about eight beers, a bag of chips, and you'd still have enough for the bus fare home. For a young married man with a wife and child to support, this was big money."

Following a few weeks of rehearsals, Rose took his new band out starting in June 1968. Still building his English fan base, Rose primarily stuck to small clubs and outdoor festivals, but the critical write-ups were solid. "If anyone comes close to the rather vague definition of 'Folk Rock,' it must be Tim Rose," wrote *Melody Maker*'s Tony Wilson. "Powerful singing backed by his own electric, augmented by bass and drums on folk-based numbers, such as 'Morning Dew,' 'Long Time Man,' and 'Hey Joe,' provided a stirring session at Blaises in London last Sunday. These heavy, soulful numbers were balanced by lighter songs, such as 'Hello Sunshine' and five-string banjo number, 'Foggy Mountain Breakdown,' which have a chance for drummer John Bonham and bass guitarist Steve Dolan to take solos.'"

Now part of the backing band for a bona fide star, John settled comfortably into the role of Tim Rose's official drummer throughout that summer, unaware that his career would soon be upended yet again. On July 31, Tim Rose and his band were booked to play the Hampstead Country Club. In attendance that night was old friend Robert Plant, who had brought with him two guests—a renowned twenty-four-year-old session guitarist named Jimmy Page, who had recently taken hold of fading British blues-rock band the Yardbirds, and his manager, Peter Grant. The two wanted to reinvent the Yardbirds into a relevant, experimental rock-blues hybrid and attended Tim Rose's gig at the behest of Robert, who swore that John Bonham was the drummer the new ensemble desperately needed. Tim Rose knew of Jimmy's reputation as one of the best guitarists in England and initially assumed the trio was there to see him. But, as he later recalled, "They didn't say a word to me, but spent a long time talking to John."

Mick Bonham later remembered that night. "It didn't take too long before Tim put two and two together and realized that these infiltrators were out to steal his drummer. [Tim] was worried enough to confront John, asking, 'Are you going to leave me to go with them?' 'No way' was the reply he got. 'Not only do I love this life, but the money's too good.'"

John spent his time offstage catching up with Robert Plant and answering all sorts of questions aimed at him by Page and Grant—

but kept his mouth shut as to the line of inquiry. Across the club, Tim Rose eyed the scene skeptically, but when John inquired as to their next booking, he felt reassured that his group would remain intact. The tour continued on to its next date in Middlesbrough. It wasn't until they arrived at the venue and conducted a head count that the other members of the band realized John wasn't there. "Luckily for Tim, Steve was aware of what was going on with their drummer and had another chap ready to fill in," Mick Bonham recalled. "John was in Scandinavia with the New Yardbirds."

Later, John himself remembered of that Scandinavian trip, "It went so well that the group became very strong, and we felt we could start again—and change the name."

PART TWO

WILDFIRE

1968–1974

Into the Din of Hordes

Chapter Three

SEPTEMBER 1968

I"**rang Jimmy when I read that he was going to form a new band, because I was** doing sessions at the time, and I asked him if he needed a bass player," John Paul Jones later explained. "He told me he was going up to Birmingham to see a singer who knows a drummer and that we might have a band by the time he gets back. When he got back, he rang me to say that John was playing with Tim Rose."

Born John Baldwin to a show-business family in 1946 in Sidcup, Kent, Jones became the final piece of Page's mysterious puzzle when he rang up his old studio mate in 1968. Like many young English musicians, Jones had heard rumors that legendary Jimmy Page wanted to assemble a new group of professional hotshots to revive the Yardbirds—making full use of the band title he'd maneuvered to own with the help of his manager, Peter Grant. But before that phone call was made, Jimmy was yet to cast his roles for singer and drummer.

Initially beginning as the Yardbirds' bassist in 1966, Jimmy Page ascended to lead guitar and then sat back and watched as the band imploded on itself during two years of tumultuous world touring. By the end, Page was left as the last man standing. Having inherited the Yardbirds' mantle outright, Jimmy went into apparent seclusion after the group's public demise. His grand plan, as he admitted later, was to carefully curate an ensemble of professional players who could help him "combine blues, hard rock, and acoustic music, topped off with memorably heavy choruses"—and leave the Rolling Stones, the Who, and Cream trembling in their wake. To accomplish such a feat, he would settle for nothing less than the very best available. First, he usurped Robert Plant from his ongoing gig as lead singer in the psychedelic-rock outfit Obs-Tweedle, who in turn promptly suggested that they pursue John Bonham for drums. But as John Paul Jones recalled, "John didn't really want to leave [Tim Rose] because he thought it was steady work—so, it took a lot of time and trouble to get him to leave."

Jones wasn't exaggerating. From that first night watching John play at the Hampstead Country Club, Jimmy had instructed Grant to rain a barrage of telegrams and phone calls upon John until he'd agreed to jump Tim Rose's ship in favor of the New Yardbirds. John received nearly fifty telegrams at home, as well as at his local pub, Three Men in a Boat; eight telegrams had been sent by Robert, forty from Peter Grant. When a response didn't come quickly enough, Robert was dispatched to talk sense into John in person. "I knew there was really only one drummer I'd ever seen that was any good, and that was John. But he was working with Tim Rose and earning some money, and I had to persuade him it was going to be big."

It had been three months since John had last heard from Robert, and now he couldn't get rid of him. Evidently, having spent some quality time with Jimmy Page at his boathouse in Pangbourne, Robert was completely sold on the bright future this new group could offer. Now, he couldn't push John hard enough, regardless of the fact that John's stint with Tim Rose had provided enough money to move Pat and young Jason out of Jacko's trailer and into their own little flat in Eve Hill. Pat would never allow it, John said, now that things had finally gotten stable. But Robert was relentless, breathlessly carrying on about Jimmy's vision—and the money it promised.

"Mate," Robert said quietly, looking at John over the rim of his beer. "You've *got* to join the New Yardbirds."

✳ ✳ ✳

JIMMY WAS BURNED OUT ON SESSION WORK—A DEADENING COMBInation of exhaustion and ennui resulting in the birth of a new creative vision. For all the mystery surrounding his latest project, he relished the change after a decade of taking orders from spoiled, egocentric pseudomusicians and incompetent producers and engineers who thought four-minute pop jingles were the holy grail of musical excellence. Jimmy—a precocious guitar prodigy turned seasoned rock 'n' roll veteran—had watched them all come and go and, as was often the case, crash and burn spectacularly. For Jimmy, enough was enough.

Born James Patrick Page on January 9, 1944, in Heston, Middlesex, Jimmy's current initiative to reinvent the Yardbirds was merely the most recent ambition in a surprisingly long career. An only child, he had bounced around wherever his father's job as an industrial personnel officer dictated—first west of London in Feltham and then to the peaceful countryside suburb of Epsom, Surrey. With no siblings and few playmates growing up, little Jimmy was pampered and reveled in his own imaginative world of painting and books, and thus grew accustomed to enjoying his own company. When a family friend returned from Spain and brought a steel-stringed guitar into the Page home, Jimmy immediately set about learning to master it. Spending his nights alone, tuned in to the US Armed Forces radio network from Germany, he taught himself to play along to the rock 'n' roll songs creeping through from the foreign airwaves. More important, he discovered American blues. Jimmy started simply enough, playing along to the styles of Buddy Holly and Ricky Nelson's lead guitarist, James Burton, until he was note-for-note perfect, then introducing himself to the small community of West London rock 'n' roll hopefuls who, like him, scoured the shops for rare blues records. That was how he met Jeff Beck, the same age and almost as precocious as he was, and—more important—as dedicated to the guitar and the blues as Jimmy had become. Under Beck's influence, Jimmy took up a paper route in order to purchase his own electric guitar: a Hoffman Senator with a much-needed electric pickup. It was the best he could afford, but its lack of a solid body sounded weak, even to Jimmy's young ears, so he persuaded his father to cosign for a Grazioso, England's afford-able Fender Stratocaster knockoff. By sixteen, Jimmy was playing gigs with local bands around West London, one of which—Neil Christian and the Crusaders—convinced the teen to accompany them on tour.

Jimmy enjoyed his romantic role as a traveling rock 'n' roll min-strel, so much like the bluesmen he had come to idolize. But then di-saster struck: following a performance in Sheffield, Jimmy succumbed to the fatigue and sheer exhaustion of constant gigging. After the doc-tors diagnosed his malnourished appearance and constant coughing fits as glandular fever, Jimmy was left with no choice but to remain homebound and consider his options. Against his better judgment, he enrolled in art school in Sutton, shifting his focus to fine art and paint-ing. It didn't last long; Jimmy missed playing the guitar too much. With touring not an option, at least for the time being, Jimmy took the advice of engineer friend Glyn Johns and turned to session work, reinventing himself as an anonymous hired gun for bands that didn't hold their musicianship at as high a standard as their public image.

While the Beatles were still far and away the global phenomenon associated with post-Elvis rock stardom, they had long since aban-doned live performance, eschewing stadiums of screaming fans for the controlled atmosphere of the studio. In their place, the Rolling Stones and the Who began to climb the charts and rapidly sell out club venues. At the time, only one other London-based ensemble seemed a creditable rival: the Yardbirds, whose reputation was based largely on the virtuosity of jaw-dropping lead guitarist Eric Clapton and whom Jimmy could count among his blues aficionado friends. But by the beginning of 1965, Clapton was vocal in his disapproval of the band's shift away from traditional blues and toward more pop-

oriented radio hits like the previous year's smash, "For Your Love."
When he split from the group, Yardbirds cofounders rhythm guitarist
Chris Dreja and lead singer Keith Relf quickly approached Jimmy to
replace him. Loyal to his friend Clapton, Jimmy refused, instead offering up Jeff Beck as another suitable candidate. And at first, all was
well—until Beck's evolving ego took over, leading to crisis after crisis,
onstage and off. As the drama wore on, Jimmy continued his session
work, not only becoming the anonymous go-to guitarist for legions of
top acts—Donovan, the Kinks, the Who, and Joe Cocker, among many
others—but also honing his producing skills. Eventually, the Rolling
Stones' manager, Andrew Oldham, asked him to work as staff producer for Oldham's label, Immediate Records. And while his many
hats in the studio were profitable—and allowed Jimmy the creative
freedom to experiment musically—the work-for-hire status became
drudgery. When the Yardbirds yet again shuffled their lineup the following year, he accepted Beck's pleas to come on board as bassist.

Jimmy debuted as the bassist for the Yardbirds at London's Marquee in June 1966 and went out on his first American tour with the
band in August. They played the Whisky a Go Go in LA and San
Francisco's Carousel Ballroom, following with state fairs throughout
the Midwest and the American South. Although he was officially
the Yardbirds' bassist, Jimmy had taken his psychedelic Day-Glo-
painted 1958 Telecaster on the trip. To the surprise and excitement
of the crowds, Beck started pushing Jimmy into performing dueling guitar solos with him, each performance getting more energetic
and more spotlight stealing. Their bandmates took note. The offstage
fights among the band became increasingly worse, and after a few
particularly grueling episodes on tour that October when he was late
or refused to show up for their gigs, Beck stormed off the tour bus
and out of the Yardbirds forever—leaving Jimmy as the band's official lead guitarist.

Again, Jimmy sat back and watched the band's internal strife take
over—the drugs, egos, and touring stress all combining into a perfect
storm of narcissistic rock 'n' roll behavior, to the dismay of their fans.

When manager Simon Napier-Bell sold off his managerial interest to a wrestler turned rock promoter named Peter Grant in January 1967, the wheels were set in motion for a less than hostile takeover. Following the commercial failure of the group's *Little Games* album, the Yardbirds cut three more singles before deciding to disband and played their final show at the Luton College of Technology on July 7, 1968.

Jimmy was not as distraught over the breakup as some had expected. Jimmy had always hated the Yardbirds' producer, purveyor of bubble gum–pop mediocrity Mickie Most. "Mickie would always try to get us to record all these horrible songs," Page later recalled. "He would say, 'Oh, c'mon, just try it! If the song is bad, we won't release it.' And, of course, it would always get released!" Fully dedicated to Jimmy's vision for a harder-edged Yardbirds incarnation, the band watched as manager Peter Grant showed Most the door. Soon after, the other members of the Yardbirds jumped ship, one by one. Grant and Jimmy, the last two standing, conferred. When the smoke had cleared, they owned the Yardbirds, lock, stock, and barrel—even the name.

The trends of rock 'n' roll seemed to confirm that Grant was correct in trusting Jimmy's inclinations toward a heavier, progressive sonic trend: Eric Clapton's new supergroup, Cream, had released their debut, *Fresh Cream*, at the beginning of 1967 to much fanfare, while Jimi Hendrix exploded on the psychedelic-rock scene with *Are You Experienced* a few months later. On tour, Jimmy witnessed it firsthand: American kids wanted their rock 'n' roll *heavy*, and they wanted it loud. At the time, the best-selling band in the States was Iron Butterfly, whose album *In-a-Gadda-Da-Vida* was a long-winded blues drone. New American FM radio stations were allowing for longer, extended tracks, sometimes even playing entire sides of an album with no commercial break. Long enough to roll a joint and smoke it.

Grant understood this, and even more so understood that America was where the money could be found. Equal parts ruthless and charming, Grant had been a wrestler and character actor before entering the music business in the 1960s. As a road manager, he had worked for Chuck Berry, Little Richard, and Gene Vincent, among others. Grant had also traveled to America with the Animals and managed bands like the New Vaudeville Band, watching bitterly as record companies and promoters took advantage of the musicians. As such, Grant uniquely empathized with Jimmy Page's industry frustrations.

One afternoon in August while the two were stuck in traffic, Jimmy told Grant that he was toying with some ideas for a new band—something bold and experimental. Something akin to light and darkness. And this time, Jimmy said, he wanted to produce the music himself.

Grant was positive he could score Jimmy a record contract. He also reminded Jimmy that they held the legal rights to the Yardbirds' name and that, prior to the band calling it quits, a tour of Scandinavia had already been booked for the fall. If Jimmy could recast the entire group within the next few months, they already had a tour guaranteed. Jimmy agreed.

During the summer of 1968, Jimmy retreated to his boathouse along the River Thames in Pangbourne and devised his strategy. He didn't just want to record and produce the music as he saw fit; he wanted to *own* the music he made. That would require financial independence, and so in early September he and Peter Grant registered their own company, Superhype Music, Inc., legally distancing themselves from any leftover contractual obligations to the Yardbirds' label, Columbia Records, or producer Mickie Most.

Now, all Jimmy needed was a band.

Word quickly spread that Jimmy Page was scouring the scene for promising young musicians, igniting all sorts of rumors about what tricks he might have up his sleeve. When members of the Who heard about Jimmy's mystery project, drummer Keith Moon predicted the guitarist's ambitions to push the boundaries of heavy rock would go down "like a lead balloon." Bassist John Entwistle corrected his bandmate; Page's project would be more akin to "a lead Zeppelin."

※ ※ ※

"MATE, YOU'VE *GOT* TO JOIN THE NEW YARDBIRDS."

It was August now. Robert was insistent. Not only was the band that Jimmy Page was cooking up the most exciting musical concept on the horizon, but he also claimed it was a surefire means to the steady income that Pat, Jason, and their new flat in Eve Hill required—as well as the big-time fame that John had long coveted.

These guarantees had been made to Robert a few weeks earlier, when Jimmy, Peter Grant, and old Yardbirds mate Chris Dreja first sought out Robert at the suggestion of Jimmy's first-choice lead singer, eighteen-year-old Terry Reid. That singer proved unavailable due to his commitments to Mickie Most, but well understood what Jimmy was looking for in a front man: an androgynous figure with the sexuality of Rod Stewart and with a vocal range that could offer a counterpoint to Jimmy's guitar pyrotechnics. Reid sent Jimmy up to Birmingham to check out the young man playfully called "the Wild Man of Blues from the Black Country," Robert Plant, who was booked to front Obs-Tweedle at a college gig in Birmingham that weekend. After finishing a set list composed of Moby Grape and Buffalo Springfield tunes for the two dozen students in attendance, Robert asked Jimmy what he had thought of the show. Noncommittal as ever, Jimmy had mumbled, "I'll call you this week," and vanished back into the night. But he did call, however, and extended to Robert an invitation to stay over in Pangbourne for a crash course in Jimmy's favorite blues and rock 'n' roll influences, including Little Walter, Chuck Berry, Joan Baez, and Muddy Waters.

To the delight of both, their musical tastes were nearly identical, and Jimmy knew he had found his lead singer. During his stay in Pangbourne, Jimmy told Robert all about the group he envisioned: a rock quartet steeped in American blues, but with softer shades of the new, acoustic California sound that was climbing the US charts. A rock 'n' roll chiaroscuro, or "light and shade," Jimmy's theoretical sound that would incorporate both heavy, loud progressive drones and lighter, acoustically driven compositional touches. Best of all, Jimmy could guarantee a built-in tour of Scandinavia with any musicians he wished to call the New Yardbirds. There was nothing to lose.

Now, all they needed was to fill the last two crucial available spots within the band. For this, Jimmy needed powerful drums, a complementary backbone and counterpart to his unique sound. When Robert asked whom he was considering, Jimmy admitted he was still looking. At first, he had approached B. J. Wilson, whom he knew from their work on Joe Cocker's "With a Little Help from My Friends." Wilson was immediately interested in joining up with Jimmy for this conceptual new band, but, like Terry Reid before him, he was unavailable due to prior obligations (Procol Harum). Fortunately, Robert had an even better suggestion. "Don't make any decisions about your drummer until you've seen him play," Plant told him. "It's hard to describe. I don't think anyone plays the drums like him. I know no one plays them any better."

Immediately leaving Pangbourne, Robert hitchhiked up to Oxford to look for his friend John Bonham, who he heard was playing somewhere that night with Tim Rose.

※ ※ ※

"Well, I'm all right here, aren't I?" Admittedly, John wasn't nearly as impressed with Jimmy's proposal as Robert appeared to be. To John, the Yardbirds represented a once-popular band that was well past its prime. Why else would all the original members have let it fall into his hands? And besides, the forty pounds John was making with Tim Rose had finally brought along the type of stability that his small family required.

"I went with Robert over to John's flat in Eve Hill," mutual friend Bill Bonham later recalled. "Pat was not happy to see Robert because John had a good job with Tim Rose. Every time John went with Robert, the money stopped coming in. So, John took some persuading to join this new group."

Finally, John acquiesced and called Jimmy at home. He told him in no uncertain terms that he was happy right where he was in Rose's group. "When you've got a good thing going, you don't throw it out the window," John told Jimmy. "I'm content right now. Things seem to be working for me."

Jimmy wasn't one to take no for an answer. "This could be a break-through band, John," Page insisted. "We have wonderful manage-ment. . . . I think this is an incredible opportunity for all of us. Think about it and let's talk again." Although he didn't say it outright, Jimmy later remembered just how impressed he had been seeing John play that first time. John's playing was "beyond the realms of anything I could have possibly imagined," he later claimed. "He was superhuman."

With Pat's permission, John at least agreed to meet with Jimmy in person and hear him out. The first week of August, he drove down to Pangbourne to meet with the guitarist. Once there, John was given the same treatment as Robert—hours of Jimmy's curated stroll through his vast LP collection, each representing a facet of the sound he was aiming for. Jimmy also emphasized how important a drummer would be within his new group. It was that latter appeal that John took to heart—hearing the lead guitarist and bandleader expressing his un-derstanding of a drummer's importance. John suddenly began to reconsider.

After a few more days of Peter Grant's continued telegrams and ap-peals, John was finally able to get the needed green light from Pat to ac-cept Jimmy's offer. Her permission came with the unexpected evidence of the New Yardbirds' profitability; John was unceremoniously granted an advance of pay—unknowing that, like much of the burgeoning band's earliest expenses, Jimmy had actually paid him out of pocket.

John called up Jimmy. "You win! Let's do it!" he exclaimed.

The guitarist was overjoyed to have nabbed the drummer. "You won't regret it," he promised his new bandmate.

✳ ✳ ✳

"I saw [John and Robert] only a few weeks later in the Rum Runner," friend Mac Poole later remembered. "I said to John, 'Don't tell me you're in the band.' And he said, 'Yes.' I said, 'Oh, here we go again.' That's when he told me they'd got an advance. And it was a lot of fucking money, three grand each! And from there, it was really a move into a different dimension because nobody had ever got that sort of money. 'We're doing some recording,'" John told Poole. "'This chap Peter Grant has got us in the studio.' And I thought, 'Blimey, that was quick.' Then, three weeks later, John told me, 'I just earned three thousand quid.' And I said, '*What*?' He said, 'Yeah, we had a bundle of money given to us.'"

Poole added, "All of a sudden, John's got the jag and the latest stereo system. For Pat, it was like winning the pools, though she was very philosophical about it. She thought it wouldn't last long."

John celebrated his newfound wealth around Birmingham. Together, he and Robert would hit the Plough and Harrow pub in Kinver, John gleefully behind the wheel of his new Jaguar wearing a chauffeur's cap so as not to alert police to his suspended license. But for weeks, John lay awake at night, wondering if following Jimmy Page like the pied piper was truly the right way to go. Up until that point, John hadn't really considered jumping ship of Tim Rose's tour for any other offers, even though they'd been coming in. "I had to consider so much," John later admitted. "It wasn't a question of who had the best prospects, but which was going to be the right kind of stuff. . . . Chris Farlowe was fairly established, and I knew Joe [Cocker] was going to make it, but I already knew from playing in the Band of Joy with Robert what he liked, and I knew what Jimmy was into, and I decided I liked that sort of music better, and it paid off."

✳ ✳ ✳

WITH JOHN OFFICIALLY IN AS THE NEW YARDBIRDS' DRUMMER, AND only weeks until the group was expected to make their hasty debut in Scandinavia, there remained one vacancy within the band—that of a bassist who could match the prowess of the other three members.

Like Jimmy Page, twenty-two-year-old John Paul Jones was, despite his age, an old pro of the studio-session scene. And like Jimmy, he was also incredibly burned out on the grueling and rigorous routine that accompanied the profitable work. In fact, having worked dozens of sessions together since 1965, Jones and Page had even shared their mutual jadedness toward the important, yet anonymous, work. "I was working at the sessions for Donovan's 'Hurdy Gurdy Man,' and John Paul Jones was looking after the musical arrangements," Jimmy later said. "During the break, he asked me if I could use a bass player in the new group I was forming. Now John Paul Jones is unquestionably an incredible arranger and musician—he didn't need me for a job. It was just that he felt the need to express himself, and he thought we might be able to do it together. . . . I jumped at the chance of getting him."

Music ran in John Paul's blood. His father had been a theater piano player in his youth, providing the accompanying live music to silent films, and taught his son to play at the age of six. A decade later, John Paul and his father formed their own piano-bass duo act, working bar mitzvahs, weddings, and cocktail parties as a team. While away at Christ's College boarding school, John Paul started his first band and discovered his natural ability for orchestral arrangement. Deviating from his father's musical tastes, John Paul soon became fascinated with jazz bassists, like Charles Mingus and Scott LaFaro. He became convinced that, in the right hands, the bass could be used as a solo or lead instrument, a belief that carried over into his first few jobs as a professional musician—one of which brought him into a lineup with jazz guitarist John McLaughlin. At the age of eighteen, with a few major studio sessions already under his belt, he officially changed his name from John Baldwin to a more adventurous stage name, "John Paul Jones," and developed a reputation as an impressive session arranger, working for the likes of the Rolling Stones, Dusty Springfield, and Tom Jones. But it was his session work for folk rocker Donovan, and his producer, Mickie Most, that brought him to the attention of guitarist Jimmy Page.

In total, the sheer number of tracks that John Paul either arranged, directed, or played on well outnumbered the full output of the Beatles—or so Most later claimed. But such a track record corresponds with hours and hours of grunt work, and, now happily married,

John Paul sought more fulfilling work. "I had started running and arranging about forty or fifty things a month. I ended up just putting a blank piece of score paper in front of me and just sitting there and staring at it."

John Paul's own disenchantment with his work was evident enough for his wife, Mo, to encourage him to quit the session game and take up with a band. "My missus said to me, 'Will you stop moping around the house?'" he later recalled. "'Why don't you join a band or something?' And I said, 'There's no bands I want to join. What are you talking about?' And she said, 'Well, look, I think it was in *Disc*, Jimmy Page is forming a group. . . . [W]hy don't you give him a ring?'"

John Paul took her advice. Not only was Jimmy delighted to hear from his old mate, but he also promised to keep him in the loop regarding the drummer he was about to check out—the hotshot from Tim Rose's band that Robert Plant kept raving about.

Toward the beginning of August, Jimmy called up John Paul Jones, who quickly agreed to come to the first rehearsal. If that first jam turned out as well as Jimmy expected, John Paul even agreed to front a bit of investment money his way.

And there was a lot riding on that first rehearsal. The New Yardbirds were booked to play in Scandinavia in just over a week.

✳ ✳ ✳

ON AUGUST 12, 1968, THE BAND MET UP FOR THEIR FIRST SESSION together. "The first time we all met in this little room to see if we could stand each other," John Paul Jones said, "the first thing to strike me about Bonzo was his confidence, and you know he was a real cocky bugger in those days."

John Paul Jones, Jimmy, and Robert may not have known it, but John Bonham was as nervous as ever walking into that low-level basement, just beneath a record shop on Gerrard Street—a makeshift rehearsal space that Jimmy had loaded with wall-to-wall amplifiers in preparation for the day's test run. "It was quite strange meeting John Paul Jones and Jimmy, me coming from the Midlands and having only played with local groups," John mused. "I was pretty shy, and I thought the best thing was not to say much, but suss it all out."

John Paul Jones added, "So, Jimmy said, 'Well, we're all here, what are we going to play?' And I said, 'I don't know. What do you know?' And Jimmy said, 'Do you know any Yardbirds tunes?'"

As it turned out, they were all familiar with "Train Kept a-Rollin'," and—following Jimmy's count off—the room "exploded," according to John Paul, into wall-to-wall energy. "And we said, 'Right, we're on, this is it, this is going to work!'"

Later, Robert recalled a similar sense of the instant chemistry permeating the session. "I've never been so turned on in my life," Robert admitted. "Although we were all steeped in blues and R&B, we found out in the first hour and a half that we had our own identity."

Robert later added, "I could feel that something was happening to myself and to everyone else in the room. It felt like we'd found something that we had to be very careful with because we might lose it, but it was remarkable—*the power*."

"It was great—instant concentration," John Paul Jones recalled of seeing John at the drums for the first time. "He wasn't showing off—but was just aware of what he could do. He was rock solid."

No one was more pleased than Jimmy Page, the group's architect and chief visionary. If that day's first jam session was any indication, his time, patience, and investment seemed destined to pay off. "Four of us got together in this room and started playing—then we knew," Jimmy later recalled. "We started laughing at each other. Maybe it was from relief or from the knowledge that we could groove together." And, most important, with just enough time to whip the group into proper shape for their nearly immediate tour. "At the end, we knew that it was really happening . . . really electrifying. *Exciting* is the word. We went from there to start rehearsals for the album."

✳ ✳ ✳

ENTHUSIASTIC OFF THE SUCCESS OF THEIR FIRST PRACTICE, THE group arranged to meet at Jimmy's Pangbourne home for a one-shot marathon rehearsal to learn the set list for the Scandinavian tour. Since the foreign audiences would be expecting old Yardbirds hits, bandleader Jimmy used those tunes as the new lineup's starting point. He opened with "Smokestack Lightning" and then slowly integrated some songs from Robert's various bands, such as "As Long as I Have You," from the Band of Joy. Finally, Jimmy showed the boys a surreal, psychedelic composition he had begun to write—"Dazed and Confused"—which would introduce his new band, and later audiences, to his signature bowing technique. But this last song was abandoned for the time being when John and John Paul were confounded by the lengthy tune's bizarre and intricate chord structure. Regardless, it was apparent to all four musicians that their coming together was something special. John Paul Jones was particularly relieved and excited at the prospect of being half of a rhythm section with a player as talented as John Bonham. "When I was doing sessions, I played with three different drummers every day," John Paul remembered. "As soon I heard John Bonham play, I knew this was going to be great—somebody who knows what he's doing and swings like a bastard. . . . We had a mutual respect when we both realized we knew what we were doing. I listened to his bass-drum foot, and he listened to what I was doing. It was one of those rhythm-section marriages."

John Paul added, "[John] only used a small kit, but he used to play large drums. He never played a large kit in terms of number of drums—he only ever used four drums most of the time, and never had racks of stuff. . . . It didn't matter what drums they were, I'd hear him sit down on all sorts of strange drum kits, and he'd immediately sound like him. It was just the way he hit them, plus an impeccable sense of timing."

The other three musicians immediately recognized how John's approach to the drums differed from his peers. While drummers often opted to remove the bottom heads, plastering their top heads with sticky tape and stuffing their bass drums with pillows and other cushions for sound buffering, John kept to using a massive kit with the heads intact. He would also only change the heads when truly necessary. And while "close miking"—placing a microphone an inch from the top head of each drum—had become the normal studio practice throughout the 1960s, both John and Jimmy were kindred spirits in their shared belief that doing so only emphasized the less flattering aspects of the instrument's sound. The ringing and buzzing that would trail off a note remained audible and distracting.

John's friend and fellow drummer Dave Mattacks later commented that John's signature "sound" was a perfect combination of drum tuning and Jimmy's microphone placement. "John adopted a variation on a [live] big-band type of tuning—big drums with high 'jazz' tuning, wide open with no damping. Kits tuned that way don't sound quite so good in small rooms and close-miked. You have to get the mikes away from the drums to 'hear' the full sound properly— hence the contemporary love affair with large rooms and ambient mikes. But it's essential for the kit to be balanced with itself for this to work—for instance, so the cymbals don't overpower the drums."

John Paul Jones took notice of John's unique approach to playing very quickly in order to adapt his bass and keyboards to the sound. "[John] used to hit hard, and he was loud, but he was actually a very subtle drummer in a lot of ways," Jones recalled. Echoing Jimmy's own theories on production, Jones added, "There was light and shade, color and groove."

John usually played his backbeats with his left hand thumbs-up, more akin to a timpani style, and kept his right hand palm-over, with the fulcrum slightly higher up on the stick, thus producing a perfectly balanced stroke. While many assumed John's sound was the product of brute force, his real strength came from the flexibility he had in his wrists—along with his superhuman stamina. Still, other drummers were in awe of John's use of the bass drum, which not only defined his signature triplets, but also gave the false impression that he was always playing with a double-bass setup. In reality, John would actually experiment with such a kit only in 1969, until the rest of the band told him he was loud enough with a single bass.

His natural inclination to use his right foot often and his masterful bass technique enabled John's flawless execution of at least two complex drum moves—his bass-drum "doubles," such as on "Good Times Bad Times" wherein he played the doubles as sixteenth-note triplets, and a similar technique referred to as the "Value of Three," allowing him to lay down triple strokes, or triple bass-drum groupings. After Zeppelin's first tour, John would exclusively use Ludwig Speed King pedals on all his future kits.

And unlike many other drummers—especially jazz and big-band players who shared many of his playing characteristics—John preferred to sit low at the kit, even when on a riser. His large frame hulking behind the set, John was unmistakable, even in silhouette.

❋ ❋ ❋

FROM THE BEGINNING, IT WAS SILENTLY AGREED THAT JIMMY WAS the band's chief soloist and leader, with the others woodshedded to become his best-possible backing band. More confident in Jimmy's project than ever, John Paul Jones made good on his promise to cough up extra expense money for the band's upcoming trip and initial recordings. But Jones also finagled his new bandmates into a last-minute commitment he had made to another artist, ensuring John and Robert would be able to garner some additional pocket money. "I must have still been doing some arrangements or had some other commitments left over because, after a short break at rehearsal at Page's house by the river in Pangbourne, I had to go back and finish off a P. J. Proby record which I had already done the arrangements for," John Paul remembered. "So, to keep the coffers full—because no one was earning any money—I booked all of us onto the session. I told them, 'You know Jimmy and I have this great new drummer you ought to have,' and I even got [Robert] in on tambourine just so he wouldn't feel left out. So, our first professional engagement was that P. J. Proby record."

❋ ❋ ❋

ON SEPTEMBER 14, THE NEW YARDBIRDS BEGAN A TOUR OF COPEN-
hagen.

The act consisted of "Train Kept a-Rollin'," which was soon mor-
phing into a high-speed original jam track that, up to that point, had
not been set to lyrics. By then the group had learned Jimmy's version
of "Dazed and Confused"; Jimmy's old Yardbirds centerpiece "White
Summer"; a slow, seductive blues ballad that Robert ate up called "I
Can't Quit You Baby"; and a long medley of early rock 'n' roll and
R&B milestones by their own favorites artists, both to pay homage
to the music they'd grown up loving and to get the Scandinavian
audience up on its feet. To John's delight, he was able to jam out
with his new mates to such fare as "We're Gonna Groove," by Ben
E. King; "Shake," by Otis Redding; the Isley Brothers' "Your Thing";
and—to Robert Plant's particular joy—a vast multitude of Elvis Presley classics, all souped up to meet the style of the New Yardbirds'
high-adrenaline hard rock. Even as time passed and the group had
its own esteemed discography of hits, their long stroll through rock
'n' roll's history would prove to be a signature encore during nearly
every set list.

It was soon very apparent that this quartet of hard rockers wasn't
the Yardbirds, and Jimmy had long had it in mind to change the name
of the group the first chance he got. Although it hadn't been discussed
during rehearsals, a new name had to be selected, and many ideas
were thrown around during the trip, including early ones like Mad
Dogs and Whoopee Cushion, which were both quickly tossed aside.
Finally, Jimmy recalled the little joke that his mates in the Who, John
Entwistle and Keith Moon, had made when word first leaked of his
new group's formation—the thing about the "lead balloon." As memory served, they had refined it to "Lead Zeppelin," but giggled that
Americans would mispronounce the term as *leed*.

"Eventually, it came down to the fact that the name was not really
as important as whether or not the music was going to be accepted,"
Jimmy later claimed. "I was quite keen about 'Lead Zeppelin'—it

seemed to fit the bill, [and] there's a little of the Iron Butterfly light-and-heavy connotation."

John Bonham, John Paul Jones, Jimmy Page, and Robert Plant left for Scandinavia as the New Yardbirds on September 12, 1968. They returned home three weeks later, just in time for the October 4 start of their first UK tour, commencing at the Mayfair Ballroom in Newcastle upon Tyne. When they played the Great Hall in Guildford's University of Surrey eleven days later, the advertisements still read the New Yardbirds, but the band insisted the organizers bring them onstage by the name all four members had agreed upon. Old Way of Life mate Reggie Jones volunteered to drive John and Robert to the Surrey University gig in his new Jaguar. "There was a huge banner hanging outside that read—in big letters—'*Tonight! The Ex-Yardbirds*,'" he recalled. "Underneath, in small lettering, it said, 'Led Zeppelin.'"

Chapter Four

SEPTEMBER 1968–DECEMBER 1968

Peter Grant hadn't been privy to the first Gerrard Street jam session of the New Yardbirds in August. He trusted Jimmy Page implicitly, and when his star client informed him that the session was "magic," the world-weary, three-hundred-pound mountain of a manager had no reason to doubt it. But still, he did; prior to seeing Jimmy and his new roster of talent, Grant was plagued by waves of depression and apprehension that his financial investment in the group could have been for naught. The Yardbirds weren't a particularly valuable commodity over the last several years, and his dual management of Jeff Beck's new band was a safer bet. But all those fears were brushed aside during the debut Scandinavian tour of the New Yardbirds featuring Jimmy Page on September 14, 1968.

Grant was particularly impressed by the drummer, "Bonzo." It seemed everyone had a nickname these days—Jimmy was "Pagey," John Paul Jones was "Jonesy," that effeminate blondie singer Jimmy swore would work out fluctuated between "Planty" and "Percy." Even Grant was amused to be addressed as "G," as the title seemed to be a form of respect.

But that drummer was a ripe one, John Bonham. First, he wouldn't shut up about some side gigs he'd had to decline for Chris Farlowe once he committed to Jimmy. Then he went back and forth between regretting his abandonment of Tim Rose and reassuring himself it was the right way to go. Grant also heard the drummer worry incessantly about whether the New Yardbirds would sustain his young family. He was already getting fifty bloody pounds a week, for Chrissakes— and then he offered to drive the band's van himself for an extra thirty quid! Where did Jimmy find these people . . . ?

Still, so far, Grant had had to rope the little bloke in only once.

John quickly acclimated to his new band and soon let his penchant for loud volume get the better of him. Having just returned from Scandinavia, the group met at Jimmy's house in Pangbourne on September 23 and 24, running back over the set list from the tour in preparation for their first English shows. They'd all had their fair share of drinks by that point, easing into their tight but loose fashion. After a little too much artistic liberty with the tempo on John's part, Jimmy sidled up to the frenzied drummer for the first time. "You're going to have to keep it a bit more simple than that," he cautioned John, unaware that John had been given the same warning by Tim Rose during their own rehearsals six months prior.

When Jimmy's words didn't seem to sink into John fast enough, Peter Grant, who had been watching from the side of the room, strutted over to John's kit. "Do you like your job with the band?" the massive manager asked the drummer.

"Well, yeah," John answered.

"Could you play drums in a wheelchair?" Grant asked, stone-faced, pausing to let the meaning of the words sink in. John remained silent. "Do as this man says. Behave yourself, Bonham, or you'll disappear—*through different doors.*"

For all his years on the Brum scene, John had never been spoken to like that, and the words hit hard. It he wanted to stay with Led Zeppelin, he would have to learn to take orders from not one but two masters.

Word got around regarding the episode, which only seemed to amuse John's old musician mates back in Birmingham. As Mac Poole later recalled, the story evolved over time, until it eventually revolved around Peter Grant threatening to drop John from the window. "I think Peter must have fired him about half-a-dozen times," Poole later remembered. "Whenever John did something stupid, Peter would have to pay the bill. . . . He wasn't too enamored with all his behavior, but he realized it was the best way for John to let off steam."

It was apparent to everyone that Peter Grant was a very special kind of manager. His unconditional devotion to client Jimmy Page was more than a financial investment; more often than not, it resembled a father-son bond. But instead of alienating the other members of the newly named Led Zeppelin, the other three saw it as a kind of reassurance: if you were on Jimmy's side, you were on Grant's side—no matter what.

Surprisingly, Grant never had a written contract with Led Zeppelin, or with Jimmy as a solo artist, for that matter. "We just had a gentlemen's agreement," John Paul Jones clarified. "He got the normal management fees and royalties from records as executive producer. [It was] all pretty above board, and as a result, it was a really happy band."

Once John got back on track, yielding to Jimmy's original vision for each of the songs that would eventually constitute the group's first attempted LP, the original magic from the Scandinavian stage show only progressed. None of the others seemed to take issue with John's bombastic tendencies, and John's playing and behavior were never seen as anything less than professional. "I used to enjoy locking into John Bonham's drums very tightly," John Paul Jones later recalled of the time. "I really wanted the drums and bass to be as one unit—that's what drove the band along. It was important to be rock solid so Jimmy and Robert could be more free to improvise and experiment. . . . [Onstage] I would start at that front, and I would just move backwards and backwards. I would always end up in my favorite position, which was as close to [John's] bass drum as possible."

※ ※ ※

"Bonzo turned up one day in his mother's [station wagon] with a copy of the album just out of the blue and said, 'You've got to hear this,'" Dave Pegg reminisced. "It was fantastic. . . . The following week, he turned up in a solid-gold S-type Jag. They obviously took off really quickly and became huge, because Robert bought a similar S-type Jag. The two of them had identical cars for a while." As Pegg would realize once he put the needle onto the album, John and Robert had reason to celebrate.

Technically, it had been the New Yardbirds that entered Olympic Studios in Barnes, South London, on September 25, 1968, to lay down their first album; they were still three weeks away from their public rebirth as Led Zeppelin. As Jimmy was paying for the studio time out of his pocket, he also sat himself in the producer's chair, assisted by an old friend, engineer Glyn Johns. The sessions were more or less composed of the songs that the band had been perfecting both during the Scandinavian tour and at Jimmy's boathouse: their touring set list set to wax.

Of the members of Led Zeppelin, it was the Midlands duo of Robert and John who had spent the least amount of time in a studio. Jimmy and John Paul Jones were old pros, but the other two would have to adapt to the controlled setting quickly; Jimmy was apt to remind his band that the meter was running and they needed a finalized LP for him and Peter Grant to shop to record companies. To save on time, John was instructed to *just play*—Jimmy, as producer, would handle the rest, regardless of John's unfettered energy and volume. "Essentially, it came down to mic placement—moving the mic away from instruments in order to give the sound a chance to breathe," Jimmy later said, recalling how he'd often witnessed drums improperly recorded—the result of which was a tinny sound lacking lush reverb. "Drums are an acoustic instrument, and acoustics need to breathe. It was as simple as that. So, when I recorded Zeppelin, particularly John Bonham, I simply moved the mics away to get some ambient sound. I wasn't the first person to come across that concept, but I certainly made it a big point of making it work for us."

Jimmy's goal for the band's debut album was to replicate what had worked best onstage and simply get it on tape. In a further attempt to save on time—and harness the group's unbridled stage energy—the tracks were largely recorded "live," with minimum overdubs or special effects. Playing into Jimmy's "light and shade" visionary theory, many, but not all, of the tracks used a common thematic model: opening as gentle acoustic "etudes," building a quick crescendo led by John's bass-drum-driven stomps, and finally meeting again with Jimmy's gritty, electric blues lead guitar.

Breaking from that arrangement template: the heavy opener, "Good Times Bad Times," kick-started the album like a starter's pistol fired into the air—that is, if the gun had been substituted for an atomic bomb and John was the one lighting the fuse. His incredible control of the bass drum, intermingled with a melodic, yet appropriately heavy, use of the tom-toms, hi-hat, and cymbal crashes—all perfected due to his carefully honed drum tuning—made the track explode from the album's very first moment. An intuitive composer in his own right, John opened with hi-hat and cowbell, following with a solid triplet fill, clockwise around the kit, leading through with a syncopated pattern that was unusually funky for a heavy-rock track. His signature three-stuttering bass-drum sixteenths, quickly followed by sixteenth-note broken triplets, turned the heads of any first-time listeners. After about a minute, John effortlessly segued into a second pattern, a stabbed tom-tom riff that punctuated Robert's beautifully shrill vocals. John brought the cowbell back into the rotation and then another tom-tom-infused return to the second pattern.

To the trained ear, it was like Buddy Rich on acid.

"The most stunning thing about that track, of course, is Bonzo's amazing kick drum," Jimmy later commented. "It's superhuman when you realize he was not playing with a double kick. That's *one* kick drum! That's when people started understanding what he was all about."

Following their rendition of the old folk ballad "Babe I'm Gonna Leave You"—which, in turn, was their own spin on Joan Baez's 1962 cover—John showcased his power of control and dramatic restraint on the third track (a slow blues originally penned by Willie Dixon, "You Shook Me") and the one right after (Jimmy's first true Led Zeppelin showpiece, "Dazed and Confused"). In the case of "You Shook Me," John opened with a slow, dotted shuffle, which he carefully maintained until nearly the four-and-a-half-minute mark, and then a short stop-time passage and two thunderous drum fills—both played at shotgun speed.

Much to John's credit, it was rare for a rock 'n' roll drummer to add the bass drum into a fill along with the rest of the kit; only one of John's favorite contemporaries, Ginger Baker, was known to do so, albeit rarely. But John soon began incorporating the all-encompassing fill into nearly every song and, in doing so, not only developed his own signature sound, but also slowly began to morph a jazz-style technique into a harder-edged form of rock 'n' roll. Although it wouldn't be referred to as such for a few years, the subgenre's name properly called to mind both Jimmy Page's vision of a weighted rock sound and its logical origin within the industrial Midlands—"*heavy metal*."

"I'd recorded Jimmy and John Paul nine million times, but I hadn't recorded the other two," recalled engineer Glyn Johns. "The sound from Bonham's kit was phenomenal because he knew how to tune it, and not many rock 'n' roll drummers know how to do that."

During one segment in the following track, Jimmy was keen to show off a parlor trick he'd been perfecting since his Yardbirds days, taking a violin bow to his Telecaster, crafting a distinctly sinister effect like a demonic moan. Recorded primarily in a single take, Jimmy needed little else than the Telecaster, a Vox amp, a Sola Sound Tone Bender for distortion, a wah-wah pedal, and the surprisingly effective violin bow in order to simulate a one-man orchestra of hellish, textured hypnotic drones.

For "Dazed and Confused," John smoothed out the tempo, playing the in-between hi-hat notes in counterpoint with John Paul Jones's slow, seductive walking bass line. Two minutes in, Jimmy's showpiece composition shifts into a dramatic call-and-response between John and Jones. John follows their sonic communion by counting off a four on the hi-hat, leading the band into a breakout jam featuring Jimmy's high-pitched wail over John Paul's reverberated, thumping bass. Not to be outdone, John morphs the overall feel into a heavy boogie and then explodes into another four-bar fill, using his triplets between the kit and bass—his hands and feet cycling in union.

For the group's first tried-and-true fan favorite, "Communication Breakdown," John maintained three-in-a-row eighth-note bass-drum figures to push the boundaries of speed and tempo, creating a furious, adrenaline-fueled pattern that, arguably, rocked harder than any other song on the band's debut. This along with "How Many More Times" (a lengthy jam turned jazz-blues shuffle) became calling cards for Led Zeppelin during some of their earliest stage and rare television appearances.

When taken as a whole, the group's finished debut album was able to reinvigorate a sense of exploration and atmosphere within the confines of drastically heavy blues rock, all while leaving just enough room to highlight the unique abilities of each of Led Zeppelin's four members. Still, while all four were able to shine, many early listeners were instinctively drawn to John's innovative jazz-rock hybrid technique. While John's style was all his own, properly recording the drummer's natural propensity toward high volume—while not drowning out the other three players—required real innovation. For this, Jimmy Page had long considered the methods that would have to be used in the studio and worked closely with engineer Glyn Johns to ensure accurate levels, all while keeping John Bonham's lush sound intact.

"I only used to use three mics—the idea was to capture the sound the guy was giving you and not fuck with it," Johns later recalled. "I did put Bonham on a riser, however, to try and get the maximum out of his kit. On those sessions, I stumbled, by accident, across stereo drum miking, and it made him sound even bigger. Your jaw was on the floor from the minute he counted off."

As restrained as John was able to play during the sessions, the raw power of his drum methods still needed to be roped in. Even with the concessions Jimmy allowed, in putting John's sound to wax the guitarist-producer still instituted a studio configuration that would keep the sound balanced—sometimes to the chagrin of John himself, unaware that Jimmy had selected Olympic Studios specifically to accommodate his style. "John told Jimmy, 'Don't put me in one of those egg-box studios,'" friend Mac Poole later remembered. "And, of course, Jimmy knew all the studios and knew which one would be the best for drums. When I heard the album, I was surprised by how simple the drumming was. Bonzo told me, 'I couldn't do anything, man.' I said, 'Why not?' He said, "'Cos Pagey wanted it really simple.'"

Like many others who had known John for years, Poole believed that it was Jimmy's insistence on restraint and simplicity that had successfully recorded the "unrecordable" John Bonham. "I still say that that was the reason Zeppelin made it, because Bonham had somebody to control him," Poole added. "In Birmingham, nobody could do that."

Additionally, John was finally able to demonstrate firsthand that his abilities at the drums far surpassed expectations of mere rhythm and timekeeping. Everyone in the studio quickly noticed the young drummer's innate talent for arrangement, crafting percussive melodies within the patterns—another extension of his earliest jazz and big-band influences. "I can't ever remember being quite so excited," Glyn Johns recalled. "[The band] blew my fucking socks off. . . . Cream was nothing like them, because of the sophistication of Zeppelin's arrangements—that was the key. There was very little free-form anything; it was all very carefully arranged, by some pretty shit-hot arrangers."

John's old friend Birmingham bassist Glenn Hughes agreed. "John was *the* most musical drummer I ever heard or had the opportunity to be friends with. He was a huge *arranger* for the band. People talk about Entwistle and Moon, but the subtle aspect of Zeppelin was the way John and Jonesy played together."

Indeed, as half of Led Zeppelin's powerhouse rhythm section, much of the heavy atmosphere on the tracks was the chemistry between John and Jones, who later admitted an excited relief at finding balance with his new rhythmic partner. "In all honesty, I'd say that I probably should have paid much more attention to the writing credits in the earlier days of Zeppelin. In those days, I'd just say, 'Well, I wrote that, but it's part of the arrangement,' or something like that, and I'd just let it go. Not realizing at the time that that part of the arrangement had more to do with the writing than just arranging something. John Bonham's contribution was always much more than he even received credit for. In fact, I know it was."

And while the sound of what would become Led Zeppelin's eponymous debut was truly the work of each member's individual contribution, the monumental task of capturing the raw energy was the work of producer Jimmy and engineer Glyn Johns. Jimmy had rarely been given the freedom to experiment with the techniques now used, but he had been theorizing each element for years. Now, on his own dime and on his own turf, the polished demo he took back to Pangbourne was proof that his many musical intuitions had been right all along. "The whole idea, the way I see recording," Jimmy later explained, "is to try and capture the sound of the room live and the emotion of the whole moment and try to convey that across. . . . You've got to capture as much of the room sound as possible. That's the very essence of it."

Glyn Johns forever remembered that recording Led Zeppelin for the first time was an experience unlike he'd ever had as an engineer, before or since. "I'd never heard arrangements of that ilk before, nor had I ever heard a band play in that way before. It was just unbelievable, and when you're in a studio with something as creative as that, you can't help but feed off of it."

But no excitement could compete with what the band's four members felt at the session's end, wrapping up three weeks' worth of studio time into a blazing thirty-hour process—fifteen for recording, fifteen for mixing, according to Jimmy. When all was said and done, the band couldn't wait to unveil the polished album to the world. "That first album was the first time that headphones meant anything to me," Robert Plant remembered. "What I heard coming back to me over the cans while I was singing was better than any chick in all the land. It had so much weight, so much power—it was devastating. It was all very raunchy."

All of Led Zeppelin—still recording under the dubious banner of the New Yardbirds—knew they were sitting on something special. Now, Jimmy and Peter Grant just had to sell it to the highest bidder.

✳ ✳ ✳

THE BAND HAD RECORDED THE ENTIRE ALBUM BETWEEN TOUCH-down from Scandinavia and with only a few days' respite before the small introductory tour of English venues—primarily clubs and universities—that Peter Grant had been able to scrape together. Still contractually known as the New Yardbirds, the band suffered a combination of kickback and indifference from club owners and moderate-size audiences alike.

No one could have been aware that the group's imminent rebirth as Led Zeppelin would ignite a windstorm of demand. Least of all, John Bonham. "We made the first album as soon as we flew back from Scandinavia," Bonham later noted. "We had only been together for a month, but at that time, I don't think I had any idea the group would achieve so much. . . . It was at least 1969 before there was any reaction in England. Our manager would try and get some dates, and they'd say, 'Who are Led Zeppelin?'"

As usual, Jimmy Page had a grand plan to enact. To him, all exposure was good exposure, as the eventual release of the group's first album would ensure accusations of "hype," and prerelease gigs would only add credibility and word of mouth. He instructed Peter Grant to accept any offer, fee, or billing, and, against every instinct the manager possessed, Grant agreed to the University of Surrey's meager offering of 150 pounds for Led Zeppelin's official debut. Depending on each individual venue's insistence, the group fluctuated between billings as both the New Yardbirds and Led Zeppelin for the duration of the tour; at the Marquee on October 18, they were Yard-birds—and when they returned to the London club at the tour's end on December 10, they were Led Zeppelin.

"The Yardbirds make their farewell London appearance at the Marquee Club tonight," one local paper announced on October 19, "and their final performance is set for Liverpool University tomor-row—after which the group disbands. Leader Jimmy Page has now decided to name his new group Led Zeppelin, and this will make its stage debut in late October."

The only real consistency was the low pay each stop provided: the band was still earning between 75 and 125 pounds a night, while television producers continued to refuse booking them for air.

However, by the end of 1968, music magazines like *Melody Maker* were publishing rave reviews, and teenagers were looping around the block for admittance to Zeppelin shows. One paper described Led Zeppelin as "the most exciting sound to be heard since the early days of Hendrix and Cream." The first Marquee concert was also reviewed positively (especially the erroneously labeled "Days of Confusion"), but most critics continued to chide the "heavy music group" for play-ing too loud.

※ ※ ※

AS JOHN AND THE OTHER MEMBERS OF LED ZEPPELIN CONTINUED to slog along that first string of UK dates, Peter Grant headed off to New York in early November in order to nail down the band's promised record deal and worldwide distribution. Armed with early audition tapes, a Jimmy-approved rough mix of the still in-progress album, and concepts for its cover art, he would settle for nothing less than complete acquiescence to Jimmy's laundry list of demands: con-trol of every album's production, cover art, and design, publishing rights, tour scheduling and venue selection, and unanimous band approval of promotional strategy and execution—in essence, com-plete and total control of the entity now known as Led Zeppelin.

There were two main contenders in the ring for Led Zeppelin distribution rights, the first of which, Columbia Records, appeared the most logical; the renowned home of Miles Davis, Bob Dylan, and Janis Joplin already had the North American rights to the Yardbirds through its subsidiary Epic Records. Columbia's president, Clive Davis, also figured he owned the New Yardbirds—or whatever incarnation of that group Jimmy Page reconjured. But Davis figured wrong; the Yardbirds had been with the EMI label in England and Epic solely in North America, and while the latter company held the band's individual solo rights, EMI didn't. Early on in his negotiations in first joining the Yardbirds, Jimmy had fought for—and won—the rights to his own recordings. And since Jimmy was never signed to EMI as a solo artist, Columbia held no rights to his new material—giving Peter Grant the full legal go-ahead to court Ahmet Ertegun and Jerry Wexler at Atlantic Records from his comfortable suite at the Plaza Hotel.

Under Ertegun and Wexler's control, Atlantic Records had branched out from its already-prestigious reputation as the purveyors of culturally significant R&B; Ray Charles, Aretha Franklin, and Otis Redding had all found crossover mainstream success on the American charts thanks to the label's creative nurturing. Jimmy Page not only was aware of this, but also knew that Atlantic had embraced the kind of heavy rock he was looking to redefine with Led Zeppelin—and considered bands Iron Butterfly and Vanilla Fudge to be logical label mates. Unbeknownst to Clive Davis at Columbia, Peter Grant and Wexler had already started their negotiations, with Wexler prepared to give Led Zeppelin an unprecedented advance of $200,000, plus a royalties agreement five times higher than that of the Beatles—all this in addition to Jimmy Page's original demands. They even agreed to a last-minute one, guaranteeing that Led Zeppelin would be on Atlantic's flagship parent label, not its smaller Atco imprint—a first for any rock band. More than satisfied, Grant summoned Jimmy to New York to sign on the dotted line.

Before completing his victory lap around the winner's circle, Grant had one last piece of unfinished business to take care of—hammering a final nail into the obsolete Yardbirds coffin, once and for all. Keeping his Atlantic cards close to his chest, Grant accepted an invitation to visit Clive Davis at Columbia Records, the label head under the false impression that he was about to attain the rights to Jimmy's Led Zeppelin. Delaying his gratification to the fullest effect, Grant coyly exchanged industry chatter with Davis, until the president finally spoke up. "Well, aren't we going to talk about Jimmy Page?"

"Oh, no," Grant offered in faux innocence. "We've already signed the Zeppelin to Atlantic." A firestorm of verbal rage was exchanged between the two mountainous moguls, with Grant returning to the comfort of the Plaza Hotel to await Jimmy's arrival.

✳ ✳ ✳

JIMMY TOUCHED DOWN IN NEW YORK TWO DAYS LATER AND WENT straight to the Atlantic offices, with Peter Grant in tow. The guitarist happily signed the needed contracts and handed over the completed masters of Led Zeppelin's debut album. Following the meeting, Grant informed Jimmy that Jeff Beck was in town that night, playing with his band over at the Fillmore East. Feeling celebratory, Jimmy decided to join up with his old friend—and play him a copy of Led Zeppelin's upcoming release.

Jeff Beck was unaware that for the album Jimmy had deliberately chosen to record the old Willie Dixon blues tune "You Shook Me." For years, Beck had killed with that very song in live performances, as he and lead singer Rod Stewart perfected a duet of guitar and seductive vocals into a menage of oozing counterpoint; it had become a signature piece of the Jeff Beck Group and a showstopping fan favorite and was even on the group's new album, *Truth*. And now Jimmy and new partner in crime Robert Plant had rerecorded the track, deliberately outdoing Beck's rendition with his secret ingredient—John Bonham on drums.

According to Beck, Jimmy brought the LP backstage after the Fillmore show. "Listen to this, listen to Bonzo, this guy called John Bonham that I've got!" Jimmy said to him. Tears filled Beck's eyes as he listened to the Led Zeppelin cut. "I looked at him and said, 'Jim, *what*?' and the tears were coming out with anger."

※ ※ ※

NOW WRAPPING UP THEIR TOUR OFFICIALLY AS LED ZEPPELIN, JIMMY led the group through the last few UK stops that offered small pay at small venues. The band was undeterred, however, as their Atlantic advance was proof to Robert and John Paul that their fearless leader, and manager, Grant, had come through with their early promises with flying colors.

Most of all, John's initial concern about leaving the comfortable job in Tim Rose's traveling road show in favor of joining up with Jimmy Page's pet project had been a gamble that paid off—and he relished finally being able to pamper Pat and Jason.

"John still lived in a council flat in Eve Hill, which was quite fascinating," remembered Dave Pegg. "In a couple of months, he'd transformed it, and it had got an oak-paneled sitting room and gold chandeliers, and all the taps were gold."

Pegg humorously recalled that John and Pat's flat soon looked like the young drummer had purchased everything in Rackhams, the most expensive store in Birmingham.

"A chap from the Midlands—and all of a sudden he's got all this dosh!"

Chapter Five

DECEMBER 1968–JANUARY 1969

"I s this your idea of Christmas?" John asked Richard Cole as the new road manager careened the rental car along the Sunset Strip.

Now performing exclusively as Led Zeppelin, the boys had flown coach from London, both Grant and Page adamant that the band cut corners during this inaugural visit to America. In his new position, Richard Cole was determined to entertain the young men with every temptation and luxury their meager budget could afford. Having forfeited the holidays with their families, Cole figured they deserved it.

"I didn't pack any fuckin' T-shirts or a swimsuit!" John yelled. "You better change this weather before I get really pissed off!"

A week earlier, Peter Grant had called an impromptu band meeting and announced the Jeff Beck Group had flaked out on a shared tour of the States with Vanilla Fudge—thus creating a lucrative vacancy for a replacement band and backing the American promoters against the wall. At Jimmy's insistence, Grant persuaded the venues to accept Led Zeppelin in Beck's place. Now it was December 23, and the band hoped to begin the new year by conquering a new continent.

As the only ones who had ever been to the United States, Cole and Page knew to expect subtropical weather in the middle of winter. Cole had aided the Yardbirds during their tour of American colleges' select countercultural venues in late January 1968 and, even then, sensed big things ahead for Jimmy. "He knew he was going to be a big leader in rock," Cole later commented. "You could tell. When the Yardbirds finished—somehow, although he'd only been in the group for a year—he ended up owning the name. Don't ask me how, but he owned the name, and it was a gold mine and he knew it. He also knew what he wanted to do with a group, and he just needed the people to complement him."

Richard Cole was born in East London in 1945. He started his career as a scaffolder, but in a pub one day in 1965 someone offered him a job as a roadie for an English band called Unit 4 + 2. By 1966 he was making twenty pounds a week road-managing the Who and later worked for Procol Harum. In late 1966, he took a job with the New Vaudeville Band, then managed by Peter Grant, and kept the job until the following year, when he temporarily relocated to the United States to work as sound engineer for Vanilla Fudge. Homesick, he contacted Grant back in England as soon as a position managing the Yardbirds became available. And when that band had mutated into Led Zeppelin, Cole was a shoo-in to act as their tour guide into American debauchery.

The twenty-two-year-old Cole had only briefly been introduced to the band back in October, stopping by Peter Grant's Oxford Street office for introductions. At one time in his youth, he had aspired to play the drums and was keen on getting to know John Bonham better. Sharing a love of Gene Krupa and Buddy Rich—and a mutual appreciation for fun and mayhem—they immediately clicked.

✳ ✳ ✳

DURING THE FINAL FEW DAYS OF 1968, JOHN READIED HIMSELF FOR his first taste of America. But what should have been a time of incredible optimism was, instead, a frantic rush to check off last-minute tasks and swallow any trepidations regarding leaving Pat and Jason at home for the holidays.

John would also have to come face-to-face once again with a growing fear of flying—this time across the Atlantic, no less. In the days prior to leaving from London to Los Angeles, John busied himself with Christmas shopping and packing, then was off with the rest of the band.

The band had three days to kill in Los Angeles before their official US debut in Denver. They'd agreed to a couple of carefully selected press interviews but opted to skip rehearsal time; their small tours of Scandinavia and English colleges had already provided all the finishing school they needed.

Richard Cole had little choice but to yield to Grant's belt-tightening. "We flew coach in commercial planes and pinched pennies on airfares by milking TWA's 'Discover America' plan," Cole later remembered. "[It] allowed us to buy airline tickets that routed us through the U.S., saving us 50 percent on every connection. . . . In most cities, we stayed at Holiday Inns or other reasonably priced hotels. At the airports, there weren't limos waiting for us, but rented cars, usually Ford LTDs from Hertz or Avis."

Grant had budgeted for an infinitesimal road crew of two to aid Cole, who also acted as the band's driver. Alongside Cole, whose chief responsibility was Jimmy and Robert—the "faces" of the band—were Kenny Pickett, former singer with 1960s band Creation and whom the group soon nicknamed "Pissquick," and his drummer friend Glen Colson, who had slugged gear for the group during the UK winter dates. "I did about six or seven gigs with them," Colson later remembered. "Basically, Kenny and I had to do everything. We had a Transit van, and, between us, we had to carry a Hammond organ, a PA, a drum kit, and two Marshall stacks. We had to carry this B3 Hammond organ, and yet John Paul Jones never used it. . . . We never traveled with them. We'd turn up at the gig with the Transit and set up the gear, and they'd arrive later in a car driven by Richard Cole."

Colson soon noticed that throughout that first tour, the band's dynamic was a seesaw of power and direction always tipped in favor
of leader Jimmy Page. "As far as I could see, Jimmy was the boss,
and none of the others said a word," he mused. "Although Kenny
introduced me to them, they never spoke and only smiled. They'd sit
around the dressing room saying nothing. I guess they were sort of
smoldering, ready to explode onstage."

Aside from employing two hired hands, Cole was allowed one
other small concession. Thanks to his previous tours with the Who,
the Yardbirds, and Vanilla Fudge—whom Led Zeppelin would be
joining in only a few nights—Cole was well acquainted with the
tawdry luxury of the notorious Chateau Marmont and purposely
selected the infamous hotel as their temporary base of operations.
There, the band members shared outdoor bungalows, John insisting on rooming with his only true friend in the band, Robert, while
Jimmy bunked with Cole.

"We ended up in the suite Burl Ives had just vacated," Robert
Plant later recalled. "Down the corridor were the GTOs, Wild Man
Fischer, and all those Sunset Strip characters of the time. . . . I was
teleported." For Robert, LA's across-the-board acceptance of hippie
culture was a much-needed change of scenery. While visiting Page in
Pangbourne only a few months before, Plant had been berated on the
street by an old woman cursing his long, flowing blond locks; when
he went to a nearby policeman to report the harassment, the cop had
sided with the woman. Now in sunny California, Robert could let out
a sigh of relief and, very literally, let his hair down.

The Chateau Marmont was just the place for Led Zeppelin to dive
headfirst into a pool of free love and decadence. The West Hollywood
haunt was first built in 1929, specifically designed as an oasis for the
town's wild elite. Four decades later, it still accommodated a wide
range of clientele, from the posh to the perverse, and in doing so
became a hybrid stomping ground where mainstream stars could
hobnob with bohemians, iconoclasts, and wannabees alike. Under
normal circumstances, it was the ideal place to provide the members

of Led Zeppelin an exotic distraction while low on funds, but, in the thick of the 1968 holiday season, the only thing the young men craved was a home-cooked Christmas turkey. Surprising his mates, John happily obliged, stepping up to the challenge of using the Chateau suite's deluxe kitchen to prepare one of his mother's holiday specialties for the others.

There was little talk while the band ate. Absent was John Paul Jones, who would soon make a habit of booking his own accommodations elsewhere; he and his wife had flown to the States separately and made plans to spend Christmas with singer Madeline Bell in New York. Later on when he joined his bandmates for the rest of the West Coast shows, he bunked with Pissquick.

With no guarantee that the US tour would go as well as Jimmy and Peter Grant had promised, and without the comfort of family to fall back on, the loneliness hit John and Robert the hardest. John had been excited for the first Christmas he'd be able to truly pamper Pat and Jason, and Robert had just become a newlywed weeks earlier; following a November 9 Led Zeppelin show at the Roundhouse in London, for which longtime hero John Lee Hooker had opened for the band, Plant and Maureen had an impromptu wedding ceremony immediately following the concert. Now alone in America, that night felt like ages ago to them all.

"I hate to dwell on it, but this is really shitty being this far away from my wife on Christmas," Robert finally offered, breaking the silence. "Really shitty!"

Jimmy quietly agreed but remained assured of the payoff to follow. He and Grant had staked their entire musical venture on American audiences—and Page had personally sunk a fortune into it. John quietly remained hopeful, but the homesickness filled him with wavering doubt. After years of promising Pat that he could make good on the drums, the past few months had finally proved his instincts might have just been correct—but with America the litmus test for potential superstardom, this was the trip that could make or break the dream. Just as Jimmy had put his faith in Zeppelin, John put his faith in Jimmy and Grant. Uncharacteristically, Grant had opted to stay home with his family for Christmas, leaving Jimmy the sole agent of optimism; in anticipation of the upcoming Denver debut, morale was decidedly low.

Grant's decision to sit out Led Zeppelin's US launch left everyone confused and doubtful, and the manager immediately regretted the move. Ever their protector, Grant instead spent the entire time at his Oxford Street office on the boys' behalf, making consecutive international calls to every FM station in the next town the band was set to appear, gently "reminding" the respective program directors of Led Zeppelin's imminent arrival. Strategic by nature, Grant also asked the DJs which tracks from the new album American listeners favored; Jimmy insisted on knowing how to give the people what they wanted come showtime.

The morning after their blue Christmas, the band loaded up at LAX for their TWA flight to Colorado, again flying coach. Backstage at the Denver Coliseum, they finally met up with a well-rested but similarly anxious John Paul Jones. Despite their nerves, all were encouraged by their placement on a strong triple bill, as Led Zeppelin was slated to open for Vanilla Fudge and Spirit. John was particularly keen on becoming acquainted with Fudge's behemoth drummer, Carmine Appice; he'd spent hours studying Appice's solos and fills on the group's 1967 self-titled album, as well as their hit follow-up from earlier in the year, *The Beat Goes On*. And tonight, at long last, John could finally count the heavy drummer among his professional peers.

Led Zeppelin was allotted forty-five minutes of stage time, just enough for a half-dozen songs combined with Jimmy's lengthy violin-bow solo routine. For his part, John had been working on his own drum solo as well, a lengthy composition he often entertained Pat with back home. Tonight, American audiences would get their first taste of the virtuoso composition, which John had cheekily named "Pat's Delight."

As the clock ticked toward showtime, the Zeppelin boys were all sweating bullets. While Jonesy leaned against a wall of the shared dressing room, staring silently at the floor with his arms crossed over his chest, John nervously tapped on some cardboard boxes piled up on the floor like drum skins. Finally, they heard the show's promoter, Barry Fey, bellow from outside: "Ladies and gentlemen, give a warm Denver welcome to Led Zeppelin!"

Jimmy, Jonesy, Robert, and John glanced at one another for a long moment. In unison, they strutted single file down the concrete stairs toward the stage. John trailed behind, eyes on the floor and stick twirling in his right hand. America was to be the band's salvation or their doom.

* * *

"THE CONCERT WAS CRANKED OFF BY ANOTHER HEAVY, THE LED ZEPpelin," wrote *Rocky Mountain News* music critic Thomas MacCluskey the following morning, "a British group making its first U.S. tour. Blues oriented, although not a blues band, hyped electric, the full routine in mainstream rock—done powerfully, gutsily, swingingly by the end of their set."

MacCluskey went on to laud all four members, only singling out the Midlands boys for criticism, adding that while Robert was "a cut above in style," he held "no special appeal in sound." As for John, he was "a very effective group drummer, but uninventive, unsubtle and unclimactic in an uneventful solo." John would challenge that consensus in the coming year.

Jimmy was the only one who got raves for the performance. Ironically, the review ran alongside an ad for *Blow-Up*, the Italian suspense film that had featured an extended cameo by the Yardbirds during the later era of Jimmy Page. Later, Fey would retrospectively recall the evening very differently: "They started playing, and it was incredible. . . . It was an unbelievable show; people were gasping. . . . That was a big day in Denver history."

But regardless of a few kind words offered to soften the blow, that review kick-started what would become Led Zeppelin's lifelong mistrust of music critics and journalists—especially John's, who would often find his apparent aloofness and behavior the subject of most printed coverage, as opposed to his innovation and aesthetics. In the world of jazz, a zipped lip had worked for the mystique of Miles Davis; not so for rock stars.

Although the band was reluctant to admit it, early word of mouth would be crucial in breaking into the American market. Their first LP wasn't due to hit US shelves for another five weeks, unfortunately missing the Christmas season, but it still provided a worthy kickoff to the new year ahead of the competition. Jeff Beck, Birmingham mates Black Sabbath, the Rolling Stones, the Who, Jethro Tull, the Doors, and Clapton's latest ensemble following the demise of Cream, Blind Faith, were all working on secret projects that were slated to go head-to-head during 1969, each embracing the heavy sound Jimmy Page wanted to dominate. If that wasn't enough, rumor was the Beatles would be releasing their final work within the same year.

An extension of Page's "let the music speak for itself" philosophy, all Led Zeppelin could do was outrock them all—but that had to be done in person.

As had been the case in Scandinavia and at home, audiences were lining up to see Zeppelin's high-octane blues and hard rock, but it was early enough in their American baptism that music journalists could do a significant amount of damage if they were given an inch. The best possible strategy, as Jimmy repeatedly reminded his bandmates, was to simply go out and keep playing—and keep faith in the album come mid-January.

In Portland, Oregon, a few days after their Denver debut, the depth and energy of John's ability would no longer be left up for debate among audiences. Midway through the show set, John unleashed a savage marathon drum solo for a full ten minutes. "Pat's Delight" was already mutating and evolving into a longer one-man performance piece. From the wings, his three bandmates plus Richard Cole were transfixed watching the manic performance.

"Jesus Christ," Cole said as John finally brought "Pat's Delight" to a thundering halt. He turned to John Paul Jones. "Bonzo is incredible!"

Jonesy gave a sly grin, then joined the other two as they walked back onto the stage.

John's bandmates weren't the only ones noticing John's newfound confidence and self-assurance; the members of tour partner Vanilla Fudge had taken notice, too—particularly their own virtuoso drummer, Carmine Appice.

"John got on those drums, he was like a ball of fire," Appice later said. "I heard Bonzo's foot thing, the triplet on 'Good Times Bad Times,' and was blown away. When I finally got to meet Bonzo, I said to him, 'I love that foot thing you did,' and he said, 'What do you mean? I got it from you.' I said, 'I never did that triplet.' He said, 'Yeah, you did. It's on 'Ticket to Ride' on the first Vanilla Fudge album.' I went back and listened to the Fudge record again after that and found that, yes, I did a triplet between the hand and foot. But he did it all with his foot. *That* blew me away."

During the next five tour dates, John and Appice "became like brothers," recalled John Paul Jones. Not only were Led Zeppelin and Vanilla Fudge similar in their aesthetic approach to "heavy" rock, but both were also connected by a shared label—Atlantic, although Vanilla Fudge was released through the Atco imprint Peter Grant and Jimmy had fought to avoid—and were mutually represented by attorney Steve Weiss. Additionally, Richard Cole had even acted as Fudge's road manager during his earlier years living in the States— just as Fudge had returned from a few UK dates, opening for none other than the Yardbirds featuring Jimmy Page. Now that Fudge was reciprocating the favor, the bands' two powerhouse drummers had ample time to express their mutual appreciation.

"I used to do a thing in 'You Keep Me Hanging On' where I'd spin the stick and grab the cymbal with my arm," remembered Appice. "When [John] saw me do that, he started mimicking me. In those days, we'd all hang around the side of the stage and watch each other play. He'd look at me and go, 'Watch this'—he'd do the spin and grab the cymbal with his arm—so I'd give him the thumbs-up. 'Yeah, cool!'"

Ever since hearing Vanilla Fudge's debut album the previous year, John had been particularly fascinated with a mysterious technique Appice seemed to be applying with his right foot at the bass drum. Listening to the record endlessly, John spent weeks attempting to replicate the sound that his American idol seemed to produce, and, as old friend Mac Poole later recalled, John's early attempts to mimic it produced little more than confusion among his bandmates in A Way of Life. "In his attempt to get it right, he'd fuck up the band," Poole recalled. "I saw him fuck up so many bands trying to do a particular stunt, which, if it came off, would be wonderful—but it never did. Eventually, over a period of several gigs, he got it off, and you'd see the end result and think, 'Brilliant!'"

It wasn't until touring alongside Appice that John finally learned the real secret of the drummer's elusive sound—Appice was one of the few rock drummers of the time to play with not one but two bass drums. Months after Led Zeppelin's tour with Vanilla Fudge ended, John met up with Poole at the Rum Runner in Birmingham and shared the revelation over drinks. "I said, 'How was Carmine?'" Poole remembered, "and he said, 'Fantastic, but you won't believe this—he's got *two* bass drums!' We had been thinking he was playing it with one foot. It fooled us all. Now everyone talks about John Bonham and his bass drum—truth is, it was [because of] a mistake."

During the time Led Zeppelin opened for Fudge, Appice's drum arsenal was a Ludwig setup he'd acquired only six months prior to the tour, which featured a double-bass drum—both of which were a whopping twenty-six inches in diameter. From the 1940s through the early 1960s, larger bass drums were commonplace among jazz and big-band players, and drummers as diverse as John's first hero, Buddy Rich, and contemporary Louis Bellson had already brought such massive equipment into the fold. In rock 'n' roll, however, such size gear was quite a rare sight. Appice deliberately applied the jazz method to create a percussion balance with the growing demand for greater guitar amplification; if Bellson could still be heard alongside Duke Ellington's orchestra without the need for microphones, so Appice could be heard alongside his bandmates in Vanilla Fudge by replicating Bellson's twin-bass setup.

For his efforts, Appice scored a prestigious Ludwig endorsement and, in meeting John, quickly requested that same sponsorship and gratis equipment be granted his new friend. John was still playing the same setup he'd used on tour with Tim Rose, the green-glitter Super Classic kit that included only one twenty-two-inch bass drum; consequently, he jumped at the chance to get his own gear on par with Appice's custom setup—the first Ludwig constructed in gorgeous maple ply.

"When Bonzo saw my drums, he just freaked out," Appice later recalled. "'Oh my God, what a beautiful kit.' . . . So, I called Ludwig and said, 'Listen, there's this group on Atlantic opening up for us called Led Zeppelin. I think they're going to be big.' What an understatement, eh? So, I sent them a copy of Zep's first record. A week later I called them up: 'So, what's the story?' 'Great, no problem—we'll hook 'em up.'"

John asked one small favor of his new corporate sponsor: while the American rocker opted for a twenty-two-inch bass-drum setup, John wanted to go bigger and louder and insisted on a setup based on Buddy Rich's specifications. Adhering to the request, Ludwig supplied him with two twenty-six-inch basses, a mounted tom and two additional floor toms, a bass-drum-mounted ride cymbal, and two horizontal crash cymbals to mirror Rich's big-band effects. John Paul Jones quipped he didn't understand why John needed the two bass drums; he was already doing more with one foot than most drummers did with two feet and two hands.

According to Appice, it didn't take long after the kit's arrival for him and John to properly bash the supposedly durable set into smithereens. "After getting the endorsement, John and I were testing out some new Ludwig stands while playing at the Kinetic Playground in Chicago. By the end of the night, we had both broken the stands, so we gave them back and said, 'They're gonna need to be a lot stronger;

we broke them.' You should have seen the look of shock on the faces of the people from Ludwig!"

For that first American tour, it had been roadie Glen Colson's job to act as John's drum tech, and he was present the day John's prized maple-finished Ludwig kit was delivered. "I think it was custom-made for him. The first time I set it up, he did his nut on the kit—and Jimmy Page couldn't figure out what Bonzo was doing. There was so much drumming going on that he couldn't concentrate—he couldn't keep time. So, Jimmy ordered me never to set up the double-bass drums again. They freaked everyone out."

Along with the maple set, Ludwig surprised John by throwing in stronger, thicker sticks to match his reputed playing style. "A huge box of sticks was delivered—the thickest I'd ever seen," Colson recalled. "John would break two or three drumsticks a night, and I'd have to hand him a new stick while standing at the side of the stage."

While acting as crew during the band's small English tour, Colson witnessed one small episode that seemed to foreshadow John's future fury at being away from home for extended periods. "I do remember Bonzo smashing up a dressing room, which was the first time I'd ever encountered anything like that," the roadie later admitted. "I arrived at some college gig just before they went on, and he'd pulled all the Tannoy speakers off the wall. . . . They were obviously only doing these gigs to warm up for America. A lot of the gigs were only a third full, so it wasn't a big deal."

John's erratic behavior was usually chalked up to his natural stage fright, fueled only more by his massive tolerance for drink. At first, it was a source of humor to the group, until road manager Cole finally pulled John aside during a calmer moment and asked about it. "Bonzo used to say that it was impossible to come back to the hotel after a performance and sip tea or hot chocolate and watch the telly," Cole later recalled. "After flailing at the drums with the force of an atomic bomb, Bonzo literally needed hours to calm down and unwind."

"I'm too hyper," John admitted. "I gotta get loose and blow off some steam."

※ ※ ※

THE BAND PLAYED ANOTHER SUCCESSFUL GIG IN PORTLAND, ORE-gon, on the final day of 1968. There, a blizzard prevented them from flying back to Los Angeles, forcing Cole to drive them all back through the sluggish weather. Returning to the Chateau Marmont a painstaking twenty-four hours later, Jimmy's weakened immune system finally gave out, and the band's fearless leader found himself temporarily bedridden with the flu. While he recuperated, the rest of the band celebrated New Year's and readied themselves for their imminent Sunset Strip debut the only feasible way: drinking to pass the time. And according to Richard Cole, each of the four young men had their own liquid preference: "John Paul like gin and tonic, Robert would drink mostly wine and sometimes Scotch, Jimmy was attached to Jack Daniels. . . . But Bonzo and I weren't as fussy—from Drambuie to beer to champagne, we'd drink just about anything."

Drinking quickly became the group's way to cope with jitters and stage fright at the front end of the tour, but it was soon coupled with the copious other substances that flowed through the Marmont on a constant basis. "With all the stresses that come from launching a new band—and from touring in general—alcohol became our con-stant companion," Cole admitted. "We had plenty of marijuana, too, and occasionally a snort or two of cocaine. But alcohol was nearly an everyday indulgence. It helped pass the time, [and] eased anxieties."

All four members were admittedly nerve-racked, as their next chosen venue, the famed Whisky a Go Go, could make or break their reputation around the LA scene. The Whisky building had once been a branch of the Bank of America; it was then sold and repainted a distinctive green, and the teller counters and desks were replaced by a stage and glass cages constructed to house dancing girls. Through-out the late 1960s, the chic club became one of the hippest vanguards for breaking new acts, introducing West Hollywood to the likes of the Doors, the Byrds, Buffalo Springfield, Arthur Lee's Love, and Frank Zappa.

Led Zeppelin's three-night Whisky engagement proved to be a massive success. Among the chic stars who had attended were Steve McQueen and drumming icon Buddy Miles, reported local society writer Carol Deck in *Hollywood*. Los Angeles had officially embraced Led Zeppelin, soon viewing the band as the town's adopted favorite sons. In return, the venue became the group's unofficial hangout whenever in LA, "where we could drink to the point of near collapse," Richard Cole recalled, something they "could all do quite well," unaware that John had already been honing such a skill for years.

※ ※ ※

ON JANUARY 9, 1969, JIMMY'S TWENTY-FIFTH BIRTHDAY, THE BAND replicated their three-night Whisky residency at the Fillmore West in San Francisco, opening for Country Joe and the Fish and Taj Mahal for another three consecutive nights as the larger acts' officially labeled "Support Group." While the Whisky run had boosted the new band's confidence, more important, those shows had relayed the critical word of mouth to the other hip cities of California, something that Led Zeppelin saw firsthand opening in San Francisco. "Bonzo and I looked at each other during the set and thought, 'Christ, we've got something,'" Robert Plant remembered later. "That was the first time we realized Led Zeppelin might mean something. . . . [T]here was so much intimacy with the audience, and if you could crack San Francisco at the height of the [Jefferson] Airplane–Grateful Dead period, then it meant something."

On the way back to the hotel, John toweled off his face, from ear to ear. Much to Plant's amusement, his Midlands mate howled into the night air, "The show hit them like a thunderstorm!"

Later, Jimmy described the importance of that night more eloquently to a reporter. "We went to California and caused a bit of a fuss there, especially at the Fillmore in San Francisco," he claimed. "All of a sudden, the name of the band traveled like wildfire."

Chapter Six

FEBRUARY 1969–AUGUST 1969

Mick Bonham hadn't heard from his older brother since dropping him off at Heathrow back before Christmas. While John was in the throes of homesickness and nerves, he mainly called Pat to check on her and Jason's welfare, as they'd spent the holiday season with her family. Now, with Led Zeppelin's nonstop tour schedule picking up steam as they moved over to the East Coast, any communication back home became all the more infrequent.

Mick kept busy waiting for John's return, having taken on his brother's old job at Osbourne & Son tailors. Knowing that Led Zeppelin was scheduled to play Chicago, followed by two dates in Memphis and, finally, a tour-ending gig in Miami on February 15, he didn't expect to see John for weeks, so "it came as quite a shock when John came marching into the shop" to surprise his little brother on February 4.

"He told me he just had to get home to see his family and proceeded to tell me all about the exploits of the previous six weeks during my lunch hour," Mick later recalled.

Following the Fillmore East dates at the end of January, Zeppelin played the Rock Pile in Toronto on February 2.

"Led Zeppelin . . . is a descendent of the last edition of The Yard-birds," wrote Ralph J. Gleason on January 19, "the one which survived the departure of [Jeff] Beck. Jimmy Page is the lead guitarist, and he is, I suspect, a better guitarist than Beck. . . . The failure of the group for me is in the vocals, which are really weak"—but nary a mention of the drummer.

After that show, John's homesickness took a desperate turn, and he pleaded with Jimmy and Richard Cole to allow him a short re-spite back to England. Even amid the band's incredible momentum, they had acquiesced and canceled a three-night marathon at the Scene Club in New York City.

John admitted as much to Mick and complained that in three days he would have to cross the Atlantic yet again, just in time for Zeppelin's Chicago debut at the Kinetic Playground, followed by the Miami Beach Thee Image Club grand finale. With bated breath, the young Bonham listened as John spilled his guts about his adven-tures over the past six weeks. Aside from the band's triumphant first US show in Denver, he went on and on about Los Angeles and the Whisky, San Francisco and the Fillmore, San Diego, and Toronto. But Boston and New York were John's proudest anecdotes.

On January 28, the boys had played their most well-received booking yet—a four-night residency at Massachusetts's famed Boston Tea Party, a club housed in a former temple in Boston's South End. Both Peter Grant—who had finally flown in from England to join the tour—and Jimmy considered this a crucial show, specifically due to its location in one of America's most influential college towns and tremendous student population. Both were aware that when Fleet-wood Mac arrived from London earlier in the year, they had been welcomed into the hearts of American youth with open arms, as had Jeff Beck soon after. In Boston, John admitted, Grant's instincts had been dead-on; Led Zeppelin had been called back for an average of seven encores by the riotous crowd each night of the engagement. During the first night, Jimmy nudged John Paul during an encore performance of "How Many More Times," just in time to witness the entire first row of boys smashing their heads against the edge of the stage.

Jubilant to be present for such a resounding success, after the final encore Grant had literally lifted all four members of the band and squeezed them tightly in a paternal bear hug.

"I can't really comment on why we broke so big in the States," Page later recalled. "I can only think that we were making an impression after the incredible response at the Boston Tea Party and the Kinetic Circus in Chicago, but it was the Fillmore West when we knew we'd really broken through. It was just . . . *bang*!"

Four nights later, they opened for Iron Butterfly at the Fillmore East in New York City. Aware that Butterfly was still the most popular "heavy" act on the American rock 'n' roll scene, Grant had pulled Jimmy aside before showtime and advised him that it was Led Zeppelin's responsibility to blow the headliners off the stage. Clad in his extravagant red-velvet suit, Jimmy led a coup against Butterfly, leading Zeppelin for two hours, plus encores. High on drink and adrenaline, at the show's climax John had leaped as high as his legs could muster into the air, screaming at the top of his lungs.

Mick roared with laughter as John shared the story's punch line: terrified at having to follow Zeppelin's performance, Iron Butterfly had refused to take the stage.

"And then," Mick recalled, "he was gone again."

✳ ✳ ✳

BY THE TIME THE BAND'S DEBUT ALBUM, *LED ZEPPELIN*, HIT AMERIcan shelves on January 12, 1969, it had already won over young men in a number of metropolitan areas. Not only had the band's concerts helped generate the necessary word of mouth to make the debut album a highly anticipated event, but progressive FM stations had jumped on bootlegged copies of "Communication Breakdown" and "Dazed and Confused" for weeks, sending teenage rock lovers into a frenzy. Jimmy and Grant's "no singles" dictum had also paid off, as new audiences hungry for a taste of Zeppelin had little issue with having to shell out for the full LP. But while many critics had accused the band of "hype" motivated solely by financial success, when the album's solid sales garnered critical backlash, the band not only was stunned—all three were confused, hurt, and, finally, pissed.

Long considered by the band to be the greatest of the American rock magazines, *Rolling Stone* set an early precedent of aiming verbal vitriol in the band's direction. "The latest of the British blues groups so conceived offers little that its twin, the Jeff Beck Group, didn't say as well or better three months ago," wrote *Stone* house critic John Mendelsohn in the March 15 issue, adding that Led Zeppelin was little more than a combination of "an excellent guitarist who, since leaving the Yardbirds and/or Mayall has become a minor musical deity, a competent rhythm section and a pretty soul belter who can do a good spade imitation."

Despite the criticism, John couldn't be prouder of the band's public debut and couldn't wait to share the final product with his closest friends and family. "On February 18, I received a phone call from John, telling me that he was back home and that he had a copy of their first album," Mick Bonham recalled. "He was so enthusiastic about it all and asked if I'd like to pop over that night to hear it—of course I did, but I'd made plans to go out. 'That's fine,' said John. 'Bring them all over. We'll have a bit of a party.'"

Mick picked up his friends and headed straightaway to John and Pat's Eve Hill flat, nervous that his friends—devoted soul and R&B fanatics—wouldn't offer John the kind of reception he was obviously hoping for. But once introductions were made, Pat tucked Jason into bed, while John poured himself a glass of wine and popped a brand-new copy of *Led Zeppelin* onto the turntable. "For the first couple of tracks, we just sat there giving quizzical sideways glances at each other, as John eagerly gave a running commentary of who was doing what on each track," Mick remembered. "I think it was John's total enthusiasm for the band, the music, and the unbelievable time he'd spent in America that really made me start to enjoy the work. . . . [U]ltimately, it was the fact that by the end of the tour, the band had made the break-through they desired. They were the band that everyone was talking about."

John was slated to leave on tour again in only a matter of days. Starting February 24, the band would pick up where they'd left off in gigging around the UK club circuit. Before Mick and his three friends left that night, John informed his brother that he had booked the posh Lafayette Club to celebrate Pat's upcoming twenty-first birthday party the following Monday—and that Led Zeppelin would be acting as the evening's entertainment. To their shared surprise and delight, John invited the whole gang to attend the rowdy soiree.

As Mick walked to his car outside, he heard John yelling to him from the apartment window. "Oi! What d'yer think of the new mo-tor?" John called down, pointing to a brand-new, sleek black S-type Jaguar parked at the curb.

"'*Bostin'*, *innit?!*" John yelled, flashing a wide grin beneath his beard.

✳ ✳ ✳

WHEN THE BAND HEADED BACK OUT ON THE ROAD FOR THEIR MARCH 1 show at the Van Dike Club in Plymouth, they were just beginning to feel like champions. Grant reported that *Led Zeppelin* had entered the American charts at number 90, but was rising steadily by the day. More important, their shows were all becoming sold-out events, and even if the critics were confounded by the album, their concert reviews more than made up for their growing reputation. Jimmy Page was no longer regarded as a mere "session man" extraordinaire, but a legitimate guitar rival to Beck, Clapton, and Hendrix. Although he hadn't conquered the world just yet, his meticulous assembly of Led Zeppelin was truly a sum of its parts. John Paul Jones, likewise, had emerged from the shadows as a bona fide musician's musician, his sly mastery of multiple instruments winning him universal critical accolades, and although Robert Plant was usually the brunt of frequent critical nitpicking—more often than not due to his androgynous, flamboyant posturing and way of dress—his stage presence and sex appeal had made him an overnight star.

And while the money and fame were glorious enough, no one appreciated the mere recognition of his talents more than John. It had taken him years of serious practice and concentration, independent study, and grueling nights onstage with failed band after failed band. Numerous music writers had already predicted his arrival as that of heir apparent to Keith Moon. Rock 'n' roll fans were accustomed to English drummers small in stature, small figures built with wiry strength—men like Ringo Starr, Charlie Watts of the Rolling Stones, or even John's personal favorite fellow wild man, Keith Moon himself. John, however, displayed his years as a construction builder throughout his torso and wore his hours bashing against the skins and toms on his large, hulking frame. Other drummers looked like human metronomes; John looked every inch the brawler, and his playing style matched his physical appearance: *brutal*.

But that was largely in America. Back home in England, the same type of superstardom continued to elude them. "They had conquered America, and all of a sudden, they were back on the little English circuit playing to four hundred people," Richard Cole later remembered. Jimmy was depressed by the English response. In London's West End, skinheads in suspenders would shout obscenities at him.

In the band's own home country, the debut album had been unceremoniously pushed back for a March release, and, once on the British shelves, it was completely ignored by the country's most significant radio network, BBC Radio 1. The members of Led Zeppelin took notice. For the next two months, the band attempted to reintroduce itself to England, kicking off their second UK tour at the Fishmongers' Hall in London. After playing nearly every major club in the city, they returned to Denmark and Sweden for a string of seven more concerts, as well as their first television appearance in Copenhagen. Exhausted, they returned home again for one more night, stubbornly trying to make a dent in the British market.

Mick Bonham vividly remembered his brother's frustrations of the British indifference, as well as the band's continued strategy to garner domestic publicity. "When they arrived back, it was into the Maida Vale Studio in London to record for the BBC World Service, and then do their first TV appearance on the BBC show *How Late It Is*," Mick recalled, noting that when he heard from John that week, the elder Bonham was excited at the prospect of playing in his own hometown on March 22—this time as the headlining act at Mothers, a popular venue in the heart of Birmingham. Originally called the Carlton Ballroom, then the Carlton Club in 1963, it had been one of John's regular stomping grounds during his wilder years in the early 1960s. In the years since, the venue's entertainment had changed with the times, and it now boasted such big names as the Who and Pink Floyd.

"John phoned me to tell me to come along and see them, as it would be the only local gig on the tour," Mick said. "For Robert and John, it would be a great return to their roots, as it would also be their first gig in Birmingham together since their Band of Joy days. The place was packed, and, as the band launched into their opening number, the venue erupted."

For months, Peter Grant had been trying to coerce John to move with Pat and Jason out of Eve Hill in Dudley, West Midlands, and into posher digs closer to London. According to Grant, it would make it easier for John to "stay close to the action and be available to fly out to America from Heathrow at short notice." But receiving that warm welcome home at Mothers in the heart of Brum—as opposed to the cold indifference Led Zeppelin had gotten throughout the rest of the United Kingdom—only solidified John's adamant decision to remain within Birmingham. He told Grant in no uncertain terms that he wouldn't budge, although things had been going well enough financially for John and Pat to begin considering a move somewhere larger and farther away from the madding crowd.

❋ ❋ ❋

ON APRIL 20, JOHN PACKED UP AND FLEW BACK TO LOS ANGELES with the band. Although they hadn't given up on cracking the United Kingdom, it was growingly apparent that America held their biggest demographic. This time around, Led Zeppelin would be offered four times more money and larger venues and, on only their second US tour, elevated to coheadliner at each stop. For just over five weeks on the road—and after paying the booking agents, lawyers, accountants, roadies, and publicity agents—the members of Led Zeppelin and Grant would split about $150,000 total. It was more money than any of them had ever seen in such a small amount of time.

The twenty-nine-concert tour was set to commence on April 24, 1969, with four nights at the Fillmore West, two gigs at the nearby Winterland Ballroom in between, and ending up weeks later, on John's twenty-first birthday, no less, at the Fillmore East in New York.

"Britain's hard, hot, electronic rock quartet, Led Zeppelin, headlines the Fillmore West show which opened before an unexpected overflow audience last night," reported Philip Elwood, blues and jazz critic for the *San Francisco Examiner*. "Drummer John Bonham has become much more visually demonstrative and less rhythmically interesting."

To John, who was already slightly weary from the road, the fact that they would be reuniting with Vanilla Fudge softened the anxiousness and imminent boredom.

Never settling, Led Zeppelin's stage show was expanding by leaps and bounds. Their original hour-long show now stretched to an hour and a half onstage. Already bulging with original material off their first album, the members' respective solos plus numerous encores ballooned each night's event to two and a half hours. Knowing that they would need to tour for much of 1969, the band also had little choice but to begin writing and refining songs for their follow-up album while on the road, leaving Jimmy the additional responsibility of finding various local studios for the band to stop and record as needed. Atlantic was already hungry for another album to push.

Between their massive stage show and unrivaled work ethic, Led Zeppelin soon garnered equal parts respect and jealousy from their rock peers. "When Led Zeppelin first came out, I thought they were fantastic," Who singer Roger Daltrey later said. "They supported us on one of their first gigs in the States in Maryland. I stood on the side of the stage and watched their set, and I thought they were brilliant. I was impressed with the whole band. . . . Throughout our early history, we used to do loads of gigs with Hendrix and Cream, that three-piece-band-and-a-singer formula. We were well schooled in that, but Zeppelin took it to another level. There was a power there. All of a sudden, there was a new form of music."

When the band touched down in LA for their triumphant return to the Whisky a Go Go, Cole again booked bungalows at the Chateau Marmont. This time, however, loyal hordes of hangers-on and groupies knew to look for them, and the onslaught became a source of guilty pleasure and distraction. But the lines of half-naked girls camping out throughout the Marmont's lobby and hallways were nothing compared with the band's in-suite indulgences. "We were in the Los Angeles area for almost a week," Cole later recalled, "and at the Chateau Marmont, we ran room service ragged with our appetite for booze." He recalled John turning to him smirking, offering an aside. "Los Angeles is something special," John told him. "It's different. It's decadent."

Los Angeles also provided them with opportunities to meet their own music idols in the flesh. John got the chance of a lifetime to record with the old hero of his teen years, Screaming Lord Sutch. On May 1, Jimmy was invited to stop down at Hollywood's Mystic Studios, also known as Mirror Sound, for a session Sutch had booked alongside Jeff Beck and Noel Redding; *Lord Sutch and Heavy Friends* was an album that would include various rock 'n' roll masters of the moment, and Jimmy was contacted by Sutch directly.

John had a lot of fun collaborating with his longtime hero, adding his signature heavy drumming to six of the album's total tracks. He even told a reporter of his adventure to acquire Sutch's autograph back in his teen years, marveling at how far he'd come since then. "To get him to sign, I cycled from my home in Birmingham to Stratford-on-Avon, where he was speaking. I couldn't afford the fares. The whole thing added up to a round trip of forty-eight miles. I never guessed when he signed that, years later, I would be one of his Heavy Friends on an LP!"

John and Jimmy were impressed with the acoustics in Mystic's facilities and returned there five days later to lay down John's drum solo, "Pat's Delight," for inclusion on the next album. And the band's budding relationship with Sutch wasn't just behind the scenes, either; on May 8, the members of Zeppelin attended the Lord's performance at hip venue Thee Experience on Sunset Boulevard—and even carried him out onstage as the flamboyant performer's "pallbearers."

Before Led Zeppelin headed over to the East Coast, they had two sold-out shows booked at the Rose Palace in Pasadena—one of which was set for John's twenty-first birthday. Acknowledging John's melancholy at having to spend his own milestone birthday away from his family, Peter Grant and road manager Richard Cole ordered the band's entourage to run out and score the most logical gift they could imagine: a four-foot-tall bottle of champagne.

Only half aware of John's tolerance and penchant for excess, the men stood idly by as the drummer single-handedly guzzled nearly a third of the bottle before showtime. As John took to the Rose Palace stage, he dragged both his body and the bottle with him to the drum kit. "Bonzo got totally wasted, to where he really couldn't play," remembered Led Zeppelin roadie Henry Smith. "And when we got up onstage for the second show, I was holding his seat and holding him up by the scruff of his collar, just so he could get through the set."

Throughout the performance, John raised the bottle over his head every other song, pouring the alcohol over his face and torso. By the concert's end, the bottle was empty—and John had crashed off his stool twice. Smith later recalled, "I think after that show it was like, 'Bonzo, if you don't clean up, you're out of the band.'"

But it was in the third week of the tour that Led Zeppelin's stop in Seattle upped the ante of their dubious reputation for debauchery. When they learned that none other than Chuck Berry would be opening for them at the Green Lake Aqua Theatre, John and Robert were particularly enthused. They watched, enthralled, as the consummate rock 'n' roll legend emerged from his Cadillac (which Berry had personally driven himself from his home in St. Louis), unpacked his lone guitar, effortlessly played a set of all classic tracks with a backup band he'd never met before, and then tossed the sum of his cash payment into an old briefcase before driving off into the night. To Robert and John—whose youths were lush with dreams of rock stardom and romantic visions of becoming mysterious traveling agents of the blues—this scene of Berry embodying those very ideals was a defining moment.

The band was staying at the unique Edgewater Inn, which was constructed directly on a pier over Puget Sound's Elliott Bay, allowing the guests staying on its north elevation to literally fish from their hotel-room windows. Playing into the gimmick, the waterfront inn housed a bait-and-tackle shop in its lobby, welcoming curious tourists with an unspoken challenge to land a fish during their stay. By this time, Led Zeppelin had earned a reputation for being the most rambunctious and decadent of all traveling rock bands, both for their collective love of partying and mayhem and for the sheer number of devoted groupies who seemed to magically appear wherever the band was staying. Although details of the event remained vague, the band's stay at the Edgewater Inn introduced a startling new mythos into the band's growing mystique: according to rumors, members of the band had tied one willing female fan to a bed and proceeded to stuff her orifices with pieces of a shark snagged from the water outside. Although John wasn't one to indulge in extramarital affairs—especially ones that included bizarre orgies and depraved ritualistic behavior—the story, nevertheless, included one incriminating detail: ever the competent fishmonger, he was the band member accused of catching the shark.

As time passed and the legend of "the shark episode" grew—Frank Zappa had even been inspired to write a rock anthem, "Mudsharks," about the circulating rumors—road manager Richard Cole later felt it necessary to set the record straight and absolve the band of the night's most nefarious rumors. "It wasn't Bonzo; it was me," Cole later reported. "Robert and Bonzo didn't know anything. They were kids, [and] yeah, and the shark was alive! We caught a big lot of sharks. . . . But the true shark story was that it wasn't even a shark. It was a red snapper, and the chick happened to be a fucking redhead broad with a ginger pussy. And that is the truth. Bonzo was in the room, but I did it. Mark Stein [of Vanilla Fudge] filmed the whole thing."

Whether the shark story happened to be true or not, factual accuracy proved irrelevant to Led Zeppelin's global reputation. The band was now regarded as the very worst of rock 'n' roll bad boys, and their very real penchant for drinking, drugs, and hotel-room destruction only gave credibility to the more outrageous rumors of Faustian pacts in exchange for stardom and human sacrifices. Cole later added, "I'll tell you how much we used to drink—I think we bankrupted Steve Paul's Scene in New York because we never paid our bar bills. . . . All the so-called Led Zeppelin depravity took place the first two years in an alcoholic fog."

Music venues and hotel management alike soon began to fear Led Zeppelin, and the band wouldn't have it any other way. In only a year's time, they had become infamous. That label, however, came with a price. While the old adage claimed that any press was good press, Led Zeppelin soon learned there were exceptions to the rule—and very real consequences that could impact their personal lives back home.

Jimmy was the only remaining bachelor in the group, and he was aware that the drinking and debauchery enacted by John Paul Jones, Robert, and especially John were mere attempts to battle their desperate homesickness and loneliness. Led Zeppelin may have reveled in their cheeky reputation as notorious troublemakers, but the presence of other women within those gossipy tales could pose serious problems for the band's married majority. As such, Jimmy and Peter Grant began to consider installing a press secretary of sorts, someone to officially monitor the information leaking to the public while also supplying local media with officially sanctioned, band-approved tour updates. Zeppelin's first attempt, one that brought the band face-to-face with the most mainstream of American media, *Life* magazine, backfired epically, as a proposed chronicle of their exploits in Detroit and New York made matters much worse.

Upon landing in Detroit, the group was met by a journalist/photographer team sent by *Life*. But Led Zeppelin wasn't the first choice for twenty-four-year-old reporter Ellen Sander, who had initially pitched full coverage of the Who's ongoing US summer tour to her editors. At the last moment, that band became unavailable, and the lesser-known Zeppelin was thrown out as a replacement. Peter Grant in particular latched on to the pitch, as *Life* had a significantly larger readership than any of the American music publications, and an in-depth piece on Zeppelin's second US tour could elevate the band to becoming a household name. In many ways, it did—but not for the reasons he had hoped.

It started when Richard Cole initiated a pool to determine which member of the band, or its entourage, would be the first to take Sander to bed, and her impressions of the group only diminished from there. "No matter how miserably the group failed to keep their behavior up to a basic human level," Sander wrote, "they played well almost every night of the tour. . . . [T]his time around, on their second tour, from the very beginning, they were almost stars." She later admitted to fearing the band during their time together, mostly due to the brooding presence that the group seemed to exude, and John in particular, who, she observed, "played ferocious drums, often shirtless and sweating like some gorilla on a rampage," and was often intoxicated. Additionally, Sander was less than impressed with the cavalier attitude the four members seemed to demonstrate toward their female fans, most of whom, she noted, were barely of legal age.

Following successful shows in Athens, Ohio, and Chicago, and a triumphant return to the Boston Tea Party, it was decided that the band would book some much-needed studio time in New York prior to the tour's final two-night engagement at the Fillmore East on May 30 and 31. There, the evening's success was horrifically overshadowed by an incident that not only rivaled "the shark episode" in signifying the group's spiral into the darker regions of celebrity, but would also cause Ellen Sander to renounce her *Life* assignment altogether.

Following the second night's Fillmore gig, Sander headed backstage to formally thank Grant and the band for allowing her access over the past few weeks and to announce the completion of her research for the article. After entering the band's shared dressing room, however, she recalled being attacked, hearing "shrieking and grabbing" at her clothes, and "totally over the edge." Within moments, a dogpile ensued, led, Sander claimed, by an inebriated John Bonham. "Bonzo came at me first," she later insisted. "My clothes were half torn off—they were in a frenzy. I was absolutely terrified that I was going to be raped and really angry."

Sander claimed she was saved in the nick of time by a furious Peter Grant, who wrapped his massive arms around John and pried him off of her, profusely apologizing for the band's behavior. "They didn't hurt me," she later revealed, "except for my feelings."

The article never ran, but afterward Sander published her own embittered account of the night's incident: "If you walk inside the cages of the zoo, you get to see the animals close up, stroke the captive pelts, and mingle with the energy behind the mystique. You also get to smell the shit firsthand." Even without the *Life* article hitting the public, word spread among journalists to steer clear of Led Zeppelin, especially the unpredictable John Bonham.

Perhaps making excuses, perhaps rationalizing the behavior to which Sander was witness, John Paul Jones attempted to explain to her the psychology that changes within a person living on the road. "The touring makes you into a different person," Jones told her. "I realize that when I get home. It takes me weeks to recover after living like an animal for so long."

※ ※ ※

To CELEBRATE THE FIRST ALBUM REACHING GOLD STATUS, ATLANTIC Records hosted a posh event in the group's honor at the Plaza Hotel during their stay in New York. But the party had also been organized to deliver them a message: a second album was expected to be delivered soon, so as not to miss the Christmas rush two years in a row. Frenzied, the band rushed to A&R Studios straight from the party and immediately laid down the rough mix for a new track, based on one of Jimmy's riffs, "Heartbreaker."

On the surface, the band appeared to be riding high, yet their morale was at an all-time low. Jimmy, who continued to function as the driving force behind the songs' composition and production sessions, became a full-blown workaholic. John Paul Jones kept quiet and busy with new arrangements and instruments, while Robert kept his own yearning for home at bay by daydreaming about home, often mumbling about how much he missed his wife, Maureen, and his newborn daughter, Carmen Jane. But it was John whose anxiety and homesickness began to take on a dark, morose edge. Without his wife and child around to keep him on the straight and narrow, John's propensity for drinking and mayhem became the constant companions to his frustrations.

Witnessing his boys' lewd behavior firsthand, Grant attempted to fly the bands' families in whenever budget and schedule allowed. He needed to keep them content and focused, especially considering that the coming year would yield even more shows and larger venues. "There was an urgency to being in the States," John said later. "I remember we went out to the airport to meet our wives, got them back to the hotel, and then went straight back to the studio and did 'Bring It on Home.' We did a lot that year like that."

During Led Zeppelin's first tour of the United States, the band had barely broken even. Grant was determined that this go-round would show a profit—and the next would be record breaking. Although he and Jimmy didn't draw too much attention to the fact outside of the band's innermost circle, this spring tour had only truly been conceived to whet the public's appetite for a third, more extravagant one the following year—wherein Led Zeppelin had the potential to gross almost a half-million dollars by the end of 1969.

※ ※ ※

CIRCUMSTANCES WERE LOOKING UP FOR THE BAND WHEN THEY RE-turned home the first week of June. *Led Zeppelin* had just cracked the *Billboard* Top 10, and ticket sales within their homeland had noticeably increased since their last sojourn across the United Kingdom. With only two weeks to rest, they were slated to head back out on the road by midmonth, commencing with a June 13 performance at Birmingham's Town Hall—a particular point of pride for John, who had seen so many of his own personal heroes at the venue during his youth.

During their time back home, the band also appeared on John Peel's popular *Top Gear* radio show as well as *Rock Hour* for the BBC, the latter of which was recorded live at the Playhouse Theatre in London. The group used both occasions to further entice English listeners, rocking as hard as ever with a brief taste of their three-hour concerts and giving the world its first listen to a few select tracks from their nearly completed second album. If the group was weary from the road, it didn't show during either performance, as Zeppelin earned enough rave reviews to push ticket sales for the next half-dozen performances through the roof. Those six concerts would act as a litmus test for one of the crown jewels of this, their fourth, UK tour—the prestigious Bath Festival on June 28, wherein twelve thousand people were set to gather at the Recreation Ground and Pavilion, advertised in all the British newspapers as "The Big One." It was to be the band's largest audience yet.

As nervous as John was at the thought of playing to such a large crowd, his few weeks with Pat, Jason, and his parents worked to shake off much of the depression that had instigated his rowdy behavior in the States. By the beginning of the following month, however, he would have to face his inner demons yet again, as Grant had almost immediately booked the third American tour for the remainder of the summer—this time to large stadiums and open-air concerts, for which the Bath Festival had been a glorified rehearsal.

The tour opened on July 5 at the Atlanta Pop Festival, but was followed by one of the major highlights for John the next day—Led Zeppelin's booking at the Newport Jazz Festival, alongside one of the greatest heroes of his youth, James Brown. As Mick Bonham later recalled, "After all the times John had played James Brown records on jukeboxes in clubs and cafés, he was finally up there playing the same venue." Also slated on the bill were Jeff Beck, B. B. King, and Jethro Tull—but it was for Led Zeppelin that hundreds of kids rushed the stage to get close to the players. It was a sight replicated at both the Baltimore and the Philadelphia Jazz Festivals the following week.

As had been the case with the previous tour, Zeppelin welcomed Vanilla Fudge onboard as their tour mates. However, as Carmine Appice later recalled, Led Zeppelin was outshining all the bands out for their summer tours by this point—including Fudge. "The band got so big, so fast, we were on equal billing," Appice remembered. "We would close one night, and they would close another."

As Appice explained, sometimes having two separate bands that featured such heavy drummers on the same bill couldn't help but provoke a certain amount of competition between the two camps—leading John to come up with a theatrical signature move that, at the time, no other drummer dared replicate.

"Bonzo used a double bass-drum set on that tour, and I always thought it must have seemed pretty funny to the audience," Appice explained. "The kits looked much the same, [and] we had the same cymbal setup as well, and we also had the six-and-a-half-inch snare drum, and one tom-tom in the middle—and a gong." John and Appice both used gongs manufactured by Paiste, designed to take an appropriate beating, but not necessarily on a nightly basis by two of the foremost innovators in "heavy" rock 'n' roll. In an effort to up his stage game even more—and perhaps in a competitive bid to challenge his friend Appice—it was during this tour that John began igniting his gong in a fiery blaze midperformance.

John's flair for the dramatic carried over to all of Led Zeppelin's stops on the tour, culminating with an episode on July 13 at the Singer Bowl, an open-air stadium in Flushing Meadows, New York. Led Zeppelin was booked along with Vanilla Fudge, Jeff Beck, and a band they hadn't yet been introduced to, Ten Years After. While even Jimmy was enraptured watching their lead guitarist, Alvin Lee, during the set, the combination of heat, booze, and boredom began to whittle down John's reserve. He soon began to grow fidgety, pacing beside the buffet table. He had been drinking all afternoon and was eager to leave. "Hang in there, Bonzo," Richard Cole cautioned him. "We'll be outta here in an hour or so." John couldn't stand the waiting around and grabbed one gratis beer after another in the hundred-degree heat. Soon, Cole noticed "a devilish gleam" in John's eye and what the road manager perceived as "trouble on the horizon."

Pointing to Alvin Lee onstage, John shouted, "I'll fucking fix him!" to no one in particular. Then John grabbed a carton of orange juice from the buffet table and walked just far enough onstage to get a clear shot of the guitarist in midsolo. "Alvin, do you want some juice?" John yelled, and proceeded to hurl the open juice carton at the focused musician, splashing him and his instrument—and igniting a wave of laughter both on- and offstage. Soaked with the sticky liquid, Lee shot John a dirty, threatening look. Still chuckling, John wagged his finger back at Lee, silently warning him against enacting any form of revenge.

With the juice caked to his fingers and frets, Lee had to slow his usually virtuoso rapid playing, struggling through the remainder of the band's set. "You're an asshole, Bonham," Lee mumbled as he walked back into the wings. "A real asshole." To the amusement of the other musicians, John's only response was a fit of uncontrollable laughter.

Jimmy Page had been enjoying Lee's performance and wasn't quite sure what to make of John's vicious prank. "Bonzo's got to get a grip on things," he whispered to Cole.

"He's just blowing off steam," Cole responded. "If he didn't let it out this way, he might be punching somebody."

But with hours left of the Singer Bowl's daylong bill, John, stricken with boredom and drink, was only getting warmed up. When Jeff Beck and his band finally took to the stage an hour later, Jimmy headed onstage to join his old Yardbirds mate for a star-studded jam—but was soon followed by a very inebriated John. Fearing an even worse act of mayhem, Richard Cole desperately grabbed John by the shoulder, but it was too late. John broke free of his grasp and ducked toward the stage. "Don't worry," he called over his shoulder. "I'll be just a minute, Richard—I'm coming right back."

Seeing John rush out from behind the stage, Beck continued to solo through his band's recent hit, "Rice Pudding," but watched out of the corner of his eye as John approached drummer Mickey Waller and got him to vacate his place at the drum kit. The guitarist stopped playing as John perched himself on the stool and then began bashing a sultry Shelly Manne–styled striptease beat. Thoroughly entertained, the crowd began clapping in time to John's rhythm, only encouraging his behavior even more. Watching from offstage, Robert Plant and Richard Cole giggled like schoolboys, but were tempted to rush out as John leaped out from behind the drummer's chair and began to peel off his clothes layer by layer. "More?" John laughed into the microphone after he'd gotten down to his underwear.

With everyone else frozen in disbelief, Peter Grant rushed the stage with both arms outstretched. "You son of a bitch!" he shouted, having noticed a half-dozen uniformed police officers making their own way to John's X-rated exhibition. Peter wrapped his arms around John and ran him backstage to a nearby dressing room. "You fucking bastard!" Grant snarled, locking the door behind him. "If you aren't dressed by the time the police break down this door, you're out of the band!"

Immediately sober, John lowered his head and pouted, putting on the pair of wayward slacks and T-shirt Peter threw at him. Like a schoolmaster, Peter led John out of the room, both silent as they marched passed the confused cops.

Carmine Appice was one of many musicians who were properly amused by John's impromptu striptease—even if the feeling wasn't shared by the older members of the audience. "My mother and father were there, out in the audience," Appice recalled. "My mother said, 'What's wrong with that guy?' So, I said, 'Aw, well, you know, man—they get a little drunk and they get a little crazy.'"

The members of Led Zeppelin were already aware that most of John's erratic behavior was to combat homesickness, but it didn't just manifest in drink. Richard Cole recalled that both John and Robert, each yearning for the comfort of their wives and families, would insist on bunking together at the hotels and would refuse to go to sleep if the other wasn't also there. When news of the August 9 "Manson Family" murder spree reached the band during their stay at the nearby Chateau Marmont, John and Robert were adamant about sleeping with the light on.

The so-called Helter-Skelter murders of starlet Sharon Tate and a group of her Hollywood friends only added to the band's nerves and a growing sense of paranoia. Under orders from Peter Grant, Richard Cole moved the band to the more secure Continental Hyatt House on Sunset Boulevard—quickly dubbed "the Riot House" by John to match the boys' collective misbehavior—and rented out the entire ninth floor of rooms, making them significantly inaccessible to fans and those outside of Led Zeppelin's entourage.

But homesickness and fear of dangerous fans weren't the only things keeping the members of Led Zeppelin up at night. Just before arriving back in Los Angeles for the West Coast leg of the tour, Atlantic Records told them they had an unbelievable four hundred thousand advance orders for the new album. The pressure was on to deliver something amazing.

Chapter Seven

AUGUST 1969–JANUARY 1970

The band started working on the second album only weeks after the release of the first one, and so out of necessity their new song ideas were developed on the road and fine-tuned after each gig. Audiences of Led Zeppelin's late 1969 shows were often unknowingly treated to onstage jams that were, in reality, public brainstorming sessions to work out songs recently hatched in Jimmy's or Robert's hotel room or during a stolen moment in one of many recording studios. If a new riff or hook seemed to work during a concert, it could find its way into the album version. As Jimmy noted, "[The album] began with rehearsals at my home in Pangbourne. Those sessions provided the foundation for the rest of the tracks that were recorded and overdubbed at various studios while touring America. We recorded and overdubbed our way from West Coast to East Coast. Part of the excitement of the album is due to the fact we were completely energized from the live shows and the touring."

Unlike their debut, which drew heavily from repurposed blues songs and extended jams built around Jimmy's completed compositions, the follow-up was intended to showcase the group's united chemistry, while demonstrating each individual member's strongest suits. This time around, Jimmy wouldn't be the only member given ample time to solo; John Paul Jones's various hats as bassist, keyboardist, and arranger would also be given room to breathe—and John's drumming, which had garnered so much attention at the band's lengthy shows, would be memorably featured on a solo track of his very own.

In order to meet Atlantic's deadline, Jimmy met with Eddie Kramer at A&R Studios in New York, fitting the recording sessions in between Zeppelin's nightly concerts. After that particular mixing session, Jimmy immediately caught connecting flights and arrived to perform in Phoenix with only hours to spare. Much of the album was fastened together in a similarly piecemeal fashion. Conceptually, if *Led Zeppelin* was an intentional representation of the band's raw stage energy set to wax, *Led Zeppelin II* sought to harness their frenetic globe-trotting.

"We mixed it at A&R Studios in two days on a twelve-channel Altec console with two pan pods, the most primitive console you could imagine," engineer Eddie Kramer later explained. "The tapes were from everywhere—'Whole Lotta Love' had been recorded in Los Angeles, some were from London, Robert had done voice-overs on the run in Vancouver in a studio with no headphones, and some, like 'What Is and What Should Never Be,' I had recorded myself in New York in obscure studios like Groove Sound and Juggy Sound, anyplace we could scrounge studio time. It was a wild scene, and the band was very boisterous. I left the depraved side of it to them."

Jimmy clung to the master tapes for dear life, preparing the final versions as the band trekked across America. As frazzled and hectic as life was becoming for the famous four, their productivity on what would become *Led Zeppelin II* was birthed out of that itinerant, gypsy lifestyle.

Although sifting through material constructed from this seemingly disorganized method, Jimmy had the order and structure to the album's tracks already in mind—beginning with its heavy opening blast. A deliberate, attention-commanding rock anthem, "Whole

Lotta Love" originally began as a composite from jamming sections of "Dazed and Confused" during the group's stage show. Its lengthy "middle section" was an abstract sound collage made up of an electric organ of higher pitches to complement the growling, evil tones and Jimmy's wailing guitar, meticulously cut and seamlessly woven into the more radio-friendly sections of the song. The eerie, descending guitar was produced by Jimmy taking a metal slide to his new Fender Telecaster and then treated with backward echo effects left over from his experimental Yardbirds days. It was also coupled with a Theremin, an electronic oscillator first used in pop music to literally produce the "good" vibrations described in the Beach Boys' titular megahit years earlier.

For John's part, he began the song using a simple doubled-up rock-infused backbeat, placing the first backbeat on a slowly counted two, and then holding back the second backbeat until the "and" of four—producing a groovy rollover effect. As much as "Whole Lotta Love" was a solid representation of Led Zeppelin's "heavy" intentions, John adapted a true R&B, funk effect to drive it home. During the psychedelic sound collage of the song's middle section, John pedaled hard on the hi-hat with upstrokes, coupled with Jimmy's added reverb, deceptively producing the effect of a rolling eighth-note rhythm. Never one to be outdone, John could reproduce the sound even playing onstage.

"[John] had a lot of input into the riffs we played, more than he was credited for, I'd say," recalled John Paul Jones. "He would change the whole flavor of a piece, and lots of our numbers would start out with a drum pattern. We'd build the riff around the drums. He would play a pattern that would suggest something.

"Lots of things happened onstage to alter the songs," Jones added. "In the fast part to 'Dazed and Confused,' John and I would turn the riff 'round backwards, and Pagey would come across and shout, 'What the fucking hell do you think you're doing?' That was good fun."

On the next two tracks, "What Is and What Should Never Be" and "The Lemon Song," John found ways to use his gong in the compositions, proving once and for all that the oversize centerpiece was more than just onstage theatrical gimmickry. "The Lemon Song" had been a direct by-product of their live concert jams, although Jimmy finalized his solo later, in one of the album's few overdubs. During the studio session at Mystic Studios in Hollywood the previous May, John wowed his bandmates toward the song's end with a single-bar fill consisting of thirty-two "mommy-daddy beats" between hands and feet, fired off in rapid succession. As lush as the final track sounded on tape, it had actually been recorded quickly in Mystic's tiny sixteen-by-sixteen-foot studio. "The room, where Ritchie Valens and Bobby Fuller once recorded, had wooden walls and a lot of ambience," Page later reminisced. "It was a small room, but the energy of the band really comes through."

Demonstrating the practical use of the gong was a particular point of pride for John, who reveled in showing off his improvisational skills by creating a perfect, memorable rhythm on Robert's *Lord of the Rings*–inspired folk-rock combination "Ramble On," by simply playing the bongos atop a plastic garbage pail he'd found in the studio.

Another fan favorite among the band's debut of works in progress, "Heartbreaker" saw John take a mid-tempo jam session pacing and jazz it up with a swinging, spiraling riff for the first two minutes, powerfully launching it into a virtuoso stream of bass-drum sixteenth notes over four bars, built to a sudden halt as introduction to Jimmy's solo.

But it was on John's tour-de-force solo, "Moby Dick," that his abilities were truly showcased. For what had first been lovingly titled "Pat's Delight" in honor of his wife, John used the band's now hundreds of live performances to refine the composition into a marathon showpiece that could last up to twenty minutes in duration. Deceptively cut down by Jimmy into a tight five-minute track for the album, "Moby Dick" had been the product of numerous takes of John fully letting loose upon his kit, beginning months earlier at Mystic Studios in LA. "I didn't actually sit there and play a solo especially for the record," John later admitted. "They just pieced it together."

After changing the song's title in favor of an observation that his young son, Jason, had made while listening to his dad rehearse at home—"*It's big like Moby!*" the boy had joyfully cried, comparing the massive sound to Herman Melville's nautical classic, one of his favorite bedtime stories—here John tried to play something different each time, mixing up the novelty of the solo with traditional kit playing, his bare hands, and, later, Jimmy's electronic effects.

John insisted he had been doing his hand drum solo for a long time—despite claims by any number of drummers that they had done it first. "I was doing it before I joined Led Zeppelin," John later claimed. "I remember playing a solo on 'Caravan' when I was sixteen. Sometimes you can take a chunk out of your knuckles on the hi-hat, or you can catch your hand on the tension rods."

Despite John's reputation as a mischief maker, on one notable occasion his Led Zeppelin mates played a trick on him. During a show, one of them took away his sticks while he was playing with his hands—and he couldn't find them to complete the solo. At the same time, Robert, Jimmy, and John Paul completely disappeared. Confused, John looked around in desperation, reaching the point of total exhaustion where he had nothing left to play. Then he spotted the other three—sitting in the front row of the audience, all grinning back at him and holding his missing sticks.

"Once we'd seen a few solos, we would go offstage and take a break," John Paul Jones later recalled. "But he was always such an interesting drummer. . . . Normally, I would listen to Bonzo either on record or onstage. So, hearing him in a live situation where it was actually well recorded was fantastic. I could sit back, not have to work, and hear him do all the stuff that made him special."

The "Moby Dick" sessions themselves revealed John's lifelong admiration for jazz greats: one unused take of the composition opened with a recognizable riff cribbed from Max Roach's solo piece "The Drum Also Waltzes," and when using his bare hands later in all versions John deployed signature drum riffs first played by old hero Joe Morello on his solo on Dave Brubeck's 1963 *Live at Carnegie Hall*,

"Castilian Drums." As a tip of the hat to a more current favorite, later on in "Moby Dick" he reproduced hand-and-foot alternations craftily lifted from Ginger Baker's "Toad." Jimmy bookended the track with a hard-rocking guitar solo inspired by an old Sleepy John Estes blues riff.

Although John's live solos earned him equal parts praise and accusations of self-indulgence—the length of the solo on a given night could dictate audience response—Jimmy Page had always wanted to innovate studio practices in recording drum tracks, and he had no issue in granting John proper carte blanche. "Not everybody likes or understands a drum solo," John later admitted. "So, I like to bring in effects and sounds to keep their interest—like 'phasing' on the pedal timpani."

Up until that time, not only were the drums viewed as just another component of a band's rhythm section, but on many recordings of the era the kit was rendered largely inaudible, sometimes due to the limitations of the recording technology standards of the day, sometimes due to the incompetence of the engineers. But in Jimmy Page, John had found the perfect collaborator in introducing new techniques that would emphasize the drums' importance and impact on an entire ensemble—and "Moby Dick" proved to be their first across-the-board successful experiment.

"I try to play something different every night," John explained, "but the basic plan is the same—from sticks to hands, and then the tymps and the final buildup. . . . I usually play for twenty minutes, and the longest I've ever done was just under thirty. It's a long time, but when I'm playing it seems to fly by. Sometimes you come up against a blank, and you think, 'How am I going to get out of this one?' Or sometimes, you go into a fill and you know halfway through it's going to be disastrous."

He added, "There have been times when I've blundered, and I got the dreaded look from the lads—but that's a good sign. It shows you are attempting something you've not tried before."

"One usually thinks of a dynamic album being translated into a dynamic live performance, but in the early days, it was the other way around for us," Jimmy Page later said. "I think part of the key was that we miked John Bonham's drums like a proper acoustic instrument in a good acoustic environment. . . . The drums had to sound good because they were going to be the backbone of the band—so, I worked hard on microphone placement."

Page added, "But then again, you see, when you have someone who is as powerful as John Bonham going for you, the battle is all but won."

※ ※ ※

Led Zeppelin's third American tour ended on August 31 at the Texas International Pop Festival at the Dallas Motor Speedway, where the group earned a high-end $13,000 for their show. They returned home to the United Kingdom for a brief respite, but as Atlantic rushed production of *Led Zeppelin II* toward an October release, the group had little choice but to circle back for a swift return to the States—their fourth visit to the country in less than a year.

In order to prepare for the trip, the band played five warm-up shows: three in the Netherlands and a single show at the Lyceum Theatre in London. More than a half century earlier, on October 13, 1915, the German naval Zeppelin LZ-15 had bombed the British city, one explosion nearly destroying the venue. When Led Zeppelin brought their bombastic stage show to the Lyceum on October 12, 1969, it sounded as if they'd come to finish the job.

"Led Zeppelin stormed London's Lyceum with a marathon two-hour, action-packed show on Sunday," wrote Chris Welch, a young writer for *Melody Maker*. "The group were in tremendous form. . . . John Bonham's drum solo was exceptional, drawing bursts of applause throughout, especially for his hand-drumming interlude."

Welch added, "Led Zeppelin don't do anything that is so revolutionary or new. They just do what the public want very well. They play heavy rock the best, and no arguing!—proving that early listeners of the new album hadn't nicknamed it 'The Brown Bomber' for nothing."

"The Led Zeppelin appear, tumultuous applause," *Rolling Stone*'s UK edition reported. "'Communication Breakdown' smashes into the consciousness, not perhaps as clear as the album, but the visuals make up for it. . . . Yet, despite the criticism, Led Zeppelin still provided a beautiful concert. Musically, one need not try to fault them. By the end, they had the whole audience on its feet, most of them were dancing. Two encores were called for and provided. A third would have been loved."

For their efforts, the band got what was reported to be the largest fee paid to an English group for a single performance. Five days later, Led Zeppelin opened its fourth American tour with two shows at New York's Carnegie Hall, making them the first rock band to play the world-famous theater since the Rolling Stones a half decade earlier.

"I first met John Bonham and Robert Plant in a taxicab that took us from Euston Station in London to Heathrow Airport," recalled Chris Welch. "We were due to fly to New York, where Led Zeppelin was scheduled to play at Carnegie Hall. . . . [T]heir second album was eagerly awaited, although as Plant told me en route, its release had been delayed due to problems with the artwork."

Welch's early praise of the band earned him rare access to their backstage process, including this return trip to the United States. He accompanied the band on their TWA flight and shared in their first-class dining of champagne and caviar; he was also invited to check into the same New York Hilton hotel where the group was staying. The following day, when tickets for Zeppelin's two-night Carnegie Hall appearance were completely sold out, Welch was granted free access to the band's sound check. Prior to the performance, John revealed to Welch that he was especially nerve-racked to be playing the venue where so many of his heroes had famously performed.

"So, there I was, standing next to Bonzo on the hallowed boards where Benny Goodman's 'Sing, Sing, Sing' was recorded live back in 1938," Welch remembered. "'This is it lads,' said Bonham, adjusting his cymbal stands, as the audience began to file in early and take their seats. 'Gene Krupa and Buddy Rich—they've all played here. So, I'd better be good tonight!'" Aside from the ghosts of John's former influences that inhabited that famous stage, another of his heroes had even flown in from England to attend the show—the shock rocker himself, Screaming Lord Sutch.

At showtime, the audience—made up of teenagers and older, curious New York culture critics—lit up at the breakneck opening to "Communication Breakdown." Robert met the crowd dressed in a black, girlish chiffon blouse, and Jimmy was decked out in antique Edwardian-inspired white satin. For his big night in the renowned theater, John donned a dramatic leather fedora. The concert was a bona fide smash. Not only was there dancing in the aisles—a rarity for a posh venue such as Carnegie Hall—but during Jimmy's solo on "White Summer," someone walked up and put a bottle of expensive champagne on the stage, an offering to the rock gods.

When it came to that evening's rendition of "Moby Dick," John pumped it up to its maximum length of thirty minutes, pounding out his signature on the maple Ludwig kit at lightning speed—incorporating his full arsenal of sticks, beaters, and bloodied hands. "But what was truly impressive," Welch recalled, "was the moment he launched into a fast, single-stroke roll on his trusty Ludwig snare drum. . . . It was very much in the style of Buddy Rich—a relentless barrage of accents and rolls that threatened to ignite the sticks.

"As the thud of his booming bass drum echoed around the hall," the journalist added, "through a roar of cymbals, Robert Plant stepped forward and paid tribute to his old pal—'Ladies and gentlemen . . . John Henry Bonham!'"

Welch wasn't the only impressed reviewer that night. As *Cashbox* magazine reported, "Drummer Bonham and bassist Jones are also masters of their instruments and stunned the audience with the driving sound that they create together as the backup for Page and Plant. Led Zeppelin has landed!" And in the *Schenectady Gazette*, Mike Hyland wrote, "John Bonham did a drum solo that lasted about 15 minutes, and it was better than Ginger Baker could ever imagine. . . . Pick up their new album, 'Led Zeppelin II' on Atlantic Records, it is a very heavy trip."

✳ ✳ ✳

FOLLOWING THEIR NEW YORK ENGAGEMENT, ZEPPELIN criss-crossed the States yet again—Chicago, Cleveland, Boston, Buffalo, Providence, Syracuse, and Kansas City, with stops in two of Canada's major cities, Toronto and Vancouver.

"I urge you to remember their names, the Zeppelin flew as represented on its Atlantic albums," noted Vancouver critic Bob Smith of the May 10 show. "Included were Jimmy Page, several types of guitar, John Paul Jones, bass, and John Bonham, drums. . . . These young men are going to perform next month at the Newport Jazz Festival. Based on what I heard Saturday night, this recognition is worthy."

"Both Zeppelin and Fudge are prominent bands on the 'heavy' scene," Steve Poulson wrote on the July 30 double bill for the *Summer Chronicle*. "The British group, Led Zeppelin, was billed second to the well-known American group Vanilla Fudge. But Zeppelin went over, noticeably better than Fudge. This is somewhat encouraging to followers of the rock music cult, many of whom believe that Zeppelin deserves more attention." Poulson added, "The members of Led Zeppelin are accomplished musicians and true artists."

John took a few moments to speak with Dallas reporter Jayne Ferguson following the band's August 4 show in Dallas, expressing some of his more critical impressions of the American rock scene. "Drummer John Bonham was impressed with the freedom American musicians have compared with what British bands do and sing," Ferguson noted, offering John's quote: "'There are a lot of reasons Americans have this freedom. The big one is probably just about anyone can get on record over here. Companies will take just about anyone, where in England you have to be pretty good before anyone will even listen to you.'" Luckily, there was no immediate backlash from the band's contemporaries.

On October 22, "the Brown Bomber," *Led Zeppelin II*, was released to the American market. At the time, the band's debut album was still clinging to the sales charts at number 18. *Led Zeppelin II* entered the *Billboard* chart at number 199; a week later, the album skyrocketed to number 25.

"Members of the New York 'in' crowd have said Led Zeppelin II is the best white blues album ever made," Ritchie Yorke wrote, in conversation with Jimmy. "Few would disagree that it's the heaviest rock album around at the moment, brimming with disciplined excitement." Following one of the more enthusiastic assessments made of the album, Jimmy told Yorke that the band was currently working out early ideas for the third album, claiming, "It's going to be more of a challenge, because it must be better than both the first and second."

Despite the incredible sales, the band still received harsh criticism from much of the press. *Rolling Stone* belittled the album, accusing the group of stealing from authentic bluesmen and robbing them of acknowledgment and royalties, and implied their form of "heavy" rock attracted a demographic of post-'60s burnout stoners seeking a droning, hypnotic soundtrack primarily for drugging, drinking, and fucking. "[Robert] Plant is described as the sexiest singer in Rock," wrote C. C. Cakebread of the August 18 Toronto show for Trinity College. "You can tell he knows it and wants everyone else to know. . . . John Bonham [is] not to be missed on drums," the reporter claimed, adding that John looked like "a freaked-out version of Richie Yorke."

The band played the Boston Garden on October 25, for which Nathan Cobb of the *Boston Globe* reported, "'Moby Dick' featured a long solo by drummer John Bonham, technically superb by ANY drumming standards." When Zeppelin played Buffalo's Kleinhans Music Hall five days later, Barry Rekoon agreed, stating, "John Bonham, in his seemingly endless drum solo, proved to be a virtuoso in his own right. I could definitely dig seeing a drum war between him and Ginger Baker of 'Blind Faith.'"

From the group's very beginning, Jimmy and Peter Grant decided that whatever incarnation the New Yardbirds was to take, it would never be a singles-driven band. Jimmy had seen the negative effects that corporate mandates for radio-friendly single tracks had done to the overall quality of studio experimentation—plus, now as owner of his own music, deliberately making fans purchase the entire LP instead of individual songs would help bolster album sales. Now that Led Zeppelin had proved itself as a musical sensation, however, Atlantic wanted to see their investment meet its highest potential and began to lean on Jimmy to release a stand-alone track.

Seeing the song's massive overnight popularity, executives were pushing for a "Whole Lotta Love" single. But in America, many radio stations had begun to simply edit out the psychedelic middle section of the song and play the spliced, non-Jimmy-approved version of "Whole Lotta Love" over the air to meet listeners' demands. When Atlantic released its own edited version as a single, Jimmy and Grant were livid—despite the fact that within five weeks "Whole Lotta Love," coupled with "Living Loving Maid" as its B side, sold more than a million copies. Still, the band was able to prevent such corporate interference in their home country, and British fans continued to gobble up the full *Led Zeppelin* and *Led Zeppelin II* LPs.

※ ※ ※

THE FALL TOUR WORE ON, AND WITH EACH STOP THE BAND GREW more anxious to return home. Even with both albums climbing up the charts and the money pouring in, all four members—John in particular—were growing restless to begin 1970 back in the United Kingdom.

The first week of November, the band was booked for a show at Memorial Hall in Kansas City. First, they made one stop in Toronto, where they had been well received on the previous tour. For that show on November 5, Jim Albright of the *York University Newspaper* wrote, "After a long and absorbing drum solo called, 'Moby Dick,' the Led Zeppelin wound up with the last important component of good rock—audience reaction, as they moved us out of the theatre, still rocking and clapping our hands, the formal and straight atmosphere of the O'Keefe [Centre] blown to kingdom come." In his own review of the show, local critic Peter Goddard added, "Most of their songs were simply the exuberant and talented posturings of a relatively new group. 'Moby Dick' was fundamentally a 10-minute drum solo by Bonham that was extended to 15 minutes." Archie MacDonnell wrote, "'Moby Dick' was John Bonham's 15-minute drum solo and his dynamic finish done with bare hands brought a complete standing ovations at both shows, calling up the usual comparisons with [Ginger] Baker and [Mitch] Mitchell."

At the next gig, Richard Cole had set them up at a historical inn for the night, the Muehlebach, and following that night's concert all five of them settled into the hotel bar for numerous rounds of Scotch, champagne, and gin and tonics. Eventually, John Paul, Robert, and Jimmy headed up to their rooms, but Cole stayed behind while John continued to knock back drinks later into the night.

"Eventually, we became so intoxicated that I doubted we would ever find our way to our rooms," Cole later recalled. "Bonzo couldn't stay on his feet any longer and collapsed into an oversized chair and refused to budge." Cole went up to his own room and popped a few Mandrax in order to grab some sleep. At about three in the morning, the phone beside his bed rang, jolting him back awake. Groggy and hung over, it took a few moments to recognize the voice on the other end. "It's me, Richard," said John over the line. "Come down and get me." John explained frantically that he had been arrested for being drunk in a public place—the hotel's lobby—only moments after Cole had left him alone to sleep it off. He needed the road manager to get out of bed and bail him out. Cole listened as a cop took the phone from John and filled in the details of the station's location—about two miles down the street. "I was furious," Cole recalled, "but my anger was related more to being awakened than to a concern over Bonham's well-being. Cursing under my breath, I got dressed and stuffed $5,000 in cash into my pocket."

Once Cole had successfully stumbled his way to the police station, falsely identifying himself as the drummer's manager in order for an easier release, the on-duty officers nonetheless refused to spring John from his cell. They ordered Cole to return in the morning after John had sobered up. "So, at nine the following morning, I returned," Cole remembered. "Bonham had a sheepish look on his face as they led him to the waiting area of the police station. His face was bruised with one contusion below his left eye and another on the cheek next to it."

"I think the cops roughed me up a little," John whispered to Cole as they walked outside. "I really don't remember."

✳ ✳ ✳

THE TOUR ENDED THREE NIGHTS LATER AT THE WINTERLAND IN San Francisco. By that point, Led Zeppelin had spent nine months on the road, six of which had been strategically mapped out through America, after which the English musicians would have to vacate the country due to tax regulations. With the tour completed, Jimmy, Robert, and Richard flew to Puerto Rico to unwind. John, however, couldn't wait to get home to Pat and Jason, eager to buy Pat her long-promised larger home. After a year and a half of being in the public eye and having to face near-nightly stage jitters, homesickness, and loneliness, John's conception of a dream home had morphed into a vision of quiet seclusion, a place in the country where he could dis-appear with the warmth of family and solitude after the inevitability of future frantic touring.

Robert had been the first to invest in similar real estate, seeking something secluded and whimsical. He and Maureen found it in an old property in the Blakeshall hamlet of Worcestershire, one of the an-cient townships in Wolverley near Kidderminster—the centuries-old Jennings Farm. Far removed from the growing groupies of the Sunset Strip, Robert settled in nicely with his wife and baby daughter—as well as a coop of chickens and goats.

But it had been John who most yearned for the normalcy that came with getting his hands dirty and working the earth. A great part of him had never truly left the construction sites of his youth, and even when out on the road or onstage, hearing his name chanted from the rows of onlookers, John would reconsider the lifestyle he'd passed up for the glitz and glamour of rock 'n' roll. Now, with four US tours under his belt and two smash albums having gone platinum, he could finally afford the large piece of God's country that he'd always wanted—the bankroll allowing him to own and work a farm on his terms: ample acreage and not a face in sight that he didn't want to see. John at last found his dream home in an old farm in West Hagley, approximately seven miles from Robert's old farm.

As quaint as both John's and Robert's new homesteads were, John also indulged in reaping the more obvious rewards of having hit the rock 'n' roll big time. He may have relished using his newfound wealth on friends and family, but he had one major passion aside from drumming that he could finally afford. "John loved cars," Richard Cole remembered. "Bonham bought twenty-six cars in the band's first successful year in 1969, [then] he'd get bored with them. . . . One day, he'd turn up in a Maserati, and the next day it would be a Jensen, an E-type Jaguar, or a Rolls-Royce. If he'd see Tony Iommi of Black Sabbath with a new car, he'd say, 'I've got to get one of those.' The car dealers in Birmingham loved him." John famously purchased the Maserati after marching into a Birmingham showroom with two suitcases flush with 10,000 pounds in cash, shocking the salesman by admitting the money had come from only three American concert dates.

As time passed, John's instant gratification for fine automobiles became a source of humorous legend. While in LA during the previous tour, he had been driving on the Sunset Strip with Peter Grant and Zeppelin roadie Henry Smith. As the three passed a Rolls-Royce dealership, John demanded they pull over so he could browse. A brand-new Silver Shadow instantly caught John's eye, but the stuffy Rolls salesman didn't recognize the rock superstar. "Sonny, don't put your hands on it unless you can pay for it," the snobbish salesman condescended to John.

"How much is it then?" John asked.

"Eighty-five thousand dollars," the man said, ready to move on to the next potential customer.

John immediately turned to Grant. "Peter, quick, give me eighty-five grand."

Ever the showman, Grant dipped into the cash-filled paper bag he seemed to always have on hand as "petty cash" and handed his ace drummer the money. Grinning from ear to ear, John dumped the cash on the table, and the sales rep stood with his mouth agape.

As much as John enjoyed putting his money where his mouth was, especially when it came to stuck-up snobs, he was sure never to flaunt it outright to his old friends. "I went to his house one night, and he was very worried about money—because he'd never had so much!" Bill Harvey later recalled. "Even though his dad was a builder and they weren't badly off, John never had much cash to play around with when he was young. Then suddenly, he was landed with all this money. He said to me, 'I just don't know what I'm going to do with it all.' He was car mad, of course, and had just got a Rolls-Royce."

With Led Zeppelin's hectic touring and recording schedule, John hadn't seen Harvey in more than a year and was overjoyed to have the time off to catch up with him. "He was on his way up from London and sent me a message saying, 'Come 'round. I'll be there,'" Harvey remembered. "He arrived at the house and said, 'Come on, help me unload.' And he had a crate of champagne in the back of the car. . . . He was showing me paradiddles and playing them on this polished coffee table, which must have cost him a bomb. He wasn't bothered, and Pat didn't scold him either. She was good as gold."

Bev Bevan recalled a similar night with John and Pat when they were all invited to the home of Phil Ackrill, the guitarist from Birmingham-based band Denny Laine and the Diplomats. "[Phil] and his wife had a little terraced house in Tamworth, and they'd never met John before," Bevan recalled. "John asked if he should bring anything, and I said, 'Oh, just bring a bottle of wine or something.' In typical Bonham fashion, he turned up with Pat, his wife, and they had a cardboard box each. They must have brought two dozen beers, half-a-dozen bottles of wine, a bottle of brandy, and a bottle of Scotch. There was just so much booze."

Bevan added, "John and I had this five-minute drum battle with serving spoons on the table. . . . You can imagine the state of the table when they took the cloth off next day. It was totally covered in dents and scratches. But our hosts saw the funny side and didn't care. Phil actually said, 'I'll auction this at Sotheby's one day!'"

※ ※ ※

IN AN EFFORT TO TURN AROUND SOME PUBLIC OPINION, THE BAND acquiesced to Grant's nudging and offered the press a few more opportunities for one-on-one access. In December, John and Jimmy gave a rare joint interview to their now trusted journalist friend Chris Welch, at *Melody Maker*. As a year-end review, both Zeppelin mates had their own perspectives on what the band had achieved in its first year—as well as their goals for the next album and tour. "When we got back from the States last month, we started recording again for the next album," John revealed to Welch, "and we have only done one gig since then in Paris. . . . I thought the solo I played at the first Carnegie Hall concert was about the best." Of their visit with the members of Traffic soon after, John added, "It's nicer than jamming in a club with a group where the audience think you are just showing off."

As the year 1969 came to a close, John and the other members of Led Zeppelin had much to celebrate. Together for only a year and a half, they were already being touted as the next major band to come out of England, eclipsing the likes of not only Cream and the Jeff Beck Group, but the original Fab Four themselves. Brother Mick Bonham later recalled, "After a family Christmas at home, news came through on December 27 that *Led Zeppelin II*, which had been released in America in October, had knocked the Beatles' *Abbey Road* off the top of the *Billboard* album chart."

On December 11, the band was invited to the Savoy Hotel to receive the presentation of gold and platinum records, symbols of the incredible sales the first two albums had scored for Atlantic. John spoke briefly to *Melody Maker* at the event, saying, "We try to record a lot when we're not doing gigs, so we don't get stale. The awards are really great. Twelve months ago, I didn't expect we would get one. It's been complete chaos for us recently, as Robert, John [Paul Jones], and I have all been busy buying houses and getting ready for Christmas."

John also gushed about finally being able to pamper his family, adding, "It will be the first Christmas at home for me with my son, Jason (age three). Last year, I was away, and before that, he was too young to know. He's music mad, and I've bought him a great set of miniature drums. It's an absolutely perfect replica down to the bass-drum pedal and hi-hat. Even I can play them. . . . They are Japanese made, and I saw them in a shop in Toronto. They weren't really for sale and were just on display—but I offered them a hundred dollars and bought them."

✳ ✳ ✳

NEWS OF THEIR SUCCESS, COUPLED WITH HAVING SPENT THIS YEAR'S holiday season at home with their families, reenergized the members of Led Zeppelin and softened the blow that their brief gap in between touring was near its end. By the second week of January 1970, Grant had already booked the band for another long string of dates in the United States, solidifying their dominance of the British rock scene with the biggest public demand for live performances and skyrocketing sales of *Led Zeppelin II* even after the Christmas rush.

In anticipation of meeting scores of adoring Americans yet again, Zeppelin commenced this run with a small UK tour, their fourth, and to John's personal delight its kickoff was set for just down the road from the Bonhams' new Hagley home. "They were opening their third UK tour just up the road at Birmingham Odeon on January 7," Mick Bonham later recalled.

By this time, John and Mick's parents had separated, and, although never formally divorced, Jacko had moved into an apartment with his younger son, while Joan and Debbie had settled into a small place in town. Thinking it best for their three children, the two remained cordial friends and continued to get along at family events—and John's concerts were such occasions that the full Bonham family unit could always provide a united front. "Although Debbie was just eight years old, there was no way she was going to be left at home, so Mum decided she could come, and Jacko and I met them with Pat at the venue," Mick remembered. "It would be Mum and Debbie's first time seeing John playing with Zep, and by the end of the show, they were both stunned."

Joan and young Debbie stood in awe of John as he was praised by the audience, primarily made up of the very community that had watched him mature from mischievous local teen into world-renowned musician and rock superstar. "John received three standing ovations that night, and the look on Jacko and Mum's faces was a picture," Mick recalled. "[Their] eyes filled with tears of pride as they realized, watching their son take the deserved acclaim, that all the arguments, pranged vans, and other escapades had all been worth it."

"Zeppelin, the group that conquered the States, was opening its first British tour for many months," wrote Toby Raba in the *Birmingham Express and Star*. "It was fitting that the group should have chosen Birmingham to do this and must have been pleasing for the boys to receive such a reception. . . . Then things really got going with 'Moby Dick,' featuring Dudley's John Bonham with a tremendous ten-minute drum solo. Discarding drumsticks, he added to the magnificence by playing barehanded, and brought the audience to its feet. . . . The group performed its two and a half hours without a break, and when it finished, all four looked as though they had given everything they had, although I imagine they would have willingly carried on for an extra two and a half hours."

John and the members of Zeppelin had everyone in the Birmingham audience up and dancing in the aisles. Amid the cheers and ovations, the townsfolk of Brum wouldn't let their favorite son leave the stage until he and his mates had given a total of four encores.

Chapter Eight

JANUARY 1970–APRIL 1970

"John Bonham, Led Zeppelin's fabled drummer, has no time for swinging London," wrote the *Evening Telegraph*. "While he is steadily amassing a sizable fortune, as a quarter of one of the world's highest paid acts, he stays clear of the capital of pop."

John had agreed to a rare interview on January 8 for the issue, a bit of a kick-start to the publicity that the new year would surely bring. "Interviews and business had taken him south from his Worcestershire home," the article continued. "Bonham has been down on other occasions to work on Zeppelin's third album. A proud member of the Birmingham scene, John couldn't resist a few slights towards the posh London crowd. 'It just doesn't appeal to me at all going 'round the in-clubs,' he said. 'They are just gossip shops. Whatever you are is all over the place the next day. Back home, I can go out for a night without any fuss or bother and have a really good time.'"

He wouldn't be back home for a while, however. Led Zeppelin began 1970 with a short experimental tour of England. Over the past year, the band had repeatedly outshone any other band sharing the bill, and while no true rivalries ever developed, there was always the chance of animosity between the respective bands' management camps and the venues. By now, Led Zeppelin's stage show ran a minimum of two hours, and with their large fan base secure, Peter Grant opted to send the boys out this time alone.

Traveling as a lone road show had its advantages, including the autonomy to play around with set lists, lengths of each member's solos, and potential for onstage special effects—all of which would begin to define Led Zeppelin's unparalleled concerts. This time around, Jimmy's bowed violin exposition wasn't the only showstopper; John Paul Jones now traveled with a Hammond organ for a few of the band's latest songs and was given ample time to solo with a few of his extended arrangements, and John's mammoth drum solo—by now a fan favorite and often a critical darling—was a mandated addition to every set list.

Following successful shows in Birmingham and Bristol, the band took particular pride in selling out world-famous Royal Albert Hall— the best gift Jimmy Page could have gotten on the night of January 9, his twenty-sixth birthday. Backstage after the show, Jimmy was also introduced to French model Charlotte Martin, one of England's hottest and most pursued "It" girls. Charlotte had first come to the attention of the rock 'n' roll world months earlier, showing up at the trendy venue Speakeasy on Eric Clapton's arm—to the unmistakable envy of the Who's Roger Daltrey. Months later, it was with Daltrey that Miss Martin had attended Led Zeppelin's Royal Albert Hall performance. Soon afterward, however, she was all Jimmy's, as his days as Zeppelin's carefree bachelor would come to an end.

Melody Maker's Raymond Telford gave the Royal Albert Hall show a solid review, calling attention to the power of the extended jams and a rock 'n' roll medley the group improvised midconcert, adding of John's turn in the spotlight, "Marathon drum solos can be the most boring experience on earth. Happily, however, John Bonham's 'Moby Dick' steered clear of the cliches." *Disc and Music Echo* shared the observation, claiming, "Solo honours went to John Bonham, who made a frantic 15-minute drum solo seem like five, with none of the embarrassment and boredom usually aroused by drum solos." Never settling, Led Zeppelin's ambition only soared from there. Following the performance, John told local critic Paul Wallace that Led Zeppelin wanted "to be known as the pop group that launched the 70's."

Amusingly, John's lengthy drum solos were a source of minor controversy between a writer covering the band's Sheffield City Hall performance on January 16 and a young fan who was at that same show. When the *Star's* culture critic wrote, "A robust drum solo by John Bonham is an excuse for an interval—or to leave," the angry fan soon penned in a letter to the editor: "Your reporter had the cheek to say John Bonham's drum solo was an excuse for an interval. The drum solo was one of the highlights of the night, as he ought to have noticed with the roar of appreciation."

✳ ✳ ✳

ZEPPELIN'S TOUR OF THE UNITED KINGDOM CONTINUED FOR THE rest of the month, which was ideal, as John was still preoccupied with getting his new home in order. Coming from a family of construction builders, he had left the necessary remodeling and additions in the capable hands of Jacko and brother Mick, both of whom were happy to help the family's budding superstar. "As the tour carried on around Britain, Jacko and I were doing the carpentry at John's, and he himself, when he wasn't playing, would do the decorating," Mick Bonham later said. "We sorted out all the other work that needing doing at his new house. I was to put a large panel fence around the garden, which was about a hundred yards long, while Jacko replaced the doors. . . . It was decided the work should start while John was away on their first European tour."

John admittedly took great pride in his new home and its construction and placed necessary outside work into only capable, trusted hands; when Jacko and Mick required additional assistance, John called on old friend and roadie from his Brum-scene days Matt Maloney to join the crew, instructing him to quit his job and begin working exclusively on the new Bonham estate. According to Mick, "Matthew didn't need asking twice."

Between Led Zeppelin's final UK date at Leeds University on January 24 and their sojourn to Scandinavia at the end of February, John worked alongside his three-man crew, getting the old farm in perfect working order and furnishing it with the best that money could buy, to Pat's delight.

Aside from the home remodeling and design, John's flush paychecks afforded him two other substantial new purchases: another Rolls-Royce and a new drum setup for Zeppelin's upcoming return to the United States. He put the maple kit in storage and turned instead to a Ludwig Sparkle Green, which he would use onstage and in the studio for the next half decade. This theatrical setup that would become synonymous with John's heavy playing style and sound—a twenty-six-by-fourteen-inch bass drum, a fourteen-by-ten-inch mounted tom (which was soon upgraded to the larger fifteen-by-twelve model for an even more powerful, reverberated sound), sixteen-by-eighteen-inch floor toms, and a fourteen-by-six-and-a-half-inch snare drum.

John was pleased enough with the setup that he purchased three of them.

Being one of the most famous drummers in the world had additional perks. He had been introduced to Paiste cymbals through his ongoing endorsement with Ludwig, the Swiss cymbal brand's US distributor, and during Zeppelin's Swiss tour a few months later, John was able to pay the company headquarters in Nottwil, Switzerland, an unannounced visit for a private tour—and some new gratis toys.

"We went through the factory and checked some cymbals," recalled Swiss drummer Fredy Studer, who worked at Paiste drummer services during the time of John's impromptu visit. "It had to sound big to him. . . . He was looking for a big sound that was pitched and would blend with his drum sound. The main thing was that they were cutting through, but not in a sharp way."

Studer recalled that John was given a set of the company's newly developed "Giant Beat" cymbals for testing on the upcoming US tour. "The company tried out different alloys because the music had changed," Studer said. "When rock music came out, Paiste developed 'Giant Beat' because they were looking for a sound that could cut through the amplified guitars more."

✳ ✳ ✳

WHEN THE TOUR ENDED IN LEEDS LATER IN THE MONTH, JIMMY AND Charlotte settled in their Pangbourne home. There, they enjoyed a reclusive existence, surrounded by Jimmy's vast collection of pre-Raphaelite furniture and expensive antiques. Jimmy's long hair and mysterious style often garnered hostility among his village neighbors, making him ever-more reclusive. His quiet bliss was interrupted one night in early February when police banged on his door, inquiring if he knew Mr. Robert Plant, who had been injured in a serious automobile accident. Jimmy was instantly terrified, wondering if Led Zeppelin had lost its singer and, more importantly, he had lost his friend. When Jimmy contacted Kidderminster Hospital, he was told Robert's Jaguar had skidded off the road following a Spirit concert at the Birmingham Odeon. Still estranged from his mother and father, Robert had given Jimmy as his next of kin.

The accident forced the band to cancel a concert in Scotland, although thankfully his injuries were minor—he had been badly bruised and received a cut over his eye. While Robert recovered, the rest of the band headed off to Copenhagen without him, using the extra time to rehearse. Robert swore he'd join them soon, and if necessary he'd even perform alongside them in a wheelchair.

Awaiting Robert's return to the tour, a bizarre incident occurred. The three members had been rehearsing in the studio when they were interrupted by a woman claiming to be Eva von Zeppelin—a descendant of Count von Zeppelin, the very designer of the first German Zeppelin airships. Causing a scene, Lady von Zeppelin threatened legal ramifications if the band continued using "Zeppelin" in their name. "A couple of shrieking monkeys are not going to use a privileged family name without permission," she vowed to the local press. Fortunately, Peter Grant had successfully subdued the hysterical woman, but just as she was exiting the studio she spied a copy of the band's debut album nearby, her temper tantrum reigniting at the sight of the *Hindenburg* going down in flames.

Robert returned to the tour just in time for all the drama, although not one of the band members was amused. Potentially facing expensive lawsuits in a country where they had very little legal knowledge, Led Zeppelin safely played the rest of the Scandinavian tour as "the Nobs," Cockney slang for "cock," which was inspired by one of John's favorite ways to greet an unsuspecting member of Zeppelin's innermost circle. "How's your nob?" a properly inebriated Bonzo would ask, while slapping a mate's genitals by way of "Hello."

Before leaving Scandinavia, the Zeppelin boys had one final night to blow off some steam. Their Danish record licensee had booked a press conference at a nearby art gallery, but well-educated connoisseur Jimmy Page was far from impressed. Ever the agreeable mischief maker, John accepted Jimmy's challenge to desecrate the works, enraging the gallery manager—and forcing Peter Grant to once again dip into his bag of "petty cash" to pay for the expensive destruction. Nonetheless, a fistfight ensued between John, Richard Cole, and two local reporters—all of whom were forcefully ejected from the premises.

✳ ✳ ✳

FOLLOWING THIS EVENTFUL GALLERY INCIDENT, THE BAND HAD TWO weeks off before they were set to perform at Switzerland's Casino de Montreux on March 7. As Jacko and Mick Bonham continued to labor away on John's new property, the drummer himself decided to take Pat on a long-overdue honeymoon, sweeping her away for a short, romantic holiday across Europe before the reality of another year on the road with Zeppelin sank in.

At this point, all the members of Led Zeppelin had used their hard-earned fortunes to solidify proper homes for their families. John and Robert had their farms in Birmingham, while John Paul Jones and Maureen had established a large, comfortable home in Chorleywood, Hertfordshire. This left Jimmy Page as the final holdout in laying down roots. He had long since asked Charlotte to move into his Pang-bourne home by the Thames, but when she brought up the prospect of starting a family, Jimmy was on the lookout for a more suitable home. In addition to the home itself, he was excited to collect rare pieces to put on display inside of it. A lifelong admirer of historical occult-ist and self-described "magus" Aleister Crowley, Jimmy ventured to obscure locations around Europe and the rest of the world in order to see places of interest to Crowley buffs while collecting a fortune's worth of the writer's memorabilia and artifacts. Although Led Zep-pelin's original plans to perform in Scotland had been cast aside due to Robert's car accident back in January, Jimmy Page had nonetheless found his own bizarre dream home within that country—"Boleskine House," a decrepit estate on the shore of Loch Ness that, a century earlier, Crowley himself had once called home.

It was a perfect place of solitude and meditation for the likes of Jimmy Page, as the history of Boleskine House was as entwined to that of its original owner as it was fascinating. Like Jimmy, Aleister Crowley was born into a middle-class British family and spent his life in mystical and artistic pursuits—most of which were controversial, to say the least. A globe-trotting adventurer and hobbyist explorer, the philosophic writer spent the bulk of his life amassing esoteric knowledge on ritualistic "*magick*," long suppressed by the church and that Crowley believed could be unlocked from within man's will, providing otherworldly powers to conjure all sorts of spells and rituals. Crowley was also known in underground circles for his belief in the transcendent nature of sexual intercourse and lived a hyper-sexualized form of polygamy, all while experimenting with hashish, opium, cocaine, and heroin. Essentially, Crowley was a rock star a century before such a concept existed.

After a loyal follower staying with Crowley at his Sicilian abbey died under mysterious circumstances, the self-proclaimed magician was exiled from the country, labeled persona non grata, and ordered never to return. It was in exile that Crowley discovered Boleskine House, which was built upon the former site of a church that had burned to the ground, killing a full congregation of parishioners in the blaze. Once settled into this home beside Loch Ness, Crowley held séances and black masses and sought to control legions of demons and armies of the dead. Not long after Crowley's death, a former groundskeeper of the site was driven mad by the mysterious sights and sounds he encountered at the house, caused by the ghosts and demons Crowley had set free, according to superstitious locals. Crowley's famous motto, "Do what thou wilt shall be the whole of the Law," had long been the beloved mantra of Jimmy Page—who sought to buy the house from his very first visit.

Jimmy was adamant that it wasn't necessarily the house's haunted vibes that drew him to the place, but rather its fascinating history, panoramic view of the loch—he was accustomed to a waterfront view of the Thames, after all—and, equally important, the structure's wonderful acoustics for rehearsal and recording. The latter reason was of the upmost importance to the young guitarist-producer, as he claimed all facets of a place's atmosphere could dictate its quality of inspiration and sound. Comfortably settled into Boleskine House with now-pregnant Charlotte, Jimmy planned to harness his affection for a given building's history and individual character into inspiration for future Led Zeppelin recordings.

That same month, in anticipation of Led Zeppelin's return to America, prestigious British trade paper the *Financial Times* ran a lengthy profile on the band, focusing on their successful financial strategies and marketing tactics in their two-year ascent through the ranks of rock 'n' roll. The article claimed that the group was set to earn $800,000 playing twenty-one concerts over one month, a fact that helped the band's families struggle less with having to see them off once again as they ventured across the Atlantic. The article did not, however, make mention of the underground rumblings regarding Peter Grant's and Richard Cole's dubious behavior when it came to the nuts and bolts of ensuring their boys received every dime they had coming to them. Grant, in particular, was known among local record-shop owners for showing up in person if he heard they were selling Led Zeppelin bootlegs. Also known for usually packing a gun under the jacket of his suit, the enormous and intimidating Grant once broke the microphone of a concertgoer caught illegally recording the band's stage show—by smashing it over the offender's head. Soon after, when *Melody Maker* made the error of running a story on a local shop owner who was distributing a particularly high-quality Zeppelin bootleg out of his storefront on Chancery Lane, Grant and Cole took it upon themselves to pay the man a visit. In true mobster fashion, Grant locked the door behind him and flipped the sign to "Closed"—then proceeded to threaten the man's life until the entire stock of bootlegged Zeppelin albums was handed over.

When new Zeppelin fans read the glowing reviews of the band's live performances, it was easy to see why bootlegged records were in such high demand. The critics may have continued their harsh assessments of the musicians' achievements, but their live set was already acknowledged to be a genuine spectacle—a brash, heavy experience unmatched in the studio recordings.

"Even the Led Zeppelin was obviously not prepared for the reaction they caused Saturday at the Pacific Coliseum as nearly 19,000 rock fans jammed the building for the group's first concert in a 19-city tour," the *Vancouver Express* reported on March 24. "Drummer John Bonham demonstrated his talent in a 15-minute stick-twirling and barehanded exhibition that exhausted both himself and the listeners."

Following the band's March 25 show in Denver, early fan Thomas MacCluskey at the *Rocky Mountain News* wrote, "Led Zeppelin has made a long flight since its first trip to Denver less than a year and a half ago. At that time, LZ, a British affair, was playing its first concert in the U.S. They were just getting their thing together, but it hadn't jelled fully. Now—thousands of hours of wailing together, hundreds of concerts and three record albums later—they've arrived. The group of four gents proved it thoroughly for 11,500 happy fans crammed into the Coliseum Wednesday night. Proved it for nearly two hours non-stop!" Of John, the critic added, "John Bonham has polished his drumming technique tremendously since he was here more than a year ago." On March 29, Jill Melichar of the *Houston Chronicle* complimented "Moby Dick," which "called on drummer John Bonham's mammoth stamina reserves. Especially towards the solo's end did Bonham finally show his added capability to also produce a thoroughly captivating beat." And despite erroneously identifying John as "Richard Bonham," Clark Deleon noted of the Philadelphia Spectrum performance, "Led Zeppelin's drummer . . . got it on in a thirty-minute solo. His speed on the drums seemed to rival Ginger Baker and his rhythm seemed more practiced and accurate than the sometimes sloppy 'Toad.' Bonham used drumsticks for the first fifteen minutes and then abandoned them to play only with his hands. It gave the impression of a modern revolutionary beating the war drums—but whatever the impression, the huge Spectrum crowd dug it, and gave him a standing, clapping, shouting, whistling ovation at the end of his half-hour ordeal."

Bonham continued to rack up critical acclaim with every stop on the tour. Less than a week later, the *Charleston Review* in West Virginia noted, "Led Zeppelin brought the frustrated Charleston rock community sweet release at the Civic Center Thursday night in a brilliant, bombastic contemporary blues recital. . . . Drummer John Bonham also triumphed in a solo, demonstrating a tenacious capacity to muster and sustain high-density sound at high volume. . . . He drummed for 20 minutes, paying respects along the way to jazz deans old and new, and ended it flailing the skin with his flesh." In Indianapolis two nights later, *Times* reviewer Zach Dunkin wrote, "Bass guitarist John Paul Jones soloed on a switch to the organ, followed later by drummer John Bonham's 20-minute act in which he played two sets of drums, bongos and a Chinese gong with and without the drumsticks. The drummer was applauded nine times during his performance and earned a standing ovation." John Klein in Cleveland's *Chronicle Telegram* later claimed, "As the rest of the group left the stage, Bonham did everything possible to make his drums talk, plus a few new things that weren't in the book."

By the time the band played their Phoenix concert in April, John finally got the headline all to himself: "Zeppelin Plays 25-Minute Drum Solo for 14,000 Youths."

But even with the fame and fortune brought on by the US tour, both proved little compensation for what was truly the most horrific tour the boys had experienced thus far—at least as far as John admitted to his brother and father upon Led Zeppelin's return home.

"He looked very tired as he told us that the tour had been a tremendous success, though there had been a lot of trouble between fans and overeager riot police," Mick Bonham recalled. "There had also been one occasion where a guy pulled a gun on them after a run-in at a restaurant, which prompted them to hire several bodyguards to accompany them through the Deep South."

Indeed, Zeppelin had unintentionally booked their fifth American visit during one of the most turbulent times in the country's history. Amid the mass protests provoked by the younger generation's disapproval of US involvement in Vietnam, the ongoing civil rights movement had taken a darker, more violent turn. Led Zeppelin, by their own definition a progressive hard-rock band, attracted the very demographic that was in the midst of social alienation, and the band had already been flagged as an instigator of near-riotous behavior, drug use, and rebellion wherever booked to perform. As such, the band wasn't always made to feel entirely welcome by the authorities or members of the older generation. The American police took particular offense to Zeppelin's public denouncement of traditional social norms, as well as their perceived championing of sexual deviancy and unapologetic advocacy of marijuana and psychedelics; they soon began inviting themselves to the concerts already decked out in riot gear and permanent snarls.

At Pittsburgh and several other later concerts, Led Zeppelin was forced to stop playing and quit the stage until a violent group fistfight stopped in the front row of the audience. This was especially frustrating for the band, since the tour had been organized with precision to come off like an efficient military campaign. As expected, the band faced their biggest problems in an area of the United States that was regarded as both the most intolerant of their hippie clothing and behavior and the largest hotbed of conservative backlash against the current waves of social protest: the American South. Stopping at a roadside diner for breakfast, they were refused service by numerous waitresses and were spat on and ridiculed by many locals who didn't recognize the millionaires in their midst. Much more serious, anonymous death threats had been made against the band at more than one hotel where they were staying, and even after the band members received honorary citizen status in Memphis on April 6, their concert that very night was canceled halfway through the show by a promoter who feared violence and community backlash.

"Go and fuck yourself, I'm not pulling them offstage," the everprotective Peter Grant told the promoter in the band's defense.

In response, the man pulled a gun and shoved it into Grant's ribs. "If you don't cut the Goddamn show, I'm gonna shoot ya," he was reported to have said.

Grant was never one to be easily intimidated. "You can't shoot me, you cunt," he laughed in the man's face. "They've just given us the fucking keys to the city!"

But a dangerous precedent had been set, and the members of Led Zeppelin wondered if it was worth their lives to continue onward. After all, each member now had a loving family awaiting their return, Grant included.

At the band's next gig in Raleigh, North Carolina, crew member Henry Smith stopped into the men's room to wash up, only to overhear a team of overzealous local cops talking about the group. Silently crouching in the stall so as not to draw attention, Smith distinctly heard the officers joyfully planning to "bust those fuckers, Led Zeppelin, tonight." Only a swift emergency call to Zeppelin's lawyer, Steve Weiss, in New York prevented catastrophe, as the toughas-nails Weiss immediately dispatched a private army of Pinkerton security agents to the show to watch his boys' backs. For the rest of the tour, each limo the band used came equipped with two security men apiece.

John had grown up as a rough-and-tumble teen in Birmingham, but nothing prepared him for this level of violence. As he later recalled, "We were leaving after the show, and the same guy shows up at the door. He pulls out this pistol and says to us, 'You guys gonna do any shouting now?' We cleared out of there tout de suite."

In an effort to boost morale, Grant invited the band members' wives to join them for the final stretch of the tour, but, as Richard Cole later recalled, their presence only dragged the boys lower; on top of everything else, now the boys had to be on their best behavior. "The atmosphere was just different," Cole later admitted. "Fucking business is business. That was the last time the wives got to go along."

With twenty-nine shows down, the tour, miraculously, was coming to a close. At their last stop in Phoenix, Arizona, Robert lost his voice, causing the band to cancel their grand-finale show in Las Vegas. "More than anyone, Robert seemed on the brink of collapse at times," Richard Cole recalled. "His voice had taken a beating. It had become so ragged and hoarse that he could barely speak, much less sing. . . . We had humidifiers operating around the clock in Robert's hotel room to try and soothe and preserve his voice. But nothing seemed to help. Each night, he had to struggle a little more than the previous night to get through the show."

Within an inch of their lives, Led Zeppelin put a cap on their fifth sojourn to America and, thoroughly exhausted, flew back home. "The violence does frighten me, mainly because the U.S. is the biggest power in the world," John Paul Jones explained to the British press. "It just seems to be in a terrible mess at the moment."

Richard Cole, on the other hand, blamed other factors for the weariness and disenchantment felt by the members of Led Zeppelin: "Too much traveling, too little sleep, too much alcohol, too many drugs."

Led Zeppelin was thoroughly exhausted after over a year of nonstop touring, mostly the major cities of America. John couldn't have been more relieved to finally be back in Birmingham with Pat, following up with Jacko and Mick on their renovations of his new home—the new home he hadn't yet had an opportunity to enjoy. With a few precious months at his disposal, John promised his family and himself that that was about to change.

Besides, Jimmy and Robert were preoccupied. Following the return home, the two had turned around and hopped a flight to Wales together. They needed inspiration. They had a new album to write.

Chapter Nine

APRIL 1970–JUNE 1970

The first week of April 1970, British reporter Ritchie Yorke ran a full-page interview with John, the third in a consecutive series profiling each member of Zeppelin. Under the banner "Led Zeppelin's Super Drummer," Yorke pumped John for information on his influences and ambitions for the group's future, adding that John was "surely the finest drummer to emerge since Ginger Baker."

"I was very influenced [by Baker] in the early days," John admitted, "because when I first started, Baker was a big image in England. He was the first rock guy like Gene Krupa. In the big band era, a drummer was a backing musician and nothing else. And in the early American bands, the drummer played with only brushes in the back and Krupa was the first drummer that was noticed. . . . Rock had been going on for a while, but Baker was the first to [prove that] a drummer could be a forward thing in a rock band and not a thing that was stuck in the back and forgotten about."

Praising close friend Carmine Appice as "one of the best [drummers] I've ever seen in a rock group," John also spoke to Zeppelin's relentless touring schedule. "Sometimes, it gets to be a bit wearing, but that's only because I'm married and got kids at home. But I've never gotten bugged with the actual touring—I could play every night. It's just the being away that gets you down sometimes."

They had been away from their families and their homeland long enough, so it was Robert who suggested he and Jimmy venture to nearby Wales for a writing retreat. The two opted for a remote cottage in the mountainous wild of rural Snowdonia called Bron-Yr-Aur. As a child, Robert visited that spot of idyllic country and had never forgotten its literal translation—"the Golden Breast," for the golden shafts of sunlight that would sneak through the green, mountainous terrain.

Jimmy had first conceived of hopping a flight to Northern California with Robert, hoping that the exotic locale would influence their new album with the soundtrack they both adored—Crosby, Stills & Nash, and especially Joni Mitchell, whom both men coveted as muse and songwriting siren. But Jimmy acquiesced to Robert's pleas to stay relatively close to their families in England and even permitted Maureen and Charlotte to come along. Not long afterward, the invitation was extended to trusted Zeppelin roadies Henry Smith, Clive Coulson, and Sandy MacGregor, who maintained the instruments and luggage brought along for song sketches and demos. For weeks, Jimmy and Robert went on extended hikes, brainstorming new material. Their evenings were filled with fireside songwriting, sipping cider that was warmed by the hearth's flames.

"Zeppelin was starting to get very big and we wanted the rest of our journey to take a very level course," Robert later said. "Hence the trip into the mountains and the beginning of the ethereal Page and Plant."

Only one thing was certain: the deliberate lack of electricity at the Bron-Yr-Aur cottage dictated that the new material would be composed acoustically. And with that dictum in place, it wasn't long before the thematic form and structure of *Led Zeppelin III* began to take shape. Once Jimmy and Robert were content with the first few songs they'd prepared, the men sent word to Peter and Richard Cole to help them lock down a studio to record Led Zeppelin's first predominantly acoustic folk-rock album—and summoned John and John Paul Jones to that chosen spot.

※ ※ ※

BY THE MIDDLE OF MAY, JOHN FOUND HIMSELF ROUGHING IT WITH his Zeppelin mates, far away from the rest of the world in an old country house in Hampshire. The band was hard at work, showcasing their diversity as musicians through softer, more folkish material—the "light" to the heavier "shade" of Jimmy's ideal dynamics, the whisper to the thunder.

The four were working out of a small Hampshire manor, known as Headley Grange, recording by way of a borrowed mobile recording studio and left alone from the world, with only their crew, Peter Grant, and Richard Cole sometimes present. In his role as producer, Jimmy raced back and forth between the makeshift-studio setup and the mobile unit parked alongside the Grange.

"Headley Grange was found by our secretary, Carole Browne," Richard Cole said later. "She used to read those magazines like the *Lady*, and she'd read that this place was for rent. . . . It wasn't very comfortable. I mean, the band was used to five-star hotels and had lovely homes by now."

Then again, comfort hadn't exactly been Jimmy's first priority when he fell in love with Headley Grange's atmosphere, acoustic capabilities, and colorful history. Headley Grange was originally built in 1795 as a "House of Industry" to shelter impoverished elders without anywhere else to turn, along with orphans and illegitimate children. In November 1830, rioters besieged the house, after which it was repaired and rebranded as a workhouse. It was sold in 1870 as a private residence to the owner of a small construction company, who finally gave it the proper name of "Headley Grange." A century later, the Grange was used as both a hostel for foreign travelers and an occasional rehearsal hall rented out to musicians—most recently used in that capacity by blues troupe Fleetwood Mac.

Led Zeppelin had roughly one month to lay down the tracks for their third album; they were already due to appear at the Bath Festival in June and, from there, launch another soul-crunching trek across the United States. These past few months had done the four members of the band good, as each entered Headley Grange properly rested and eager to record Jimmy and Robert's new material.

Earlier in the month, the band had gathered at Olympic Studios in London and Basing Street in Notting Hill as a kickoff to the recording sessions, recording the album's first two tracks, "Immigrant Song" and "Poor Tom," before packing up for their rural adventure into Hampshire. On "Poor Tom," John flexed some jazz-ragtime muscles, opting for a New Orleans–style rock 'n' roll side-drum groove: rapid eighth notes played on the snare instead of the hi-hat, while John locked syncopated bass-drum beats tightly beneath. Well rested from their long-overdue break, the band—John in particular—was in excellent form by the time they reached Olympic Studios; by the end of the session, they were ready for their trip into the great outdoors.

Robert and Jimmy had already prepared a few tracks—"Bron-Yr-Aur," "Down by the Seaside," "Jennings Farm Blues," and "The Boy Next Door," later renamed "That's the Way"—from their Welsh retreat. Jimmy also wanted to rerecord a ballad of his, "Tangerine," from his final year with the Yardbirds. When taken as a whole, the two sides of *Led Zeppelin III* would demonstrate to both fans and critics that the group was composed of truly versatile musicians, not merely the brash heavy rockers that they were often typecast as.

Despite the album's folk leanings, they would still start the record off with their bombastic best, a new rock anthem with which to open future concerts. With "Immigrant Song," John's thunderous drums remain consistent throughout, heavily married to the riff imposed by Jimmy's syncopated guitar and John Paul's bass. "A bit of backwards echo makes [the song] a bit more complete," Jimmy reminisced. "I have to say that Robert's input on that song was also absolutely magnificent . . . John Bonham and I playing the riff, putting the E to A 'Rumble' chords, and Robert singing his wonderful melodies."

Robert's epic lyrics saw the musicians as Viking warriors, raping and pillaging through the countryside, literally conquering a new world, while bragging of their tales of warlike glory. Robert's high-pitched wails of "Valhalla, I am coming!" were tongue-in-cheek when recorded in the original studio but worked to instantly rally young fans when the group launched into the song in concert.

Heavily inspired by Crosby, Stills & Nash, "Friends" was the first track on the album to offer listeners the lighter acoustic aspects that Jimmy and Robert had intended to evoke. With the inclusion of minstrel-like orchestration and group chanting, the song became an inadvertent blend into atmospheric, folk psychedelia, and its lush drone wove seamlessly into the introduction of "Celebration Day." Here, John needed little more than a standard eighth-note rock beat, but took the opportunity to show off around the two-minute mark, hammering out a distinctive sixteenth-note snare-drum fill, which would be nearly impossible in any hands other than John's. The first take was sadly lost due to a careless engineer, but luckily for John, his flamboyant flourishes later in the song had been preserved.

"The rhythm track in the beginning of 'Celebration Day' was completely wiped by an engineer," Jimmy lamented. "I was listening through the headphones, and nothing was coming through. I started yelling, 'What the hell is going on?' Then, I noticed that the red recording light was on what used to be the drums. The engineer had accidentally recorded over Bonzo! . . . And that is why you have that synthesizer drone from the end of 'Friends' going into 'Celebration Day,' until the rhythm track catches up. We put that on to compensate for the missing drum track."

Later on in the album, John played into his natural inclination for jazz technique with the slow blues song "Since I've Been Loving You," a lengthy torch number seemingly composed in the same vein as "Dazed and Confused." John's smooth introduction conveyed his control and restraint—a subtle tap on the snare drum, followed directly by a series of hi-hat eighths, later punctuated with his signature snare and bass drum combo. Throughout the sultry number,

John gave listeners a lesson in dramatic tension, holding back on the natural groove of the tempo, in line with Robert's seductive whispers. Playing into Jimmy's blues groove, John utilized a long-learned big-band technique by setting up the guitar riffs at the base of each verse's turnaround—a delicate lick on the snare acting as an audible cue for the upbeat syncopation of the Telecaster. It was an old trick used by Buddy Rich, signaling the larger horn sections in keeping their phrases and stabs on point. A lengthy song, "Since I've Been Loving You" also gave John enough time to incorporate a few of his beloved triplets, in this case nine, after the six-minute mark.

"Bonzo is one of the few drummers, to this day, who plays the drums like an instrument," Zeppelin roadie Henry Smith marveled. "He doesn't just play drums to hear the sound. I could listen to him play by himself and be totally enchanted by what he's doing. He took a lot of rhythm 'n' blues drum licks and put them into rock—which at the time was different."

"Bonzo loved Gene Krupa," recalled *Led Zeppelin III* engineer Terry Manning later. "In my opinion, Bonzo was playing the hardest jazz ever as simply as anyone ever did. He really wasn't bashing like a rock drummer. There was a finesse to the bashing.

"He made the drums important all the time."

John also wanted a drum-heavy centerpiece track to work as a follow-up to the previous album's "Moby Dick." Jimmy based the new riff on a playful drinking song John sometimes sang in the studio. "Yes, John Bonham had quite a bit to do with 'Out on the Tiles,'" Jimmy remembered. "I wrote the opening descending riff, but the guitar part behind the vocal was based on a song [John] used to sing that went something like, *'Out on the tiles, I've had a pint of bitter / and I'm feeling better 'cause I'm out on the tiles.'* You know what 'out on the tiles' means? It's slang for hitting the bars, and a bitter is a sort of dark pale ale."

Page added, "Robert's lyrics took it in a different direction, but the vibe is still there."

For the recording, John playfully used one of his favorite funk grooves, a tip of the hat to soul and R&B styles—something he would bring back for "Gallows Pole"—with paradiddle-derived combinations between snare drum and foot, in essence truly a swing technique. Although the song wasn't played in live concerts for years, the hard-driven guitar duet that opened and closed the track eventually became Jimmy's onstage cue for John to begin his long "Moby Dick" solos.

All the tracks for *Led Zeppelin III* were completed by the middle of June, with Jimmy planning to mix the final version while on the road in America. A week later, John and the boys flew to Iceland for the start of the new tour. The band planned to gently introduce songs from the unreleased album into the set list, including an acoustic section wherein Jimmy, Robert, and John Paul would sit at the base of the stage and John would take to the bongos.

In the wake of the previous tour's violence and accusations of sonic hooliganism on the band's part, this time Led Zeppelin hoped to show their softer side to the world.

※ ※ ※

"DO YOU THINK THESE CARS REALLY FLOAT?" RICHARD COLE ASKED, nudging John in the ribs.

Cole was referencing Volkswagen's latest advertising campaign, showing a photograph of the rounded coupe bobbing atop a lake beneath a printed declaration that the vehicles were "airtight." In the daylight hours before Zeppelin's performance that night, John, Cole, John Paul Jones, and roadie Jim Dobson had opted to do a bit of sightseeing to ward off the boredom, polishing off a bottle of champagne between them as they wandered the streets of Reykjavik. It was a special occasion, after all; Led Zeppelin had been more or less dispatched to Iceland as cultural ambassadors. The first week of June, Peter Grant had been contacted by a talent agent named Jasper Parrott, on behalf of the British government. As a show of goodwill, he was tasked with organizing a British cultural event in Iceland and immediately thought to bring in the biggest, most successful band in the empire to represent the country's musical prowess. Led Zeppelin had been instructed to be on their best behavior.

"I'll drive mine into the water," John said, finishing off the last of the Dom Perignon straight out of the bottle. "Let's find a lake somewhere and give it a try."

Initially, Cole requested a small fleet of Land Rovers for the band's trip, but the rental company was clean out. In their place, the road manager settled for two brand-new Volkswagen Beetles, hopping in one with Dobson and handing the other set of keys to John and Jonesy. After three hours of driving around looking at frozen landscapes of glaciers and geysers, the four men were willing to take on Richard Cole's experiment.

"This could be a historic moment," Cole announced when the group had settled on an appropriate lake. "Will it float, or will it sink?"

In keeping with the rules of the Volkswagen advertisement, natural-born automobile enthusiast John made sure to roll up the windows. Ready as ever—and with Jones beside him in the passenger seat—John veered to the river's edge, did a swift 180-degree turn, and flew backward fifty feet into the lake. "Finally, he shifted into first and gunned the engine, aiming for the water," Cole later recalled. "The VW left land—and hit the river with a thud! It bounced, it bobbed atop the water for a minute or two, and then it settled into a peaceful, rocking float as the engine stalled."

At first, it appeared that the advertisement had told the truth; John and Jonesy sat wide-eyed in the car as it gently bobbed atop the water. After a long, tension-filled moment, however, Cole and Dobson watched as the waterline reached the exterior's door seals—and water slowly began to fill into the car with both superstars locked inside.

Frantically, Cole and Dobson rushed into the water, still shallow enough for the two men to stand upright. Inside, John was cackling at Cole, who proceeded to push the car with all his strength back onto the slope of the water's edge. Touching land, John turned the key in the ignition, and the car sprang back to life.

The men stood around laughing, amazed that the car was as durable as the company claimed.

※ ※ ※

"Two months passed before I saw John again," Mick Bonham later remembered. "This time, he arranged to pick me up on his way to the Bath Festival on June 28. . . . This time, we would travel in another of John's acquisitions, a sleek new Jensen Interceptor, which Matthew was driving so that John could get some sleep on the back-seat, along with a case of Dom Perignon champagne, just in case we got thirsty on the trip."

Following the successful gigs in Iceland, John and the band returned to England for the year's massive Bath Festival, where they'd play for an expected audience of 150,000 people. That year's event had become so big that the show was relocated twenty miles from its original venue in Bath to the Showgrounds at Shepton Mallet. The band turned down a quarter of a million dollars to play in Boston and New Haven, Connecticut, that same weekend, as they were certain that a triumphant display at Bath could garner the long-overdue praise they still sought from their English audiences.

"Bath was a turning point in recognition for us," Peter Grant agreed. "I remember Jonesy arriving by helicopter, [and] we had to get the Hell's Angels to help us get them on site."

Led Zeppelin was in excellent company at the Bath Festival, which was regarded as the largest and most prestigious of all British music fests; Jefferson Airplane, the Byrds, Carlos Santana, Frank Zappa, and John's fellow Birmingham mates the Moody Blues were all booked on the same Sunday bill. Though it had been raining that morning, the sun finally broke out in time for the festival's second half. Predicting a beautiful sunset, Peter Grant pushed Zeppelin's allotment for precisely at sunset—an added special effect care of Mother Nature. The band booked just before them, the Flock, was running long, forcing Grant to go out onstage during their performance and coerce them back into the wings. When a member of the Flock's crew objected, Grant punched him square in the face, allowing for Jimmy and the band to greet the crowd. Grant was determined not to let anyone fuck up Zeppelin's place in the sun. When he spotted someone in the audience taping the performance with a video camera, he had the video pirate manhandled into the backstage area, where Richard Cole poured a bucket of water into his camera.

Even so, listeners were delighted when Led Zeppelin took the stage. "I found a spot on the side of the stage," Mick Bonham recalled. "It was obvious when [Led Zeppelin] did appear that this was what the crowd had been waiting for, and a huge roar echoed around the Somerset countryside."

It was a crucial show for the group—the first British unveiling of *Led Zeppelin III*. As the dipping sun provided a magnificent natural backlit landscape behind the band, they launched into "Immigrant Song." The sunset peaked at the most perfect moment: the band's epic rendition of "Dazed and Confused."

Thankfully, the reviews reflected what Led Zeppelin had prayed for all along—validation and recognition from their home country. More than satisfied with the outcome of that weekend, it was with a new energy that the band prepared, once again, to head back to the States.

Chapter Ten

JULY 1970–OCTOBER 1970

By this point, John's parents had been separated for a number of years, but he remained close with both of them. However, as Joan lived with young daughter Debbie and Jacko had become roommates with Mick in nearby Studley, Warwickshire—living only a few doors down from two of John's favorite pubs, the Duke of Marlborough Pub and the Studley Conservative Club—it was a reunion of the Bonham boys that was more common. As Mick later recalled, "John would get away from the hustle and bustle of the rock scene by coming over for a quiet drink and game of snooker with us at the club and then crossing over the road for some George Rafters at the Duke of Marlborough Pub."

Although now a millionaire and bona fide superstar, John clung to his hometown Birmingham roots for dear life, always yearning for acceptance from the same townsfolk that had watched him grow up. Thankfully, he was still considered a local by most of his fellow Brummies, and when he wasn't traveling the globe as a member of one of its biggest rock 'n' roll groups, he was relatively easy to find around town. Only a few days before leaving with Led Zeppelin for Germany, John happily agreed to take part in the annual summer fair hosted by the local house of worship the St. Mary's Parish Church—after he and the head of the parish, the Reverend David Acheson, downed a few pints at the Duke of Marlborough Pub.

"It was John's job to help raise money by signing autographs and judging the Queen of the Fayre contest," Mick remembered. "An added bonus was that John had got Atlantic Records to sign some hundred assorted albums so that they could sell at knockdown prices to help raise more money for charity."

Only a day following the church's charity event, John was back in work mode, traveling with the band for some warm-up gigs in Germany—preparation for their sixth US tour the following month. In a rare show of trust toward a member of the press, Led Zeppelin extended an exclusive invitation to old friend Chris Welch from *Melody Maker* to join them, hoping that his account of their first few European dates would keep the enthusiasm and momentum high in England after their successful show in Bath.

"We spent five days on the road, traveling by car, train, and plane," Welch recalled. "We flew from London to Düsseldorf through heavy cloud layers. It was a turbulent flight, and almost immediately after takeoff, Bonham—who hated flying even under the best conditions—left his seat and lurched to the toilet to be violently sick. It was moments like these where I saw a different side of Bonzo, 'the tough hell-raiser.'"

Jimmy had been feeling ill even before leaving England, and following the turbulent flight John was so nervous about getting onto another airliner that he begged the band to travel to the other gigs by any other means. In order to calm John's growing airplane phobia, the group instead opted for five-hour trips by train to Berlin, Essen, and Frankfurt.

※ ※ ※

As Welch was soon to discover, when it came to John and his behavior, "most of his bravado and drinking stemmed from nerves, worry, or boredom." He continued, "On our arrival, Bonham stomped around Germany looking somewhat menacing in his black mustache and black leather hat. Yet when he got to the Düsseldorf Sporthalle, he was clearly nervous, as was the rest of the group. . . . And yet Bonham sat silent and edgy, as if waiting for the boxing bell to ring for round one of the big fight."

Nervousness among the band was understandable during the concert in Cologne; about a thousand fans had rioted outside the Sporthalle, throwing rocks and breaking windows when they couldn't get into the concert.

Next, in Frankfurt, the band performed at Festhalle in front of eleven thousand fans—the biggest rock 'n' roll turnout in German history. After the concert, the band and its entourage celebrated the success by finding the closest bar and closing it down with their table's bar tab alone. "The six of us—John Paul, Jimmy, Robert, John, Peter, and I—could all tolerate liquor quite well," Cole remembered fondly. "Only the bartender was keeping track of just how much we were drinking. When I finally went to pay the bill, I was shocked. 'Are you sure you added this up right?' I asked. 'There were just six of us at the table.'

"'I know there were just six of you!' the bartender exclaimed, 'but you guys almost cleaned me out. I've never seen anyone drink like you!'"

During a four-hour period, the six-man Zeppelin crew had consumed a total of 280 drinks—120 slivovitzes (plum brandies) and about 160 beers. Cole recalled this number as a particular point of pride to the band—and to John especially. "At one point," Cole remembered, "Bonzo exclaimed, 'Let's keep running this fucking bartender ragged! By the time the bar closes, the poor bastard might be too tired to throw us out when they close!'"

However, as the *Melody Maker* writer observed, Led Zeppelin's hard partying came with a price. "We went on to Berlin, where barbed wire and 'the Wall' was still in place," Welch recalled. "By now, the tour was taking its toll with Page ill and Bonham a nervous wreck. . . . After the show, I went with John to a Berlin cabaret full of people who could have been men, women, or both. It was hard to tell. 'There's some weird-looking people about,' he observed sagely. 'There's nowhere for a decent bloke to have a pint of beer!'"

According to Richard Cole, the band's disenchantment was a combination of nervousness and a form of "comedown" following their triumph at Bath, where not only had the crowd been three times as large as those in Germany, but it was completely populated with the band's own native Englanders voicing unanimous approval. "As enthusiastic as the crowds were in Germany, Zeppelin was experiencing an emotional letdown after the Bath Festival," Cole admitted. "It was hard to top the two hundred thousand people who had seen them perform a few days earlier."

✳ ✳ ✳

FOLLOWING ANOTHER MONTH OF REST BACK AT HOME, LED ZEPPElin began their sixth American tour on August 5, 1970, in Cincinnati, Ohio. Unhappy as ever strapped in for the long transatlantic flight, John had taken to knocking himself out with alcohol until touchdown.

Playing for a minimum of $25,000 a night with no opening act and no stage props other than their amplifiers and lights, the band sold out each gig in rapid succession. Thirty-five performances into the tour, the band scored a record high—and made international news—when they played at New York's Madison Square Garden (MSG), earning more than $100,000 for their appearance.

The band used the Bath Festival set list as the working template for the tour, with "Immigrant Song" blasting the audience as the ultimate call to arms, following with tried-and-true fan favorites off the first two albums. "Dazed and Confused" was mandatory, as was Jimmy's violin-bow routine—his own psychic, spiritual bond communion with the adoring, enraptured crowd.

"Communication Breakdown" was now a medley comprising "Good Times Bad Times," Buffalo Springfield's "For What It's Worth," and the Beatles' "I Saw Her Standing There"—a shout-out to two other bands that Zeppelin considered rock 'n' roll canon—leading into the new, sultry blues ballad "Since I've Been Loving You" and a few others before John and Jimmy's tumultuous near duet, "Out on the Tiles." From there, John would segue into his "Moby Dick" solo oblivion, which was pushing its epic length to just under a half hour, now including a five-minute drum roll John performed with his bare hands. Following the solo, Robert summoned the audience's applause for "The Big B!"—or, to John's amusement, his full given name: "Ladies and gentlemen, John Henry Bonham!" Each night was a standing ovation.

New to the group's stage show was the acoustic centerpiece set approximately at the set's middle half, allowing for the four members to each grab a chair at the foot of the stage and feign a sort of quiet intimacy with the thousands in attendance.

On the same night Zeppelin was selling out the Forum in Los Angeles, the band learned that their old friends in the Fairport Convention were recording a live album during a three-night residency at one of their old Sunset Strip stomping grounds, the Troubadour. Not only were Jimmy and Robert great admirers of the folk-rock ensemble's acoustically driven work, especially vocalist Sandy Denny, but John's closest Birmingham mate, Dave Pegg, had since joined up with the Fairports as their bassist. On September 5, the night after their massive show at the Forum, the members of Zeppelin surprised their Fairport cohorts at their Troubadour gig, even joining them onstage for a crowd-pleasing jam session—although, to avoid recording legalities, Zeppelin was playfully billed on the eventual Fairport Convention live album, *Full House*, as the Birmingham Water Buffalo Society.

"They were all coming down to the Troubadour to see us," Dave Pegg later said, "[and] for our second set, they all turn up after their gig, and it was, 'We wanna have a play.' So, I went, 'That's fantastic,' so, they all got up. Jonesy had my bass, [and] Richard Thompson stayed onstage with them, and Simon Nicol gave Jimmy his Gibson. . . . We had to buy Mattacks a set of new heads for his kit because they were heavily indented by Bonzo's playing."

As Pegg remembered, if John got wind of any musicians he loved playing locally, he'd make it a point to be in the audience; in this case, blues rockers Savoy Brown were also due in Los Angeles that same weekend, and John wasn't going to miss the show. "There was a club opening the following day where Savoy Brown was due to play," Pegg continued. "Bonzo said, 'We're all invited back there. We're going back for a game of pool and for drinks.'"

Coming off another Fairport gig on the Strip, John and "Peggy" didn't arrive at the Savoy Brown show until after the performance had ended, around two in the morning. Partying with the British band, however, the time flew by, and eventually the club's management informed the group that it was well past closing time. As had been the case in Germany, John wasn't nearly ready to leave. "Bonzo said, 'I'll go if you beat me on the pool table,'" Pegg recalled. "So, they had this game of pool, and Bonzo won. He beat the guy, and it got to be five o'clock and the same thing happened—and now it's six in the morning."

Unamused by John's show of skill, someone called the Los Angeles police to scare the musicians off. At the sound of a squad car pulling up, the various band members scattered out of the club, leaving John and Pegg to get inventive in their escape. "The room just clears, and Bonzo says, 'Come with me!' So, I follow him and go onto the stage, and we're hiding behind these four-by-twelve barstools, a big stack. I'm slumped behind one, and he's behind the other. I pass out, and the next thing I know, the sun is streaking through the window. It's 9:00 a.m. and the place is deserted, and Bonzo is passed out next to me. I go, 'Shit! What happened? Where the fuck are we?'" He goes, 'Oh, it'll be all right. My driver will be outside.' There's nobody in the club, so we creep out of the club, and outside there's a big limo. The guy's been waiting all night."

John instructed his limo driver to bring the two to Pegg's room at the Tropicana, informing his old friend during the drive that Led Zeppelin was actually booked to play in Honolulu the very next day—and his flight to Hawaii was only hours away. After being dropped off, Pegg was resting in his hotel room that afternoon when the phone rang. "It's Bonzo," Pegg laughed, remembering. "'Fancy a drink before I go?' I say, 'Oh, all right.' So, he comes 'round, and we go to Barney's Beanery just up the road. We have a few beers, and Janis Joplin comes in and sits down next to us. It was unbelievable." As evening began to set in, the two thoroughly inebriated friends suddenly remembered John's flight to Honolulu. "I'm going, 'You should have gone.' Bonzo says, 'Ah, fuck it. I can get a later flight, whatever.' I say, 'You really should go.' 'Fuck it. Fuck 'em.' He really didn't give a shit."

Instead, the two headed back to the Tropicana and hung out with Andy Warhol and a few tourists by the hotel pool. John may not have cared much if he was late to his Led Zeppelin gig the following day, but Pegg was still due at the Troubadour with the rest of Fairport Convention in only a few hours. "I've got to go in an hour and a half to do the first set that's being recorded," Pegg added, "and Bonzo pushes me into the pool, fully dressed. I think, 'I'll get you, you bastard,' so I push him in the pool, and then he gets out and takes all his clothes off, except for his 'Y' fronts, and he's having a swim, and he's left his clothes by the side of the pool. He comes out, and we're befriended by two Texan girls with a big bag of grass, which we take back to our room and carry on partying for a bit. . . . Then, I have to go back to the Troubadour to do the first set. I'm drinking black coffee, cold water, in a fucking dreadful state.

"Just before the second set starts, there's a phone call from Bonzo, going, 'Where am I? Can you help us out?' He was in my room at the Tropicana, and he'd gone out to the pool in his wet 'Y' fronts, and all his clothes had been nicked. So, he borrowed some of my clothes out of my suitcase and came down to the club, and we had to loan him the dosh to get the ticket to get to Honolulu. I thought, 'Peter Grant's going to fucking murder us.' . . . Bonzo made it to Hawaii. Don't ask me how."

✳ ✳ ✳

WHILE IN HAWAII, ZEPPELIN GOT WORD THAT *MELODY MAKER* HAD just published its reader poll, running with the stunning headline "Zeppelin Topple Beatles"; after eight consecutive years, the Fab Four had been officially dethroned. Robert had also won Best British Male Vocalist, and *Led Zeppelin II*—"the Brown Bomber"—nabbed Best British Album.

By all accounts, it appeared that Led Zeppelin's antagonistic relationship with the press was turning around. Throughout their US tour, the positive reviews abounded. But the band's love-hate relationship with music journalists took a decidedly sour turn on September 18, due in large part to a press conference held in New York, which announced the band's record-shattering compensation of $100,000 for their upcoming Madison Square Garden performance the following evening. That figure didn't sit well with a room full of music writers, and the band quickly grew defensive before the skeptical scribes, a terse preamble to the big event.

"The lights went out and Zep began to play," one reviewer wrote of the Madison Square Garden show. "What does one expect from a true 'supergroup'—an act who for the first time toppled the Beatles from their perch as Most Popular Group in the annual Melody Maker poll in Britain? Zep are like anyone else, just four musicians making music. The crowd reaction was fantastic, but I wonder sometimes whether people have come to hear music or see stars like Jimmy Page? . . . And how many groups can sell out the vaunted Garden twice in one day? It's true what they say: nothing succeeds like success." Still, the review went on to concede that "when Zep get it together, they are amazing. . . . John Bonham's fifteen-minute drum solo was anything but tedious. And showed him to be a much-underrated drummer."

New York critic Larry Hutchinson added, "In brief, everything that has ever been right with live rock and roll is right with Led Zeppelin in concert. . . . After some slightly lackluster acoustic material and a John Bonham drum solo that brought down the packed house, the group got into the best extended live rock playing I have ever heard anyone do, and that includes the Stones."

Jimmy didn't have much time to give the critics much thought. After all, he had an album to mix—the deadline for *Led Zeppelin III* was rapidly approaching, Atlantic adamant that an October US release would kick off the holiday season. Long accustomed to multitasking, the young producer set to mixing the master takes on the road, completing the bulk of the work at Ardent Studios in Memphis.

As expected, Jimmy made the deadline, and *Led Zeppelin III* greeted the American public on October 5. The band waited with bated breath; more than the previous albums, both of which were still placing well on the *Billboard* charts, their third endeavor was a deliberate attempt to branch out and demonstrate their serious dedication to their craft. They made a name for themselves with *Led Zeppelin* and its immediate follow-up—but this one was a labor of love.

Jimmy was immediately disappointed with the album's cover, which had to be a compromise when initial designs proved too time-consuming to complete. The band's preferred artwork was discarded and replaced with an intricate—and expensive—die-cut psychedelic wheel that, when spun, revealed headshots of the band.

However, Jimmy was pleased with a cheeky inclusion that he'd been able to sneak in, having added a personal touch to the album's master pressing only moments before its mass printing: scratched into the runoff matrix of the first side, he'd slyly included a maxim attributed to Aleister Crowley—the very philosophy Jimmy himself practiced in every one of his artistic undertakings: "Do what thou wilt. So, mote it Be."

Ultimately, none of the four musicians cared for the artwork, or the overly ambitious packaging. But there was no time to tinker with it: following a massive hit like "the Brown Bomber," there was an enormous amount of advance orders for the album, and the group's current tour was strategically scheduled to coincide with *Led Zeppelin III*'s highly anticipated release.

Yet nothing could have prepared them for the reviews. The critics often criticized Led Zeppelin and took potshots at their quick rise to stardom and financial success. When the more aggressive of the poisoned-pen journalists grew weary of putting the members of Zeppelin down, they instead turned their cold stares in the direction of the group's fan base. The *Los Angeles Times* suggested that Zeppelin's devout popularity among American teens could be chalked up to the drug use associated with the band's concert atmosphere and lyrical content, of "barbiturates and amphetamines, drugs that render their users most responsive to crushing volume and ferocious histrionics of the sort that Zeppelin has dealt exclusively." Admittedly antagonistic in their assessments, most US critics lamented Zeppelin's musicianship and innovations within Peter Grant's management strategies.

Most shocking of all, it seemed, was the backlash against the album from Led Zeppelin's own fans. Prior to the album's release, preorders had guaranteed placement on the *Billboard* charts—which it did receive. However, after a few weeks of negative word of mouth and even more negative critical press, the album stalled, then slowly dropped. As the band's first two records were still comfortably placed on the same chart—and the songs of *Led Zeppelin III* had been granted a stirring welcome when publicly debuted during the tour—the Zeppelin crew was at first confused, then hurt.

The band, especially Jimmy, took it very personally. Predictably, the band largely blamed each tier of the album's perceived failure on the press—the journalists who had all but declared war on the band once word of their MSG payday went public. After each member of the band had toiled away years of their respective youths in scores of failed rock 'n' roll bands, hours of thankless session work, and deep sacrifice on the part of their individual families, Led Zeppelin was erroneously perceived as an "overnight success"—and the American press would never completely forgive them for it.

"The third LP got a real hammering from the press, and I really got brought down by it," Jimmy later recalled. "The press didn't like it, and they also went on about this enigma that has blown up around us. I admit we may have made it relatively quickly, but I don't think we overplayed our hand in the press or anything. Yet we were getting all these knocks and became very dispirited."

Against Grant's learned experience from working with previous bands, he went along with Jimmy and the rest of the group's insistence to ignore the press entirely—at least for the time being. Instead, he sided with Jimmy's growing desire to simply put out an even bigger and better album, one that the critics—or, at the very least, the sales charts—couldn't ignore. More concerts, more music, more Zeppelin, and a surefire rock album that would draw back all the devoted fans who felt strangely betrayed by the softer balance of *Led Zeppelin III*.

For the next album, Jimmy and Robert planned to retain the folk sensibilities, but agreed to amp up the hard-driven shadings that Zeppelin addicts had come to expect. Jimmy would soon discover his compromise between the two realms of music, the acoustic and the metallic. He would settle for nothing less than Led Zeppelin's masterpiece.

Determined, Jimmy and Robert returned to the Bron-Yr-Aur cottage to write new material. In Wales they began to develop fragments for a new epic that would replace "Dazed and Confused" as the show's centerpiece. "It's an idea for a really long track," Jimmy told the press in November. "We want to try something new with the organ and acoustic guitar building up and building up, and then the electric part starts. . . . It might be a fifteen-minute track."

Chapter Eleven

OCTOBER 1970–FEBRUARY 1971

"**J**ohn Bonham, the extrovert drummer with Led Zeppelin, remains a down-to-earth individual who retains his Brum accent, his sense of perspective, his flamboyant nature," wrote local Birmingham newspaper the *Record Mirror* in October, after John agreed to a full profile. "Like colleague Robert Plant, he is at home in the country and spends whatever spare time his hectic schedule allows at his home near Birmingham." John told the paper, "I have ambitions in all sorts of different ways. As far as the group is concerned, I think we can be a lot better; I believe the group can get 100-percent better in the next twelve months. . . . So many groups . . . work hard for a certain amount of time, they make it and then they sort of say, 'we've made it now, we're OK.' This attitude is completely wrong. Achieving success makes things harder."

As the year wound down, the band continued to push themselves, both to make even better music and to create an even bigger album. By December 1970, while proving less popular than its two hit predecessors, *Led Zeppelin III* had nevertheless inched its way to platinum status—something that would have ended the year as a success for any other band. Led Zeppelin, on the other hand, still had something to prove. The veiled accusations of early hype still cast a shadow on some of the concert write-ups the band received throughout the tour. Critics would both acknowledge the skill of the members and note the audience havoc the music seemed to invoke.

And most notably, *Led Zeppelin III* had been a very personal album, at least to Jimmy and Robert, who poured their own love of acoustic instrumentation and folk themes into the record. It wasn't as if the album ignored their heavy reputation completely; "Immigrant Song" was a well-received smash that was used to open their show, and John's drums-driven "Out on the Tiles" was played, at least in part, as the intro for his twenty-minute "Moby Dick" solo. Still, the band craved universal critical and public acclaim.

Reflecting on the experience of recording *Led Zeppelin III*, Jimmy noted that using the mobile unit for the bulk of the sessions had produced some of the most successful tracks on the whole record, and he was particularly fond of the distraction-free Headley Grange. The building's history alone fascinated him, and even when the other three opted for Cole's suggestion of a hotel for the evenings, Jimmy was quite comfy reveling in the house's character each night.

"It was very Charles Dickens," Page recalled. "Dank and spooky. . . . Headley Grange freaked Robert and John Bonham out, but I liked it, actually."

More important, Jimmy found the place inspiring and was impressed by the sounds the acoustics had produced during the band's previous sessions. This time, however, they would rock more and harder—and save the poetic fingerpicked "light" of the album's folkish balance for one epic multisection ballad. Headley Grange would be perfect for that recording, too.

"We thought it would be interesting to record someplace with some atmosphere and just stay there," Page later remembered. "[Wales had been] very beautiful, and there was nothing to distract us. . . . This time, we thought it would be fun to bring the whole band somewhere and hire a mobile unit to capture that moment in time."

The band again booked the Rolling Stones' mobile unit, and Jimmy hired engineer Andy Johns to help with its operation, after the two had worked well on the last album's mixing sessions. Andy was particularly enthusiastic about working with John again and continued to play with microphone placement and the drummer's thunderous approach. "[John] was a great drummer, whether it was a heavy death march or an acoustic thing with small animals cavorting in a meadow," Andy recalled. "[He was] a naturally fantastic timekeeper and not a trudge merchant, very creative with sound."

At the beginning of December, the band recorded a few isolated sessions at London's Island Studios—including the six-stringed introduction for the unnamed epic ballad he was working on with Plant. After Christmas, they headed for Headley Grange.

John Paul Jones opted to drive himself, while Jimmy and Peter Grant hired a driver to take them down to the manor. John offered to drive Robert from the Midlands out to Hampshire, but couldn't decide which of his twenty-one cars would keep him the most entertained the longest during the extended stay: the AC Cobra, the Rolls-Royce, the powder-blue Jaguar XKE, the Maserati, or one of the Jensens.

Upon arriving at Headley Grange, John started wandering from room to room. He sighed aloud, "The house seems more dilapidated than it was the last time we were here."

According to Richard Cole, during their stay the band ate "like million-dollar boy scouts" and drank like fish. "There weren't any serious drugs around the band at that point," he recalled. "Just dope and a bit of coke." In between sessions, the band hiked around the surrounding woods, shooting small game or sometimes trekking farther into town to visit the local pub, where John would eagerly swap his jeans and T-shirt for his "country best"—an expensive tweed jacket and cap. "We had an account at a shop in the village, and we'd go down there regularly and collect huge quantities of cider," Richard Cole reminisced. "They found an old shotgun and used to shoot at squirrels in the woods, not that they ever hit anything. And there was this lovely old black Labrador wandering around [that] we used to feed." The regal canine eventually inspired a complex blues jam by Robert and John Paul Jones called "Black Dog."

Jimmy loved the quick turnaround that self-producing in the remote manor provided. "What we found exciting about our time at Headley Grange was the ability to develop material and record it while the idea was still hot. If the track isn't happening and it starts creating a psychological barrier, even after an hour or two, then you should stop and do something else. Go·out—go to the pub or a restaurant or something. Or play another song."

"Black Dog," in fact, was once such instance. Jonesy was inspired for the basic riff of the heavy blues track by repeatedly listening to Muddy Waters's "psychedelic blues" album, *Electric Mud*, an underappreciated crossover album that delighted fans like Jimi Hendrix.

The band jammed extensively over the fragments that Jonesy brought with him, Robert improvising the first round of lyrics while Jimmy continued to experiment with guitars and sound. Later, Jones admitted that "Black Dog" caused John some problems while ironing out the song's complex time signature. "I told [John] he had to keep playing four-to-the-bar all the way through [it]. . . . But there is a 5/8 rhythm over the top. If you got through enough 5/8s, it arrives back on the beat. Originally, it was more complicated, but we had to change the accents for him to play it properly."

Despite the deceiving simplicity of the song's call-and-response composition, it proved to be one of the group's most rhythmically complex works. Following along, each musician began by counting an extra beat—a total of five—at the end of each instrumental "response" riff following Robert's vocal "call." "I seemed to be the only one who could actually count things in," Jones later said. "Page would play something . . . and you'd say, 'That's great. Where's the first beat? You know it, but you've gotta tell us. . . . ' He couldn't actually count what he was playing. It would be a great phrase, but you couldn't relate it to a count. If you think of 'one' as being in the wrong place, you are completely screwed."

Initially, John attempted to keep his percussion in step with Jimmy's lead, which only added to the initial confusion of the early takes. But Jimmy continued to tinker with the guitar parts, finally choosing a "direct" technique similar to Neil Young's recording of "Cinnamon Girl." Engineer Andy Johns said that the experiment would be more easily accomplished at Island, and the group agreed to finish "Black Dog" when they returned to the London studio once out of Hampshire. There, the resulting final cut contained numerous overdubs, with Jimmy layering up to four separate guitar tracks.

Johns also later remembered the experimentation that led to Jimmy's satisfaction with the proper guitar voicings. The aggressive snarl effect of the song's signature riff was created by plugging Page's sunburst Les Paul into a direct box and, from there, into a mic channel on the studio's mixing board. According to Page, "Andy Johns used the mic amp of the mixing board to get distortion. Then, we put two 1176 Universal compressors in a series on that sound and distorted the guitars as much as we could, and then compressed them. . . . Each riff was triple tracked—one left, and one right up the middle. The solos were recorded in a more standard way. . . . I ran my guitar through a Leslie and miked that in the usual way."

"I remember 'Four Sticks' was obviously in 5/4, but I couldn't work out where the first beat was, and he couldn't tell us," John Paul Jones added. "But somehow, we all did it—and foxed each other. We never played it live. . . . And it took [John] ages to get 'Four Sticks.'"

Jimmy was equally meticulous regarding the guitar parts of "Four Sticks"—another challenging composition that featured multiple riffs, which switched between 5/8 and 6/8 time signatures. He later admitted, "I can see certain milestones along the way like 'Four Sticks,' in the middle section of that. The sound of the guitars—that's where I'm going."

John Paul Jones, on the other hand, had his hands full as the band's de facto arranger with the Indian-influenced song. "Rhythmically, it was quite unusual, but I was the only one in the band who could do that because of my background as an arranger."

For John's part, "Four Sticks" presented him with one of the most unusual compositions for the band yet. For the recording, he showed serious flourish using four drumsticks, gripping two in each hand like a mallet, and produced unique sounds by tapping the rims of his drums while continuing his rolling tom-toms. By concurrently pedaling "fours" on his hi-hats, he sounded like a one-band percussion section. But showing off with four sticks presented an odd problem, because in order to keep all the sticks within his hands, John was unable to hit them with his usual brutality. Utilizing this softer, rapid technique—coupled with the added heavy compression—instead produced a distinctive rippling effect on the toms.

"It was two takes, but that was because it was physically impossible for him to do another," Page explained. "I couldn't get that to work until we tried to record it a few times, and I just didn't know what it was and I still wouldn't have known what it was. We probably would have kicked that track out." After venting his frustrations with a wave of cussing and stomping around, John finally "just picked up the four sticks and that was it."

Again, the band opted to lay down the rhythm section at Headley and save the more intricate pieces for their final trip to Island. There the following month, John Paul Jones overdubbed the VCS3 synthesizer solo on the song's second middle-eight section. "It was a bastard to mix," confessed Andy Johns. "When I originally recorded the basic tracks, I compressed the drums. Then, when I went to the mix, I couldn't make it work. I did it five or six times." The band also made the tragic discovery that a quarter-inch tape of the track was missing, as well.

Halfway through the seemingly endless process of trying to make "Four Sticks" work, John began to lose his patience, primarily with himself. He needed a breather, but with no bar or lounge area anywhere in Headley Grange, there was little to do but bash away at the drum kit. While Jimmy and Andy Johns continued to tinker, John knocked back the rest of his Double Diamond lager, twirled his sticks, and, for fun, launched into the signature count off to an old Little Richard favorite of his, the rollicking "Keep a-Knockin'." Hearing this improvised burst of creativity, Jimmy grabbed his 1959 Les Paul and started riffing over it. With the aggravation "Four Sticks" was causing for the band, a little jam session was certainly in order.

And so, in this high-energy jam session reminiscent of their first time ever playing together in that cold basement in London three years earlier, the band reconnected psychically, and the seeds for "Rock and Roll" were sown. "That's how it was going back then," Page said later. "If something felt right, we didn't question it. If something really magical is coming through, then you follow it. It was all part of the process. We had to explore; we had to delve."

The band's timing couldn't have been better, as another skilled musician just happened to be present for that particular session. Ian "Stu" Stewart occasionally played piano for the Rolling Stones, but was known primarily as one of their recording technicians and one of the only engineers trusted with the task of keeping their extremely valuable mobile recording unit in proper working order. As an agent of the Stones, he was also one of the few outsiders allowed to drop in on Zeppelin while recordings were under way, and he had been assisting Andy Johns when John began his impromptu R&B bashing. Without having to be asked, Stewart playfully strolled to an old piano pushed off in the corner, another furnishing relic of Headley Grange, and hammered out a distinctive boogie-woogie part—which Jimmy Page instantly loved. The band retained Stewart for the Ritchie Valens–inspired jam "Boogie with Stu" and later invited him down to London to rerecord the piano section he'd concocted for what Robert Plant initially titled "It's Been a Long Time," later renamed "Rock and Roll."

As Page remembered, "At Headley Grange, there was this old piano that had fallen into a state of disrepair and was almost unplayable. It was so bad, we never even thought to use it. But Ian came in and just started improvising this amazing lick on it. So, I went over to him and I did my best to tune my guitar to the piano, and the other guys started playing tambourine, handclaps, and stomping in the hallway, and before you knew it, we had recorded 'Boogie with Stu.'"

John's hard-driving intro set the stage for the amped-up boogie on steroids, both hands shuffling in-union eighths on snare and half-open hi-hat, accenting a rock "clave"—played primarily to shake off the restraint of having to previously balance four sticks in his hands for the bulk of that day's recording. Let loose on "Rock and Roll," John now tackled two-handed shuffles with energetic ease, allowing the band to explode in creative expression and, finally, let out a sigh of relief. The recording sessions were back on track.

※ ※ ※

DURING THEIR NIGHTS AT HEADLEY GRANGE, THE BAND—ALONG with Richard Cole and the few roadies who accompanied them—would wander outdoors and unwind by building a fire and enjoying an acoustic jam amid the peaceful serenity of the surrounding woods. In such an atmosphere, Jimmy and John Paul Jones continued their work on the chord charts for Jimmy's epic-to-be, the acoustic "light and shade" masterpiece he'd since started with Robert. And finally, one morning, the band ran through "Stairway to Heaven" for the first time.

The song, with its six-string and twelve-string solo, was another complex arrangement. At the kit, John initially had problems with the timing on the twelve-string section before Jimmy's solo; again, it took ample rehearsal time for Jimmy to conduct it just the way he envisioned the delicate shadings.

"We were going over and over it from the beginning to the end quite a few times, with Robert sitting on the stool," Jimmy recalled. "Then we all threw in new ideas—things such as Bonzo not coming in until the song was well under way to create a change of gear—and the song and the arrangement just came together. . . . For some unknown reason, [at one point] Bonzo couldn't get the timing on the twelve-string intro to the solo. Apart from that, it flowed very quickly."

Engineer Richard Digby Smith was assisting Andy Johns during the "Stairway" sessions and recalled the interplay between John and Jimmy in getting the song's drum parts perfected for the recording. "They run up the stairs for the playback, [then say] 'Sounds wonderful.' Bonham says, 'That's it, then!' But Pagey's quiet. He's a man of few words anyway. His hand's on his chin, he's going, 'Mmmm, mmmm'—you never knew what he was thinking. So, Bonham looks at him and says, 'What's up?'

"'Nothing.'

"'No, something's wrong. What is it?'

"'No, there's nothing wrong.'

"'Well, is that the take or isn't it?'

"'It's all right.'

"'It's all right? So, you want us to do it again?'

"'I think we've got a better take inside us.'

"Well, Bonham's not yet pleased. 'This always happens—we get a great take, and you want to do it again.' They go back down. Bonzo grabs his sticks, huffing, puffing, muttering, 'One more take and that's it!' He waits and waits until he makes his grand entrance, and, of course, when the drums come in, if you thought the one before was good, this one is just explosive. And when they play it back, Bonham looks at Jimmy, like, 'You're always right, you bastard.'"

As the drama played out, Robert remained offside and continued to pour out his particularly poetic lyrics. "He must have written three-quarters of it on the spot," Jimmy said later. "He didn't really have to go away and think about them. . . . [It was] amazing, really."

Ever inspired by his love of fantastical mythology and medieval folklore, Robert drew on such imagery for his lengthy tale of a quest for spiritual liberation. He had recently been enraptured with British antiquarian Lewis Spence's voluminous books on mythology, particularly *The Magic Arts in Celtic Britain*, and saw "Stairway" as his opportunity to prove his own worth as a songwriter. The object of his lyrics worked as a poetic amalgam of Spenser's Faerie Queene, mixed with other such Celtic heroines—the Lady of the Lake, Diana of the Fields Greene, and Rhiannon the Nightmare.

"Stairway to Heaven" began as a ballad, but Jimmy was insistent that the rock bursts would be more effective the longer John waited to fully join into the ensemble's flow. As such, the lengthy composition was the most delicate opening the "heavy" group had yet attempted in a new track. John's drum section didn't begin until the four-minute mark, and even then he was instructed to pace his accompaniment until the epic guitar solo another minute and a half later. Finally, John entered the fold, playing an inspired snare-drum phrase to re-introduce Robert's returning vocals; by the end of this section, John's drumming perfectly mirrored the other members' parts, bringing the four men into sublime unity.

This recording would be the only track on the new album to fea-ture the full of Jimmy's guitar arsenal. Hoping to replicate the subtle nuances of a true rock orchestra, he varied each part with another stroke of his sonic brush: the song's gentle intro was played with his Harmony, the rhythm part on a Fender electric twelve-string, and many of the song's heavier riffs and turnarounds on the '59 sunburst Les Paul given to him by Joe Walsh. For the epic guitar solo, however, Jimmy deliberately played his old Telecaster, which he'd also used on the first album, plugging it through a Marshall amp.

The delivery of a new Ludwig kit to the Grange soon inspired one of John's most standout performances of the sessions on a track called "When the Levee Breaks." Earlier that day, John and Jonesy headed into town for a pub break, and the two then set up the new kit upon their return in the house's large entrance hallway, playfully referred to as "the Minstrel Gallery." "There was a lot of leakage from the drums," John Paul Jones recalled. "So, we moved [them] out into the hall where there's a big stairwell."

Jimmy later remembered, "We were working on another song in the front room of Headley Grange when a second drum kit showed up. Rather than stop what we were doing, we told the people bringing it in to just set it up in the entrance hallway."

The hallway in question was "massive," according to Jimmy, and dead center was a spiral staircase that ascended a full three stories. When John went to test the kit, the echo and reverb throughout the hall were so lush, Jimmy immediately decided to keep the second drum set right there.

Andy fondly recalled John's excitement at experimenting with the sound on the track. "We'd done a couple of takes of 'When the Levee Breaks,' and the sound pressure was building up, as it always did with those buggers. One night, they're going down the pub, and I say, 'All right, but Bonzo has to stay behind.' He says, 'Why?' I say, 'I've got this idea. You're always moaning about your drum sound, and I think this is going to work.' So, we carted his kit out into this huge lobby, where the ceiling is at least twenty-five feet high."

Johns then hung two ambient Beyer M160 stereo microphones over the kit, one ten feet up, the other about twenty. "[John's] kit was very well balanced internally. Each drum's volume was consistent with the others. In the truck, I put him into two channels and compressed the drums." Johns ran the resulting signal through the Binson echo unit he'd used on a previous track, "The Battle of Evermore," and the echo effect immediately stood out as incredibly powerful. "I remember sitting there thinking it sounded utterly amazing. I ran out of the truck and said, 'Bonzo, you gotta come in and hear this!' And he came in and shouted, 'Fucking hell! That's what I've been hearing!'"

Johns and Jimmy added more echo to the compressed signals—and then compressed the echo. "The acoustics of the stairwell happened to be so balanced that we didn't even need to mic the kick drum," Jimmy recalled. "Jonesy and I came out in the hallway with our headphones and left the amps back in the room and banged out the rhythm track."

Jimmy considered this new sound tantamount to creating a track that would signify his long-believed theory that "distance equals depth," and John's reverberated drums could hold all the presence of thunder when recorded properly. "I knew the drum, being an acoustic instrument, had to breathe, so it was always paramount in importance that the studio had to sound good," Jimmy said. "The drums are the backbone of the band. . . . But while Headley was great for drums, it wasn't always the best for the guitars. A lot of the guitars recorded there were used as guide tracks and rerecorded later at Island. However, 'Levee' was an exception."

Originally written by blues singer Memphis Minnie and her husband, Kansas Joe McCoy, shortly after they left Tennessee for Chicago in 1929, "When the Levee Breaks" spoke of the devastating floods that swamped the American South during the '20s—and it had long been a favorite of Jimmy's. Zeppelin attempted to record a version of it back in London, but they were unsatisfied with the earliest takes. Now, at Headley Grange, the depth of John's drums made all the difference.

"The whole idea was to make 'Levee' into a trance," Jimmy later explained. "If you notice, something new is added to every verse . . . and at the end, everything starts moving around except for the vocal, which stays stationary. . . . That was it—it was going to be *the* drum song. As soon as it was set up, it was the one we went for, and it worked."

"Bonzo started playing, and we said, 'Jesus, will you listen to that sound,'" John Paul Jones added. "Then we started the riff, and that's how the song came about—through experimentation."

John and Andy decided not to add a separate microphone for the bass drum—John's sheer power didn't need it. "[Bonzo's] kick sound was that powerful," Jimmy remembered. "And his playing was not in his arms; it was all in his wrist action. Frightening! I still do not know how he managed to get so much level out of a kit."

While John's beat is played relatively simple, his fills were incredibly distinctive; the use of the bass drum syncopated on the last sixteenth of the beat added a funky turnaround that Jimmy lovingly called John's "sex groove." But, as was John's signature sound, he still retained a triplet feel—gorgeously lush amid the compressed echo.

According to Jimmy, each twelve-bar of the blues composition added a new effect: for example, the slow backward integration of phased vocals and harmonica solos, elements added in as the song went along. The backward echo was a favorite trick of Jimmy's and something he had been experimenting with since his Yardbirds days on a track titled "Ten Little Indians." Now, in the producer's chair, he was finally able to expand on it, creating a disorienting effect that was nonetheless melodious and hypnotic. "That's my electric Fender twelve-string in open G," Jimmy later clarified. "It sounds lower because we slowed the track down to make everything sound more intense. . . . That's also part of what makes that track sound so huge."

He added, "When Bonzo was in the hall, Jones and I were out there with earphones; the two sets of amps were in the other rooms and other parts, such as cupboards and things. A very odd way of recording, but it certainly worked."

Another Plant original was a riff-based swinging blues tune, loaded with more of the increasingly confident singer's Welsh mythology included. Like its sister track, it was also started in the studio and retained for the band's venture into the Hampshire wild. Once there, John crafted a more subtle tapping pattern that showed off his restraint, but grew heavier and more recognizable at the chorus and turnaround. To achieve that denser sound, he included some strong sixteenth-note fills over the snare and toms at the end of each eight-bar chorus—which Robert also composed to act as a bridge—and left just enough room for John to insert some flourish. In the eighth bar at the climax of the final chorus, John seemed to begin another recognizable fill, but tricked the ears by continuing for a few extra bars, starting with one of his famous snare triplet rolls, then exploding over seven beats before opening out across the kit.

Begun as a mandolin-driven instrumental, "The Battle of Evermore" became another lyric epic once Robert's current fascination with the Scottish border wars got the better of him. The band recorded some rhythm parts in advance but saved the vocals—which would require a female to sing the second half—for the eventual trip to Island. Robert and Jimmy also composed their true love letter to the mutually appreciated Joni Mitchell with a ballad, "Going to California," which didn't leave as much space for John's drumming acumen, but whose lyrics reflected each member's love of the American state—and state of mind—that had embraced their music the strongest. During the group's final weeks at the Grange, Zeppelin recorded a version of "Down by the Seaside," brought from Bron-Yr-Aur; "Jennings Farm Blues," penned by Robert as inspired by his recently purchased

Kidderminster farm, later renamed "Bron-Y-Aur Stomp"; and another dark travelogue, "Night Flight." After laying down the last song, Led Zeppelin ventured out of the woods, exhausted, and returned to civilization.

✳ ✳ ✳

UPON THEIR RETURN, THE BAND TOOK A FEW MONTHS TO REST, ALL satisfied with the material that Headley Grange had inspired. With all the rhythm and backing tracks safely recorded, Led Zeppelin returned to Island Studio in London at the end of January 1971. There, they recorded the many songs' overdubs and guitar solos, and Robert laid down the vocals. For "The Battle of Evermore," Jimmy and Robert approached the Fairport Convention's Sandy Denny to contribute the other half of the duet's voicings.

Finally, Jimmy recorded his guitar solos alone. By the end of the following month, the still-unnamed fourth album had wrapped, and all that was needed was a proper mix.

Before wrapping on the album's final sessions, John was adamant that he have one last go at "Four Sticks." Having attended a London concert of beloved rival Ginger Baker's new solo act, Air Force, John returned to the studio properly inspired to finally tackle the new album's most elusive composition. "I'll show Ginger Baker something," he grumbled under his breath as he sat behind the Ludwig kit. Grasping four drumsticks—two in each hand—he forced himself into a state of hyperfocus and, with Jimmy recording, nailed the track in two consecutive near-perfect takes.

With that, Led Zeppelin's fourth album wrapped by the middle of February 1971.

Chapter Twelve

MARCH 1971–NOVEMBER 1971

Speaking about *Led Zeppelin IV* to *Melody Maker's* Chris Welch, John confessed that "my personal view is that it's the best thing we've ever done."

But as anxious as the band was for the public to hear the new album—especially with the lackluster response to *Led Zeppelin III* still fresh in everyone's minds—there were numerous production delays. It was accepted among all four that the release had to be perfect; there would be no room for critical naysaying this time around, and while the group insisted that their musicianship and acoustic abilities be acknowledged with the few softer tracks, the album had to satisfy the group's core fans, who largely craved Led Zeppelin's heavier blues.

For the final mixing sessions, engineer Andy Johns convinced Jimmy to take the master tapes to Sunset Sound in Los Angeles. That would add weeks, or even months, to the potential release date, but at this point the band hadn't even settled on a proper title. For all involved, it was largely referred to as "Four."

In an effort to rally early anticipation for the album's eventual release, the band headed out on the road again at the beginning of March—nearly a year since their last tour. With each member of the group relishing their time back at home, Peter Grant and Jimmy opted to start small, booking a monthlong tour of local universities and small clubs throughout the United Kingdom. Aside from appeasing the true diehard fans, many of whom had shown their earliest support for the group in those smaller venues, this would be a testing ground for the fourth album's new material—including a midconcert acoustic set that the band was dead set on retaining for performance of the new ballads and their favorites from *Led Zeppelin III*. Sitting on three chairs at the front of the stage, Robert sang while Jimmy played lead guitar and John Paul Jones took up mandolin. During "Going to California," John sat out.

By this point, the band had been away from the public long enough for rumors of a split to emerge in the music trades. Beginning with Zeppelin's first show of the tour on March 5 in Ulster Hall, Belfast, Ireland, Robert Plant—decked out in a flamboyant red-and-black blouse—playfully dispelled the rumors from the stage at nearly every stop. "A lot of those musical papers that come down from across the sea say we are going to break up," Robert belted into the microphone. "Well . . . we're *never* going to break up!"

The tour marked Zeppelin's first visit to Ireland, and, upon touchdown, all four were instantly apprehensive. The violence and civil unrest they'd seen previously in the United States were a mere precursor to the riots and crime that were visible on the ride from the airport. In truth, many British rock groups avoided playing gigs throughout Northern Ireland due to reports of such political upheaval, the streets literally engulfed in violent acts between the Catholics and Protestants. As Zeppelin made their way to the very first gig, word spread that a gasoline tanker had been hijacked and lit on fire right beside the venue hall and a teenager had been gunned down nearby. From the car window, the band could see the sky lit by high-flung Molotov cocktails.

Zeppelin ventured on, and, luckily, their Belfast performance went off without incident. Indeed, the world premieres of both "Black Dog" and, most appropriately, "Stairway to Heaven" seemed to calm the restless crowd, a promising sign of the latter song's spiritual potency.

For the tour, Jimmy had to have a custom-built double-neck Gibson constructed, as the epic's many guitar parts could be replicated on-stage with only such an instrument; the fans loved it.

When the time came for John's first live performance of "Moby Dick" in more than a year, the crowd grew rabid. "Here comes something that gets a little better every night," Robert joyfully proclaimed for John's introduction, leading into a near half hour of Bonzo unleashed—and the first of many standing ovations throughout the tour.

"A new kind of riot hit Ireland last weekend," wrote Chris Welch in his lengthy feature for *Melody Maker*. "A riot of fun, laughter and excitement, when Led Zeppelin paid their first visit to the troubled isle. . . . Violence and explosions raged only half a mile away from their concert in Belfast on Friday night. But the young people of the town, unconcerned with ancient conflicts, used their energy to celebrate the worthwhile cause of peace, love and music."

Welch continued, "Then came 'Moby Dick,' featuring John Bonham—the Compleat Drummer. Said Robert, 'Here comes something that gets just that little bit better every night.' John edged forward on his stool, crouched down and tore into his marathon. His hi-hat jigged a merry dance, while his colossal bass drum rumbled to a climax. He played with his bare hands and his sticks. . . . Bursts of applause punctuated the phenomenal feats of sweat and dexterity."

As a security precaution while in Northern Ireland, road manager Richard Cole hired individual cars for each member of the band. Regularly anxious while on tour anyway, John insisted that he be allowed to provide his own driver rather than the fleet of Irish chauffeurs the band retained. And so John brought along old friend Matthew Maloney, who promptly made a disastrous wrong turn following the Belfast show, which landed the two face-to-face with the worst of the ongoing violence: the Falls Road riot area where the Irish Republican Army and British were locked in urban combat.

"Hey, mate, what do you think I should do?" Matthew asked, trying his best to remain calm.

"Get us the fuck out of here!" John shouted back.

Richard Cole had ensured that each departing Zeppelin car had at least one bottle of Jameson's whiskey, and John knocked back as much as needed while Matthew navigated the harsh terrain. "The street was covered in glass," John later remembered, "and there were armored cars and kids chucking things. . . . We just kept our heads down and drove right through."

Rattled by the violence, John wasn't the only band member who needed liquid courage to make it through; by the time the band and its entourage arrived at Dublin's Intercontinental Hotel later that night, they all greeted each other properly inebriated.

Already feeling sick, Peter Grant checked in and promptly sequestered himself in his private suite, sipping Irish coffee and trying to catch some sleep. Likewise, Richard Cole was exhausted from the flight, the show, and the balancing act that the Belfast violence had called for in last-minute changes. But once again, as soon as his head hit the pillow, his phone rang. It was Matthew, John's friend and driver. Apparently, John was in the hotel's kitchen, running amok. "You better get the hell down here before John kills somebody," Matthew warned Cole, "or vice versa."

Evidently, John had been unable to wind down after the night's performance and subsequent nightmarish trek through Belfast. Having only liquor for dinner, the drummer and his dutiful chauffeur had gone to the hotel's internal restaurant seeking a late-night supper, only to be turned away. At that hour—and in a rare mood—John wasn't about to take no for an answer. "Matthew had assaulted the hotel's chef, who, in turn, pulled out a carving knife," Cole later recalled. Throwing his clothes back on, the road manager raced down to the kitchen to prevent catastrophe. When he got down there, John and the chef were facing one another on opposite sides of a table.

"I told you that we're closed, you jerk!" the chef shouted. "We can't serve food after eleven thirty!"

"I'm not asking for a five-course meal," John yelled back. "I'll settle for a fucking sandwich. I'll even make it myself if you're too damn lazy to do it!"

"After I get through with you," the chef said, "you're gonna look like you went through a bread slicer!"

Threatened, John began to round the table in the chef's direction, and Cole ran in between the two men. "I quickly stepped in front of Bonzo and shoved him backward," Cole recalled. "He resisted and tried to push me aside." Accustomed to John's forays into mayhem, Cole was unafraid of grabbing John by the back of his T-shirt, his right hand on Bonham's shoulder. "Shut your fucking mouth," Cole yelled. "It's not worth going to jail for, Bonzo. Let's get out of here."

"Hey, you asshole," John yelled past Cole to the chef. "All I wanted was a goddamned meal. What kind of crap are you trying to pull?"

According to Cole, "That's when I swung at him with my right fist, aiming right at his nose." He punched an enraged John hard in the face, shattering his nose and covering him with his own blood. Then "Bonham staggered back a few steps, tripped on a chair, and dropped to one knee."

"Fuck!" John screamed, holding his hand up to the bleeding nose. "Cole, who's fuckin' side are you on?"

More shocked than embarrassed, John stormed up the flights of stairs to Peter Grant's door. "That's it," John yelled through the door to the half-sleeping giant. "I'm leaving the fucking band!"

"Go and fuck off," Grant bellowed back through the door. "Don't give me that shit at this time of night!"

As Cole remembered it, even in the middle of the night, they were able to find a local emergency room for John's broken nose. "How can I ever thank you?" John asked Cole sarcastically as the two waited for a doctor. "Maybe I'll tell Peter to throw you out on your ass! If I had my way, Peter would fire you!"

"There were several bottles of champagne in his room," Cole noted. "Neither of us counted how many—and we finished them off in a three-hour drinking binge. Later that day, we downed thirty Irish coffees, which didn't do much for our condition. . . . Bonzo could be the most headstrong, the most defiant, member of the band, even though there was a gentle, loving side to him."

The following night, Zeppelin was booked to play the National Boxing Stadium in Dublin. Stephen Averill was a twenty-one-year-old aspiring artist and freelance writer for independent fanzine *Freep* when he took a shot of interviewing the band before their concert. "The gig was sold out, and I had no ticket," Averill later recalled. He arrived in the late afternoon and was ushered backstage by an elder member of the stadium's boxing club. "This was in the days before heavy security. . . . I went to the dressing room and met the only member of the band who was there at the time, drummer John Bonham."

Averill remembered, "I politely asked for an interview, and he said he would, as long as we didn't talk about music!" Much to John's delight, Averill—who was only a few years younger—was another automobile enthusiast, and the two talked cars the entire time. Soon, however, Zeppelin was due to meet the crowd. "I thanked him for his time and said I would have to go, as I didn't have a ticket. He told me not to worry about it [and] that I could sit on the stage behind his drum kit!"

Keeping his promise, as the band was announced, John led the young journalist to a cozy spot right beside the massive gong. During the show, Averill snapped away using his cheap Instamatic Kodak camera, and afterward the band invited him out to a nightclub for the after-party. "I had to refuse," regretted Averill. "I had to be in class early the next morning and had no way of getting home."

Despite his backstage access, when Averill presented his exclusive feature story of his adventure with John Bonham to the magazine's editors, they refused to print it. They claimed no one would be interested in an interview with the band's drummer.

Back in England, the group carried on with Peter's conceptual "Return to the Clubs" tour, "a way of saying 'thank you' to those fans who have been with us since '68 and '69," as the manager described it. Zeppelin was booked at the Mayfair Ballroom in Newcastle, the Boat Club in Nottingham, and Stepmother's in Birmingham, all with crowds averaging three to four hundred people—a huge contrast to the arenas to which the band had become accustomed. Additionally, there were violent scenes, as angry fans tried to force their way inside the small venues. They wound down the mini tour at the Marquee in London.

"The clubs tour . . . was much better as a concept than as a reality," Richard Cole later admitted. "None of us particularly enjoyed it. The clubs were small, and the demand to see Zeppelin was, of course, much larger than it had been in the early years."

The band introduced its new songs to the British radio audience with an hour-long concert on the BBC at London's Paris Theater on April 4. "Black Dog" opened the set to great fanfare, and new softer songs like "Going to California" and "Stairway to Heaven" were very well received, encouraging the group that this time around, the album was sure to be a hit with both fans and critics. A second leg of the promotional tour was set to begin May 3 in Copenhagen.

Despite all their success, the past year had been exhausting for John, and he made the most out of his full month off with family and friends. "During the break between the UK tour and flying off to Europe for their second tour, John and Pat came over to the flat to see me and Jacko," Mick Bonham recalled. "With that usual grin plastered across his face, he told me he'd brought my birthday present a couple of months early, as he would be in Europe for my twenty-first birthday. He then proceeded to hand me an envelope, which I assumed was my birthday card but which, to my surprise, contained the logbook for a brand-new MGB sports car, which he had parked 'round the corner."

Home for the month of April, John made the rounds in Birmingham, spreading his generosity and cheer—and resting up for the grueling year ahead. He missed the comfort of his farm and the nearby pubs where he didn't always have to be the center of attention and could enjoy the quiet laughter of those locals who truly knew him best.

"I remember one night we went to the Elbow Room in Birmingham, where we knew the owner and were always welcome," old friend Bev Bevan recalled of this time. "A friend of ours called Nicky was the DJ for the night. He kept playing all this disco stuff, while John and I kept requesting the Allman Brothers and Chicago or Blood, Sweat & Tears. He wouldn't play any of our requests, and John said, 'If he plays one more disco record, we're having him.' So, Nicky put on the Jackson Five, and we grabbed a soda siphon each and absolutely drowned him in soda water.

"Unfortunately, the water got into the record decks and his equipment and shorted out the whole pub—it fused all the power, and the place was plunged into darkness. We weren't thrown out, but some heavy bouncers escorted us out and told us not to come back for a while."

Aside from his many musical projects with the Birmingham-based groups the Move and the Electric Light Orchestra, Bevan was another local star who enjoyed being around his old hometown more than anywhere else. By 1971 he had opened his own music shop in town, an investment that he hoped would inspire a countercultural demographic to come and check out the progressive bands that Bevan not only was a part of but also loved. "We had a big opening day in 1970 when Tony Iommi and Ozzy came from Black Sabbath, as well as a couple of guys from the Move, and John Bonham."

As a proud member of the Birmingham community, John was happy to patronize Bevan's shop whenever he was at home in between Zeppelin's seemingly never-ending tour cycles. And when he did visit Bevan, he was sure to make the visit worthwhile. "Whenever John came to my house for dinner on a Sunday, we'd open up the shop for him, and he'd buy loads of records at a discount price," Bevan fondly recalled. "He was very much into his music and loved to listen to other bands and drummers. The shop was a great place for a couple of years. . . . It was good fun but commercially a bit of a disaster, and the business fell by the wayside."

While John, Robert, and John Paul caught some rest at home, Jimmy had a fire under him to get the fourth album finished and marketed as soon as possible. In the month's gap between the UK tour and their next visit to America, Jimmy and Andy Johns flew to Los

Angeles to mix the Headley Grange and Island sessions. In an interview around that time, Jimmy finally referred to the upcoming release by its tentative title—*Led Zeppelin IV*. Initially, Jimmy and Peter Grant toyed with the idea of releasing all the new material as a series of EPs, but, as the band had long rejected the corporate push for singles, the idea of forcing Led Zeppelin's devoted fans to shell out for multiple albums at the same time was quickly dropped.

Jimmy and Andy Johns spent the bulk of April in Sunset Sound in LA, which the engineer swore was the best mixing studio in the world. The earthquake that greeted the duo once in California was a dark omen of things to come. "I remember lying in bed while it was shaking up and down," Page later said. "I immediately flashed on 'Going to California,' where Robert sings, 'The mountains and canyons start to tremble and shake,' and all I could think was, 'Bloody hell, I'm not taking any chances—I'm going to mix that one last.' Which I did."

Once completed, Jimmy triumphantly returned to England to play the finished album for his bandmates—all of whom were aghast at the poor sound quality that the mix presented. A notorious perfectionist, Jimmy—along with the other three—was furious.

"It didn't sound anything like it did in LA," Page later complained. "I was astonished. At the time, there were all these stories of tapes that had been wiped out by the magnets used on British subways. . . . All I can put it down to was that the speakers and the monitoring system in that room [at Sunset Sound] were just very bright . . . and they lied. It wasn't the true sound."

With the clock ticking—and with John, Robert, and John Paul suspiciously needling Jimmy regarding what could have happened during those three weeks in California—the guitarist had little choice but to immediately sequester himself at Island Studios in London and redo the entire mix. There, however, he became terrified that one of the greatest sessions to come out of Headley Grange—John's incredible drumming innovations on "When the Levee Breaks"—could never be properly recaptured. To make matters worse, Jimmy also knew that John would be furious to have his shining performance lost.

Frantic, Jimmy listened to the Sunset Sound mix of "Levee" one more time to determine if any of it would prove salvageable. To his shock, the original "Levee" mix was the only song completely intact—including John's astounding, thunderous reverberated echo from the Grange's cavernous hallway. With a sigh of relief, Jimmy made "When the Levee Breaks" the only original Sunset mix to make it onto the album still known as *Led Zeppelin IV*.

❋ ❋ ❋

THE BAND'S EUROPEAN LEG WAS COMPARATIVELY SHORT, WITH ONLY a handful of stops: Copenhagen and Odense in Denmark, then a return concert in Liverpool. Audiences were well receptive to the combination of acoustic elements from both *Led Zeppelin III* and its unnamed follow-up, but with additional time in the United Kingdom prior to a show in Milan, Italy, on July 5, the band was again unprepared for the violence and overall crowd behavior that their shows seemed to provoke.

On that date, the band was booked to perform at Vigorelli's bicycle stadium. Zeppelin had been paid in advance but hadn't been offered any prior notice that they were billed along with twenty-eight other rock acts. As the band arrived at the stadium, prepared to give their usual hard-driven stage show to twelve thousand people, they immediately noticed hundreds of uniformed police officers toting riot gear posted outside.

Having witnessed the extreme social unrest in America in April of the previous year, and the all-out rioting of Belfast only two months earlier, the members of Zeppelin were instantly wary of the circumstances they found in Milan. Jimmy and Peter Grant—neither too pleased with the gig, having agreed to play sight unseen—headed backstage to have it out with the management. Not only was the image of an army of riot-expectant police the ultimate deterrent in their fans enjoying the show, but Grant claimed it was unwarranted as well. For his part, Jimmy added that the backstage area—packed to the brim with other bands' entourages and hangers-on—was entirely unacceptable, as was Zeppelin's slot following more than two dozen other acts. Expressing an extension of the band's concerns, road manager Richard Cole recalled the manic atmosphere prior to showtime. "It was getting very fucking hectic," he later noted. "And we said, 'Fuck this, we aren't waiting here all fucking night for you fucking wops with this fucking madness going on here. Bollocks, we're fucking going on when we wanna go on.'"

Grant and Cole led the band to the stage, bypassing the other acts, much to the apparent joy of the crowd. That was the end of that—or so it seemed. Only a few songs into the set, however, Jimmy and Robert spotted smoke billowing among the crowd. "The promoter came out onstage and told us to tell the kids to stop lighting fires," Jimmy later remembered. "Like twits, we did what he said." Unsure of the proper course of action, Robert obediently took the microphone and repeatedly asked the members of the audience responsible for the fires to behave themselves. However, after every song was finished, the members of Zeppelin watched aghast as more smoke rose from the crowd. "Stop lighting those fires, please," Robert begged.

It was only then that the band saw the actual cause of the smoke signals: a tear-gas canister was hurled toward the stage, and the band quickly realized that the riot police had been gassing the crowd. Terrified, the band launched into "Whole Lotta Love," causing only more havoc as the police increased their attacks upon the dancing Italian teenagers. Panicked, many of the kids began to charge the stage—leading to a full rush toward the band. Richard Cole led the way as Peter Grant signaled him from the wings to get the boys to safety. Confused roadies were unsure if they should attempt to grab the band's gear, but Cole yelled for them to abandon ship and make a run for it. Once underground, the band and its crew barricaded themselves past a long escape tunnel in a medical office, attempting to catch their collective breath and watching each other's responses to the madness.

Once the smoke had literally cleared, the band resurfaced—only to find that their equipment had been thoroughly destroyed. John was furious; amid the pandemonium, his new drum tech, Mick Hinton, had been assaulted and smashed over the head with a broken bottle. But it wasn't just the equipment; a roadie had also been taken to a local hospital on a stretcher to receive treatment for the cuts he had received.

Back at the hotel, John was visibly shaken. As the band tried to regain their composure in the bar, a reporter made the mistake of approaching John and asking about the incident with Hinton. John warned very quietly: piss off, or *he'd* be the one getting a bottle broken over *his* head next.

On the plane back to England, Robert Plant was in tears.

✳ ✳ ✳

THERE WAS ANOTHER BATTLE IN STORE FOR THE BAND WHEN THEY returned home—but for this one they were rightly prepared. Weeks earlier, Jimmy hinted that the fourth album would likely be named *Led Zeppelin IV*. However, all four members were convinced the album represented their strongest material to date, and, in that regard, the music should—and could—speak for itself. With that in mind, the band decided to conceptually release the album without a title at all. At Atlantic, the executives weren't quite sure at first that they'd heard the band correctly.

Had they said, "No title"?

No title. And what was more, there would be no corporate "Atlantic" insignia—or a catalog number. In fact, Jimmy explained, there was to be no mention of Led Zeppelin anywhere on the album whatsoever. If the music was as good as the band believed it to be, then let the music's quality dictate sales.

Jimmy, however, would be credited as the producer on the inner sleeve.

Atlantic was incensed and quickly tried to appeal to the band's business sense. "They told us we were committing professional suicide and threatened war," Jimmy later explained. "But the cover wasn't meant to antagonize the record company—it was designed as a response to the music critics who maintained that the success of our first three albums was driven by hype and not talent. We wanted to demonstrate that it was the music that made Zeppelin popular. . . . What matters is our music. We said we just wanted to rely purely on the music."

Nor was the label enthused when presented with Zeppelin's concepts for the cover art. Having visited an antique shop on their way to Headley Grange, Jimmy and Robert had come upon a nineteenth-century painting of an old villager, bent over to a ninety-degree angle from the weight of sticks affixed to his back; the figure, although unnoted, bore a striking resemblance to historical figure "Old George" Pickingill, an early occult mentor to Aleister Crowley. Jimmy immediately conceived of the painting as the new album cover, with the LP sleeve unfolding to display the painting as plastered to a decaying, old building, while a modern landscape of the Birmingham tower could be seen in the distance and older slums sprawled in the foreground. With a gatefold displaying the hermit card of a tarot deck prominently displayed before the printed lyrics for "Stairway to Heaven," and four bizarre symbols given in place of the band members' names, Atlantic was rightfully disturbed by the occult imagery the designs suggested.

The executives' opinions were of little consequence to the band. According to Robert, the four adamantly told Atlantic they wouldn't get their hands on the master tapes unless Led Zeppelin be given final say in the cover and overall album design. With their backs against the wall, Atlantic finally relented.

The final creative dictum attached to the album used symbols representing each of the band members, rather than their actual names or any mention of Led Zeppelin. Jimmy had presented a dictionary of ancient historical designs to each of the musicians and allowed them to pick their own. John Paul's single intersecting circle, the "triquetra," signified competence and confidence. Robert's feather encased with a circle was known to represent Ma'at, the Egyptian goddess of justice. Jimmy's obscure symbol, which caused confusion due to its visual similarity to the word *zoso*, represented Saturn, the planet ruling over the guitarist's Capricorn sign. John's iconic seal of three interlocking circles was meant to signify the father-mother-child bond—but the drummer playfully pointed out its resemblance to the logo for Ballantine beer.

Contractually obligated, Atlantic credited the LP to the four symbols. Prior to the album's release, the company sent out media packets that included the font pressings for the symbols, guaranteeing that newspapers and magazines could replicate the designs in print.

✳ ✳ ✳

THE BAND HAD SIX BLISSFUL WEEKS BEFORE THEIR US LAUNCH. THEY opted to take their families to the island of Jersey in the English Channel, hanging out most nights at the Royal Hotel in St. Helier. Conspicuously keeping to the back, drinking and laughing with their wives, the group took in performances of the Jersey Folk and Blues Club and was sometimes even invited to come and jam onstage. Out of the public eye for more than a month, the band was well rested before the biggest American tour of their career: twenty shows at venues accommodating a minimum of twelve thousand people each. At those numbers, the band was in line to gross more than $1 million for the one tour alone.

Leaving for the States in less than a week, John tried to soak up as much of his beloved Birmingham before another trek across the world. This time, however, there was a difference: all four members of Zeppelin were adamant that their new album would be the biggest success of their career thus far. Proud of the band and their efforts, John couldn't help but brag about the upcoming album to all his old friends.

"My band, Trapeze, was playing as a trio, and we end up playing Mother's [in Birmingham]," recalled John's old friend Glenn Hughes. "We were coming to the end of the set with the final number, [when] fifteen or twenty feet in front of me, walking up to the stage as bold as brass, is Bonham with his assistant, Matthew.

"'Ey, we gonna 'ave a knock, then?'

"Bonham gets onto the stage and—without missing a beat—takes the sticks, nicely, from Dave Holland and says, 'Right, play that outro section again.' And we played the outro section for about fifteen minutes until we'd gone through all the formats of the arrangement the way he wanted it. . . . That was my real introduction to John."

Aware that John's behavior was all fun and games, following the concert Hughes accepted John's invitation to come back to his home for a nightcap—and an early listen to Led Zeppelin's upcoming album. "That night, he took me back to West Hagley," Hughes later remembered. "He wasn't out-of-his-mind 'nasty-drunk,' [but] he was in a really good frame of mind. He told me in the car that Zeppelin had just finished recording the fourth album, and he wanted to play it for me.

"We got there," Hughes continued, "and he proceeded to play an acetate of the album from tip to toe, 'Black Dog' to 'When the Levee Breaks.' We must have played it ten times, the whole album, and he was grinning and crying and smoking and backslapping and dancing."

Hughes was blown away by the tracks he was hearing, and the two men—drinking and laughing, all while John rambled on and on about the recording sessions themselves—completely lost track of time. In John's case, he had also forgotten that he was due to leave with Led Zeppelin that very morning. "What I heard—on an amazing stereo, turned up to eleven—was life changing," Hughes marveled. "'When the Levee Breaks' just did me in. It became embedded in my soul. . . . [John was] giving me a historical lesson on the making of Led Zeppelin's fourth album, and it was one of the biggest moments of my life. The next morning, Robert's standing over me and waking me up because they're about to leave for the States, and he's come in a car to pick John up."

✳ ✳ ✳

THE GROUP'S US TOUR—THEIR SEVENTH—BEGAN ON AUGUST 19, 1971. The shows immediately sold out. With the band having been away from live audiences for more than a year, the enthusiastic response was a constant everywhere they went.

"Led Zeppelin still plays music that sounds like a haunted cathedral singing the blues," wrote Brian McLeod of their Vancouver show. "Only now they play it better. In addition to their familiar pulsating pillars of rhythm, they have learned to penetrate every nook and corner of the sound spectrum, with a resulting versatility rarely found in a rock band. . . . With seemingly ceaseless energy, bassist John Paul Jones and drummer John Bonham drove at top speed for more than an hour, making enough racket along the way to sound like a stampede of elephants from an early Tarzan movie."

Jeani Read wrote, "There was a great maniacal burst of sound framed in a bright stainless-steel scream: there were four figures on stage moving in the glare of the music. . . . Again the sudden rough plush into two-and-a-half hours of mesmerizing roller coaster rides for guitar, bass, drums, and voice. . . . Led Zeppelin construct their roller coaster with massive gestures, blunt workmen, John Bonham on drums erecting the scaffolding."

During the same tour, however, the budding violence of their riotous crowds only continued to grow. "About 35 young people and two policemen were injured Thursday night as a crowd crashed a Pacific Coliseum rock concert," another newspaper reported. "Twenty policemen, 12 of them equipped with riot helmets but no sticks, attempted to stop a crowd which police estimated at 3,000 from forcing its way into a concert by the British rock group Led Zeppelin."

The band played a massive event at New York's Madison Square Garden on September 3, garnering the attention of some of the city's more influential media outlets. "Led Zeppelin, British blue-rock combo in its first U.S. tour in about a year, packed Madison Square Garden while many of the more than 19,000 (at $7.50 top) crowded towards the stage," noted *Variety*. "The group, especially lead singer Robert Plant, kept things under control with remarks to the crowd. The group was generally overpowering musically without much variation despite a welcome acoustic bit. . . . Drummer John Bonham had a strong, well-received number in 'Moby Dick,' while John Paul Jones, generally in the background, was steady at bass guitar."

Reviewer Rick Atkinson wrote of the MSG concert, "'Moby Dick' spotlights drummer John Bonham in a 15-minute solo that is just magnificent. He starts off the same way every other drummer in the business does, but the similarity ends there. By the time he is done, your arms feel tired just watching him, but that never stops you from giving him the standing ovation he always gets and always deserves."

Despite its success, the concert wasn't without collateral damage, as the *New York Daily News* reported: "Two incidents marred the Led Zeppelin concert at Madison Square Garden Friday night, and at least two members of the audience were injured when the stage collapsed. . . . In the middle of the second and final encore, the bouncers who had been keeping the huge crowd off the stage all night suddenly let about 40 get through. The weight proved too much, and part of the stage collapsed."

Only two days later, the band was in Chicago, playing a sold-out show at the International Amphitheatre. One local review noted how during "Moby Dick," Robert, Jimmy, and John Paul took their leave of the stage, "while Bonham worked over his drum kit. Halfway through the song, he threw away his drum sticks and played the drums with his hands." The review went on, "Bonham's solo effort was longer and better than the studio version." On September 7 at the Boston Garden, Maxine Simson from the *Boston Herald* observed, "John Bonham scored with a 20-minute drum solo. Never losing a beat, he threw his sticks away and completed the riff with his hands." However, the band "had to deal with hysterical fans rushing the stage. . . . At one point, a frenzied devotee executed a perfect swan dive from center stage to the crowd below."

On September 14, Led Zeppelin finally made their way to California, performing at the Berkeley Community Center and earning John some of his best reviews. "John Bonham, the drummer in the group, presented one of the most phenomenal drum solos this reporter has ever witnessed," wrote John Wasserman. "The half-hour solo had the crowd in a frenzy, and they roared its approval until his conclusion."

✳ ✳ ✳

As had long been the plan, the 1971 tour was the longest and most extravagant to date, with each show pushing the running time further and further out. By the time the band ended their run with two consecutive dates in Honolulu, all four were in serious need of rest. When the group had taken an extended holiday to the British island of Jersey earlier in the year, their spouses had been invited, making the trip a true celebration and group vacation. Grant and Jimmy decided to keep the band's morale high and, in that same spirit, allowed the Zeppelin wives to come along to Hawaii. While still in a committed relationship with Charlotte, Jimmy remained the only unmarried member of the band and opted to have the Diamond Head mansion the band had previously rented all to himself; the other three, joined by their wives, stayed at the nearby Rainbow Hilton. While the hotel was not nearly as secluded as the mansion, Richard Cole ensured that the band's stay would, nonetheless, be as luxurious as possible, renting out a floor's worth of high-rise suites, fully equipped with Pacific Ocean views and fully stocked liquor cabinets. Of course, with Led Zeppelin, by the end of their four-day vacation, the cabinets had been drained, restocked, and drained again multiple times.

According to Cole, having their wives along on the trip this time around didn't do much in the way of keeping the band from their usual forays into playful misbehavior. On their very first night at the hotel, John and Robert removed a fire hose from the wall and flooded John Paul Jones's suite.

Much of the mischief was due to the abundance of liquor readily available. Road crew member Johnny Larke had been assigned the job of keeping the band members' liquor cabinets in constant supply of top-shelf booze. One afternoon during the group's holiday, Larke stopped by Cole's suite to inquire if his services were needed.

"Larke," John had responded to the roadie, "we've been here almost twenty-four hours, and we haven't gotten into any mischief yet. . . . What's there to do around here?"

Larke thought a moment, then responded, "Well, the exotic drinks are good . . . "

Peter Grant immediately inquired as to what was on the vast menu of exotic mixed cocktails, and Larke handed a copy over. "It takes too long to read this fucking thing," Grant said, shoving the menu away. "Larke, have room service send up four of every drink on the menu. You can join us."

In less than a half hour, nearly a hundred mixed cocktails were brought up on multiple room-service carts—Hawaiian highballs, "green dragons," mai tais, and "Waikiki wowees"—and, according to Cole, "not a single one went to waste."

Even in their condition, Zeppelin was ready to give Hawaiian audiences their money's worth, and the shows were a great success. Following the Hawaii series, the band flew off to their first bookings in Japan at the end of September. Finding "Immigrant Song" number one on the local charts immediately put the band back into a celebratory mood, including Atlantic Records' UK representative Phil Carson, who was along for the trip; on their first night booked into the Tokyo Hilton, John tossed a room-service cart into Carson's shower—while the label executive was still naked inside.

That night, the band opted to soak in the Tokyo nightlife, beginning with dinner at a traditional Japanese restaurant—geisha girls included. John quickly grew impatient at having to sip his drinks out of the small, delicate, thimble-like serving mugs from which the girls demurely served. "Can we get some bigger cups?" he finally pleaded impatiently to one of the geishas. "Maybe a coffee cup. Or a beer mug—or some buckets!"

The following morning, John had to stumble his way back to the hotel, after Richard Cole had left him passed out on the Tokyo sidewalk.

John's exuberant behavior was only beginning. The following night, he and Cole went sightseeing around the Japanese capital and, properly inebriated, purchased authentic samurai swords. Returning to the Hilton, John immediately went to work chopping every piece of his suite's furniture to ribbons. "With our swords in hand, we began swinging them at one another like a couple of maniacs," Richard Cole laughed. "[We were] slashing anything in the room that would cut . . . the drapes, the bedspread and mattress, the wallpaper, the paintings. With each swing, we probably added hundreds of dollars in damages to our hotel bill."

With nothing left to destroy, John went on to John Paul Jones's room down the hall, chopping the bassist's door down and dragging him out of bed. John and Cole then continued their rampage, destroying the hallway itself while Jones continued to sleep on the floor. The following morning, Richard Cole was called to the hotel manager's office. "I know you are very good musicians," the manager told him, "but we can't have this kind of behavior in our hotel. There was a lot of damage in your rooms. . . . [O]ne of your people got drunk in the gutter; another one slept in the hall. I'm sorry, but I cannot let you stay in this hotel ever again." The band was tossed out and banned for life.

At the band's first Japanese performance at Tokyo's Budokan Hall the next night, reporters were quick to notice that the flaxen-haired lead singer was sporting a freshly split lip. Although the minor injury had no impact on Robert's performance, journalists eager for gossip continued to push for an explanation. Finally fed up, Robert tossed over his shoulder to one reporter, "It's really none of your fucking business—it's just between me and Bonzo."

To his credit, Robert was being honest, as the true story behind the busted lips would have been almost too embarrassing to admit publicly. With a friendship that harked back to their youthful days in Birmingham, John and Robert were close enough that they often behaved more like brothers or—as an ongoing joke with the Zeppelin camp described—an old married couple. In this instance, the incident that had occurred backstage at Budokan Hall was regarding a topic as trivial as could be: gas money. For weeks, John pestered Robert for the thirty pounds owed to him for having filled up a tank during a joy ride through Scotland. With a substantial amount of booze in both men, the topic had resurfaced in, of all places, the dressing room in Japan only moments before Led Zeppelin was due to take the stage. Robert not only disputed the minor debt but couldn't believe John would even bring it up at the concert hall. To everyone's surprise, the argument escalated—ending with John's fist right in Robert's jaw. As Robert dabbed blood from his mouth with a handkerchief, the band was called out to meet the massive Japanese crowd.

Hand to his bleeding mouth, Robert continued to curse his old friend as they both staggered out onstage. Later, John admitted to Richard Cole, "Robert and I have known each other for so long that there's never any maliciousness in these fights. . . . We just lose our tempers sometimes."

The two Budokan concerts on September 23 and 24 were smashing successes for the band, garnering some of the best foreign reviews they had ever received. In a show of goodwill, Zeppelin then traveled to Hiroshima, performing at a benefit concert at Shiei Taikukan Hall for the victims of 1945's destruction. Following the show's final encore, they were presented with a peace medal by the mayor of the city.

"Throughout Japan, Zeppelin's music was remarkably well received," Cole observed. "Even though rock music was relatively new in Tokyo and throughout Japan, the kids obviously knew our music well. While the Japanese have a reputation for being quieter and more reserved than Westerners, fans loosened their kimonos and let their hair down when they came to Zeppelin's concerts."

Following their performance in Hiroshima, Zeppelin took the Bullet Train and headed over to play their dual bookings in Osaka and Kyoto. Their Japanese Atlantic Records distributor had sent along two gifts—a personal tour guide named Tats Nagashima, who acted as the promoter-host for the concerts, and, somewhat naively, a dozen flasks of hot sake and a full case of expensive Japanese whiskey known as Suntori. Zeppelin downed it all while still en route to Osaka.

That night, John led the way as he, Robert, and Jonesy planned to make Jimmy the next recipient of the now notorious Led Zeppelin late-night pranks. The group had bunked up together on the tightly packed Bullet Train, and Jimmy was sharing a cubby with Peter Grant. At three in the morning, John whipped together his own "cocktail" of sorts: a disgusting mixture of cold tea, stale sake, and soggy rice—all of which was destined to be dumped over Jimmy's head as he slept. Robert volunteered to do the honors. Drawing back the cubby's curtain, Plant doused the unseen, sleeping victim—unaware that he'd accidentally poured the slime on Grant. Enraged, the huge former wrestler chased the three giggling bandmates down the Bullet Train's corridor, bellowing profanity and promises of revenge. First, he pummeled Robert; next, he took a swing at Richard Cole, who peeked out of his own cubby to inquire about the cause of all the commotion. Cole ducked, and Grant connected with John, square in his face.

Atlantic's Japanese executive stood back, terrified that Led Zeppelin was breaking up—and on his watch. As he stood back in shock, British executive Phil Carson sidled up next to him. "Don't worry," he comforted his fellow executive. "This is Led Zeppelin. This stuff happens all the time."

The following night in Osaka was no different. During the band's acoustic interlude midconcert, Japanese audiences were treated to a rare live rendition of "Friends," but were completely unaware what had led to the necessity for the impromptu number. Jimmy recalled John's alcohol-induced disappearing act years later, explaining, "During the acoustic set of 'That's the Way,' 'Going to California,' and 'Tangerine,' John Bonham nipped offstage and hadn't returned for the electric 'What Is and What Should Never Be.' So, we continued the acoustic set with a quick retune for 'Friends'—the first and only time we were to play this song live."

According to Jimmy, the band's all-around behavior during the Japanese excursion, while all in the name of fun, set a defining precedent for the "anything goes" attitude that would encapsulate much of

Zeppelin's later touring excesses. "We did things [in Japan] that you just wouldn't believe. For example, there was a night when one of us got our clothes tossed out the window, and the person took advantage of that opportunity to run around on the rooftops of Japan naked. . . . In retrospect, our Japanese hosts were probably completely horrified, but they were so polite, they just kept bowing to us!"

The band wasn't due back on the road for more than a month, and, to the relief of all involved, it was slated to be a brief tour around the United Kingdom—meaning that all members could go home to their families. To John and Jonesy, this sounded like bliss, but not so for the band's two leads, Jimmy in particular. Whereas Jimmy and Robert had a love of exotic travel, John and Jonesy were quite content to remain home safe and sound in the company of their families—especially John, whose love of alcohol-fueled mischief seemed the only way to stave off his homesickness. When his family was brought up in conversation, John seemed instantly sober and saddened to have had to leave them at all.

"That surprised a lot of people," recalled Cole. "After all, on the road, he would sometimes behave like a raving lunatic, but his wife, Pat, provided him with stability and a haven that allowed him to just be John Bonham. A lot of people never saw Bonzo's warmth, [but] I thought it was one of his most precious attributes."

And so, following the six Japanese shows, John caught a flight back home with John Paul Jones and Peter Grant; meanwhile, Jimmy, Robert, and Cole decided to continue venturing around Asia—Hong Kong first, followed by Bangkok. When Cole opted to book a flight to Australia alone to scout venues for the band's future tour there, Jimmy and Robert pushed onward, flying to Bombay. The two hoped the Indian culture would inspire new lyrics and exotic sounds for the eventual fifth album.

"Robert and I were just really keen to see what it would be like to go into a studio with some musicians from Bombay and see what we would come up with," Jimmy later remembered. "We tried recording versions of 'Friends' and 'Four Sticks' with some percussionists, a half-dozen string players, and a thing called a Japan banjo, and boy, was that tricky! They were great musicians, but they were used to counting and feeling rhythms in a different way."

Unfortunately, nothing much came from these experimental rehearsals.

✳ ✳ ✳

JOHN WAS THANKFUL TO BE ABLE TO SPEND THE MONTH OF OCTOBER with Pat and Jason, who was getting bigger by the day. He hadn't seen his siblings, Mick or Debbie, in months, and spent as much time catching up with them as he could before the band was expected to take up the UK shows. For that, John wanted Mick along to catch some of the new material performed live.

"On November 27th, I joined up with John, and we headed north to Preston, where the band was appearing at the town hall," Mick Bonham later said. "I watched the show perched on the stairs leading to the stage and, as the performance reached its climax, [John's drum tech] Mick Hinton came over and said that John wanted a pint of mild and wanted me to fetch it for him."

John's younger brother was happy to oblige, returning from the bar with the drink. Hinton told him to walk it over to John, who was already at his drum kit, midperformance. Quietly, the younger Bonham crouched down next to his brother to place the glass carefully next to the stool. "Like lightning, John grabbed my arm, pointed to a set of congas behind his kit, and shouted, 'Play them!'" Mick Bonham recalled. "Before I could reply 'How?' the opening riff for 'Whole Lotta Love' had kicked in."

Mick continued, "So, there I was, stranded and thinking how not to look like a prat, so I started to play. . . . I looked up and saw a sea of faces looking back at me. At this moment, my arms went into overdrive, and my legs decided they weren't with me and wanted to leave. As the number came to a close, all I could think of was getting the hell off that stage, but John and Robert had other ideas, escorting me to the front of the stage to take a bow alongside Jimmy and John Paul."

For Mick Bonham, it was a rare instance to bathe in some of the spotlight to which John had grown so accustomed, the same spotlight he wanted to share with his beloved kid brother, even for a brief moment.

Later, Mick recalled, "After beating a hasty retreat to the bar, John looked at me while I was still visibly shaken, grinned, and said, 'Good, ain't it!'"

Chapter Thirteen

NOVEMBER 1971–APRIL 1972

A fter countless delays, Led Zeppelin's fourth album was finally released in November 1971.

The band's premonitions of a smash hit, even without a proper title or artist attribution, proved to be correct—the music spoke for itself. For lack of a proper title, fans took to calling the album an assortment of nicknames, *Led Zeppelin IV* or *Four Symbols* proving the most popular. And it was with this record that Jimmy and Grant's long-standing strategy of not releasing singles truly proved its worth; those who desperately needed their own copy of "Stairway to Heaven" had to rush and purchase the LP, quickly driving the album to number two on the American *Billboard* charts.

Every stop on the group's UK tour sold out within the first twenty-four hours. They launched north at Newcastle's City Hall on November 11 and expanded upon the Japanese tour's time allotment, but minimized the format: no opening act, no stage set or props—just hours upon hours of their biggest hits. Zeppelin made one notable exception, opting for state-of-the-art theatrics when playing consecutive nights at Wembley on November 20 and 21 and modeling the shows after a Roman circus, complete with jugglers and acrobats. Advertising the large-scale spectacle as "Electric Magic," Zeppelin provided the massive crowd with three hours of music off all four of their albums. Critics, as usual, were apprehensive—but the fans ate it up.

"When you're Britain's biggest band, you get the heaviest critics," Roy Hollingworth observed in *Melody Maker*. "If Jesus was still about, we'd expect a miracle every week, right? But no matter what the rock society says. What matters are people. An entertainer performs for people. . . . Led Zeppelin performed to the people on Friday night, and 9,000 of them put their hands above their heads and got their Saturday night rocks off." Hollingworth humorously noted, "Mid-evening: Performing pigs, Circus acts, beasts that do clever things are brought out for the audience's amusement."

Of John's Wembley performance, the *Melody Maker* writer claimed the drummer's playing was "like thunder," and as a member of the audience he could "feel the force of the combined volume hit" him physically. "It's painful," Hollingworth added, "but it rips out an emotion common to most everyone in the hall. Excitement, and something rude, something so alive it smells. Rebel-rousers, that's it. . . . My how fat John Bonham gets, as he tightens up screws."

※ ※ ※

NOW THAT LED ZEPPELIN HAD, FOR ALL INTENTS AND PURPOSES, assumed the mantle as the biggest rock band in the world, they were in the unique position to dictate their own touring schedule. After that first US tour at the end of 1968, the band promised themselves, as well as their families back home, that there would never be another holiday season spent on the road. With that in mind, the tour ended promptly on December 11, allowing the band to spend a much-deserved Christmas holiday home in England.

As part of spreading the holiday cheer, John visited a tailor friend in nearby Redditch and purchased the bulk of his Christmas presents for the men in his family from the single shop—a surprise act of generosity that perked the interest of the local newspapers. "Pop star John Bonham did not forget the tailor who let him have his wedding suit on tick five years ago when he could not afford to pay for it in cash," opened the playful article. "So when John, drummer with Led Zeppelin, decided to buy 500 [pounds] worth of suits as Christmas presents for his family, he headed straight to the tailor—Peter Robinson in Unicorn Hill, Redditch." Robinson himself recalled, "Five years ago, he came to me for his wedding suit, which cost about 35 pounds, and he couldn't afford to pay for it. . . . He managed to pay me back, in time, and he remembered me when he wanted some suits as Christmas presents."

Robinson noted that John also bought four suits for himself, one of which was custom-made in velvet.

※ ※ ※

"WE ALL LIVED IN DIFFERENT PARTS OF THE COUNTRY, SO WHEN WE came off the road, we didn't really see each other," Jimmy later claimed of the band's lack of camaraderie once back home. "We really only socialized when we were in the studio or out on the road. We really came to value our family lives, especially being on the road so much, which is how it should be. . . . It helped create a balance in our lives. Our families helped keep us sane."

John Paul Jones later shared similar sentiments. "The band was very close, which fostered a feeling of 'us against them,'" he later said. "[Peter Grant] did a very good job of keeping everyone away from us, which allowed us to focus on our work. . . . We always got on well. We never socialized when we weren't touring, but we were always pleased to see one another." By now, John Paul Jones was father to three little girls and was happy to spend as much time with them— and in his extensive home recording studio—as Zeppelin's obligations allowed.

Likewise, Jimmy was a father now, too, and after amassing a lifetime's worth of antique collectibles and artworks, he sold his Pangbourne home on the Thames outright and acquired an eighteenth-century estate in rural Sussex designed by Sir Edwin Lutyens called Plumpton Place for a half-million pounds. Ever the purveyor of secrets, Jimmy's new home had ample space for a home recording studio—and even came equipped with a moat.

But while the band may not have socialized much while at home, John and Robert's genuine friendship was an exception. The two lived as neighbors in Worcestershire, where both enjoyed the outdoors and operated their working farms. At one point, so in love with the lifestyle, Robert even considered buying a second farm, a working sheep farm near the coast in Wales. Likewise, John was so enthralled with country life, he began researching bull breeding.

Of Led Zeppelin's members, John and Robert were recognized as the true friends, the only two who would spend their off time in each other's company. When not on tour, the original Midlands boys would head into Birmingham, as they had in the old days. As local celebrities, "Bonzo" and "Planty" were beloved by the community that continued to see them patronizing the local businesses or visiting their old stomping crowds—not allowing superstardom to go to their heads. Often, John and Robert could be seen grabbing drinks at any one of their favorite pubs or checking out local music venues, championing up-and-coming bands.

One such Brum band they liked was called Bronco, whose guitarist was an old Kidderminster friend named Robert Blunt. Robert and John soon took to attending Bronco rehearsals at the village hall and then inviting the band out to the local pub for celebratory drinks.

During one such evening out on the town with Robert and the boys from Bronco, John bumped into an old friend, *Melody Maker*'s Chris Welch. Welch sat with John for a few candid minutes, listening to the superstar drummer vent his frustrations and insecurities regarding Zeppelin's lengthy tours of America, Japan, and the United Kingdom. Admitting to the reporter that he feared having lost his drumming ability before the tour, John added that the entire band was left "drained" by the extensive travel and looked forward to taking the rest of the year off.

Furthermore, "I've never tried consciously to be one of the best drummers and I don't want to be," John told Welch. "A lot of kids come up to me and say, 'There's a lot better drummers than you,' or something. But I enjoy playing to the best of my ability and that's why I'm here doing it. . . . I don't claim to be more exciting than Buddy Rich, but I don't play what I don't like. I'm a simple, straight-ahead drummer and I don't try to pretend to be anything better than I am."

Amid the rumors that Led Zeppelin was always one step away from calling it quits, Welch had no choice but to bluntly ask John about the group's future. "Oh, he's come out with a gem!" John barked, laughing. "I knew it!" After a long moment, he added, "We might be on top next year, or I might be back on the buildings!"

Deep down, many in John's inner circle knew he sometimes missed working with his father and brother at the construction sites. He often said that he would willingly give up rock stardom for the normal life his parents had once envisioned. Robert even told a reporter that John once admitted to the band that he "could go back to a building site anytime . . . and we all agreed."

On the occasion when John would break character and drop the tough facade to a journalist, making veiled promises to take up carpentry and farming, one never really knew if he was joking.

✳ ✳ ✳

AROUND THE TIME JOHN WAS APPROACHED BY *MELODY MAKER*, JIMMY was being sought out by a satanic American filmmaker named Kenneth Anger, whose underground film *Scorpio Rising* had become a cornerstone of independent filmmaking over the past decade. Like Jimmy, Anger was an Aleister Crowley aficionado and collected much of the same memorabilia and many of the same relics and collectibles. In fact, the filmmaker learned of Jimmy's shared dark passion only when an agent representing Jimmy outbid Anger at Sotheby's for the original galley proofs of one of Crowley's manuscripts. Eventually able to meet in person, Anger convinced Jimmy to assist him by creating an original soundtrack to his current film project, a mysterious work in progress he'd dubbed *Lucifer Rising*. Appealing to Jimmy's vanity, Anger claimed that something along the lines of "Dazed and Confused," only the full length of the movie, would be ideal. Intrigued, Jimmy agreed, but warned the director that Led Zeppelin was his full-time gig. The two formed a loose agreement, but no deadlines were set. Before the year was out, Jimmy would be touring with a rough cut of footage, which he played, along with the creepy, chant-driven music he was composing to match the footage, only to his most intimate friends. By the following year, Kenneth Anger took up residence at Jimmy's home while he struggled to complete the final editing of this bizarre labor of love.

✳ ✳ ✳

Meanwhile, the band lined up their many projects for the coming year.

In January 1972, the four members met at Olympic Studios in London for the preliminary rehearsals of both the upcoming tour and their hotly anticipated fifth album. Richard Cole's scouting trip of the Australian continent had been a huge success, and he was proud to report that Led Zeppelin had many fans eager to see them perform live there for the first time. Peter Grant quickly lined up a string of five dates for the country, as well as concerts in nearby New Zealand.

Zeppelin was due to arrive for their performance at Subiaco Oval, in Perth, on February 16. First, however, Grant booked them for a one-off show in the former British colony of Singapore on Valentine's Day. Things got off to a rotten start, as the band was denied entry into the country due to the length of their hair. According to the Singaporean customs agents of the ultraconservative country, the local government was taking a firm stand against the negative influences of Western culture—typified, so they claimed, by the lyrics, behavior, and, yes, appearance of Led Zeppelin. The band wasn't even allowed off the plane.

The band was surprised, but not particularly offended. After all, the upcoming Australian dates would be much more lucrative, with three consecutive nights in Perth, Adelaide, and Melbourne, then one side trip to Auckland, New Zealand, before returning to Australia to appear in Sydney and Brisbane. Each venue was huge, and each show broke records in ticket sales—something that Grant ensured by booking only indoor venues for the Australian dates. But that strategy was only half of the manager's reasoning; although he offered no true explanation, Grant was forever fearful of allowing his boys to perform in inclement weather. With the massive amount of electrical equipment, fuses, and wires used for every element of the group's full stage show, he considered playing in the rain to be an unacceptable risk. On this tour, only the Adelaide show on February 19 was booked for an outdoor amphitheater, Memorial Drive, and when a slight drizzle developed into a full storm, Peter Grant postponed the concert until the following evening.

Following the cancellation, John was forced to find other distractions to kill the time. "In Adelaide, Creedence Clearwater Revival had performed the night before us and were still in town when we checked into our hotel," Richard Cole recalled. "Creedence's drummer, Doug Clifford, had a practice drum kit in his hotel room, and Bonham and he took turns pounding out a thunderous beat until almost daybreak. Amazingly, no one from the hotel complained."

Though John had confided in Chris Welch weeks earlier that he had no compunction in chucking the rock 'n' roll lifestyle for his old job as a carpenter, his actions on the Australian tour proved he wasn't necessarily kidding. Throughout the tour, Richard Cole made it a habit to arrive at the concert sites hours before the band in order to inspect the stage area and security barriers; following the many riots on the last tour, the tour manager figured he couldn't be too careful. When he got to the Western Springs Stadium in Auckland on the morning of February 25, Cole was dissatisfied with the stage's stability and requested a hammer and nails, planning to perform some quick fixes himself. Spying Cole's thoroughness, John ran over, grabbed another hammer, and began to make a few expert adjustments of his own.

"Once the repairs were made, Bonham and I started looking for something to do until the gates opened," Cole later reminisced. "We raided the liquor cases backstage, and after a few beers, Bonzo spotted a pair of Honda motorcycles parked near the stage. 'Well,' he said, 'don't just stand there. Let's take 'em for a spin.'"

Hoping to avert a potential disaster, Cole inquired as to who owned the bikes in question. Informed that they belonged to the concert promoter, Rem Raymond, Cole asked permission for John to take them for a spin. Not looking to upset the talent, Raymond agreed. After a few minutes, however, John grew bored merely riding up and down the stadium parking lot. "There's one more thing we should try," John said to Cole. "I've never played chicken before. Let's do it with the bikes."

"Forget it, Bonzo," Cole replied. "I don't feel suicidal today." He was also very much aware that both men had been knocking back beers during their repairs to the stadium's stage.

But John was adamant. "Richard, do it for your old pal," he begged.

Cole reluctantly agreed, and the two rode to a nearby field. There, they separated 150 feet apart and aimed the bikes at each other. Cole later recalled, "I gunned the engine, turned up the throttle, and, like a couple of lunatics, Bonham and I sped toward one another. Rolling at about thirty miles per hour, we were nearly on top of each other almost immediately. But about twenty feet away from Bonzo, despite my promise, I must have flinched. . . . My bike skidded into the dirt, and I rolled over it."

Cole was uninjured, but Raymond's motorcycle was destroyed. "Just then, I spotted an ax lying near some tools about twenty yards away. I walked over, picked it up, and hovered over the bike for a few seconds. 'It's like a horse with a broken leg,' I said. 'You gotta put it out of its misery.'"

To John's amusement, Cole completed the bike's demolition, swing by swing. Raymond, however, was much less amused. "But there must be a good repair shop around here," Cole innocently said to the furious promoter. "Send us the bill."

"Once we were out of Rem's earshot, Bonzo mumbled, 'Sure, send us the bill. We won't pay it—but go ahead and send it anyway!'"

Mischief achieved, the Auckland show proved to be a tremendous success for the band. Having waited years to see Led Zeppelin live, some people traveled by train nearly a thousand miles from the other end of the continent just to make it to the concert. In total, Led Zeppelin played for twenty-five thousand eager fans. Cole recalled, "Bonzo came away from the concerts so energized that he proclaimed, 'I won't be able to sleep for days,' [but] sometimes, it seemed as though he hadn't."

Lynne Barber covered the Auckland show as a special correspondent for *Groove* magazine. "The group themselves were just as incredible as their music. John Bonham, who made the concert memorable with his fantastic 12-minute drum solo, arrived at Auckland airport in a far-out black and white check suit with white shoes and a red carnation and immediately asked where he could buy a two-feet long cigarette holder! At a party the night before the concert, he had everyone in fits with his impersonations of whomever happened to be singing on the record. He also insisted that he have a record player in his room and played Heedband's latest LP which he was very impressed with.

"The word is that they'll be back within the year although it's unlikely they'll be staying at the same hotel," Barber added. "Apparently, they made a bit of a mess of it by having food fights. They also got the porter drunk and then threw him into the pool."

Brisbane's show days later offered a more forgiving review, focusing on the night's performance. "Let's begin by studying the name itself," Tom Zito wrote. "Sounds pretty heavy, doesn't it? Even heavier, you might say, than an 'iron butterfly?' . . . Well heavy is what Led Zeppelin is all about—four young British musicians who play VERY loud and VERY frenzied rock music."

Zito went on, "Two songs later, on a tune entitled 'Moby Dick,' Bonham took a 20-minute solo during which he played the drums not only with the usual two sticks, but also with his hands and finally with two sticks in each hand. Pretty heavy, huh? Someone in the audience threw a beer can at him near the end (which might serve as a warning to all drummers everywhere on the hazards of such under-takings). But the crowd finally came to life and cheered wildly (for the drummer, not the beer can)."

John also used the trip to Auckland as a rare opportunity to drop in on his aunt Dorothy, Joan Bonham's sister, who had immigrated to New Zealand when John was only a child. Finding her rock 'n' roll nephew waiting for her backstage after the concert proved a surprise for the older woman, and John had even come bearing a gift. Mick Bonham remembered, "They caught up with each other at the gig in Auckland, and he gave her the Gold LP for *Led Zeppelin* he'd received for Australian sales." For John, it was a proud moment and a high-light of the trip.

John Paul Jones recalled one other highlight that took place on their way back to the United Kingdom. "We had to catch a plane from Brisbane to Sydney and then fly from Sydney straight back to En-gland," Jones later explained. "The plane was very early in the morn-ing, [and] we had stayed up all night. . . . Bonzo and I ended up in a bar with all these Fijians. They looked like a sort of rugby team, and they were all lounging about obviously waiting for the same plane. So, we started chatting and drinking, and it turned out they were the Fijian Police Choir, who had also just done a gig in Brisbane."

John and Jonesy bought the police choir members rounds of drinks, and, soon enough, the men had all started singing. "It was lovely stuff, and we all sat around having a great time," Jones re-called fondly. "Then, they told us it was our turn. I said, 'Hold on, he's a drummer and I'm a bass player.' They said, 'Well, you must be able to sing something.' So, Bonzo and I looked at each other and thought, 'Ah, I know,' and we went through half the 1959 Everlys' repertoire. . . . It was hilarious serenading the Fijian Police Choir with Everly Brothers songs. It had been a great night, and, as we parted, they gave us presents of necklaces and cowrie shells."

✳ ✳ ✳

THE FINAL SHOW OF THE TOUR TOOK PLACE ON MARCH 10 IN SYDNEY, for which Zeppelin performed to an audience of twenty-six thousand. Afterward, while John and Jonesy were keen to return home, Jimmy and Robert had other plans. Again, they returned to Bombay, determined to lay down the conceptual tracks with local Indian musicians, planning to play with obscure sounds and experimental time signatures. This time, they brought along the needed recording equipment, as well as Richard Cole, who tagged along to act as assistant and one-man road crew. Using his new Stellavox stereo field recorder, Jimmy led Robert and Cole along the crowded streets of Bombay, laying down any snippets of local music or ambient sounds that struck their imagination. After placing a few calls to London, they were able to book a single recording session in a Bombay studio, along with several local raga musicians—some of whom were members of the prestigious Bombay Symphony. Jimmy quickly put together a few experimental rearrangements of Zeppelin's canonical "Friends" and "Four Sticks," although, as Robert later admitted, "it was just an experiment; we were simply checking it out and sussing out how easy it would be to transpose the ideas that we've got into the raga style and into the Indian musicians' minds. As it turned out, it was very hard for them to cope with the Western approach to music."

The trip had been an inspirational pilgrimage. Robert and Jimmy returned home reenergized and brimming with fresh ideas for the group's next album—and a new shared love of Indian whiskey.

Back home at his new Sussex estate, Jimmy secured the tapes of the experimental Bombay recording sessions in storage. John Paul Jones spent the lengthy break at home with his wife and daughters, and Robert blissfully returned to his farm in Worcestershire, spending every waking moment with his six-month-old son, Karac—the Celtic name inspired by Robert's obsession with ancient Welch and English history.

John, perhaps more than the rest, was overjoyed being back in England. Although he loved having a place for his family in West

Hagley, the drummer became serious in his ambitions to take up farming and bull breeding. He and Pat searched for a new place to accommodate those dreams. "During the breaks of '72, John was on the lookout for a new home," Mick Bonham recalled, "somewhere in the country, and with a fair bit of land. On several occasions, Jacko and I went with him to look over some of the properties, and, eventually, he found what he was looking for."

It was love at first sight when John first stepped foot onto the hundred-acre property called Old Hyde Farm. Situated in the Cutnall Green section of Worcestershire, the sprawling farm was perched on top of a hill overlooking a romantic panorama of the countryside, and John had already visualized what he wanted to do with the place. Once again enlisting the help of brother Mick and father Jacko—and doing quite a bit of the grunt work himself—John quickly set to rebuilding the farm's preexisting structures. The house would be virtually knocked down and then rebuilt to about twice the size, but it would also be developed and workable once more. Jacko ran the project and assembled a team to help with the hands-on construction; an old friend from J. H. Bonham and Son, Stan Blick, along with his son, Peter, were contracted for all the brickwork. John also retained the services of Malcolm Plant—Robert's cousin, who, unlike the rock god, had stayed within the more stable career path of insurance sales—to provide the needed coverage, as well as Malcolm's wife, Grace, to do some architectural work.

Their first order of business was to repair all the farm buildings and renew the cottage, so a farm manager could move in and start to get things back in order. John also insisted on installing a few luxuries, including a lush game room equipped with an expensive billiard table and a fully functioning bar. All told, the full construction would take just over two years to complete.

"I was determined that when we had a house and garden of our own, I would keep them in wonderful shape," John later claimed. "I picked up quite a bit about house construction when I was working on building sites."

Further complementing his new idyllic homestead, John fulfilled another lifelong dream and purchased a boat. Mick Bonham remembered, "Whether it was the childhood memories of Jacko's boat, or the fact that the Old Hyde was only five miles from Stourport-on-Severn, in April, he took delivery of 'The Staysea,' a thirty-four-foot seagoing cabin cruiser that was to be moored in Stourport." Whenever John had time off from his Led Zeppelin obligations, and the weather permitted, he would take Mick and friends out on the water, usually cruising the waterways of Worcestershire.

True to his word, John soon began breeding and raising white-faced Hereford cattle. Viewing it as no mere hobby, John considered the cattle farm to be a profitable investment and took true pride in learning the ins and outs of raising prize bulls. "For a guy who made his living banging away at drum skins, I was amazed at the affection Bonzo showed for the cattle," Richard Cole later claimed. "'It's different from playing music, of course,' he told me, 'but I feel some of the same sense of accomplishment with what I've done with these bulls.'"

Surprising everyone, John was very serious about the care of his pedigree bulls, even hiring a professional breeder named Brian Treble, a young man from Lincolnshire, to take up residence in one of Old Hyde's renovated cottages with his wife, Lin. As a live-in manager, Treble would keep watch of John's functioning farm and see to it that his prized Rushock herd of pedigree Hereford cattle were always maintained for competition.

Not long after, Zeppelin was booked on a commercial flight with Rolling Stones bassist Bill Wyman and his girlfriend, Astrid. During the flight, John couldn't stop bragging to the group about his Hereford bulls, which had just garnered a number of top prizes at a national competition. "I love those bulls, just getting up in the morning and seeing them," John told Wyman and Astrid, much to the amusement of Richard Cole. "John [was] beaming with pride like a father talking about his children. On the plane, he was wearing overalls and a wide-brimmed hat that any farmer could have put to use as a daytime shield from the sun."

Bringing his prideful diatribe on the bulls to a conclusion, John excused himself to the men's room. Wyman's girlfriend leaned across the aisle to Cole. "Why did you guys bring that farmer with you?" she innocently asked. "Does he work on one of the boys' estates?"

✳ ✳ ✳

FOR A FEW MORE PRECIOUS WEEKS, JOHN SPENT TIME WORKING alongside his father and brother on Old Hyde's needed repairs and additions. At the end of April, the band was committed to begin the session work on the next album, a daunting task in the face of the untitled fourth's excellent sales and better-than-average critical acceptance. Its follow-up would consume most of that spring, and it was agreed that the group would split the recording time between the creative isolation of Headley Grange and the local convenience of Olympic Studios in London.

Being home in Birmingham for the bulk of the album's work was a healthy alternative for John, as his high jinks during the previous tour had slowly earned him a reputation for mayhem and destruction rivaling his friend Keith Moon's. Coincidentally, both drummers made dual cameo appearances as ghoulish band members in the Ringo Starr–produced rock 'n' roll horror film *Son of Dracula* earlier that same year; starring Harry Nilsson, and featuring an ensemble of high-profile guest stars, the movie nonetheless languished in the Apple Films archive until August 1974.

Although many were unaware of the fact, John's drunken misbehavior was usually encouraged by members of Zeppelin's entourage and crew; the band was well aware of John's inhibition, but they had long since ceased pushing him too far. Richard Cole later claimed, "The only time John would wreck a hotel room was if he'd had an argument on the phone, or maybe he just missed his wife and was feeling a bit moody. . . . Then he might smash up a room or something."

As Mick Bonham later explained, "The band always paid, and nobody cared. In any case, John didn't break things so much as meticulously take them apart with a screwdriver. It was all paid for, and Zeppelin spent a fortune on hotels anyway."

But between the early rumors of the band's nefarious behavior when in America and two separate Atlantic executives witnessing it firsthand during the trip to Japan, journalists had learned to steer clear of Bonzo, while other record company staffers began to grow weary of the likelihood of drama—and steep expenses—when the drummer was around. One such long-suffering member within the Zeppelin camp was stuffy, by-the-books press officer Bill Harry, whom John often enjoyed making the butt of practical jokes. A former editor for *Merseybeat* music magazine, Harry had worked as a publicist for the Beatles and still represented a number of acts for producer Mickie Most, who had in turn recommended him to Peter Grant.

Harry was well aware of John's gruff sense of humor and usually chalked the behavior up to the sheer amount of booze surrounding the band. One night at the Revolution club in Mayfair, in central London, Harry was about to head home when a call came in for him from John, all the way in Birmingham. "He said, 'I want to come down for a drink,'" Harry later remembered. "I said, 'You'll never make it—the club shuts at 2:00 a.m., and you're still in Birmingham.' About ten minutes before closing time, he arrived, went to the bar, and ordered fifty lagers. . . . The table was just covered in lagers."

That had been one occasion when Harry hadn't been singled out as Bonzo's target, but those were few and far between. The press agent later recalled the afternoon he bumped into John and his friend Chicken Shack lead guitarist Stan Webb at a restaurant in Soho—and the ensuing incident that directly led to his resignation from Led Zeppelin's employ. "Bonzo was fun, and there was nothing unfriendly about him—and he was a brilliant drummer," Harry said, "but it was a strain, I admit, putting up with his antics.

"I had [singer] Suzi Quatro doing an interview in the Coach and Horses, and Bonzo was in there drinking again. I got up to walk somewhere else, and he grabbed hold of me. I had all my things in my pocket, and he ripped the pocket off me. . . . [M]oney went everywhere. I was so pissed off and fed up, I just said, 'That's it. I'm fed up with you, and I don't want anything more to do with you. If I see you coming up the street, you better cross to the other side.'"

Furious, Harry called Peter Grant directly, informing him that he was immediately leaving the band's employ, and under no circumstances was he to have to face the likes of Led Zeppelin—particularly John Bonham—ever again.

"What did they do?" Grant asked over the phone.

Harry let out a sigh. "Bonham ripped my pocket."

After a short pause, Grant said, "Go out and buy the most expensive pair of trousers you can find and send me the bill."

Harry shrugged off Grant's generosity, choosing instead to part ways with the manager and his merry band of misbehaved rock stars. Later, however, Harry looked back on his time with Led Zeppelin, and with John Bonham, with a certain degree of perspective. "They were superstars letting off steam," he later admitted, "but when you are not a star and you don't have much money, their pranks can become very expensive—like when you walk into the Speakeasy Club and a plate of spaghetti comes flying through the air and lands all over your suit. There had been a number of incidents like that. It was just mischief, and I had to take a certain amount, as did anybody else who was associated with them."

Unbeknownst to Harry, John's behavior that afternoon was only just beginning, as he and Stan Webb continued their jovial reign of terror hours into the evening.

Still in the midst of contracting interviews with a number of his other musician clients, Harry had hung up the phone with Peter Grant and returned to his Oxford Street office. When settled at his desk, he heard "Webb and Bonham charging up the stairs," after which "they hammered on the door and eventually knocked it off its hinges, before fleeing the scene of destruction, leaving a trail of toilet rolls down the corridor."

Harry couldn't believe the behavior of the two men and was even more shocked as he peeked out his office door just in time to see John Bonham and Webb tackle Doug D'Arcy, a young executive with the adjacent Chrysalis label, wrap him "head to toe in sticky tape," carry the man down the stairs, and, finally, dump his mummified body onto Oxford Street.

John had one more expensive episode up his sleeve that day, and for that he'd need reinforcements.

"Bonzo called me when I was at my house down in the country," Richard Cole recalled. "He said, 'Look, I'm in London for the night. Get a train or drive up.' He was out with Stan Webb, who was also a friend of mine. . . . So, I went up to town, and somehow Stan came up with this bizarre idea that we should dress up as Arabs."

John also called up Atlantic rep Phil Carson, convincing the executive to book a room at the nearby Mayfair Hotel in his name. The luxury suite, coupled with the Rolls-Royce Phantom 6 that Richard Cole had been able to procure upon his arrival in the city, gave the small band of pranksters the necessary props to begin their "Arab charade."

John—joined by Cole, Webb, and now Phil Carson—drove throughout London wearing Arab costumes, looking for trouble. "We were actually barred from the Revolution Club," Cole remembered. "They wouldn't allow us in there."

Bill Harry got wind of the escapade the next day. "While they were in the lift going up to their room," Harry clarified, "they shocked some blue-rinsed American ladies by lifting up their robes. They weren't wearing anything underneath, so I think the women started hitting them with their umbrellas."

Finally getting up to their suite at the Mayfair, John called room service for more alcohol and enough steak dinners to feed fifty people. "All these waiters came up with trolleys loaded with steaks, and the 'Arabs' started throwing the steaks all over the room," Bill Harry remembered.

The following day, Richard Cole received a call from Stan Webb. Having passed out in his Arab costume, he had awoken unable to find his street clothes. Cole recalled, "He didn't have any money for a cab, so he had to get on the Tube still dressed as an Arab and go back to the Mayfair to pick up his trousers."

According to Bill Harry, it was after that night that John Bonham was banned from every major hotel in London.

After five years of fundraising efforts by the John Bonham Memorial Fund, on May 31, 2018, for what would have been John Bonham's seventieth birthday, a statue of his image was erected in Mercian Square, in his hometown of Redditch, Worcestershire. Designed by British sculptor Mark Richards, and constructed of three tons of bronze, the statue forever immortalizes the drummer in one of his most proud moments— swiping at his timpani drums at his birthday celebration at the LA Forum in 1973.

(Photographs courtesy of Elliott Brown / Public Domain.)

Emblazoned with the drummer's "three rings" symbol from Led Zeppelin's fourth album, and including a smaller likeness of the *Hindenburg*—an unmistakable reference to the band's 1969 debut album—the Redditch memorial is inscribed: "The most outstanding and original drummer of his time, John Bonham's popularity and influence continue to resonate with the world of music and beyond."

(Photograph courtesy of Elliott Brown / Public Domain.)

On March 6, 1971, Led Zeppelin made their first appearance in Dublin, Ireland. Invited onstage by Bonham himself, young local music reviewer Stephen Averill sat behind the drum kit and John's prized Carmine Appice–inspired gong for the rare opportunity to see the world from the drummer's point of view.

It was an auspicious start to a long career in rock photography and graphic design; Averill would go on to work with Depeche Mode and Elvis Costello, and not only design the majority of U2's album covers but, in 1978, give the band their name.

(Photographs courtesy of Stephen Averill.)

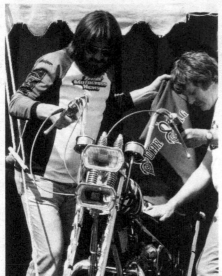

John at the British round of the 500cc World Championship Motocross Races at Farleigh Castle in July 1979. To raise money for the Schoolboy Racing motocross series, John put up for auction his prized Triumph chopper and the jacket he wore in the film *The Song Remains the Same*, as well as his gold record for the soundtrack album.

(Photographs courtesy of Mark Kiel.)

John and Jason at the World Championship Motocross Races, 1979.

Jason Bonham, at twelve years old, a chip off the old block.

John was lifelong friends with the Fairport Convention multi-instrumentalist Dave Pegg, with whom he had earlier played with in a Way of Life. Seen here together in Barmouth, Wales during the summer of 1968.

John playing host at his first home with Pat in West Hagley, entertaining friends Dave Swarbrick of the Fairport Convention and girlfriend, Vivienne, and Swarbrick's Fairport mate Dave Pegg, circa 1969.

(Photographs courtesy of Dave Pegg.)

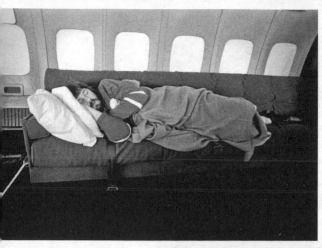

Never fully over his fear of flying, John would often drink himself to sleep during the international tours, relieved when the band would arrive at their destination unscathed. Here, sleeping soundly aboard *The Starship*, 1975.

Led Zeppelin's famed personal plane, *The Starship*, had always been intended to bring the comforts of a hotel suite into the air. With room to move around freely, Bonzo jokingly towers over Robert Plant and Jimmy Page. In the background, manager Peter Grant cranes his neck toward the playful conversation, 1975.

A somewhat more relaxed moment backstage, featuring John in full *A Clockwork Orange* threads. (L-R) Robert Plant, Peter Grant, John Bonham, 1975.

(Photographs courtesy of Neal Preston.)

With Led Zeppelin in New York, July 1973—the first tour using the amber Vistalite kit.

(Photographs courtesy of Dina Regine.)

Chapter Fourteen

APRIL 1972–FEBRUARY 1973

Their holiday over, Led Zeppelin returned to the studio the final day of April. They were also set to begin an eighth American tour in June. First, however, the band planned to cut their fifth album in its entirely.

As a warm-up, of sorts, they gathered at Olympic Studios for initial recordings of two tracks—"Over the Hills and Far Away," a ballad that turned into a hard rocker at its midpoint, and "Houses of the Holy," an up-tempo number whose title was being considered for the album's own proper name. Satisfied with the day's work, the band took the next two weeks to prepare to record the bulk of the album in one long shot.

Engineer Eddie Kramer, who hadn't seen the group since finishing his work on *Led Zeppelin II*, was summoned from New York. He had received a call from Richard Cole weeks earlier, notified that the band was going to be dividing their time among a few different locations: Olympic Studios in London and a large country house owned by Mick Jagger, known as "Stargroves," in Hampshire. For the latter two recording sessions, Zeppelin would also be paying the Stones for further use of their mobile unit.

Arriving in London, Kramer was glad to find the band in good spirits, all four men well rested from their time off and all enthusiastic about the new material they would be recording. Jimmy and Robert had put together a number of compositions from their travels to Bombay, in addition to some leftover ideas from the long Headley Grange sessions nearly two years earlier. But with the musicians fired up thanks to the positive response the fourth album had yielded in the United Kingdom and America, they were anxious to experiment with new genres of music. There was so much usable material, in fact, that in the months ahead it would take Jimmy many hours of studio time to mix it all.

"[The band was] great, inspiring, wonderful," Kramer later recalled of the Stargroves sessions. "It was just that everybody in Led Zeppelin was so confident, and so very happy about what was going on. The general feeling was excellent."

For the opening of the album, Jimmy had initially envisioned an instrumental piece that would signify the commencement of the songs ahead—properly titling the work in progress "The Overture." The intricate composition included multiple guitar voices and changes, and, under Robert's suggestion, the band retitled it "That Campaign," perhaps readying it as the opening song at each gig of the new tour. Still happy with the composition as multiple drafts were altered, Robert eventually put lyrics to it, calling the finished version "The Song Remains the Same."

According to Jimmy, the song was always meant to act as an overture to the following track, a song long gestating titled "The Rain Song." "It was originally going to be an instrumental," Jimmy later said, "but I guess Robert had different ideas. You know, 'This is pretty good. Better get some lyrics—quick!'"

As "The Song Remains the Same" would go on to garner Zeppelin more than a few comparisons in structure and execution to the Who—in particular their rock opera, *Tommy*—it would be only fair to compare and contrast John's approach to the song by his occasional references to Keith Moon. Having long discovered his own signature sound and approach, John had evolved well beyond Moon's earlier influence. Indeed, on "The Song Remains the Same," John chose to keep his rhythmic beats much tighter than the other drummer most likely would have done, as well as rode the half-open hi-hats for a sound that is unmistakably and uniquely John's own.

Most of the material that wasn't outright penned at Stargroves was, at least, constructed there into its final form. A few exceptions, however, were "The Rain Song," which Jimmy had brought from his London demos, and "Over the Hills and Far Away," the only song the group had truly worked on with great focus during their one session at Olympic the previous month. John Paul Jones likewise had worked on "No Quarter" during the band's previous stay at Headley Grange, but it was only now during their time at Stargroves that he turned his full attention to fleshing out the complex composition.

Both "The Rain Song" and "Over the Hills and Far Way" were compositions Jimmy had been working on for the previous year, each constructed from his experiments with different guitar shadings, the latter displaying his love of gentle finger style—the "light" of his old sonic theory juxtaposed with the middle crunch into heavier, electric, "shaded" terrain; "Rain" was a direct response to George Harrison, who had earlier commented to John and Jimmy backstage after a Zeppelin show at the Forum that the group needed to balance out their set list with more ballads, as the Beatles used to do. Jimmy had started "The Rain Song" at his home in Sussex, bringing the majority of the guitar parts with him to Stargroves, while "Over the Hills" in all its gentle folk glory was near completion, sans the harpsichord elements Jones would soon add. Likewise, Jones was eager to present a final version of "No Quarter" to the band, its slow, "underwater" sound effect in the same hypnotic vein as "Dazed and Confused," but with more space for the bassist's keyboard experimentations; he had purposely left the field open for Jimmy to throw in some trippy jazz guitar.

At first, it appeared that John would have little to do on "The Rain Song," with the soft ballad eschewing percussion for a lengthy three minutes, at which point the drummer utilized his rare, but master-ful, application of a gentle brush effect. Displaying the potential for brushes as opposed to sticks, when the song explodes a few minutes later, John attacked the kit, but retained brushes, his style so powerful a casual listener could be tricked into thinking he'd swapped them out for his heavy sticks. For this sonic effect, John played harder, strik-ing the lower end of the brushes, emphasizing where the strands were rooted into the stem handle—then fading his percussion out com-pletely at the song's coda, displaying a perfect control of his restraint. John's versatility was further demonstrated on the harsher parts of "Over the Hills," where he followed alongside Jimmy's heavy riff, somewhat uncharacteristically, by riding the open hi-hat, but making his place audibly clear by subtly letting his beat hang atop the shorter sounds of each of Jimmy's guitar notes.

Never a group to shy away from a challenge, Zeppelin tackled the growingly popular reggae genre with "D'yer Mak'er"—the title itself a pun spoken in a Cockney accent. In England, island fusion rock had become trendy thanks in large part to the mainstream appeal of Bob Marley and the Wailers, and Jimmy and Robert—both lovers of world music—wanted to give the distinct style a worthy attempt. Perhaps to the band's detriment, however, reggae was a sound that relied heavily on its percussion—and John was not a fan. In the stu-dio, he had been teased about his difficulty in mastering reggae's odd time signatures, to which John had simply described the genre itself as "boring" to play.

In the drummer's capable hands, however, the groove of "D'yer Mak'er" melded into a near funk-rock sound, yet John retained fills more akin to traditional reggae playing. With this song, John was at a distinct disadvantage, however, as most popular reggae and dub sounds were produced on heavily dampened drum kits or single-headed toms wrapped in tape—a muted percussion that was the very opposite of John's lifelong practice of organically amplifying his rock playing.

"When we did 'D'yer Mak'er,' [John] wouldn't play anything but the same shuffle beat all the way through it," John Paul Jones later admitted. "He hated it, and so did I. It would have been all right if he had worked at the part—the whole point of reggae is that the drums and bass really have to be very strict about what they play. And he wouldn't, so it sounded dreadful."

John felt much more at home with the next song the Stargroves sessions yielded—"The Crunge" was Robert's homage to the sexy R&B-driven grooves of James Brown, an artist and a genre John adored. The result, though far removed from hard rock, was Zeppelin played truly heavy on the sessions for the first time—primarily thanks to John's enthusiasm for the style, bookending the song with a complex circular 9/8 drum pattern, playing some heavy syncopated funk riffs in between. Both John's playing and Robert's emotional vocals pay distinct homage to Brown's improvised vocal outbursts on the previous year's smash hit "Sex Machine," giving the loose cut a jubilant jam feel. Not one to be outdone, Jimmy tweaked his own voicings by adapting to a similar smacking style as Brown's own guitarist, Jimmy Nolen. "Where's that confounded bridge?" Robert can be heard saying on the track—and apparently, amid the fun of the session, it was a question no one seemed to be able to answer.

The one undisputed hard rocker for the new album was Robert's less-than-flattering love letter to the group's own audience, "The Ocean," which used poetic symbolism to describe the singer's take on the massive seas of upturned teenage faces that would always exist in droves, in city after city, to empty their pockets for tickets for the opportunity to worship Led Zeppelin live. Just as "The Song Remains the Same" had been conceived both as an overture to the album and as a potential show opener, "The Ocean"—with Jimmy's layers of electric lead, nearly giving an effect of a rock 'n' roll choir of angels—was the ultimate Zeppelin "encore." On the album alone—and in a true twist of "progressive" rock—John clipped an eighth note off each second bar, making the hard riff 17/8 time and one of the greatest, yet most subtle, experiments with time signature from among the Stargroves sessions.

And although the sessions had yielded numerous other hard-driven songs, Jimmy made the executive decision to leave them aside for various reasons; in truth, he had long planned a double LP at some point in the band's future, and although the Stargroves "leftovers" were strong, it was agreed that some held too many similarities to others to make the cut. Outtakes like "Black Country Woman" and "The Rover" would be shelved temporarily, as would "Houses of the Holy"—a decision that left many scratching their heads, as that track would, more than likely, become the album's name—and the heaviest cut of all, "Walter's Walk." With this one, John had been allowed to unleash some of the fastest and most ferocious playing ever recorded—after only a few seconds crashing in on the end of Jimmy's opening riff with his bass and snare locked together like a hurricane. The drummer's use of the full kit, especially the thumping bass, was near violent in its extreme approach, relying on adrenaline and speed. Like the rest of the outtakes, however, Jimmy chose to shelve the heavy masterpiece for a rainy day.

Inspired by the spiritually laden Indian double-reed *shehnai* that mystified them during their stay in Bombay, "Dancing Days" was another atypical tune that Jimmy and Robert penned, a swinging, hippie vibe that got their audiences up and grooving. At least, according to engineer Eddie Kramer, it accomplished such a response from the band itself. "I have a very strong vision, from my perspective in the mobile with the doors to the truck wide open, of all four of them dancing in single file on the lawn during the first playback of 'Dancing Days,'" Kramer recalled. "It was Robert, Bonzo, Jonesy, and Jimmy dancing in a line on a green lawn, celebrating this incredible thing they'd just recorded."

According to Kramer, the Stargroves sessions were always under Jimmy's watchful, creative eye. Although the Zeppelin sound was a collaborative effort—all four members bringing their styles and ideas to the table—it was the guitarist/producer who was running the production, even in the instances when the appearance of improvisation took over, as was the case with "Black Country Woman." Recorded outdoors in the garden, the song captured the ambient sounds of a propeller-driven airplane above the band. Kramer heard the whirring plane from his place in the mobile unit. After asking if they should keep rolling and Robert said to keep it, Kramer did so only after a nod of approval from Jimmy himself. It was Jimmy's love of emotional aesthetics that kept it in the take.

Recording John was another story. Much like Andy Johns before him, Eddie Kramer was excited at the prospect of trying new innovations in harnessing Bonzo's lush, epic sounds to tape. For the recordings, Kramer varied the microphones in his arsenal, alternating between Shure SM57s, Neumann U67s and U87s, AKG C12s, and ElectroVoice RE20s—switching between the mics depending upon the song, but always putting into effect an open drum sound that ignored compression and reverb, allowing the drums to "breathe." Although natural tape compression from the massive signal was inevitable, Kramer opted to record John's playing as close to "live" as the mobile unit would allow.

"Bonzo was the easiest drummer I ever recorded," Kramer later admitted. "I had him in a room to himself, playing inside the bay window of a big conservatory, with three mics on the drums. His sound was so great that it facilitated a monumental drum sound on record. . . . Bonzo sounded that way because he hit the drums harder than anyone I ever met. He had this bricklayer's ability to bang the drum immensely hard—yet he had a very light touch."

Kramer remained adamant that John's playing was integral to the band's overall sound. He added, "In many ways, he was the key to Led Zeppelin. You could work fast with him. . . . The only reason Led Zeppelin ever did retakes was the extremely tricky time sequences of most of the songs. Once Bonzo mastered his part, everything would fall into place."

The engineer also admitted, however, that dealing with John on a personal level could be a trying experience—at least if you had a female companion with you. "Bonzo burst into my room very late one night, extremely drunk and wearing an oversized raincoat, and flashed my girlfriend and I, who were in bed," Kramer recalled, laughing. "Then, he ran out roaring with laughter. But the room didn't have a lock, and soon he was back, even more drunk, and he flashed us again. Then a roadie ran in and threw a bucket of cold water on us while we were in bed, and the other roadies were running amok, climbing in and out of our window all night. The girl left the next morning in disgust. I can't say I blamed her."

The band finished up at Stargroves in only a few days. When all was said and done, they were pleased with the full amount of completed tracks, also taking into account a few untitled rhythm tracks of mixed quality, including a hard-rock instrumental titled "Slush."

Trouble came when the group reconvened at Olympic Studios in London on May 30 and listened to the playback of the mobile unit's recordings. Stargroves had been a pleasant-enough experience, but Mick Jagger's country home lacked the rich acoustics previously captured at Headley Grange. Jimmy would have to spend many more months remixing in London and, as the clock ticked and Zeppelin was midtour, at Jimi Hendrix's Electric Lady Studios in New York City.

Luckily, the band's fourth album was still strong on the sales charts. Their fifth album wouldn't be satisfactorily completed for almost another year.

The group was set to unleash their eighth American tour on June 6 at Cobo Hall in Detroit. Having new material to introduce to the world, Zeppelin played two brief warm-up gigs in their old touring woodshed the Netherlands, on May 27 and 28, then headed for the States.

This time around, Led Zeppelin would reap the many rewards of Peter Grant's own hard work during their recordings in Stargroves. From his Oxford office, the manager had been able to solidify some of the most astounding concessions ever bestowed upon a rock band— all of which were unprecedented and, at least among those in the management business, controversial.

Formerly, major acts would split the gate with the venue where they would be performing; Grant was well aware of the practice and had had to act as an enforcer on behalf of his clients for nearly two decades. But when Zeppelin returned to London, he had a surprise for them: this time around, Grant would be demanding a whopping 90 percent of the profits from each concert—and so far, each US venue had begrudgingly agreed to the astronomical terms. Grant had presented the American promoters with simple logic: 10 percent of a sold-out Led Zeppelin show was better than 50 percent of nothing.

"He just figured that the people go to see the artist and the artist should get the money," Richard Cole later recalled. "And he took the risk. . . . [Grant] hired the stadiums with his own money. He said, 'I'll rent the halls; you do the work for me.'"

But Grant had another reason to fight as hard as he did for his boys. At the beginning of May, he had suffered a great personal loss when the lead guitarist of Stone the Crows, Les Harvey, had been violently electrocuted onstage during a performance in Wales. The band was another client of Grant's and had even performed alongside Led Zeppelin the previous year at their "Electric Magic" rock 'n' roll circus at Wembley. But more important, Les was a close friend of Grant's—and the freak accident had not only proved the manager's ongoing fears of improper stage safety sadly sound, but also kicked in his protective, paternal nature. From now on, if a venue wanted to work with one of Grant's clients, they would pay accordingly and be held accountable for any unforeseen fuck-ups that could affect the performers.

Grant's heavy-handed mandate for the band's profits made the press. Soon, all major acts would be asking for massive increases in their take of a concert tour's gross, citing Peter Grant as the chief motivator in how the rock 'n' roll world approached its business. Inadvertently, the news of Led Zeppelin's massive asking price only drove up demand among their fans; if the band was asking for that much, their new show must be incredible. Despite the fact that rivals the Rolling Stones would also be touring America at the same time, their first US visit since 1969, an update from Grant set Led

Zeppelin's mind at ease: before even touching down in the States, every show had been sold out.

Although the group was sure their music would be worth the price of admission alone, the unprecedented amount they were making off the tour called for a revamp of their normal stage act. Zeppelin had paid top-dollar Dallas-based effects company Showco to provide massive elements to their live experience, including the laser lights, mirror balls, dry ice and smoke effects, and oversize screens. Further adding to the extravagance, the group presented every song amid a spectacle of pomp and circumstance: "Dazed and Confused" was now a hypnotic twenty-minute centerpiece, while every performance of "Stairway to Heaven" saw the waves of masses enraptured as though a religious ritual was taking place.

On some nights, the show could run as long as four hours, depending upon Jimmy's health and Robert's voice; the singer had shown cold symptoms early in the tour due to the West Coast's dry climate and nursed his singing voice with a steady diet of tea, honey, and lemon. While in LA in June, John and Robert uncharacteristically made a surprise appearance on the popular "Wolfman Jack" radio show, pumping the audience for Zeppelin's appearance and putting everyone's mind at ease over Robert's vocals.

The set list leaned heavily on the newly recorded material that was unfamiliar to the fans, on the new standards from the untitled album, and on veteran Zeppelin tunes, such as "Since I've Been Loving You," "Dazed and Confused," and "Whole Lotta Love." But the show now opened with "Rock and Roll" and segued into "Over the Hills and Far Away," "Black Dog," and "Misty Mountain Hop." They opted to save "The Song Remains the Same" for the new album's release.

John's epic "Moby Dick" solo had consistently proved to be a highlight to fans and reviewers, but with the expansion of the band's shows in the coming year, John was able to increase his one-man turn in the spotlight for two very different reasons: aside from a longer all-around concert that could warrant a longer solo, with the band exhausting themselves for a longer duration, the break that John's solo provided the other three was deemed all the more necessary.

"England's number one rock group, Led Zeppelin packed the Spectrum Tuesday to give their fans a [two-and-a-half-hour] tidal wave of Zep music," Gloria Elliott wrote in the *Philadelphia Morning News*. "For those 'drum freaks' in Philly, John 'Bonso' [*sic*] Bonham had a 20-minute solo—most of it, bare-handed. He never shows he is tired. High energy percussion seems to be the name of the game." A week later in the *Sunday Oregonian*, John Wendeborn wrote of the group's Portland show, "Amazing is the word, alright. Most superstar rock bands—Led Zeppelin is doubtless in the top five along with the Stones and The Who. . . . Tons of equipment were jammed onto the stage and it all served various purposes. . . . When the Zeppelin turned to heavy music, it was announced by a number of rolls on the huge gong behind the drummer. But the tunes were mellow, then intensive, then heavy again."

Despite massive crowds and relatively strong concert reviews, the band had noticed how rarely they received coverage in the mainstream American press. Their aggressive distrust of journalists was well known by this point, but with the Stones' tour being covered for Andy Warhol's chic *Interview* magazine by none other than celebrity novelist Truman Capote, Zeppelin—Jimmy and Robert in particular—couldn't help but feel slighted.

"I must admit, it does annoy me," Robert admitted. "I must have an ego because I have to go onstage partially to satisfy it."

But the band knew the cause of the perceived media indifference: ever since New York reporters had rained down accusations of "hype" upon learning of Zeppelin's $100,000 payout for Madison Square Garden in 1970, the band had allowed their publicity to fall by the wayside. While Jimmy's "let the music speak for itself" attitude had definitely proved sound when it came to album and ticket sales, Led Zeppelin was not yet the household name that the Rolling Stones had long been.

At Grant's suggestion, Zeppelin began to proactively find a new publicist. Bill Harry had long since resigned thanks to John's misbehavior, and the group hadn't yet bothered to replace him. In their search, Robert half-jokingly told one reporter, "Without being egocentric, we thought it was time people heard something about us other than that we were eating women and throwing the bones out the window."

The band finally settled on B. P. "Beep" Fallon, a seasoned music publicist who had previously worked for T. Rex. A bit of a hipster, Fallon liked to dress as theatrically as the musicians he represented, as well as speak the same jive lingo he often overheard in the music business. Jimmy and Robert found him amusing; John disliked him immediately, especially Fallon's faux-dandy veneer—and his nickname, "Beep."

Early in the tour, they played two shows at Madison Square Garden in New York. While in town the band took in many of the small rock 'n' roll venues, getting their first taste of the harder-edged New York music scene. They then trekked up to Syracuse before the grand journey west, inevitably landing in Los Angeles.

They again set up camp at the Continental Hyatt House on Sunset Boulevard and took up their old habits, jamming and visiting rock clubs like Rodney's English Disco and the Rainbow Bar. John and Robert kept their mayhem localized to the "Riot House," where rumors of John riding his motorcycle throughout the hotel's labyrinthine stairways began to circulate—although it had actually been road manager Richard Cole who introduced the dangerous new hobby to the band.

Meanwhile, Jimmy's eye had caught hold of a fourteen-year-old teen model named Lori Maddox, whom he began to chase like a heat-seeking missile. "But the others were really against me at the time," Maddox later claimed. "They were concerned because somebody warned them that if Jimmy was discovered with a fourteen-year-old girl, he'd be deported immediately. So, Jimmy kept me locked in the room at all times."

The LA shows themselves were a smash, as was John's newly expanded "Moby Dick." Danny Holloway wrote, "From the minute the group walked out onstage, the crowd went wild, throwing firecrackers and smoking mounds of dope. . . . All in all, there were five encores because the audience screamed and stomped like spoiled babies till they got what they wanted. I was told that the group performed ten gigs of this calibre in 14 days," Holloway noted correctly. "It's easy to understand America's love for the group and vice versa."

The US gigs were completed in August, and the band touted their best profits of any tour thus far. As they prepared for the next international wing of shows—beginning with their second visit to Japan—it was discussed that publicity would have to become a larger aspect of their marketing push.

That same month, John agreed to a sit with journalist Roy Carr for a large profile in *New Musical Express* (*NME*). "Led Zeppelin, together with the Who, are one of those rare combinations in which every member plays an equal and integral part," wrote Carr. On Zeppelin's four-member unity, John was quite vocal. "That's the way we are, and that's probably one of the reasons why we work so well and stay together," John commented. "We're not like some bands—who are worlds apart. One danger is when group members start spending most of their time playing with other musicians. Sure, it's OK occasionally, but when a guy prefers to play with other musicians, it's best to forget the whole thing. . . . You see, all his creative ideas go to other people—and the group eventually suffers."

John added, "If we wanted, we could probably do 12 tours of the States each year and do extremely well on each of them—but that's not what we formed this group for. . . . Before long, your prestige goes and you burn yourself out. You must create your own demand."

Finally, John offered up Zeppelin's consensus on their presence—or lack thereof—in the mainstream media. "Look, we've just toured the States and done as well if not better than the Stones," he said, "but there was hardly anything about it in the British press. All we read was, the Stones this and the Stones that, and it pisses us off."

After a few weeks home in England, the group returned to Tokyo's Budokan Hall on October 2, then continued to Osaka. As had been the case previously, Japanese audiences loved Zeppelin's three-hour high-octane hard rock. To ensure the quality of their stage extravaganza remained intact, the band even paid for Showco's cofounder Rusty Brutsche to accompany them and act as a sound and lighting consultant.

The band then flew to Hong Kong for a brief vacation, then continued on for two shows in Montreux, Switzerland. Keeping the momentum going and the profits rolling in, on November 10 Grant announced a two-month tour of the British Isles beginning in December. With the band reminding Grant that those were the holidays, he in turn informed them that all 120,000 tickets sold out in one day. And so Led Zeppelin began 1973 on the road.

As Zeppelin's stage show had exploded to epic proportions, John's heavy style of drumming not only was gobbled up by the band's rabid fans, but called for even more amplification to meet the expectations of larger crowds coming to see the hardest of hard-rock bands.

By the early 1970s, amplification had increased dramatically, yet close-miking was still viewed as an imperfect science, forcing all rock drummers to get creative in order to be heard above the guitars, basses, and synths. Although considered controversial by purists upon its introduction, one widely used solution was to craft new drum sets from synthetic materials. As a longtime product ambassador for Ludwig, John was in a unique position to bring their latest innovation—a multicolored Plexiglas-shelled Vistalite kit.

During the 1973 tour, Ludwig had shipped a few of the multicolored Vistalite drums to John, hoping the image of him using the trendy kits onstage would help promote the controversial new product line. The switch to acrylic drums was a risk to longtime manufacturer Ludwig, but as competitors, such as Fibes, had already begun to sell synthetic-based kits, the company saw little option but to surpass the others and dominate the market. As was the style of the 1970s, Ludwig's major innovation to the acrylic design was to offer numerous dramatic colors to add a little extra theatricality to a drummer onstage.

Although John took his playing and sound very seriously, there was a fashionable edge to him that saw potential in a custom-styled kit that would match the likes of Jimmy's double-neck Gibson and sequined suits in showmanship or Robert's donning of flowing blouses. Most important, one of John's favorite modern drummers, jazz-fusion player Billy Cobham, had since switched to using a clear translucent acrylic Fibes kit during live performance. After recording with the likes of Miles Davis and John McLaughlin's Mahavishnu Orchestra, Cobham had just reinvented the very essence of jazz-rock with his debut album, *Spectrum*, recording at Zeppelin's New York stomping ground, Electric Lady Studios. John couldn't get enough of the album and was quickly convinced that he, too, could push the sonic envelope with a similar Ludwig Plexiglas Vistalite setup.

John requested that Ludwig send along an amber-colored Vistalite kit, complete with his signature "three rings" symbol from the fourth album boldly emblazoned on the front bass. He immediately noticed that the reflective Plexiglas surface made for a loud, resonant sound, much louder than the wood-shell drums. He kept his usual configuration of twenty-six-by-fourteen, fourteen-by-ten, sixteen-by-sixteen, and eighteen-by-sixteen. The full kit also came with twenty- and twenty-two-inch floor toms, plus an extra kick drum, but John found little use for those. In the recording studio, John still opted for the warmer tones of the traditional hardwood kits.

"What's an anomaly is that John played one of the worst forms of drum ever invented, and I also had a set—a humongous Ludwig Vistalite set," recalled the Police's drummer, Stewart Copeland. "It was okay, I guess, but it sounded like shit, [and] John's sound was a big part of his technique. I suspect that he hit his drums not loudly."

Copeland continued, "I've always found that when I hit my drums quietly, they sound bigger—it's really the space between the notes. His bass drum had a lot of ambiance—he'd hit it once and make it count. . . . [John] was a pioneer of ambient sound."

That same year, Paiste introduced its own innovative line of modern cymbals, and John immediately requested samples to match the new drum set. While he was used to using Paiste's "Giant Beats" cymbals for the better part of a decade, with their new "2002" line he alternated between the styles. As was the case with his drums, John opted for cymbals larger than conventional sizes, including fifteen-inch Sound Edge hi-hats, a twenty-four-inch and a thirty-eight-inch symphonic gong, along with an eighteen- or twenty-inch medium ride as his right-side crash cymbal and a sixteen- or eighteen-inch crash on his left. When the larger cymbals were paired with the new Ludwig Vistalite kit, John's sound became louder and more powerful than ever.

Before the band would even come out onstage to play, crowds soon cheered at the mere sight of the kit itself, the image of John's distinctive identifier like a superhero's emblem, now synonymous with the thunderous rock that the kit would soon somehow harness.

While Zeppelin was in Glasgow, Scotland, on December 3, Beep Fallon was beaten up by ticket scalpers; in Cardiff the band had to pay up after John trashed his room at the Angel Hotel. On December 20, the group played Christmas carols for the joyous crowd, and then, finally, they broke for a few nights following consecutive sold-out performances at the Alexandra Palace in North London. The day after New Year's, John and Robert were riding together to a show in Sheffield when their rented Bentley broke down on the side of the road. Like their old days as teenagers, the two friends laughed it off and hitchhiked to their own sold-out performance at city hall.

Glad to at least be back in England, the band was booked for a show at Trentham Gardens in Stoke-on-Trent on January 15. Set among a thousand acres of lush woodlands and gardens, Trentham Hall had been constructed in 1633 and was the ancestral home of the Duke of Sutherland. Unaccustomed to welcoming rock bands, the Grand Hall—a large ballroom complete with a first-floor balcony—was now set to host Led Zeppelin. As it was located just north of

Birmingham, John rang up his brother, Mick, and got tickets for him and their father to come to the night's show.

"John had popped in to see if Jacko and I would be all right getting there on our own, because he'd got to go early to do the usual sound checks," Mick later recalled. "Upon our arrival at the hall, a hundred or so fans were already milling around. . . . Heading for the bar, we found a space, settled, and waited for Led Zeppelin to arrive onstage. The buzz of anticipation was audible by the time the hall was half-full. . . . Eventually, the house lights dimmed, [and] John kick-started the kit into life, making it sound like a pneumatic hammer was pounding the snare." For the occasion, John had playfully decked himself out in a cartoonish checkered suit and oversize rainbow-colored bow tie, all of which brought a laugh to his family. Mick remembered, "Jacko and I stood watching proudly as the boys yet again gave their all in a show that melded talent with sheer magic."

By Mick's account, John saved his most dramatic performance of the night for after the show, a one-man encore of sorts. After the band's incredibly energetic, rousing performance, all of their fans and personal guests gathered beside the large bar in the ballroom's luxurious lobby to await the musicians' postconcert emergence—hoping to share a drink and toast them all. Amid the pleasant chatter and clinking of pints and champagne glasses, the guests heard a loud barrage of coarse words coming from somewhere beyond the ballroom walls, a shouting match taking place in the dressing-room area. "It was our John," Mick later recalled, "and he was going totally apeshit." As the crowd stood around exchanging stunned looks and scratching their heads, the band and their entourage appeared victoriously through the security doors—minus John.

"John was nowhere to be found, so it was back to the bar to figure out what to do next," Mick remembered. "Our thoughts were soon interrupted by a huge cry of 'What the fuck was that?' echoing across the hall. It was in response to a loud crashing sound from somewhere outside the hall, and everyone headed towards the exit door."

As the band had been provided with all the expected VIP treatment thanks to the Trentham Gardens management, their respective vehicles had been stored in a large private courtyard off the parking lot, secured by wooden doors by their own personal valets. John had driven himself down in his Rolls-Royce that night, and, from outside, Mick suddenly heard the unmistakable crash of the wooden gates being smashed to pieces. As he recalled, "John had stormed out of the building, jumped into his motor, and driven it straight through the large doors while they were still closed, leaving a passable impression of a large mouse hole behind him." Family and friends raced outdoors to try to grab hold of him before he could get the Rolls out onto the busy road, but it was too late.

As Mick later described it, "So, here's the picture: we're looking for a young rock drummer with a long heavy beard and is dressed like Coco the Clown, driving a Rolls-Royce at high speed down the M6 motorway on his way home."

But heavily intoxicated—and on his usual postconcert adrenaline-fueled high—John had veered onto the wrong highway, aiming his Rolls-Royce toward the exit for Scotland. Realizing his error, John quickly—and dangerously—switched lanes toward Liverpool, before noticing that the vehicle was nearly out of fuel. Now miles away from civilization, the car finally sputtered to a stop, and John had to hitch through the cold night in search of fuel and a lift back to Old Hyde alone. He eventually found a lone emergency phone booth and rang the ever-faithful Matthew Maloney to come and pick him up. Mick Bonham later remembered, "It wasn't the first time during the five years he had worked for John that he'd had to leave his bed in the early hours to go looking for him. It wasn't the last, either."

As John's brother added, the following day everyone was too scared of John's temper to bring the drunken episode up in conversation, and they "never did find out what upset him" back at the Grand Hall in the first place.

And it was a question that reporters would continue to ask regarding John, as his brilliant career at the drums would be nearly overshadowed by a concurrent career of violent outbursts and un-restrained misbehavior. Years later, a Led Zeppelin aficionado and memorabilia collector named Howard Mylett came forward with a similar story, remembering a terrifying incident that took place in Brighton on December 22, 1972. The young man had been to as many UK Zeppelin concerts as he could afford and had assembled a scrap-book of his ticket stubs and photographs. Hoping to have the band autograph his valuable memorabilia, Mylett convinced Mick Hin-ton to allow him backstage to meet John in person—but a sudden change in the backstage area's atmosphere made him quickly turn on his heel. "I heard Bonzo trashing a dressing room," Mylett remem-bered. "You could literally hear these chairs being thrown around and grunting noises being made, no words being formed. It was like a bear in a cage."

Mylett, scrapbook in hand, instead cowered outside of the theater and headed home.

The tour finished with a few return dates in Scotland at the end of the month. The band's show at Edinburgh was attended by *New Musical Express* writer Nick Kent, who covered the band extensively over the next few years. "Why, wasn't [Plant] just a moment ago working in cahoots with Bonzo Bonham to turn the place into the usual boisterous rough-house, specifically attempting to provoke a mock fight between Bonham and the Securicor representative, rejoic-ing in the nickname of 'Patsy' and generally indulging in a pleasant blend of cajolery and ribald banter," said Kent. "A beer-fight breaks out among Messrs. Plant and Bonham against road manager Richard Cole. The ubiquitous B. P. Fallon. Publicist extraordinaire, intervenes and yours truly hides behind a troupe of young girls as soggy, toasted, tomato-and-ham sandwiches, beer-cans and bottles are thrown in all directions."

Kent added, "Finally, from the wreckage of furniture, a large bucket of ice water descends over Mr. Fallon and myself, and every-one leaves in a hurry. Slowly, we pick up the remains of the wine and head back to the hotel."

It was agreed that the band needed some time away from the road. At this point, what would soon be officially titled *Houses of the Holy* was long since completed, although the cover art—as usual—was causing strife among the band and executives at Atlantic. The musicians were certain, however, that their preferred designs would eventually be accepted; according to the most recent sale figures, Led Zeppelin's previous four albums accounted for 18 percent of the record company's total sales for 1972. They'd see eye to eye soon enough.

Confident and exhausted, the band went their separate ways at the end of January, and John happily returned to Old Hyde Farm to pick up his hammer and nails to continue the home's ongoing renovations.

When childhood hero Chuck Berry brought his tour to Birmingham the following month, playing at local club Barbarella's, John grabbed Robert and Cole and got front-row seats. As the show went on, the two noticed John getting irritable and fidgety at the house drummer's mediocre performance—one of his personal pet peeves. Halfway through "Johnny B. Goode," John turned to Robert. "Chuck Berry's a rock 'n' roll legend, and they got this worthless drummer backing him. . . . I gotta do something. This guy can't play worth a damn!" Another song later, John could take no more. "The fucking drummer is useless," he said. "I gotta get him out of there!"

To the room's shock, John rushed the stage. "Chuck wants me to take over!" he said as he grabbed the drummer by his shirt and pulled him from the kit. Berry turned around, startled, and John grinned at him. Berry led into "Roll Over Beethoven," and John knew every change. He sat in for three songs, after which even Berry was cheering.

John had the month of February to himself. In March, Zeppelin would trek across Europe and—inevitably, it seemed—America again, starting in May.

Chapter Fifteen

MARCH 1973–JUNE 1973

The fifth album was finally released in March 1973.

It was the first Led Zeppelin album to be given a proper title, *Houses of the Holy*, although the title song itself, recorded at Olympic Studios in April 1972, had been deemed too similar in style to some other, stronger tracks and left aside.

As had been the case with the band's previous two albums, the cover had been primarily responsible for the months of delays. Like the fourth album, *Houses of the Holy* deliberately omitted the group's name—another point of contention for Atlantic. But the design, created by innovative London art firm Hipgnosis, caused immediate concern: depicting naked blond children scrambling up a monolithic stone formation in Staffin, in the Western Isles of the Hebrides, the album all at once suggested pagan symbolism, implied human sacrifice, and clearly displayed underage nudity. According to the band, however, it was the cover's print job that had held up production. Initially, faulty color separation had caused the children to bleed out purple; once corrected, the second attempt gave the full cover image a strange burnt-orange tone. Third time proved to the be the charm, and fans rushed out to buy the band's long-awaited follow-up to the untitled album that had become known as *Led Zeppelin IV*.

As usual, the critics were divided, yet the band was intensely proud of their work on the album. Like *Led Zeppelin III*, it had been a deliberate attempt to demonstrate their versatility; unlike the third album, however, even genre-bending numbers like "The Song Remains the Same" and "The Crunge" flexed the appropriate hard-rock muscles.

Houses of the Holy was released while the band was in the midst of circling the globe, allowing the band to revamp its set list yet again. During March, Led Zeppelin played to audiences in Denmark, Norway, Sweden, Austria, and Germany, then continued on to Japan and England. At the end of the month, they began a five-city tour of France at Lyons. There, Peter Grant was furious when he found out that the local promoter had cheapened out on providing the band with security. He quickly mobilized his own security detail, employing Benoit Gautier, an employee of Atlantic's France division who had been a longtime friend to Grant and the group.

The first gig in Lyons on March 26 was at the Palais de Sport, a twelve-thousand-seat basketball stadium accommodating four levels' worth of people. Trouble began before the band even went onstage, as waves of gate-crashers rushed the venue, screaming for free admittance and claiming that music belonged "to the people." Of course, nothing was for free—especially to Grant, who was outraged at the teenagers' behavior. During the concert, matters got worse, as kids on the upper tiers began dropping wine bottles onto the band, sending dangerous shards of smashed glass across the stage.

Without being told, Gautier rushed to the balcony and caught the ringleader, dragging him backstage by his hair. After a proper beating, Gautier and a few of the roadies tossed the boy out of the stadium. For his loyal efforts, Peter Grant hired the ironfisted Gautier to continue his security post for the next four nights, working alongside another henchman-for-hire named Patsy Collins. Collins had received his own offer to remain in Zeppelin's employ that night after Grant witnessed him break a gate-crasher's jaw.

"[Grant] had the reputation of being a tough motherfucker," Gautier later recalled. "I saw him [mis]behave many times, breaking things, breaking people physically, but every time he did it to somebody, it was because they deserved it. He was very professional, a gentleman, incredibly loyal to his acts and to the people who worked for him, and especially to people who went out of their way to help Led Zeppelin."

Still adhering to John's aversion to flying whenever possible, the band rented two cars to travel to their next gig at Nantes: a large Volvo, which Grant used to drive Robert and Jimmy, and a luxury Mercedes, for which John called dibs, along with Gautier and Collins. All was fine until the group congregated at a rest area for gas and food. Grant suddenly decided he wanted to tool around in the Mercedes, so he simply took the keys and hijacked it with his singer and guitarist. Considering that a challenge, John gunned the Volvo's engine and took off after them.

According to Gautier, John would play chicken against the oncoming traffic—lingering in the passing lane at the Volvo's top speed, then veering back into the proper lane just in the nick of time, narrowly missing the onslaught of incoming cars. At the group's next break an hour later, John got drunk on red wine before getting back behind the wheel. "I'm still surprised we didn't die," Gautier admitted later.

Finally arriving at the Parc des Expositions in Nantes for the band's sound check, Grant was angry that the backstage gates were slow to allow them through. Frustrated from hours behind the wheel, he rammed the Mercedes through the gate, ripping off the car's fenders.

The concert went off without a hitch, despite the group's condition. Afterward, however, John was more than a little disappointed with the three trailers provided as dressing rooms, as well as the quality of the meals the band was served. To properly demonstrate his disapproval, the drummer grabbed the thirty-eight-inch mallet used for his Chinese gong and destroyed the trailers. Back at the hotel, Robert was still nursing his throat with tea, lemon, and honey. Notified that room service was out of milk, the road crew mobilized on his behalf; doors were removed from their hinges, rooms were flooded with fire hoses, toilets were plugged and overflowed, and furniture was destroyed.

Amazingly, John hadn't been part of that evening's holocaust; he had skipped out with Richard Cole and a few of the band's roadies in search of local bars. While they were out on the town, Gautier had escorted Robert and Jimmy to the only all-night restaurant in the area. Staggering the streets from too much drink, John and Cole happened upon the more sober members of the Zeppelin enjoying their late-night meal and proceeded to verbally attack them for the snub. After blasting insults upon Robert and Jimmy for leaving him out, John led his own entourage into the waiting Volvo. Jimmy and Robert begrudgingly piled in after them, making Gautier an unwilling chauffer and babysitter.

As the car rolled on through the deserted nighttime streets, the passengers began to destroy the car from within—starting with the sunroof and the four doors of the sedan, the roadies soon went to work prying off other pieces of the interior, dumping it all into the street. By the time the first police vehicle flashed its lights, the Volvo had been stripped of its spare tire and trunk lid. In the rearview mirror, Gautier soon noticed more cops had joined in the chase. Panicked, he sped up and began to make abrupt turns down alleys and side streets, inadvertently initiating a high-speed pursuit—much to the amusement of the musicians. They stopped laughing when a roadblock was eventually set up, leading to their mass arrest. Evidently, the police had already paid a visit to their hotel and found their rooms thoroughly destroyed.

As wealthy foreigners, the band was eventually released, but warned to remain at their hotel until it was time to move on to the next unfortunate destination. Peter Grant quickly made new travel arrangements; both the Mercedes and the Volvo were destroyed and deemed unfit for the roads. Terrified by the group's behavior in Lyons and Nantes, their promoter disappeared into the night, not to resurface until Led Zeppelin had moved on to their next European dates.

While Zeppelin as a whole may have solidified their reputation for joyous mayhem in the French city that night, John Bonham himself had earned a personal tag for his contributions. Gautier couldn't help but be amused at the sight—and sounds—of a thoroughly inebriated John hulking around when a dark mood overcame him. Indeed, people were warned to steer clear if John was in such rare form. For this, the French security agent had coined a nickname—one that, while Robert and Jimmy found amusing, was never to be uttered if John was within earshot.

As their French promoter had gone into hiding, Grant felt they owed him nothing and canceled the next two shows contracted with his company, one in Marseilles and another in Lille. Instead, he decided to treat the boys to a few extra days in Paris before their two-night engagement there on April 1 and 2 at the Palais des Sports. Again, John insisted on road or rail, and so Grant shelled out for the train.

However, when it was discovered that the club bar was closed for the duration of their journey, John immediately trashed his cabin. Grant and the band ordered the roadies to restrain the drummer before his path of destruction made its way to the rest of the train. Behind John's back, they gave the directive using Gautier's clandestine nickname:

"*Le Bête*."

They were told to restrain "the Beast" before he could strike again.

Against his better judgment, Grant booked Zeppelin into one of the most renowned luxury hotels in the world, the Parisian Hotel George V—an elegant palace recognized for its antique tapestries and priceless antique decorum. Gautier recalled that during their stay, while he was never asked to procure drugs, he suspected they had begun to circulate among the band along with the consistent flow of booze. He was, however, asked to use his knowledge of the Parisian underground to find high-class call girls for the band's amusement. The security agent was surprised, however, that John wouldn't take part in the group's more carnal pastimes, adamant that the drummer was more apt to drink and pass away the hours until he could be back home in the United Kingdom with Pat and Jason at Old Hyde.

"[John] could be the most generous guy and the worst guy," Gautier later recalled. "Bonzo would cry talking about his family. Then the roadies would start to push him to do something, and he'd go crazy. . . . He had no natural defense against being manipulated, and nothing to protect him." According to Gautier, even John's bandmates weren't immune to winding his key. Jimmy would find it amusing to influence John in dumping food and drinks on unsuspecting people, and even mild-mannered John Paul Jones would occasionally get in on the fun. "I would say that [Jones] was the most mischievous in the band," Gautier recalled. "He was the kind of person who enjoyed mind games. He might say, 'Hmmm, Jimmy seems tense. Wouldn't it be funny if someone threw a firecracker at him?' And of course, John Bonham would then throw the firecrackers at Jimmy."

There was one memorable incident with John, however, that nearly brought the two men to blows. The drummer was known at least to indulge in some of the drugs and had once offered a large line of cocaine to Gautier back in his room. Dipping his face to the powder, the world-weary Gautier instantly recognized it to be heroin—a far more deadly substance to snort. "It's smack!" Gautier yelled angrily, knowing he could have just ingested a lethal dose. He was shocked that John's only response was a fit of laughter that brought him, rolling, to the floor in hilarity. "He thought that was the funniest thing, offering you coke and giving you smack. He would take a chance on killing you!" Gautier admitted. The next day, however, John demonstrated his sober, generous side by literally giving Gautier the shirt off his back.

Although Zeppelin had continued to outsell many of their peers and the concert tours had become only increasingly profitable, the band and Grant agreed that finally addressing their status within the mainstream media was long overdue. With the American leg of the tour coming up—and with damage control becoming more necessary amid the group's frequent forays into debauchery—Grant and Jimmy decided that someone a little more hands-on was required over "Beep" Fallon's meager news briefs and interview bookings. With this tour, Led Zeppelin needed to rival the Rolling Stones in every way, and that included media coverage.

The group was told to be on their best behavior for two guests who would be arriving from New York to see their second night in Paris: the first man, midfifties in a conservative suit and tie; the second, his assistant, early twenties and with a ponytail that could outflow Robert's own locks.

Lee Solters was regarded as one of the most influential show-business press agents in the United States; he counted Frank Sinatra among his roster of A-list clients. At twenty-three, Danny Goldberg had formerly worked as a music journalist for *Billboard* and written for *Rolling Stone*, and that experience, coupled with his youth, gave him a unique insight into acting as a liaison with the hip American music press. On the plane to Paris, Solters had asked his young protégé if taking on Led Zeppelin seemed like a worthwhile investment. Goldberg knew the band's music—and their reputation—very well and had even prepared for the trip abroad by researching the chronology of Zeppelin's negative coverage in the US press. He explained to his boss that, by all accounts, the band had a tremendous following of loyal fans, but they were perceived as "barbarians" by everyone else. Even *Rolling Stone* regarded Led Zeppelin as "crass" and tasteless, despite their incredible sales and popularity.

Solters had sat back in his seat and thought about it. Later that night, the two men attended the show at the Palais des Sports and watched as Led Zeppelin opened their show with "Rock and Roll." Solters noted the crowd reaction—the Parisian audience went insane. Solters leaned over to Goldberg. "You handle it," he yelled over the music.

"Before meeting the band, Lee and I had an audience with their legendary manager, Peter Grant," Goldberg later recalled. "Peter had the ultimate chip on the ultimate shoulder. . . . He understood, more than any of his peers, that artists had grown more powerful. . . . This shocked the nouveau establishment of rock promoters and agents. Many of them never forgave him, and Peter couldn't have cared less."

By way of first impressions, Goldberg was taken with how Grant's enormous physical stature—coupled with his scruffy beard, multiple silver-and-turquoise rings, and faded blue jeans—was in direct contrast to the old-world elegance of his Hotel George V suite where the preliminary meeting was being held.

"Peter said that he thought that contempt for the rock press had worked in the band's favor in the early years, but that by 1973, it was time to go the other way," Goldberg recalled. "I told him that Led Zeppelin had the reputation of being barbarians on the road. Peter laughed. 'Yeah, but we're just *mild* barbarians.'"

Although he hid it well, John felt deeply wounded by how he, in particular, was viewed in the press. Ever since the start of his professional drumming career as a teenager, technique and style were his greatest priorities; for all the misbehavior, he adored finally making a good living as a musician. The mainstream media seemed either to miss the innovations he brought to the instrument or to be making it a point of ignoring them completely. Only a few years later, John shared his frustration with drum technician Jeff Ocheltree, who recalled the seriousness with which John wanted to be taken.

"There was anger and a bitterness that was starting to form in him," Ocheltree later recalled. "In interviews, he was never asked questions about his playing, about the time signatures or patterns he used. In fact, he was never asked any intelligent questions."

According to Ocheltree, it was during those dreaded excursions away from home when John's insecurities would completely engulf him, the distance between his loved ones and the creature comforts and security of Old Hyde somehow bringing those inner demons bubbling to the surface. "I used to spend days and nights with him at the Rainbow Bar & Grill on Sunset Boulevard in LA where all the musicians and crews used to go," the drum tech later recalled. "I remember him saying to me, 'These idiots don't know anything about drums. All they want to know about is the gossip.'

"In fact," Ocheltree added, "John listened to Max Roach, Alphonse Mouzon, Elvin Jones, and a lot of fusion and jazz drummers. That's the thing that gets me about John Bonham—everybody thinks he was into big drums and hitting them real hard. Bonham was into swing and playing with technique."

But in 1973, very few serious music critics tended to notice John's genuine talents and acumen, or the fact that he was changing the way the drums were approached by rock players right before their eyes. Their ignorance was more than a source of frustration to John; at this point, it was a mounting depression.

The day of their formal introduction to Lee Solters and Danny Goldberg, the band gathered in Peter's hotel suite. Upon the Americans' arrival, only Robert seemed comfortable enough to address the group's frustrations regarding the US press, animatedly listing the band's requirements, should they indeed retain Solter and Goldberg's services.

"Look, we were very young when we first started," Robert explained. "You gotta realize I was nineteen years old, and I went crazy! I met the GTOs and my mind just snapped. I'm from a nowhere town in the Midlands, and here were these girls with bare breasts blatantly coming on, and of course we went crazy the first few tours. . . . But those days are completely over—we're adults now. We're successful businessmen. I got all that other stuff out of my system."

When it was all over, Grant smirked. "Peter asked me to explain what he bemusedly called 'the barbarian thing,'" Goldberg later recalled, laughing.

Despite having plenty of opinions on the subject, John was the only member of the group who had remained completely silent throughout the meeting. Seemingly comfortable with Goldberg's age, deeming his youth more approachable, John sidled to him once the room had cleared. "What you're saying," John half-whispered to Goldberg, "is that you're going to get us known to people who don't know us yet?" At this, Goldberg assured John that, yes, that was the idea.

"Well, then, thank God you're here," John finally said, quietly. "We're the biggest and we're the best—and no one knows it. . . . You gotta do something about this."

Goldberg later remembered, "Despite their affability, Zeppelin continued to view the rock press with suspicion. . . . Bonzo spat contempt as he referred to reviewers who had disparaged his famously long drum solos. 'Look, if Buddy Rich says I'm shit, then I'm shit, but what the fuck do those wankers know?'"

Goldberg agreed to begin his duties as the group's acting publicist the following month, coinciding with the North American tour's first stop in Atlanta. It was to be Zeppelin's most ambitious tour campaign yet: in just under three months—stopping for the briefest of breaks in the middle of the summer—the band was booked to visit thirty-three cities. Thanks to Grant's hardball efforts regarding ticket grosses, the band was set to take a cool $4.5 million. The manager was quoted in the press that the group was set to make $30 million that year alone. As their new publicist, Goldberg was going to have to come up with new synonyms for *unprecedented*.

But the Led Zeppelin mystique was only just getting warmed up. Primarily due to John and Jimmy's shared fear of flying, the band tried to drive or travel by train as much as possible. Of course, there was always the inescapable need to fly between countries, and it was during those excursions that John usually made himself blackout drunk to avoid his phobia. In an attempt to ease the band's nerves, Grant had previously chartered private planes, hoping that the little comforts would make the experience a tad more palatable. By 1973, he could do so much more.

Lo and behold: *The Starship*.

The converted jetliner was the first Boeing ever built. Redesigned and reconfigured as a forty-seat luxury plane, it was lavishly decorated in Las Vegas, bachelor pad–lounge style specifically for celebrity charter. The plane included a full-length bar, television screens, carpeting, sofas, and individual bedrooms adorned with working showers and faux fireplaces. But aside from publicly displaying the band's apparent stardom and wealth—which in and of itself was a grand PR stunt—Grant's decision to shell out the required $30,000 for the extravagant luxury airliner solved a multitude of pragmatic problems. For one, it didn't *feel* like an airplane; giving the band the psychological experience of being in their own hotel suite or apartment went far in the ways of curbing both boredom and—in the cases of John and Jimmy—the dreaded fear of flying. Of equal importance, having a private plane that also acted as a base of operations cut out the necessity of booking numerous hotels. Now, Zeppelin could literally live in the plane at a centralized airport, then commute to neighboring areas by car for individual gigs. It cut out confusion, saved plenty of time, and—last but certainly not least—eliminated the drama and steep expenses of trashed hotel rooms. Although *The Starship* would forever be associated with Zeppelin, covetous acts that later chartered it for touring included the Rolling Stones, Bob Dylan, Alice Cooper, Deep Purple, and Elton John—four times.

Zeppelin's entourage expanded, as well. Each member was assigned a roadie who would be primarily responsible for their individual needs, both for instrument care and, in most cases, for personal whims. Jimmy's tech, Ray Thomas, handled the safety and security of each guitar, while Yardbirds veteran Brian Conliffe took care of John Paul Jones's multiple instruments; Robert's assistant, Benji LeFevre, was a sound engineer initially hired for the singer's live vocal demands, but spent an equal amount of time catering to the lead singer's personal demands—as was also the case for Mick Hinton, John's longtime drum technician who was merely advanced in his title to "personal drum tech." Most often, Hinton would be the lightning rod for John's mood swings and pranks, but as a personal assistant his responsibilities—which included acting as John's "handler"—were probably the most challenging.

For example, on paper, the four assistants were supposedly the chief preconcert operators for each individual's instruments and stage props; however, Jimmy's necessities also included bottled water, cold champagne, and fresh flowers in each of his hotel suites—and it was left to Ray Thomas to guarantee all of it, on top of tuning a dozen invaluable electric guitars. As John's drum tech for the past three tours already, Mick Hinton knew the usual needed off the drummer's checklist, now also being on the hook for guaranteeing each of John's hotel rooms came furnished with a sheepskin rug—a comforting reminder of Old Hyde.

There was much riding on this tour. As the group landed in Miami to set up camp for the first gigs around the American South, the earliest US reviews for *Houses of the Holy* began to dribble in. Apparently, having a hands-on publicist like Danny Goldberg—newly christened by the band as "Goldilocks" in honor of his signature ponytail—had been a serendipitous decision for the tour: the album reviews were mixed at best, thoroughly angering the group and motivating their stage performances, hoping to make the American press eat their words.

The band kept reminding themselves that the press just didn't "get them" and not to take it personally. Besides, the sales for the album were hardly an issue; four years earlier, *Led Zeppelin II*—"the Brown Bomber"—had knocked the Beatles' *Abbey Road* from the top spot, and now *Houses of the Holy* had bested the undisputed king of rock 'n' roll himself, replacing Elvis Presley's *Aloha from Hawaii via Satellite* as number one in the country.

But even good news regarding *Houses of the Holy*'s sales couldn't completely boost band morale—especially John's. The fourth album had been an across-the-board smash hit, and weak early reviews for its follow-up planted the insecurities among the group that the uphill climb as the biggest rock band in the world had stalled.

The outpouring from fans on May 4 at the Atlanta kickoff spoke otherwise. "Zeppelin played a three-hour set without an opening act," Danny Goldberg later recalled, "[and] at some point during the middle, Peter pointed to a window that overlooked a highway in which cars were speeding by. 'Look at that,' he said to me. 'In here, people are screaming and jumping around and having the time of their life, and out there, those people in those cars don't have the slightest idea what is going on.'"

"About 7:00 pm on May 4th in Atlanta, Georgia, it would have been almost impossible to drive anywhere in the vicinity of the Atlanta Stadium because traffic was backed up for miles," claimed *River City News* writer Bill Read. "The mad rush was due to the fact that there was to be a rock concert . . . no, not just another rock concert—a Led Zeppelin concert!"

The show began, Read reported, and the audience "rose to its feet in a gesture of welcome, even as John (Bonzo) Bonham started the group off into 'Rock and Roll.' . . . [T]hree members of the group took their break as John Bonham gave a fantastic solo within the '69 head smasher, 'Moby Dick,' which was later transformed into the biggies—'Heartbreaker' and 'Whole Lotta Love.'"

On May 5, Zeppelin shattered the attendance record for Tampa Stadium. As *Times* staff writer Rock Norcross observed, "It had been nearly four years that the Led Zeppelin touched down in Tampa, drawing a near capacity crowd at the downtown Curtis Hixon Hall . . . a crowd of a little more than 7,000. Saturday night's show had more than that turned away at the door." Local police estimated sixty thousand inside the stadium, with another thirty thousand on top of that hanging around the stadium.

Michael Crites wrote for the *Watcher* that "John Bonham's drum roll brought on the high-volume magic of Led Zeppelin in 'Rock and Roll.' This was a selection from their fourth album, which is in the same class as their first masterpiece, *Led Zeppelin*."

Zeppelin had played for more than three hours, including four encores—and the crowd still wouldn't let them leave the stage. Morale surrounding the band had not only turned around but reached a peak; as motorcycle police had to escort the row of Zeppelin limousines off the stadium grounds, the group screamed and hollered their excitement out the windows. Back at the Atlanta Hilton, John ordered two brandy Alexanders from room service to start, and when they arrived, he told the valet, "You better bring us up four more." When those too were gone, he said, "Bring us up a pitcher as soon as you can." When the next round arrived, he told the room service attendant, "You better bring us two more pitchers."

About fifty-six thousand ticket-holding fans helped Led Zeppelin shatter the Beatles' long-standing record for attendance—which Danny Goldberg quickly whipped into a press release and sent out to national media outlets. Although Goldberg was sternly warned by Zeppelin's New York attorney, Steve Weiss, to refrain from printing the band's financial numbers in any more press releases, Peter Grant was quickly impressed with the young publicist's sharp instincts. A few days after Zeppelin's Tampa triumph, Grant beckoned Goldberg to his room. Goldberg waited nervously as the large man snorted a few large lines of cocaine. Finally, Grant spoke. "It would be really good if you could put something in the press about how Zeppelin was the biggest band to hit America since *Gone with the Wind*."

Not completely understanding his task, Goldberg innocently asked, "Do you want me to say that you said that?"

"No," Grant said gruffly. "I don't want to say that. I just thought it would be good for the press to say that." Goldberg went back to his own room and brainstormed, soon remembering that Sam Massell, the mayor of Atlanta, had been in attendance that night and had even requested backstage passes for his family. Surely, he wouldn't mind some additional press. On a hunch, Goldberg rang up a music journalist friend of his, Lisa Robinson, and ran the line past her. "I figured, accurately, that it was too trivial a concoction for the mayor to deny," he later recalled. "Although she had her doubts, Lisa dutifully 'quoted' the mayor in a puff piece she wrote for the British weekly *Disc and Music Echo*, which got me off the hook and immediately endeared her to Peter."

Robinson's ongoing coverage of the band was soon a major asset, as Ellen Sander's recent book, *Trips*, had finally divulged her nightmarish experience touring with the group years earlier, provoking a certain amount of fear of them among female journalists; Robinson's positive depictions of the four musicians slowly worked to change public opinion.

Goldberg had also inadvertently endeared himself to the band's members. Both Robinson's story and the initial wire-service report of Zeppelin's sell-out numbers made their way across the pond and into the UK's influential *Financial Times*, which the band's families all read. Robert ran up to Goldberg and threw his arm around him. "My dad finally believes I'm a success!" the singer gushed. "Now, he finally thinks I may have done the right thing not to become a chartered accountant."

Soon, London's *Daily Express* ran a similar story under the reassuring headline "Believe It or Not—They're Bigger than the Beatles," and Goldberg was fully accepted into Led Zeppelin's innermost circle. When John began greeting Goldberg with his customary locker-room signature—grabbing his crotch and inquiring, "How's your nob?"— the young publicist was certain he was part of the team.

By the time Zeppelin made their way to California, playing massive shows in San Diego and LA, *Houses of the Holy* had taken the number-one spot on the American charts. Taking note that sales both of the albums and for concert tickets always seemed to outshine the critics' views on Led Zeppelin's worth, Danny Goldberg hatched the idea that a younger member of the press—an actual *fan* of Led Zeppelin—could work wonders in boosting their print plaudits. In the United Kingdom, *Melody Maker*'s Chris Welch had earned the band's trust with thoughtful, serious commentary on their music; perhaps an American counterpart could be found.

Following the group's San Diego show, Goldberg found his writer. "My mantra was that whether critics liked them or not, Led Zeppelin was the people's band, the favorite of real rock fans," Goldberg later recalled. "I would note pointedly, *young* rock fans. . . . It was no coincidence that the most favorable major newspaper piece about the 1973 Led Zeppelin tour was written for the *LA Times*, whose music editor, Robert Hilburn, bought into the idea that there was a generational shift occurring in rock 'n' roll. Hilburn assigned Cameron Crowe."

Crowe was only fifteen years old when he was handpicked by Hilburn to cover the Sports Arena concert. His writing style and maturity were well beyond his years, and his enthusiasm for the bands he covered always shone through, making him an ideal voice for the very generation that actually listened to the music. "Just as hysteria reaches a peak, four musicians take the brilliantly lighted stage and the thunderous opening notes of 'Rock and Roll' blast through 33,000 watts of amplification, more wattage than the sound system used at Woodstock," young Crowe had written of Zeppelin's San Diego concert. "Zeppelin's three-hour set is flawlessly paced with a well-chosen crowd-satisfying cross section of the high-powered material that has characterized each of its five albums, all of them sellers and platinum discs."

The band was greatly impressed with the young writer. Although they declined Crowe's request to do a full feature on them for *Rolling Stone*, when the time came to reconsider, Jimmy and Danny Goldberg insisted the boy be given the assignment.

Goldberg later recalled, "After the story came out, Jimmy admiringly said to me, 'Well, I have a nickname for him—Cameron Crowbar.'" Within Led Zeppelin's world, a nickname was the highest form of trust.

"Appearing Monday night in the Sports Arena before a sold-out house of 16,000 persons who began to gather outside the entrances at noon," wrote San Diego reporter Carol Olten, "Led Zep attested to all the praises that have preceded its performance here, namely sold-out concerts all around the country and gold record sales that continue to mount. . . . Essentially, however, the set was as powerful as rock 'n' roll ever gets."

Following success in San Diego, the band arrived at LAX for their upcoming shows at the Forum when disaster immediately struck. Fans had lined the fence along the airport tarmac, screaming and hoping for a peek at Zeppelin as they disembarked from *The Starship*. In a jovial mood, Jimmy took notice of the enthusiastic fans and said to Richard Cole, "Give me ten minutes, and then we'll be on our way." Reaching through the wire fence to sign autographs, Jimmy snagged a finger on his right hand. "Oh shit!" he shouted, quickly turning away and heading to the waiting limousine. "I think I'm in trouble," he said to Cole. The finger was indeed sprained, leaving the virtuoso guitarist out of commission for almost a week. With no other choice, the first of the two Forum shows was pushed ahead for later in the week. Jimmy kept his hand submerged in ice water all the next day, suffering through the second Forum show on May 31.

He couldn't miss out on John's twenty-first birthday.

"Good evening!" Robert said into the microphone. "This is Bonzo's birthday party! I've known him for about fifteen years, and he's been a bastard all his life!"

As Charles Shaar Murray reported, "Suddenly the lights explode, and there they are. John Paul Jones with shortish hair, moustache and five-string bass, looking almost as if he'd just left the Eagles, Page bare-chested in black velvets sparingly sequined, carrying a business-like Les Paul, Bonham settling in behind his kit to check it out, and leonine Robert Plant in flowered shirt and jeans."

They had opened with "Rock and Roll." The Forum crowd went crazy for the revamped set list, and it wasn't until hours into the show that Robert finally divulged that Jimmy had sprained his finger, garnering an arena's worth of applause. Inspired by the outpouring of appreciation, Robert looked at the crowd and told them, "Here's a song about you," leading off Jimmy's thunderous opening riff of "The Ocean."

Afterward, the ocean itself sang "Happy Birthday" to John before the band launched into their first encore, the obligatory "Whole Lotta Love."

Immediately after the show, the band darted to their limos and headed off to the Laurel Canyon home of an FM radio-station owner, who, along with Atlantic Records' Tony Mandich and New York FM disc jockey J. J. Jackson, hosted a star-studded birthday party for John high up in the Hollywood Hills.

"A videotape machine is showing 'Deep Throat' continuously while the stereo fills the house with Johnny Winter, the Stones, Humble Pie, and Manassas. Roy Harper, one of the new people who Zep acknowledge as an influence, is there, as is Jimmy Karstein who distinguished himself during the Clapton gig at the Rainbow, and B. P. Fallon, who's flown halfway around the world since this morning when the band phoned him at Michael De Barres' place," wrote Nick Kent. An unexpected surprise was in store for John, as George Harrison swung by with wife Pattie Boyd. The former Beatle admitted to a fascination with Led Zeppelin—particularly their apparent ascent to superstardom and penchant for heavy rock—and had been in attendance for their show in San Diego on May 28. That night, Harrison had pulled one of the band's roadies aside and inquired who was booked to be the opening act. Told that Zeppelin didn't tour with an opener, he pressed to find out what time the intermission was set to take place. Led Zeppelin never needed intermissions.

"Fuck me!" Harrison exclaimed. "The Beatles were never onstage more than forty minutes when we were doing concerts."

But it was true; the band never needed an intermission—largely due to John's "Moby Dick" solo providing a long-enough break for the other three. And John himself didn't need a break at all.

As John was about to cut the tremendous birthday cake, George Harrison—thoroughly drunk and joyful—ran up to him, grabbed the cake's top layer, and gleefully plunged it into the birthday boy's face. Amid the crowd's laughter, John took it as a declaration of war, picking up the rest of the cake and lunging it in Harrison's direction. He missed, but got his revenge later that night, throwing both Harrison and Boyd into the enormous swimming pool. Soon, a number of the guests were laughing and pushing each other in—except for Peter Grant, whom everyone left alone out of fear he'd take a push personally, and Jimmy, who shied away, claiming he didn't know how to swim.

"Mr. Fallon's exquisite antique velvet costume was totaled by his immersion," Charles Shaar Murray added, "as was Rodney Bingenheimer's camera and a mink coat belonging to a lady named Vanessa. . . . Of the proceedings we will draw a slightly damp veil."

Originally, Zeppelin had been booked for concurrent nights at the Forum, but, due to Jimmy's injury, the first night was rescheduled for later in the week—which forced the band to fly to San Francisco on June 2 for a show and then return once again to LA for the Forum's contractual "makeup" concert on June 4.

In San Francisco, the band headlined an all-day show at Kezar Stadium for influential promoter Bill Graham, the impresario and mastermind behind both the Fillmore East and the Fillmore West. Even with his previous experience working with Zeppelin, Graham was shocked at the fan response the band garnered, especially in the few years since they'd last worked one of his venues. For the Kezar event, Graham had opened the gates for admittance at five thirty in the morning, only to find that more than three thousand dedicated Zeppelin fanatics had camped out for two nights just for the chance to see the band. Led Zeppelin was booked to take the stage in the early afternoon, after a trio of acts that included Jimmy and Robert's friend folk singer Roy Harper, followed by the band the Tubes and Lee Michaels.

On the day of the festival, however, Zeppelin ran late by an hour and a half, infuriating Graham. Roy Harper was reported to have silenced hecklers among the crowd, yelling back, "Zeppelin haven't even left LA yet, so fuckin' shut up!"

"There was not the audience warmth for Led Zeppelin that was evident last weekend when the Grateful Dead and friends christened Kezar as a super-show rock arena," Philip Elwood reported in the *San Francisco Examiner & Chronicle*. "A substantial number of yesterday's crowd (perhaps half) had bought tickets in agencies away from the immediate Bay Area and they were here to have a high time with the Zeppelin, not necessarily to generate the communal-like performances by locally based groups."

To compensate their patient fans, when the band arrived they played for more than three hours—then headed backstage to confront the promoter in person. As stern a businessman as Peter Grant, Graham had been irritable from the beginning, angry over the amount of money Led Zeppelin commanded for the performance; the *San Francisco Examiner & Chronicle* reported that the band had "picked up better than $1,000 a minute for their two-and-a-half hour show." As a result, there was already bad blood between him and the Zeppelin manager, which carried over to their interactions throughout the afternoon and night. As a show of authority, Graham had denied the band's recently hired photographer, Neal Preston, access to the stage midshow, further irritating Grant. As retaliation after they'd left the stage, the band set John loose, prodding the Beast to dump a bucket of ice water over the promoter's head. Graham was furious, but was too intimidated by the combination of Peter Grant, Richard Cole, and John Bonham to take the issue any further. But Graham's day for revenge against all three would eventually come.

"Much of Zeppelin's musical strength comes from the drive of their rhythm section with John Bonham," Michael Wale wrote in the *Los Angeles Times*, "a strident timekeeper on drums, who even provides the rest of the group with a 20 minute interval while he plays solo on stage halfway through their performance. He has the strength of the best white American drummers."

The reporter noted Zeppelin's ongoing frustrations with the American press, drawing as an example the known animosity between the band and arguably the country's most influential pop-culture magazine. "In America, they are conducting a splendid two-way war with Rolling Stone, that one-time leader of the alternative press, which has now become almost part of the Establishment it used to attack. Rolling Stone had a go at Zep and when I was with the group at a concert in San Francisco, the home-town of Rolling Stone, Zep attacked boldly from the stage, bringing a roar of support from the 53,000 spectators. . . . They continued the battle the next night at the Forum in Los Angeles. The second half of the American tour is unlikely to bring a peace treaty."

Wale added, "Led Zeppelin are the ultimate in heavy metal music."

Back in LA, the band took up their regular place as the kings of the eleventh floor. Jimmy stayed locked away with regular sweetheart Lori Maddox, while John and Richard Cole took turns riding their Honda motorcycles up and the down the halls. When not racing along the stairwells, John and some of the roadies passed the time in their usual fashion: trashing the rooms and throwing furniture and televisions out the windows.

"They were tired," Danny Goldberg later recalled of the band's behavior. "One of the stories that doesn't get told was how many times there weren't wild parties, and how lonely and exhausted they could get."

On top of the boredom and exhaustion, the band was also nervous regarding their safety. With each tour had come more misbehavior—not just on their part, but on the fans' as well. Each concert was a hotbed for riots, violence, and drug- and alcohol-induced mayhem. Peter Grant was also concerned about the death threats that seemed to mount against the band as their popularity and stardom grew—Jimmy, in particular. This time in America, Grant had been so concerned, he was driven to hire a fleet of private security guards, keeping them posted outside Jimmy's suite during their entire stay in Los Angeles.

"Led Zeppelin was always the focus of death threats," Danny Goldberg recalled later. "The '73 tour was the first time that significant death threats had been directed toward Led Zeppelin, so it was taken very seriously. . . . Later, the death threats became routine."

The tour wound down with a series of well-received shows. "Nobody so far has reached the level of extravaganza shown by the Led Zeppelin in concert last night at the Seattle Center Coliseum," Patrick MacDonald reported in the *Seattle Times*. "Smoke, fire, strobes, sparklers and rockets filled the stage at one time or another during the group's nonstop three hours of music. Not to mention the three-story banks of lights and speakers that surrounded the four performers and the mirrored panels behind them. . . . John Bonham, the drummer, displayed supernatural strength by lasting the full three hours without a rest, even after an energetic drum solo that must have last 20 minutes. . . . It was quite an experience."

In Boston on July 20, *Herald* writer Peter Hearst couldn't help but notice the band's exhaustion with audience behavior, which had degraded as a whole by the madness of 1973. "Led Zeppelin were somewhat appalled by the goings-on, but like the true professionals they were, continued to [play]. . . . Finally, the group played what everyone had been waiting for, the anthem of heavy-metal music—'Stairway To Heaven.' One of the classic songs of rock, 'Stairway' helped to nurture the hard, heavy, violent music currently prevalent, which serves as such a suitable backdrop for the doings of a violent audience."

As profitable as the first leg of the US tour had been, when the band returned home for the month of June, all four members let out a collective sigh of relief.

Chapter Sixteen

JULY 1973–JANUARY 1974

One afternoon, Peter Grant called Danny Goldberg into his office. There, the young executive found himself surrounded by the entire band, lined up and waiting for him. They claimed there was an issue that needed addressing. "We're sick and tired of seeing photos in the papers that don't include Bonzo and Jonesy," Jimmy said. "This is a four-person band, and I don't want this happening anymore." John nodded in agreement, and Goldberg quickly understood the request came at the drummer's insistence.

As Grant flirted with the idea of banning photographers from the concerts—a public relations nightmare in Goldberg's eyes—they struck an agreement that the young executive could scout for an "official" tour photographer, someone who would take the photos the way the band desired. He quickly contacted Neal Preston, an up-and-coming rock photographer who specialized in concert pictures. Preston was quickly making a name for himself with brilliant backstage candid shots of the performers.

"The first time I shot Led Zeppelin was way before I worked for them," Preston later remembered. "I was eighteen years old, and I guess I was a senior in high school at the time. They had done a press conference, which later became famous, when the *Melody Maker* readers' poll was announced, and they were named 'best rock band in the world' for the first time. . . . The Beatles had won that something like six times in a row, and Zeppelin taking over was a big deal, so there was a press conference. I knew the PR people, and I found myself in the front row shooting Jimmy and Robert. Later that same day, they played Madison Square Garden, and I shot that show."

Two years later, Preston had partnered with another New York freelancer, Andrew Kent, who would go on to become David Bowie's official photographer. In the early 1970s, the team shared retainer with Atlantic Records, wherein one of them would have to remain on call in case the record label needed spur-of-the-moment photo coverage for an event or concert. As Preston recalled, "I did some more work for Zeppelin through that deal. I had known Danny Goldberg for many years, and soon after, I got to know Peter Grant."

Preston continued, "I had heard early on that the band wasn't going to do television, so their still photos were going to be of prime importance. When it looked as if the band was going to take on their own official photographer, I said to Danny, 'I'd love to throw my hat in the ring.' A couple of months later, I heard from him, and he said, 'Are you still up for it?'"

"Neal got access other photographers didn't get in return for the band's right to disapprove any photos they didn't like, as well as the right to use any of them for PR or marketing purposes," Goldberg recalled. "I promised the band that Neal would spend his entire time that first night shooting pictures that included all four members. . . . To my surprise and relief, this solution was accepted by Peter and Bonzo, and the meeting abruptly ended."

"As a photographer, I try to be as invisible as possible," Preston later recalled. "I used to try and hide behind the band to get my style of shots. With Zeppelin, the trick in remaining invisible was to be *very* visible—letting them see you doing your thing, and becoming part of the fabric of the tour. . . . They would become comfortable with you, and that was the irony: if you wanted to be invisible, you would have to be present all the time."

That night, Preston arrived at Chicago Stadium for his first assignment as Zeppelin's official photographer. Only three songs into the set, he was having difficulty getting the types of action profiles the band wanted, primarily due to the dim lighting surrounding the rhythm section of John and Jones. He frantically searched for Goldberg backstage, shouting over the music that Jimmy and Robert were perfectly lit, but he could not get the other two.

Not wanting to disappoint the group, Goldberg, Preston, and Richard Cole located the lighting engineer and explained their predicament and asked if the lights on John and Jones could be raised for a single song to create a photo op. "The lighting guy looked at me as if I were insane," Goldberg recalled. "He explained to me that 'the bright lights are on Jimmy and Robert. That's always been the way it's always been, that's the way it is, and that's the way Jimmy wants it,' and walked off."

Goldberg and Preston expected to incur John and Grant's wrath, but by the next day John had forgotten the whole thing.

According to John Paul Jones, while the lighting arrangement was one matter, the band took their stage positions deliberately for optimal collaborative purposes. "I always used to start the show fairly near the front of the stage, and then during the first number, I'd move back and end up underneath John's ride cymbal," Jones remembered later. "That was my favorite place, because I could feel that bass drum, rather than rely on the monitors. And of course, I could see John from under the cymbal because he was on a drum riser, and I could look up at him. . . . You'd have to watch each other for cues. There was a lot of eye contact."

Learning the personalities of the four performers, some of the road crew found their stage behavior amusing. "When there was no singing, it was almost like Jimmy wouldn't let Jonesy near Bonzo because it was about him and Bonzo," recalled Robert's voice technician and assistant, Benji LeFevre. "[Jimmy] stood in front of the drums the whole time. He would direct Bonzo and suggest where to go. Jonesy would just be standing there and following along because he was such a fucking brilliant musician, he could handle anything.

"I think the telepathy between Jimmy and Bonzo as musicians almost extended to the drug taking," LeFevre added. "It was like, 'I wonder how fucked up we can get and still play.'"

As Led Zeppelin's official photographer, Neal Preston was now an integral cog in the wheel that kept the machine running, and, as he later recalled, the methods to get the group's press materials prepared from city to city was like a well-oiled machine. "How it was set up was very interesting," Preston said. "We would have a 'base' in certain cities, since the band had their own plane. . . . After every show, on the next 'off day,' I would put all the film into bags for the local labs we were using. We had a lab in New York, a lab in Chicago; we had one in New Orleans. So, I would get back to the room, and I'd have sixty rolls of film or so, and I'd have to write up the processing instructions, and the labs would be notified up front that they were going to get something important dropping in their 'night' drop box—and I would order six contact sheets for every single roll. Richard Cole would then give me the use of one limo for one hour after the show, so I could rush to the lab. I was not to be picking up girls in the limo; I was not to take the limo on a joyride—I only had one hour, so, it was always rush, rush, rush!"

If all went smoothly, Preston would have a delivery from the local lab by breakfast the following morning. He recalled, "There would always be a knock on my hotel room door, and it would be all the developed negatives, the six copies of each proof sheet, all the slides—and I would rarely sleep, averaging maybe forty-five minutes to an hour of sleep during the tours. So, then I would have to collate everything and make up five different envelopes: one for each band member, one set for Peter, and then one set for me to keep. I would go around and slip the envelopes under the door of each band member's suite. I never found out what happened after that, unless there were comments or notes—but I know that Jimmy kept everything and, to this day, I believe, has a complete set."

Aside from his camera and lighting equipment, Preston began traveling with a Kodak carousel projector, complete with the circular tray. "It would hold maybe eighty color transparencies at a time," he recalled, "and we could then decide which shots would get used in print. . . . I realized many years later that I'm really addicted to deadlines—I'm a deadline junkie."

With the team of Danny Goldberg handling press and Preston supplying all the band's official images, by 1973 Led Zeppelin had taken complete control of their media output.

The second wing of Led Zeppelin's North American tour was a grueling marathon of sixteen shows in nineteen days, leaving very little rest for the weary—but the end was in sight. After a full month back home in the United Kingdom, the group had to push forward only for the month of July.

While home Robert had finally made good on his old plan to purchase another farm—this one a sheep farm on the Welsh coast. Jimmy had allowed his hand the needed time to heal, spending a restful four weeks in his new abode—the famed "Tower House" in the Kensington section of London, for which he had outbid rock 'n' roll rival David Bowie. Formerly actor Richard Harris's home, each room of the majestic manor was designed to signify an all-encompassing, artistic theme: the ocean, the stars, the earth itself—and for such a cerebral fortress Jimmy was grateful, as he was under strict doctor's orders to leave his guitars alone for the entire four weeks. By the time the band touched down in Chicago on July 6, Jimmy's hand seemed to be back in proper working order.

Before the first leg of the tour months earlier, the band had been approached by experimental filmmaker Joe Massot. He had pitched an unusual concept to Peter Grant: a concert film of the group, interspersed with footage of the individual members at home with their families and then seen in dreamlike symbolic vignettes representing their innermost passions and dreams. Massot had previously made an art-house rock western called *Zachariah*, and, in retrospect, his ideas for a Led Zeppelin film didn't seem too outlandish; such an offbeat concert film could be seen as an extension of the band's theatrical live show. Nonetheless, Grant deemed the ambitious film format too expensive and time-consuming and initially turned Massot down. As the year went on, however, both the band and its manager reconsidered the potential in having a big-budget concert film in the can for future use, perhaps to take the place of a tour should the band require extended time away from the stage. In order to move ahead with the investment, Grant had coordinated for Massot and a film crew to meet with Zeppelin for the final three dates of the US tour.

Led Zeppelin and crew were joined by B. P. Fallon, whom Grant still retained for UK-based PR, and Massot's cameramen. From *The Starship* at Newark Airport, the full entourage would travel together to a given night's concert.

In New York, the band was booked into the Drake, another grand palace of a hotel situated on Madison Avenue. Massot would be filming their shows at Madison Square Garden, as well as the concerts slated for Baltimore and Pittsburgh's Pirates Stadium.

The Garden was saved for last. Because Massot had been contacted by Grant at the last minute, his crew and equipment had been hastily assembled. Without the meticulous shooting schedule usually required for such an ambitious film, the crew let the cameras roll aimlessly, mandating endless reshoots for continuity and mere narrative cohesion. Before the film was ever completed, sights of John Paul Jones's shirts changing from performance to performance were noticeable, and Jimmy, who had gotten his hair cut, would be forced to don a wig to match up various shots of footage. Cameras were rolling during the New York performance when, as would live forever in infamy, the band was robbed of $200,000 from the hotel safe.

According to Richard Cole, Led Zeppelin usually traveled with huge sums of cash, dubbing the amount "petty funds" for emergencies or last-minute necessities; reasons could run the gamut, from additional musician equipment, such as a replacement guitar for Jimmy, to large quantities of drugs for everyone. As the Madison Square Garden shows were the final stops on the tour, Zeppelin's cash stash was flush, Grant opting to keep more money on hand than usual to pay Massot and his crew. He would regret the decision later.

"I went down to the safe at two or three in the morning after one of the concerts," Richard Cole later recalled, "to get some money for a guitar that Jimmy wanted to buy, and the money was there then. Then, we slept all day. Then, on the night of the last show, when I went to get the money to work out the amounts at the Garden, when we were just about to get into the limousines, I opened the thing and there was fuck-all in there. There was no money, just the passports. I fucking screamed."

Panicked, but aware that the Federal Bureau of Investigation (FBI) would be summoned for such a large money heist, the dutiful road manager sneaked into all four band members' hotel suites and eliminated as much of their drugs as he could find. When the federal agents eventually arrived, even Cole was interrogated regarding his whereabouts, as well as administered a polygraph test. He passed.

During the Garden concert, however, the band was completely unaware of the drama unfolding backstage. Danny Goldberg noticed Cole's absence as the band played "No Quarter," then became aware of everyone's growingly suspicious behavior: the regularly irritable Peter Grant appeared even more agitated in a quiet conference with Atlantic head Ahmet Ertegun.

Knowing that the night's performance was meant for the concert film, the band thoroughly hammed it up onstage. For the occasion, John Bonham had swapped out his floor tom-toms between sixteen-, eighteen-, and twenty-inch sizes and made his "Moby Dick" solo particularly theatrical, drumming with his hands in conjunction with dub-style pedal effects, hammering out unique melodies and riffs on his ride and crash cymbals—as well as the massive symphonic gong.

As John began his solo, the band went backstage for their usual half-hour respite. There, Grant informed them about the robbery. More surprised than angry that anyone would dare steal from them, the band kept their emotions in check for the movie cameras. Jimmy later admitted, "It had reached a point where we really couldn't care that much."

Back onstage, "Moby Dick" was coming to its thunderous, crashing crescendo. As expected, the New York crowd went crazy for John's theatrics—but not as crazy as John himself once he ducked backstage and was told of the theft. "If we do a press conference," he yelled, "we'll bloody well lose both ways! If we make it like we care too much, they'll say we're only in it for the money. If we say we don't care, they'll say it's because we're too rich!"

Danny Goldberg later recalled, "The next morning, I was summoned to Peter's hotel room to help him deal with TV crews and reporters, who were gathered in the lobby. I asked him if he wanted me to call Atlantic's PR department, and he snapped that he didn't want the fucking label there; he wanted me to organize the press conference. . . . [T]he *New York Daily News* ran a boldfaced page-1 headline saying, 'Led Zep Robbed.' Lee [Solters] looked at me approvingly in the morning and said, 'You see—if we hadn't done all that work, they would have said, "Rock Band Robbed."'"

During the press conference, Peter Grant was asked why the band carried so much cash. He innocently explained the money was to keep *The Starship* on retainer. Further pressed if Led Zeppelin was insured for such a theft, Grant barked, "No, we love America!"

They did—but were nonetheless sick of it. No arrests were made in the robbery, and none of the $200,000 was ever recovered.

Led Zeppelin flew home early the next morning.

"Late in the summer of 1973, John was recuperating after a grueling thirty-six-date tour of America," Mick Bonham later recalled.

Indeed, the older Bonham was exhausted and hadn't had nearly enough time to enjoy the pleasures of his home at Old Hyde Farm, his cars, his boat, his bulls—particularly his new prized Hereford stud, Bruno—or his family and friends. "It was during the time we spent building 'the Old Hyde' that John regained his love of fishing," Mick

Bonham recalled. "On several occasions, he would arrive on site to see if Matt and I fancied a day's sport on the riverbank."

During September, John and Robert also took time to visit with their old Birmingham friends Tony Iommi and the other members of Black Sabbath, who were putting the finishing touches on their fifth album at Morgan Studios in Willesden, North London. John and Robert had recorded some of *Led Zeppelin II* there only years before and looked forward to surprising their old mates.

"When the guys from Zeppelin visited us while we were recording *Sabbath Bloody Sabbath*, we had a jam together," Iommi later recalled. "Bonham wanted to play one of our songs, I think it was 'Sabbra Cadabra,' but we said, 'No, we're playing our songs already. Let's just jam and play something else.'"

John and Robert did hang out for the afternoon, and tapes rolled as the two bands collaborated on an impromptu blues fest. "I don't know if any tapes exist of that," Iommi admitted. "That would've been a different one—*Black Zeppelin*! It's the only time the two bands played together. . . . John did get up and jam with us in the early days, but Bill [Ward] never liked him playing his kit. It was his pride and joy, and Bonham always broke something."

"Oh, Bill, let me play them," John begged.

"No, you're going to break something," replied Ward.

John was insistent. "Let me have a go, Bill!"

"*No!*"

Iommi remembered, "It was always Zeppelin and Sabbath and Purple, but the rivalry was with Deep Purple, certainly later on, when we had *Paranoid* in the charts and they had 'Black Night' out. It was then, when we were both climbing the charts, that we felt real rivalry. . . . We were such good mates with Led Zeppelin that [later] they even wanted us on their Swan Song label. . . . We would have loved to have had Peter Grant as our manager, as well, but it wasn't to be."

Before leaving Morgan Studios, Iommi informed John that he was planning to marry longtime girlfriend Susan Snowdon at the beginning of November and asked his old friend to stand up as his best man.

Before September was out, *Melody Maker* readers voted Robert as the number-one male vocalist in the world, reminding the exhausted band why they had spent the bulk of 1973 working so hard: their fans adored them and always craved more. But even while being off the road, Zeppelin had band obligations in order to keep their momentum: in October, Joe Massot announced that it was time to film the dream sequences for their concert film. One by one, the filmmaker visited the band members at their private homes, allowing each to dictate what innermost passion and symbolic acts they wished filmed to represent them. Jimmy led Massot around the grounds of Aleister Crowley's old estate on the shore of Loch Ness in Boleskine, directing the filmmaker to capture images of him climbing a nearby mountain; by all accounts, Jimmy's hand had healed nicely. At the precipice, Jimmy was dressed in a dark, ritualistic cloak, appearing to take the form of the Old Man of the Mountain, symbolically clutching the lantern of the hermit of the tarot, and deliberately bringing to mind the strange imagery from the inner sleeve of Led Zeppelin's fourth album, its masterpiece.

More simply, Robert wished his vignette to capture shots of him and his family frolicking at his farm in Wales and at Raglan Castle; John Paul Jones rode horseback clad as a Prince Valiant–esque knight in shining armor, finally reading bedtime stories to two of his daughters before turning out the night-light.

John wasn't one for fairy tales and considered himself most content and at peace when at home in Birmingham, surrounded by the things he most loved—Pat, his farm, and his now massive car collection. "After a couple of weeks' rest, John arrived at the farm," Mick Bonham later remembered, "[but] this time closely followed by a complete film crew. . . . He just wanted to do what he enjoyed the most, which was being on the farm with his family, playing a game of snooker down at the local Conservative Club, racing fast cars, and having a pint down his local."

The drummer's scene opened with idyllic shots of him and Pat walking hand in hand around the Old Hyde grounds, then boarding a horse and cart for a romantic country sojourn. From there, shots of John onstage at Madison Square Garden would be cut against his passions for auto racing. He had fun considering which of his vintage automobiles should be featured in the vignette, finally settling on two of his most recent acquisitions—a customized Model T Ford ice truck turned hot rod and an American-made chopper bike fitted with a British-built 650cc Bonneville engine. The hot rod, called the "Instant T," had previously won the Oklahoma Custom Car Show and was powered by a seven-liter engine with a "blower," which would propel the vehicle up to sixty miles per hour in just under three seconds.

Massot shot one of the movie's most memorable scenes in Black-pool, and it was so dangerous that local police had to be notified that a film shoot was in progress. John insisted his vignette end with him climbing into British Drag Racing Hall of Famer Clive Skilton's AA fueler race car and exploding down the Santa Pod drag strip in Podington, Bedfordshire. Action packed, the footage captured the drummer in the ideal machine juxtaposed with John's "Moby Dick" solo footage.

Never to be outdone, Peter Grant and Richard Cole appeared in the film's opening together, both dressed as machine gun–wielding 1920s gangsters, firing a hail of bullets into a barroom of sitting victims. When Massot screened a rough cut of the movie for the group, however, it was Grant who felt victimized.

Having financed the production himself, he exploded, denouncing the footage as "the worst, most expensive home movie ever made." Deeming the film unreleasable, Grant fired Massot and locked the raw footage away to be used for something later—if needed. Even Jimmy was furious; how on earth could the director have forgotten to film "Whole Lotta Love," of all things?

On November 3, John set aside the glitz, glamour, and superstardom of rock 'n' roll and Hollywood, accepting the honor to act as best man at Tony Iommi's wedding—his first of four.

Iommi later admitted how intimidated he was by his bride-to-be's family: old-money types who lived in an enormous stately mansion.

The day he had dropped by their manor to ask for Susan's hand in marriage, her parents summoned the help to roll out a cart of fancy teas and cakes, displayed among fine china teapots and tiny cups. As soon as Iommi's future in-laws requested the wedding reception take place in their home, the rock guitarist immediately feared presenting them with his list of invited guests—the members of Black Sabbath and Led Zeppelin, together in one room. "Oh, bloody hell," Iommi thought to himself. "What's going to happen when they see my friends?"

But that was a concern for another day. First, he had to get through the bachelor party—the requisite "stag night"—hosted by none other than John Bonham.

The night before Iommi's wedding, John had kept his word to try to make the night as harmless and free of crazed misbehavior as possible; they had to be up early the next day, and John himself was responsible for getting the groom to the church on time. To simplify the stag night, John hadn't invited any other guests, only him and Iommi, and a driver to cart them around the pubs of downtown Birmingham. The hours flew, and by the time the two men reached the last pub on their agenda, an old place on Corporation Street called Sloopy's, it was only minutes from closing time. Iommi was just about ready to call it a night.

"Let's go and have one last drink," John insisted.

"Right, one last drink!" Iommi later recalled. "[John] had the bloody bar lined up with twelve bottles of champagne and twelve glasses—and he said to the bartender, 'Pour them out!' I thought he was going to treat everybody in the club, but, no, he said, 'This is for you.'"

"Fuck off, John," Iommi tried to argue. "I'm getting married in the morning. If I drink that, you're never going to see me there!"

John thought for a moment. "Well, I'll drink them then," he said, knocking back the first in the row.

The two friends finished off as many drinks as they could, as Sloopy's was emptying out and the bartender was antsy to close up shop. "On our way out," Iommi recalled, "John grabbed the owner of the club around the neck, and of course the bloke fell down the stairs. He hurt himself, so he wasn't very happy. Our driver and me finally managed to get Bonham out of the club and into the car, and we took him home first."

Finally pulling up at Old Hyde at four in the morning, John searched his pockets and suddenly realized he hadn't brought his keys with him—and could barely stand. Iommi propped the huge drummer up next to him and tried the doorbell. No answer. Iommi rang again, still to no avail. When he tried the third time, he saw a bedroom light flicker on from the second story of the house. Pat, half asleep, leaned out and shouted to the two below, "He's not coming in!"

Iommi recalled, "I said, 'Pat, please, let him in. I'm getting married in the morning, and he's got to be there!'"

"'He's not coming in!'

"'Please!' Iommi yelled again.

"Finally," Iommi recalled, "Pat said, 'All right, but he's not coming upstairs then! If he's coming in, he can sleep downstairs.'"

Iommi agreed and propped John against the door, then waited for his weary wife to unlock it. In her nightgown, Pat unlatched the door and then bolted back up to the bedroom, leaving Iommi and the driver to carry John inside. Sitting him upright on a radiator, Iommi said to a belligerent John, "You're not going to make it tomorrow, are you?"

John held a thumbs-up and slurred, "Yeah, I'll be there."

The driver took Iommi back home, and as he sat in the backseat, the guitarist was sure his friend would never make it the next morning and that he'd be left at the altar minus a best man. But sure enough, the next day at eight, Iommi was just beginning to lay out his tuxedo when he glanced out the bedroom window, shocked to see a clean and sober John Bonham proudly waltzing up the driveway, all spiffed out in his top hat and tails. "He lived a good thirty-five minutes from my house, and I hadn't even had a shave or anything yet," he remembered. "I opened the door, and he was all chipped and energetic, going, 'I'm ready. Are you?'"

Iommi was feeling the effects of a massive hangover and couldn't believe John was not only on time but cheery and sober as a church mouse. In the car, they did a few bumps of cocaine, and Iommi rightly feared such behavior would set a mischievous tone for the rest of the day. He recalled, "I thought, 'Oh dear, so this is how the day is going to be!' We got to the bloody church, and, before we went in, all our lot kept disappearing behind the building, one after the other, having a line. Come back, snort, and go, 'Right!'"

According to Iommi, all the guests on the bride's side were left scratching their heads, wondering why all of the groom's friends kept disappearing outside the church—then returning, only to keep sniffing and snorting throughout the ceremony. When the group got back to the Snowdons' mansion for the reception, Iommi's musician buddies continued their frequent disappearing acts. Finally, his new mother-in-law pulled him aside and said quietly, "It's funny, none of your friends are eating . . . "

Iommi had taken one precaution in an attempt to avoid serious drama at the reception; knowing that John and Black Sabbath lead singer Ozzy Osbourne were the heaviest drinkers among the group, the guitarist had insisted that only a single champagne toast be offered, meaning no other alcohol would be served. The servers had been instructed to provide apple juice to anyone insisting on a "refill" of their champagne glass—which didn't sit well with the large group of rock stars once the deception was discovered.

Taking a sip, John immediately spat it out. "Fucking apple juice!" he yelled to everyone's amusement. The prim-and-proper Snowdon family never so much as used profanity in their home, so John's outburst garnered the expected dirty looks. According to Iommi, it was his dear, sweet old mother who improvised and saved the day. He recalled, "She said to Bonham, 'Don't worry, John—we'll go back to my house. I've got plenty of booze there.' They all sneaked off to Mum's house and carried on drinking there. . . . If it weren't for her, there would have probably been antiques going through the walls, on account of all that apple juice."

✳ ✳ ✳

DURING THE BAND'S EXTENDED HIATUS, JIMMY PAGE KEPT BUSY TIN-
kering with a number of projects, at least three of which would require the full ensemble of Led Zeppelin. Rehearsals were set to begin
soon for the group's next album, but in an attempt to streamline its
release, and to finally bring to fruition the guitarist's long-gestating
plan for a double-album masterpiece, he had begun to mix older material from as far back as Bron-Yr-Aur and Headley Grange. Spanning
a half decade, many of Led Zeppelin's outtakes were strong enough
to stand on their own, and Page figured a half-dozen new songs could
pump a solid album together.

Jimmy and Grant agreed that the release of such a massive album
from Zeppelin should be viewed as an event, a milestone for the band,
and a return to form after the mixed response garnered from *Houses of
the Holy*. The sales had been excellent, as had the tour, but still hard-
rock purists craved meatier heavy anthems. Just as the band's unanimously praised untitled fourth album had been a direct response to
the vocal naysayers of *Led Zeppelin III*, so the next album would quiet
the critics of *Houses of the Holy*.

Just as Jimmy was ruminating the possibilities for such a double album, Led Zeppelin's original five-year contract with Atlantic Records
was nearing its expiration date at the end of the year. Peter Grant was
already planning on playing hardball for much more money, but the
circumstances themselves could put the band into the unique position
for more than just a bigger cut—they were in line for more power. For
this, discussions began to lay the foundations for Led Zeppelin's own
record label.

Danny Goldberg later explained the thought process behind Zeppelin's new strategy. "The idea of a rock band being given their own
label started with the Beatles and Apple Records, followed by Jefferson Airplane's Grunt Records, Deep Purple's Purple Records, and
Rolling Stones Records," Goldberg recalled. "These labels, as well as
Zeppelin's, were, in reality, imprints funded by the artist's existing
label, which, in the case of Led Zeppelin, was Atlantic Records. The

theory was that superstars often spotted talent before A&R [artists and repertoire] people did, [and] unlike the Beatles and the Stones, Led Zeppelin wanted their label to be more than a showcase of their taste—they wanted to actually break artists."

After an all-night negotiating session between Peter Grant and Ahmet Ertegun, the Atlantic head agreed to the harsh new terms for which his label would distribute Led Zeppelin's next album—including their vanity pet projects, meaning the other acts they "discovered." In January 1974, Grant and Atlantic held a joint press conference in London to announce the launch of Led Zeppelin's new label, and, although no company name was yet divulged, the band offered some examples of acts they were planning to sign: a hard-rock ensemble called Bad Company, fronted by Paul Rodgers, the former lead singer from Free; Jimmy and Robert had been dying to sign their folk-singer friend Roy Harper, as well as 1960s iconoclasts the Pretty Things; and Grant was already grooming bluesy folk songstress Maggie Bell for a debut on the label. "We're going to work with people we've known, and we've liked," Robert explained. "It's an outlet for people we admire and want to help . . . people like Roy Harper, who is so good and whose records haven't even been put out in America."

Danny Goldberg was summoned to London to meet with Grant, who had called the young publicist at his office in New York but refused to go into detail until they were face-to-face. With permission from Lee Solters, Goldberg quickly caught a flight to Heathrow Airport, where he was immediately swept into a limousine and ensconced in Grant's country house in Sussex. Led upstairs to Grant's enormous bedroom, Goldberg reported for duty as the manager lay in repose, clothed in a nightgown and sleeping cap. "Jimmy likes you," Grant said, finally. "Led Zeppelin is being given their own label by Atlantic, and I need you to be my ambassador."

Grant was surprised when Goldberg responded that he needed a few days to think it over. "I agonized over it because of their bad reputation," he recalled. "But it felt right." He knew it would be a challenge, but Led Zeppelin was the biggest band in the world, and working for them in such a capacity could only be a lateral move for a young executive not even thirty years old. By the end of the week, he had accepted and was swiftly made vice president of Grant's Culderstead, Ltd., the holding company that would oversee Zeppelin's record label—once the band settled on a name for it.

"In addition to doing PR for the artists, I would be his day-to-day liaison to the promotion and sales departments at Atlantic," Goldberg later explained. "Since Peter was also managing the first few artists that would be on the label, he also wanted me to help plan the tours with the booking agents and promoters."

Meanwhile, Grant established Zeppelin's office on King's Road in Chelsea, a hip section of London.

The band itself prepared to record the first album for their new label, booking the preliminary rehearsals and first few recording sessions. Again, Jimmy had to put the fourth, and final, major project he'd been struggling with on hold: the soundtrack for Kenneth Anger's dark underground work in progress, *Lucifer Rising*. Upon accepting the job, Jimmy had clearly warned the director that Led Zeppelin would always be his top priority, but still Anger was beginning to lose his patience. Working on the film's score only during his rare downtime, Jimmy was slowly composing the music in dribs and drabs, although the compositions he'd been putting together were among some of his most experimental and atmospheric. He planned to bring the project with him on Zeppelin's next tour, so as to tinker with it back in his various hotel suites.

Announcing Led Zeppelin's record label launch at the beginning of 1974, Jimmy was immediately asked about the band's next album and plans to, again, return to the United States. It was no secret that the group was exhausted, but as the guitarist coyly explained, the four men had no plans of ever stopping. "We'll be together until one of us punts out," he told one reporter, adamant that only death could put an end to Led Zeppelin.

Chapter Seventeen

JANUARY 1974–NOVEMBER 1974

I t was a relief to the members of Led Zeppelin that at least half of their next album was already completed by the spring of 1974. Jimmy, the consummate perfectionist, was convinced that the tracks he'd saved over the past few years not only fitted well together, but, taken as a whole with some new songs, could also form a loose retrospective as the band's double LP.

Many of the songs carried over had been recorded using the Rolling Stones' mobile unit at Headley Grange and Stargroves. This year, however, the unit was unavailable; instead, they borrowed a similar unit owned by Ronnie Lane, bassist and founding member of the band Faces. Lane had carefully assembled the gear within the mobile unit with the help of American engineer Ron Nevison—who came highly recommended to Jimmy when it came time to assemble a loose crew. As Jimmy admitted later, "Who better to run a studio than the guy who built it?"

"I drove the Ronnie Lane mobile unit down to Headley," Nevison later recalled. "It was state of the art with a Helios console, the same ones the Stones had in their truck, sixteen tracks, like most of the big studios had."

The band met at Headley Grange in late January, planning to lay down about a half-dozen new songs to match the completed outtakes already in the can. Trouble began almost immediately, and accounts vary as to whether John Paul Jones became sick or had merely had enough of the rigors of Zeppelin's schedule; he'd told Peter Grant that he was considering quitting the band, citing not enough time at home with his family. Grant told the bassist to think things over for a few weeks but pleaded with him not to leave the band entirely. While Jones was gone, the band visited their families back home, nervous about the future of the next album. When Jones agreed to stay, all four returned to Headley Grange and the true recording sessions were resumed.

As the members of Led Zeppelin arrived at the Grange, it was apparent they were reinvigorated and well prepared, all hoping to make the recording process a faster one than it had been in the past. Robert's personal assistant, Benji LeFevre, later recalled being nervous for the band's well-being from the beginning, especially when he learned of the substances the group had brought to ensure their creativity and hyperfocus. "Bonzo and Robert arrived in Bonzo's brand-new BMW," LeFevre recalled. "'Arrggh, best fucking car I've ever had!'— and Bonzo goes, 'Here, Benj, look what I've got.' And he had a bag of about fifteen hundred Mandrax. . . . I thought, 'Well, this is gonna be a good session, isn't it?' He was handing them out like sweeties, saying, 'Don't tell Robert.' I said, 'Bonzo, you'd better fucking stash these somewhere.' So, a little later, he said to me, 'Come and look.' He'd taped them to the inside of his tom-tom—forgetting, of course, that it was a Perspex kit, so we could all see it."

Even from the start, the band was apprehensive about living in Headley Grange once again. They were older now and admittedly tired of the exhaustive explorations that had often led to the innovations of their previous albums. This time, Robert, John Paul, and especially John were keen to blast out some strong straightforward recordings and return home.

"There were very few takes, maybe six to eight," Ron Nevison recalled, "most of which were done to make minor adjustments to ensure the tempos were absolutely what they wanted and that the drum sound was correct. We'd start at one in the afternoon and end at around one in the morning. . . . I started living at Headley Grange with the band, but then I realized I would be better off not staying there. Sometimes, it would get a little crazy. For example, they'd wake me up and want me to start recording something at 4:00 a.m. or something."

Nevison also recalled that the frenetic atmosphere of the sessions could be at least partially blamed on the growing presence of drugs this time around—especially cocaine, which the band, in a clandestine manner, referred to as "Charlie." "I was pretty naive," Nevison admitted. "They kept saying, 'When's Charlie coming?' And I never met Charlie. . . . There was a decided change in the vibe after Charlie came. After a few days, I realized what was going on. At some point during the recordings at Headley, I made the decision not to stay nights there, but to lock up the truck and drive back to London at the end of each session."

In an effort to appease the antsy band, Richard Cole had opted to book the apprehensive three members of Zeppelin into nicer digs than the cold, dank Headley Grange. "When we went back to Headley Grange to do the next album, I put Robert, Bonzo, and John Paul into a hotel called the Frencham Pond," Cole remembered. "Jimmy wouldn't stay there. . . . He was quite happy in that fucking horrible old house."

With the band's first attempt at the Grange weeks earlier, it had been John Paul Jones who'd been the inadvertent cause of the delays; this time, the band became livid when engineer Nevison had no choice but to make good on another outside obligation. "I'd made a commitment to Pete Townshend to start the *Tommy* film in late January," Nevison remembered. "Because of Jonesy not appearing for a week, I had to ask at one point to leave the project, and I don't think anybody in the history of Led Zeppelin had ever quit a project before."

The engineer recalled that the band didn't take the news of his pending departure well at all. "When I called up and told them I couldn't continue," Nevison added, "they were really nasty to me on the phone. They all shouted and screamed at me, and it was very upsetting. Especially Bonham, who called me all sorts of names."

Regardless, the band pushed through, resulting in some of the hardest rock they'd yet recorded and some of the tightest playing the four had ever produced. And, in their never-ending attempts to top themselves as musicians, the album would also feature some of their most musically complex compositions, playing rings around the time-signature experimentation of *Houses of the Holy*.

The band made their second homage to Bukka White's classic "Shake 'Em on Down," opening the album with the heavy guitar-driven "Custard Pie," giving John ample room to put his signature on a rhythm and blues-like groove. Here, Robert's playful lyrics are matched with the drummer's echoing hi-hat sixteenths with their heavy emphasis on the eighth notes, doubling up on the atmosphere of echo effects.

"In My Time of Dying" was an old spiritual that had previously been recorded by, among others, Blind Willie Johnson in 1927 and Bob Dylan on his 1961 folk debut. Here, Jimmy modernized it with a dark, bluesy tone using a slide in its gradual buildup, leading to the signature Zeppelin crunch into a heavier tone. From there, the track ran more than eleven minutes, bringing out the best in each band member's jam qualities. John makes his entrance into the song using an on-beat pattern, again mixing it up with an innovative use of sixteenth-note bass-drum figures. He leads the heavy nature of the song's final two-thirds at the four-minute mark, structured smartly around Jimmy's electric lead riff and coming the closest to jazz fusion stylings than much of his previous attempts. Another minute later, as Jimmy launches into his epic solo, John works the bass drum beneath a sixteenth-note hi-hat. The lengthy track seems to lose all sense of time and space until, finally, John crash-lands with the cymbals exploding upon impact.

The hypnotic drone of "In the Light"—originally titled "In the Morning"—was presented as Jimmy's new centerpiece as maestro of the bowed guitar. Heavily inspired by his love of Eastern sounds and percussion, here the guitarist replicated the distinct voicings of harmonium and, again, the Indian *shehnai*. Robert's overtly spiritual words seemed like another layer to Jimmy's overdubbed choir effect, and the sounds themselves offered a small glimpse into the type of haunting atmosphere Jimmy had been long tinkering with for filmmaker Kenneth Anger's still-incomplete soundtrack recordings.

Rounding out the sessions, the band opted, with only few exceptions, to go a much more traditional hard-rock route: "Ten Years Gone" was Robert's love letter to an early girlfriend who'd made him choose between her and his musical ambitions; tracks "Sick Again" and the "The Wanton Song" were crowd-pleasers in the making—heavy on John's drums, but very lead-guitar oriented. Delicate compositions "Bron-Yr-Aur" and "Down by the Seaside" were among the earliest outtakes Jimmy pulled out of storage, both dating from the 1970 sessions for *Led Zeppelin III*; "Night Flight" and "Boogie with Stu" were Headley Grange leftovers from 1971. Appearing almost tongue-in-cheek by its mere appearance on the track listing, "Houses of the Holy" was, most obviously, the forgotten title track from 1973's album of the same name.

That left only a few more spots for John to really showcase his playing. Being back at Headley Grange, where the very structure of the manor and its lush acoustics had provided what was arguably John's greatest moment set to tape in 1971, "When the Levee Breaks," Jimmy had great plans for a spiritual follow-up: another drum masterpiece that would anchor the double album's entire collection of songs. However, as a double album, perhaps there would be room for two such new classics.

"Trampled Under Foot" started simply enough, with John Paul Jones playing around with a riff inspired by Stevie Wonder's "Superstition" on the clavinet. Led Zeppelin wasn't known for dance music, but thanks largely to John's distinct swinging approach to heavy playing, his groove-based drum riffs were open to such possibilities. Here, Jones embraced it head-on, presenting the band its first true funk track.

"I think I'd been listening to a lot of Stevie Wonder at the time," John Paul Jones later recalled. "We were also big fans of James Brown." And while previously "The Crunge" had been recorded as a deliberate homage to the style of James Brown, even the band admitted that the song somewhat failed as mere facsimile. "Trampled Under Foot," however, was pure Zeppelin—but in a funky vein. John was in his element experimenting alongside Jonesy, inserting some incredible triplet rolls on the clavinet and guitar turnarounds, and, at the five-minute mark, he playfully tossed out a rapid string of hi-hat notes, making new space for his drum effect, precisely one sixteenth before and after the fourth beat of each bar. Again, John was showing his abilities to play jazz funk with the best of them.

Thoroughly energized from the drumming he had produced on the song, John was ready for his own masterpiece—the anchoring epic of the new album that would surpass even "When the Levee Breaks" as the ultimate drum-driven recording.

During the preliminary sessions in January, John and Jimmy had noodled with a duet demo, with the guitarist playing in the obscure Celtic-Indian-Arabic tuning, something that Jimmy had used occasionally for his "White Summer" Danelectro solo. When Zeppelin reconvened in early February, following John Paul Jones's much-needed retreat home, Jimmy and John again returned to their demo tapes. The tuning itself suggested an epic sweep, and once Robert heard it he quickly began penning lyrics inspired by his previous journeys with Jimmy to the East.

Engineer Ron Nevison later recalled the intricate strategy that John insisted upon for the recording of his drum part. "The drum kit was set up where it had been set up for the fourth album," Nevison said. "I put mics all around it, and Bonham told me to take them down. I said,

'Well, just in case . . . ,' and he said, 'No, not just in case—take them down.' So, I took them down, and they showed me where to put the microphones where they'd used them before."

While Robert went off to finish his lyrics for the song, tentatively titled "Driving to Kashmir," the other three players laid down the entire backing track. With Jimmy's strangely soothing riffs inspired by the shifting desert sands, coupled with Jones's synthesized Arabian orchestra at the song's massive bridge, "Kashmir" became the ultimate playground for John's all-encompassing reverberated echo. Indeed, Headley Grange had proved its worth yet again.

"I'd heard that Eventide phasers sounded great on cymbals, so I brought one in for 'Kashmir,'" Nevison later added. "I only had two tracks for drums, so what I did was set up the phaser and put one of the tracks through it, just for the hell of it. And they loved it and kept it in, and that's part of the whole sound of 'Kashmir.'"

Even more so than "When the Levee Breaks," John's drums on "Kashmir" were cinematic and theatrical, echoes deep as a cathedral. Although neither Robert nor Jimmy had ever been to Kashmir, the searching vision quest suggested in the lyrics seemed to represent the city as more than a location; their Kashmir was a state of mind, as would be so eloquently implied by William S. Burroughs during Jimmy's audience with the writer in the coming year.

Once the song was wrapped, Robert had presented a poetic narrative of a long car journey in Morocco from Guelmim to Tan-Tan—the Saharan sun beating down from the piercing blue sky. The band left more confident than ever that the new album was their masterpiece. Of equal importance, the double LP would be a worthy signifier of their label's coming launch. Now, they were just anxious to return to their families. Gyl Corrigan-Devlin, a close friend to Jimmy and Robert, had been invited to swing by weeks before. Later, he recalled the emotional exhaustion of all four members—especially John. "I can remember the night when everything got a little scary for me at Headley," Corrigan-Devlin said. "I was worried about Bonzo, I think, because he'd finished the wine at dinner and then he'd stuck into the

Jack Daniel's. And that was the first time I'd spent time with him at the kitchen table, as it were. This wasn't on the road—he wasn't coming down from anything. And he would get sad at the end of the night and say he wanted to go home."

Although Jimmy would have the tracks thoroughly mixed by mid-June, it would be another year before Led Zeppelin's double album would be released. By then, however, the band had settled on a proper title—something that spoke of the organic nature of the songs and the personal touches each track represented as a retrospective of the past half decade: *Physical Graffiti*.

On February 14, John agreed to take part, along with Robert and Jimmy, in Roy Harper's "Valentine's Day Massacre" concert at the Rainbow Theatre. He and Robert took the train into London from Birmingham, getting nice and toasty drunk before the rail journey and spending the trip laughing and joking around in front of the other passengers. It was going to be a long night, so, upon arrival, they met up with Jimmy and decided to book rooms at the band's usual London stomping ground, the Blake Hotel in South Kensington; John liked to frequent the hotel's small basement bar, and the locals would cheer when he entered.

Although John and Richard Cole had grown tired of Roy Harper's persistent presence at Zeppelin's shows—he had affixed himself as a staple of their entourage for years—the Rainbow concert had a few additional incentives for making the night more worthwhile. For one, it was being recorded as Harper's eventual live LP, *Flashes from the Archives of Oblivion*. But more enticing, John would get to play onstage beside fellow wild-man drummer friend Keith Moon.

Local music critic Austin John Marshall attended the all-star event, running his *NME* review the following week. "'Too Many Moves,' a slow blues number by Harper out of Saint James' Infirmary, allowed the trio of seasoned rock and roll warriors the chance to show how laid-back they could be," Marshall wrote. "But there was no way of preventing John ('Bonzo') Bonham from doing anything he was determined to do. And what he clearly was determined to do during the third piece ('Home') was cavorting around the stage, with Harper's acoustic guitar, in a red coat, porkpie hat and black tights. In his face shone the fanatic glaze of a man determined that everybody is going to have Bonzo's good time, come what may. No-one seemed inclined to stop him, so it didn't really matter did it?"

Marshall added, "Anyway, Bonzo came into his own in the award ceremony which followed (after Robert Plant, resplendent in leopard skin lurex had come on to express his appreciation). I remember trying to tot up on my fingers the quantity of albums which Zeppelin, Who and Faces, had sold. The millions had run out of fingers when Bonzo presented five gold albums to Keith Moon."

While still in London later that week, the band convened at their Chelsea office with Peter Grant to finally decide on a name for their record label. Only semiserious about the task at hand, the group threw out crass suggestions such as Slut Records before finally reaching an agreement on Eclipse Records. However, a cursory search by Atlantic's legal department revealed that another entity already held the trademark for that name, proving the London meeting for naught.

As Zeppelin hadn't come up with a finalized name, Grant's client Maggie Bell was forced to release her debut on parent company Atlantic. After reminding the group they wanted to coordinate *Physical Graffiti* in time for their summer tour, Grant was relieved when Jimmy came up with "Swan Song." Previously, Jimmy had used the name for a lengthy acoustical composition he'd recorded at home and then reconsidered it as an alternate title for *Physical Graffiti*. As Led Zeppelin's record label, it seemed as strong a name as any.

Some of the Atlantic executives were confused, however, as the term itself suggested a "last gasp," or a finale of sorts; was the band sending the veiled message that they were through? Jimmy denied the interpretation, explaining to Danny Goldberg, "They say when a swan dies, it makes the most beautiful sound."

"Then came the parties," Richard Cole remembered. "To celebrate the launching of Swan Song, we flew to the States to host receptions at the Four Seasons in New York and the Hotel Bel-Air in Los Angeles."

The receptions were booked only a few weeks apart during May. As a label launch, the events were also meant to feature Bad Company, whose debut album would be Swan Song's first official release.

Although meant to be seen as elegant by the public—especially by rock 'n' roll standards—having the band venture to America without the usual concert itinerary cast a suspicious eye upon the band members: the Zeppelin wives weren't crazy with the idea of their husbands going with the sole agenda of hosting potentially wild parties. Danny Goldberg was ordered to write up fake itineraries, claiming the Swan Song events were planned for Denver and Atlanta, not the debauchery havens available in New York and LA.

New York was first. The band took up residence at the St. Regis Hotel, while the launch party was booked for the Four Seasons on Manhattan's Upper East Side. Grant's vision for the tasteful business affair had included swans present in the large restaurant's decorative pool; when Danny Goldberg had rented "swan geese" by a dubious animal trainer, however, Grant went crazy. "We all fucking live on farms!" he yelled. "Who are you trying to kid? Get these geese out of here!"

Taking this as their cue, John and Richard Cole giddily rounded up the birds and turned them loose on the pedestrians of Park Avenue.

Led Zeppelin may have thrown a lush gala luncheon to give the world a new image of them as young entrepreneurs—each member spiffed up in suit and tie—but it was a guise none appeared comfortable with during the event itself. As two hundred guests and media personalities mingled, met the members of Bad Company, and devoured expensive finger foods and pastries shaped like swans, Jimmy, Robert, John Paul, and John sat by themselves in a corner and drank, waiting for nightfall.

John was properly smashed by the time the party was over. The Swan Song luncheon wasn't his scene; his evening plans with Robert and Peter Grant were much more his speed. Mott the Hoople was playing at the Uris Theatre on Fifty-Fourth Street, featuring Queen as their opening act. The three men piled into one of Zeppelin's many limos and headed over to the show, John already belligerent when they arrived at the theater. As bigger stars than the headliners, the three needn't tickets or backstage passes, but when John insisted on going out onstage to take over from Mott the Hoople's drummer, Dale "Buffin" Griffin, things took a decidedly ugly turn.

"John Bonham was prodding me," Griffin later recalled. "I was in awe of him, and he was out of his head. In the end, I had to hide in the toilet because he kept following me around."

Mott the Hoople's front man, Ian Hunter, later remembered what a scene John caused. "It got pretty ugly," he said. "That's all we needed—our first night on Broadway, and there were pitched battles going on. Robert Plant and I just headed for the dressing room."

By all accounts, John had instigated the altercation after being denied access to the stage. It only escalated as the headliners got ready to meet their crowd, as drummer Griffin remembered. "Eventually, there was a scuffle, and one of [Led Zeppelin's] road crew booted me in the knee just before we went on," he recalled. "My knee went up like a balloon. It was our first night, and we wanted it for ourselves. . . . It was horrible playing with Bonham in the wings. I was painfully aware of his prowess as a drummer and quite froze, feeling more and more inadequate."

Ian Hunter added, "I remember I was walking out on the stage after the show, and Zep's manager, Peter Grant, came up to me as he was leaving and whispered in my ear, 'Sorry about that.' I think it's the only time Grant apologized for anything in his life."

Following a violent fistfight, Mott the Hoople's road crew had to toss John out of the theater and into the street.

On to LA and the Riot House.

"Hundreds of Zeppelin fanatics just assumed that we'd be congregating at the Riot House—and so they did, too," recalled Richard Cole. "The lobby was swarming with photographers with their cameras cocked and excited and with tawdry girls."

During the band's previous visit to Los Angeles, Peter Grant had taken the initiative of increasing their security measures, having a

round-the-clock armed guard posted at Jimmy's suite. This time, at
the suggestion of Led Zeppelin's new head of security, Bill Dautrich,
each member of the group would be bestowed with the same treatment. Zeppelin had already taken up the Continental Hyatt's ninth
floor, as well as sections of the tenth and eleventh floors, but now each
member got a corner suite and a personal guard—usually an off-duty
cop looking for extra pay. Although such measures were intended to
set the band's collective minds at ease regarding their safety, having
such drastic protocols in place only increased their anxiety about being so far from home.

The West Coast Swan Song party was booked for a few days later
at the Hotel Bel-Air. With some time to kill, Peter Grant and Richard Cole brainstormed activities to pass the time, while keeping the
mayhem and destruction to a minimum, if possible. Grant contacted
the band's promoter, Jerry Weintraub, and requested if one of his
other clients might be available to meet with Zeppelin, as they were
huge fans; after pulling a few strings, Weintraub agreed that, yes,
the king of rock 'n' roll himself, Elvis Presley, would be delighted to
meet Led Zeppelin.

This was one of the rare trips to LA when Zeppelin wasn't booked
to appear at the Forum; this time, however, Elvis was playing there
and was lodging nearby. Behind closed doors, Elvis had vented his
frustration to his closest confidants, the so-called Memphis Mafia entourage kept on the Presley payroll just to keep him company: he was
aware that the younger, sexier Led Zeppelin boys were outselling
him in both album numbers and ticket sales and had agreed to entertain them at his hotel suite mainly out of morbid curiosity. Lately, he
had even been known to quip, "Well, I may not be Led Zeppelin, but
I can still pack 'em in."

On the flip side of the scenario, John, Jimmy, and Robert were
giddy as schoolboys at the opportunity to finally meet one of their
genuine childhood heroes. Robert, in particular, had spent hours as
a kid back in the Midlands practicing his Elvis hip swivels in front
of the mirror; Jimmy had long idolized Elvis's lead guitarist, James

Burton, and John had long ago listened to Elvis's Sun Studio hits with younger brother Mick.

Prior to their audience with the king, Jerry Weintraub laid down the ground rules, first of which was that under no circumstances were they to discuss music. Also, Elvis was a "good ol' boy"—a country gentleman, as it were—so no foul language in his presence.

At the hotel, the band was shown into Elvis's suite by one of his many unnamed Memphis Mafia bodyguards. Waiting in the lush living room was Elvis, seated with his girlfriend of the moment, Ginger. As the band entered, the king deliberately ignored them, letting moments pass as he finished up some business and allowing the dramatic tension to mount. For the first time ever, Led Zeppelin was speechless.

Finally, the king turned his attention to Zeppelin. "These stories I keep hearing about you boys on the road," he said suddenly. "Are they true?"

The three young men exchanged nervous looks. Finally, Robert spoke up first. "Nah, of course not!" he said, giggling. "We're family men! What I like is to wander the hotel corridors, singing *your* songs." And, breaking the first of Weintraub's rules, Robert began to sing Elvis's own 1956 hit "Love Me." Amused, Elvis merely joined in—and the tension was over. Then Elvis gave the men the crowning achievement of compliments, admitting that he liked "Stairway to Heaven."

Naturally shy, John did the least amount of speaking, allowing Robert and Jimmy to talk shop with Elvis while he silently considered what common ground he could offer. As the topic turned to Elvis's love of fine automobiles, John was finally confident enough to chime in and, to the amusement of his two bandmates, ended up monopolizing the conversation as he and Elvis compared their favorite vehicles—hot rods, collectible vintage models, and motorcycles. The king was particularly impressed that John knew the models Elvis had driven in specific films.

When it was over, Elvis shook the hands of all three men and showed them to the door. Just before they exited, overjoyed and smiling, Elvis remembered something and quickly stopped them. His daughter, Lisa Marie, had wanted her daddy to bring home Led Zeppelin's autographs.

※ ※ ※

THE SECOND SWAN SONG LAUNCH PARTY WAS BOOKED FOR MAY 10 at the Hotel Bel-Air.

Grant and the band had provided Danny Goldberg with a long "wish list" of the Hollywood elite for him to invite to the exclusive patio party. Grant and Jimmy had envisioned themselves hobnobbing with the likes of Warren Beatty, Robert Redford, and Jane Fonda— primarily to rival the Rolling Stones. Of the dream list, the biggest Hollywood legend to agree to come was Groucho Marx. However, fellow rock stars Bill Wyman and Roxy Music's Bryan Ferry swung by.

Inspired by the kindness shown by Elvis Presley only days before, John approached Ferry and asked if he could have his autograph to give Jason when he returned to Old Hyde.

As had been the case at the Four Seasons in New York, Zeppelin was thoroughly bored having to play hosts and slumped off into a corner to drink by themselves. They were, however, in awe of Groucho Marx and sent Danny Goldberg over to ask him for his autograph. During the party, Jimmy had his hands full. Only hours before, Bebe Buell—Jimmy's new West Coast girlfriend whom the guitarist had interloped from fellow rocker Todd Rundgren as a replacement for Lori Maddox—arrived at the Riot House and took up with Jimmy in his suite. Maddox found out and, enraged at being spurned, spent the evening at both the Bel-Air and the after-party at the Rainbow Bar & Grill attempting to confront Jimmy for his behavior.

None of the band thought much of the party after they returned home to England; the four were actually quite relieved to be back on their native soil, as traveling halfway across the globe to *spend* money was quite different from touring all over the country *making* money. Unfortunately, a few weeks later, *Melody Maker* ran an article about the dual Swan Song soirees—and the dramatic confrontation between

Jimmy and his former girlfriend Lori Maddox at the Rainbow—featuring a large photo of Robert with a lovely young woman who was not his wife. Maureen Plant was not amused. When Peter Grant called Danny Goldberg in a fit of rage, relaying Robert's unhappiness and demanding to know how the photos had leaked out to the media, the young vice president appealed to his boss's sense of logic. "If the band wants privacy," Goldberg had said innocently, "they shouldn't hang out in places like the Rainbow on the Sunset Strip."

Perhaps inspired by Danny Goldberg's keen observation, the band kept a low profile for the rest of the summer. On September 1, Jimmy flew from London to appear alongside Swan Song protégés Bad Company at a concert in Austin, Texas. Two weeks later, he joined up with Robert and John to attend a massive show at Wembley Stadium: his and Robert's beloved Joni Mitchell, in concert with Crosby, Stills, Nash & Young.

The morning of the concert, John rang up an old motor-enthusiast friend of his from Birmingham, David Hadley, and told him Zeppelin had an extra spot in the royal box. Hadley had formerly worked for the *Birmingham Post* but now ran a company selling automobile supplies in Bromsgrove and shared many of John's own interests—fast cars, big-band music, and snooker. Aware that the much-hyped show was the hottest ticket in town, Hadley had told his wife, "I'm just popping out to see a show with John—I'll see you later," and ran off to meet up with his superstar friend.

John picked Hadley up in his Range Rover, and the two drove into London, arrived early, and were seated in the VIP section. Inspired by the folk-rock atmosphere, John had dressed in his country best—a debonair tweed suit and cap, looking more like a turn-of-the-century squire on a fox hunt than a member of the biggest rock band in the world.

After about fifteen minutes at the bar, the concert's first round of opening acts was due to start, and John and Hadley were notified that the bar was getting ready to close for a hiatus during the performance. "That's no good," John said to his friend. "We're going to be here all day." Knowing he'd never make it through a long day's worth of music without the proper amount of liquor, he quickly ordered a full case of lagers. "And while you're at it," he told the bartender, "give us that gallon bottle of Scotch whiskey from behind the bar."

During the afternoon, John and David played bartenders themselves from their seats in the royal box, dispensing the whiskey from the gallon jug to visitors. The opening acts for the concert included such big names as the Beach Boys, Joe Walsh, and Carlos Santana and so had attracted many English stars who had never seen the American performers in person. As arguably the biggest name in the entire arena, John, Jimmy, and Robert received their fair share of visitors, including Jeff Beck Group's former lead singer, Rod Stewart, who had since broken off for a hugely successful solo career. And every visitor was given a round of whiskey by the biggest drummer in the world.

When Crosby, Stills, Nash & Young finally left the stage hours later, Jimmy and Robert went off with Stephen Stills and Graham Nash to jam with them at a small club nearby. After a full day's worth of drinking, however, John wasn't in the mood to sit behind the drums, and he and Hadley took their leave to have a late dinner at a Chinese restaurant in Chelsea with Rod Stewart and his entourage. Not ready to go home, John insisted he and Hadley continue on to a late-night after-party at Quaglino's, a local venue where Birmingham band Mike Sheridan & the Nightriders were booked as the entertainment.

As Hadley recalled later, the next thing he remembered was waking up with a large hangover in the back of John's Range Rover, the two men parked alone at a service station. Nursing a headache, Hadley had no idea what day it was, but assumed it was the following morning, a Sunday. John gave his friend an impish grin. "No," he said through his own hangover. "It's Tuesday, old pal."

A week later, after the Wembley concert, Jimmy flew to the States for his second surprise onstage jam with Bad Company in a month, this one at Central Park in New York City. As Swan Song's first release, Bad Company's debut had been deliberately aimed at American audiences, and the strategy had paid off: their single "Can't Get Enough" had quickly risen in the charts, and by the end of September the LP was the number-one album in the country—thanks in no small part to the group's Led Zeppelin connection. In a deliberate counter-strategy to his mandates regarding Led Zeppelin's songs, Peter Grant had insisted the Bad Company track be released as a stand-alone single. It, too, reached number one.

Hoping to replicate that same type of success with the Pretty Things in England, Zeppelin threw that group a lavish—and rather blasphemous—launch party on Halloween at the Chislehurst Caves. The motif was that of a "black mass"—right up Jimmy's alley—and the reception featured such holiday fare as half-naked strippers clad in nun's habits, magicians, and carnival barkers. With gallons of booze flowing, the night ended with John inciting a food fight with Zeppelin's roadies, all of whom pelted the partygoers with mounds of Jell-O from the concession tables.

As the year wound down, the members of Led Zeppelin were content to be home in the United Kingdom, watching their investments pay off without the need for another grueling world tour. Only Jimmy was getting cabin fever. With his personal life in tatters—he had recently begun a relationship with friend Ron Wood's young wife, Chrissie; his side project, the soundtrack for Kenneth Anger's *Lucifer Rising*, was still limping along slowly; and the director had even moved into the basement of Jimmy's Gothic Revival "Tower House" in London both to edit his footage and to keep a closer watch on the guitarist's productivity—the road seemed to beckon.

John, however, was finally getting the opportunity he yearned for—to enjoy the fruits of labor on Old Hyde Farm. After many months, his brother, Mick, and father, Jacko, were nearly finished with the long list of renovations and additions to the property. The farm cottage and outbuildings were completed, and the new barns and stables had been installed; John had even converted one of the numerous barns into a functioning automotive workshop for his many antique cars and motorcycles. Manager Brian Treble had been doing a solid job of maintaining the livestock and prize Hereford bulls, and John was rightly pleased with the overall outcome of his home.

"As all this to-ing and fro-ing was going on, all Brian's hard work and sleepless nights had paid off," Mick Bonham later recalled. Toward the end of the year, a bull calf had been born to John's valuable herd, much to the excitement of the farmhands. "As a celebration, we invited Brian over to the Conservative Club along with Pete and Stan [Blick], to wet the baby's head, and although Brian didn't drink, he was so chuffed about the calf, he came over just to be with his workmates."

As Mick Bonham recalled, the young manager was exhausted from the early mornings and late nights at Old Hyde and left the party early. The next morning, Mick was shocked from the news he received: Brian had been instantly killed in a car accident on the way home from the Conservative Club. He recalled, "Everyone was devastated, as Brian had become such an integral part of the project with his enthusiasm and hard work. . . . The added tragedy was that he had left his young wife, Lin, expecting their first child."

John took his farm very seriously and regarded his workers as family. As such, the news of Brian's death hit him hard. He quickly asked his brother and Matthew Maloney to take over the management duties at Old Hyde, knowing he could trust them while he was forced away by obligations to Led Zeppelin.

"Matthew and I camped in the unfinished house so we could keep an eye on the sheep throughout the night," Mick remembered. "If we spotted a ewe in trouble, we had to go and help with the birth. . . . After two solid weeks on the farm, twenty-four hours a day, I was awarded off. Upon my return the following day, I found an irate Bonzo fuming because I was a bit late. A few short, sharp exchanges later, and I was fired, . . . but the next day, there was John on the phone asking why I wasn't at work and laughing about the events of the previous day."

John was nervous about leaving the farm that year, more so than ever before. This time, against his better instincts, he would be gone for the longest duration yet. At a meeting in the Chelsea Swan Song office a few weeks earlier, the band's accountant had given them the strange news that their widely publicized financial success had put them in the dubious position of having made "too much money"—at least according to British tax laws. At Peter Grant's insistence, the band begrudgingly decided that they had little choice but to join many of their English rock 'n' roll peers as tax exiles.

Britain's controversial tax laws had been a point of contention among the country's entertainers for nearly a decade; under the UK guidelines, the most successful pop musicians were accountable for heavy taxes on their royalty income—nearly all of their profits. The Rolling Stones had already moved abroad, as had David Bowie and Rod Stewart. For the time being, the members of Led Zeppelin would have no choice but to divide their time equally among their own homeland—and their families—and elsewhere throughout the world. Grant suggested a world tour to keep the band busy and to keep the money rolling in.

Under the circumstances of his friend and farm manager's untimely death, John had been planning to be more hands-on at Old Hyde Farm and to spend the year with his family. Now, he and the rest of Led Zeppelin found themselves victims of their own fame. The year 1975 was to be spent as gypsies.

"The last two years had been a lot of fun, working with Jacko and John and hearing about the progress of the band firsthand from stories that John told us," Mick Bonham recalled. "Now it was back to the real world of following the band through the music papers."

PART THREE

INFERNO

1975–1980

The Loneliness of the Long-Distance Drummer

Chapter Eighteen

JANUARY 1975–FEBRUARY 1975

L ed Zeppelin left England at the beginning of 1975, determined to make the year
of tax exile work for them. Having nowhere else to go, being onstage throughout America, Australia, and perhaps even South
America would ensure a tremendous payoff once the group was allowed back home. However, it had now been more than a year since
the band had performed together, and without the incentive of a quick
return home, all four were racked with nerves.

Zeppelin booked rehearsals for the seemingly endless tour for the
end of November 1974, inviting only a select few to the converted theater in Ealing, West London. This included a handful of reporters and
friends. For good measure, the band started off with some favorites,
like Elvis Presley's "Hound Dog" and "Don't Be Cruel," then segued
into newer songs meant to whet the public's appetite for the next album: "Custard Pie," "Sick Again," "In My Time of Dying," and John's
showpieces, "Trampled Under Foot" and "Driving to Kashmir."

Previously, Led Zeppelin's stage show followed a somewhat set
format: Jimmy standing on the right, Robert on the left with Jones,
and John at the drums just behind as a centerpiece, the drums the
same height as the rest of the group. However, the recent inclusion

of props and effects, such as Showco's expensive laser-works pyro-technics, inspired a bit of an overall revamping. For the 1975 tour, John's drums would be placed on an elevated riser, and he would rival Jimmy's custom-embroidered stage suits—the "dragon" suit, the "poppy" suit, and so on—with his own handpicked costume: a white boiler suit and black derby hat, straight out of *A Clockwork Orange*. Nothing said "ultraviolence" like a drummer dressed as a droog; John had an identical suit made for assistant Mick Hinton, and together the two stalked the backstage area like a gang on the warpath. As Robert's assistant, Benji LeFevre, recalled, "Most people were completely shit scared of them."

The stage shows' special effects were an expensive affair, as Showco's cofounder Jack Calmes later noted. When he was summoned to Peter Grant's Chelsea office to explain the specifications of Zeppelin's laser show, oversize screens mounted above the stage, and the seventy thousand watts of amplification that would rock every venue (regardless of size), he first waited for Grant to dip a large bowie knife into a tremendous bag of cocaine, do a line, and then consider the cost before committing to it. Perched around Grant's desk, the Zeppelin boys allowed their manager to finish his enormous toot, business as usual. "So, they were all sitting there staring at me, which was pretty intense," Calmes remembered. "We unveiled the model and showed it to them. Bonham looked at me and said, 'How much fucking money is this going to cost us?' I said, '$15,785 per show.' The room went dead silent. Not a word. They started looking at each other sideways. Bonzo got up, walked over to the window on New Kings Road, and opened it up like [he] was going to throw me out of it. Then he came over to me, gave me a huge bear hug, and started laughing. He said, 'Yeah, go for it. We're in.'"

Everyone agreed that the West London rehearsal had gone well. Behind closed doors, however, everyone also agreed that Robert's voice was different, clearly in a lower register following a clandestine throat surgery after the previous tour had worked over his vocal cords. They were concerned with John's condition, as well. He was utterly miserable about leaving Pat and Jason and the farm behind and let everyone know it. The crew noticed he was drinking a lot more than usual and had put on a lot of weight. At the rehearsal, he looked bloated and out of shape, and, aside from an increase in his alcohol intake, there were rumors he had been experimenting with heroin. But no one said anything, not yet; after all, he seemed to be playing as well as ever.

Even in his physical condition, John was adamant that with each tour, his playing—and his *approach* to playing—would continue to evolve. Zeppelin may have been in the process of incorporating all forms of new technological extravagances to their stage show, but in John's view that extended to his own gear as well. Still a proud ambassador for Ludwig—whom he'd also represented through a series of new ads—the drummer swapped out his gear during the 1975 campaign.

Though John was still happy with his various Vistalite kits, he opted to return to the classic wood-shell incarnation of the new "Sparkle Silver" kit. He didn't stop there, however, and chose to vary the Sparkle Silver's sizes among the full fifteen-inch, sixteen-inch, eighteen-inch, and twenty-six-inch range. He continued experimenting with this variation over the next few years. His 1977 drum technician, Jeff Ocheltree, later explained, "The reason [John] went to the fifteen-inch [mounted] tom was because of his health. He was a little slower, and he was going more to the bigger rack-mounted tom than he was the floor toms. . . . It makes me sad to say that, but it's what I saw—he gained weight and didn't feel well. But still, he never did a gig where he didn't play well. He really believed in performance."

✳ ✳ ✳

ON SATURDAY, JANUARY 11, ZEPPELIN PLAYED ITS FIRST MAJOR SHOW of the tour, making a surprise appearance at the Ahoy, a club in Rotterdam, Holland, the Netherlands. The audience could sense the group's nerves: Robert forgot the words to "Stairway to Heaven" and saved face by inviting the audience to sing along with him. Backstage after the concert, all agreed that they'd played too many songs for the first night. Unfortunately, the uneasiness spilled over into the following night's show in Brussels, Belgium. Forgoing the laser and lights for a straight-ahead playthrough of the set list, the band struggled through the material off of *Physical Graffiti* and gave their first-ever live performance of "When the Levee Breaks" from the fourth album.

John was hung over from the night before and surprised the crowd by not performing his signature "Moby Dick." Jimmy, too, was unwell and left out his epic "Dazed and Confused." Unceremoniously, the band left the stage after a mere two hours—and ignored the calls for an encore. Aware that the band had only a week before their first US date in Chicago, Jimmy grumbled to Peter Grant that the band was going to have to pull itself together. The audiences of thirty-seven upcoming shows and an entourage of forty-four men were all depending on them.

✳ ✳ ✳

WITH ZEPPELIN'S LATEST TOUR AND THE RELEASE OF *PHYSICAL Graffiti* pending, Danny Goldberg was pulling twelve-hour days at Swan Song's midtown Manhattan office. The vanity label had taken over the top floor of the Newsweek Building, a brick-clad skyscraper at 444 Madison Avenue. Goldberg's office consisted of minimal decor: a desk, filing cabinets, a large blue statue of Lord Krishna playing a flute, a barely used sofa, and a phone he never seemed to be able to put down. As part of the promotion for Zeppelin's return to America, Goldberg put a new media strategy into play, this time involving more members of the music press.

"When Zeppelin released the *Physical Graffiti* album and announced plans for a 1975 tour, Jann Wenner called again, offering to do a *Rolling Stone* cover story," Goldberg recalled. "Jann said we could pick the writer." Knowing the band's harsh opinions of the US press, and of *Rolling Stone* in particular, Goldberg appealed to the band that it was time to allow the influential magazine to finally have a second chance at reassessing the band's career. Jimmy agreed and requested that *Rolling Stone* send California teenager Cameron Crowe as the reviewer, since he had written the most loving review of the group's San Diego concert during the previous tour. Goldberg also convinced the group to allow British reporter Stephen Davis to cover the East Coast leg of the tour and pushed for an advance copy of *Physical Graffiti* to drum up advance praise.

Just before the band was to leave for America, disaster again struck: Jimmy caught his left hand in the sliding door of a train at Victoria Station and immediately feared the US dates would have to be postponed—or, worse, canceled. Though a series of X-rays revealed a badly sprained ring finger, Grant was quick to remind the guitarist that they had already sold out forty shows in twenty-six cities and would have to give back $5 million if they canceled. Danny Goldberg was told to issue a press release announcing the accident, stating that the shows would go on. Jimmy was experimenting with a "three-finger fretting technique," the press release read, so fans needn't worry.

Led Zeppelin arrived in Chicago on January 16, and Richard Cole booked them an entire floor of the Ambassador Hotel overlooking Lake Michigan. Their floor was under the careful watch of two new members to the band's entourage: former FBI agents. Fearing that Robert's slight cold could grow worse and disable his singing voice, the entourage grew by one more: a young doctor who had previously worked for the Rolling Stones and whose dual medical bags admittedly contained cures for everything from "overdoses and gunshots" to homesickness.

Seventeen-year-old Cameron Crowe soon flew in to Chicago to meet the band, joyfully hanging out with Robert and Jimmy and listening with them to Bob Dylan's upcoming album, *Blood on the Tracks*. Bonding with the young man, Jimmy and Robert sneaked out of the hotel with Crowe to catch a late-night showing of *Young Frankenstein*. Unsurprisingly, when the feature article finally ran on March 13, the profile was laudatory of the band, the tour, and their latest album.

The band chartered a jet to Minneapolis the following day, rehearsing at the Met Center before their January 18 concert. John played "Moby Dick" for a mere fifteen minutes. Despite the good doctor's magical bag, Robert's cold got worse, and the show ended just after the two-hour mark; the audience jeered the brevity of the performance.

The next night, John was in a particularly foul mood. At the hotel, he had been quietly reading a newspaper in his suite when one of the roadies made the mistake of showing him the results of the latest *Playboy* music poll; the magazine's music editors had Karen Carpenter nudging him out of the top spot as best rock drummer.

"Oh my God, no!" Bonham roared. "Karen Carpenter! Karen Carpenter!" he repeated, pacing the floor and throwing an ashtray against the wall. "I can't believe it! I give up! If Karen Carpenter is a better drummer, then I'm in the wrong business! I'm gonna get a job driving a taxi! Somebody, help me, please!"

According to Richard Cole, that night at the stadium, John wouldn't let up. "Clad in his ominous white boiler suit and bowler cap, Bonzo roared in the dressing room of the Chicago Stadium, 'I'd like to have it publicized that I came in after Karen Carpenter in the *Playboy* drummer poll! She couldn't last ten minutes with a Zeppelin number!'" Trusted reporter Lisa Robinson claimed that John was still incredibly depressed over the results twenty-four hours later. Once she prodded, however, he revealed the true source of his depression; of all times for him to be in exile from home, Pat had just found out she was pregnant with their second child. "Late that night at the Bistro, Bonzo was sitting quietly in a booth, alone," Robinson later said. "'You know, my wife is expecting again in July. . . . She's really terrific, the type of lady that when you walk into our house, she comes right out with a cup of tea, or a drink, or a sandwich.

"'We met when we were sixteen, got married at seventeen,'" he went on, praising his wife and letting it be known that he missed her terribly. "'I was a carpenter for a few years—I'd get up at seven in the morning, then change my clothes in the van and go to gigs at

night. How do you think I feel, not being taken seriously, coming after Karen Carpenter in the *Playboy* poll . . . Karen Carpenter . . . What
a load of shit!'"

Their first show in Chicago didn't do much to boost morale, as
Robert was running a fever and the group was certain he had the
flu. He performed anyway but apologized to the audience of twenty
thousand five times throughout the concert. When his vocal cords
grew more strained over the next two nights, it was agreed to give the
band a few days off.

Much later, journalist Chris Charlesworth observed the darker
aspects of the band's early stops in 1975, beginning with his memorable drive with John from downtown Chicago to O'Hare Airport.
John, bundled against the winter chill in a sheepskin and swigging
from a quart of blue-label Smirnoff, muttered to himself the entire
chauffeured way to the plane. "Even though it's only just past midday, Bonzo is not sober," the writer recalled. "I cannot even be certain
whether this is the first bottle of vodka he's tackled today, and, bearing in mind his reputation for unprovoked aggression toward music
writers, I am acutely aware that the situation could turn nasty. . . . I am
nevertheless on my guard and watch what I say."

Charlesworth observed, "Bonzo's main problem is that he is homesick. He wants to be back in England, on his farm in the Black Country
with wife Pat and the kids, breathing in the Albion air, tending his
livestock. . . . [T]he fact that Led Zeppelin now has an unscheduled
forty-eight hours of downtime, which leaves Bonzo bereft of a reason
to be here in the first place, just adds to his inconsolable mood. . . .
Bonzo looks out of the window at the frozen gray landscape rolling
by and closes his eyes. He might actually be nodding off, I think. Then
he opens his eyes again. 'What the fuck am I doing here,' he mutters.
'I wanna be back HOME.'"

With the band desperate to leave frigid Chicago for three days,
Grant held a meeting in his suite at the Ambassador Hotel. John sug-
gested Jamaica, which would bring them closer to home; as journalist
Chris Charlesworth recalled, "Bonzo, of course, would really like to

go back home, back to Worcestershire, just so he can spend a night with his beloved Pat, but he'll settle for Jamaica if that's out of the question." John Paul Jones suggested the Bahamas. Jimmy, nursing his strained finger with Jack Daniel's, requested LA, and since *The Starship* wasn't certified to fly out of the continental United States, Jimmy got his way. Robert, for his part, was pissed to have to remain bedridden and miss out on the fun.

During the flight to LA, the ominous nature of the tour came to a head. As *The Starship* cruised at thirty thousand feet, two pretty hostesses served drinks, and after finishing an intense game of backgammon with one of the security agents, John Paul Jones entertained at the organ. Onboard for additional coverage were British reporter Chris Charlesworth, young Cameron Crowe, and official band photographer Neal Preston. Peter Grant leaned back and sang.

Meanwhile, John had killed an entire bottle of whiskey and, now largely incoherent, had to be put to bed in the plane's large rear stateroom by Richard Cole and Mick Hinton. During the flight, Charlesworth was given a full tour of the luxurious plane, even being allowed to grab the controls for a brief, exhilarating moment. Amused, Grant replied, "That's nothing. Bonzo flew us all the fucking way from Los Angeles to fucking New York on one tour," to Charlesworth's instant relief. Suddenly, Richard Cole appeared beside the journalist. Aware that Charlesworth had ridden to O'Hare with John, the road manager was concerned what behavior the drummer might have displayed in front of a member of the press and asked what John had had to drink in the limo.

"Only vodka, but plenty of it," Charlesworth responded.

"No pills? No coke?"

"No, not that I saw," said Charlesworth. "He was just swigging vodka, straight from the bottle."

"Nothing else?" Cole persisted.

"No."

About a half hour before descent into LAX, the flight had calmed down, and a few were asleep. From the back of the plane, a loud crash signaled that John had awoken; staggering out in nothing but a robe, he began cursing up and down the plane. Full of drink, he lurched forward and grabbed one of the pretty attendants and began groping her, mumbling incoherently. After she tried to pry herself loose from his grip, John put the girl in an arm lock. She screamed. The entire flight was startled awake, and Grant and Cole raced to the scene, pulling the inebriated drummer off the girl, tackling him to the ground. They dragged him back into the bedroom and slammed the door. Alarmed at the hostess's screams, one of the pilots raced from the cockpit, demanding to know what had transpired. Told of John's behavior, he was furious. Grant took the shaken girl in his arms and calmed her down, while Cole quietly walked over to the shocked faces of Charlesworth, Crowe, and Preston. "I don't wanna see one fucking word of this finding its fucking way into your fucking magazines," Cole warned without the slightest trace of a smile. "Right?"

Journalist Stephen Davis recalled that Richard Cole once explained to him the basis for John's volatile behavior. "One was 'Bonzo,' a great pal and full of fun—the other was 'the Beast,' as in *'There's a party later? Don't tell the Beast,'*" Davis claimed. As Cole further explained, "The Beast was a psychotic bully who attacked people and then was ashamed when he found out about it later. . . . It was a real problem when Led Zeppelin went on tour. No one could predict when the Beast would surface—but it usually happened when John Bonham was drinking and desperately homesick for his family."

✳ ✳ ✳

UPON THEIR RETURN FROM LA, THE REST OF THE BAND WAS PLEASED to discover that Robert was feeling well enough to complete the East Coast leg of the tour. "The dominant feeling among the sellout Coliseum crowd Friday night was that of being part of a special event, more than just another concert," ran one review on the group's appearance in Richfield, Ohio. "Zeppelin have managed to achieve this position over a period of six years as a headline-status group. . . . Understandably, expectations were running high."

The review continued, "The level of musicianship was high throughout the show. . . . Page and *Clockwork Orange*–attired John Bonham maintained their usual high standards, the latter sending the audience into ecstasies with his soloing in 'Moby Dick.'"

In the *Cleveland Review*, Ron Weiskind noted, "A long Bonham drum solo resembles a volcanic eruption in the sheer force of his playing. He builds a crescendo of trembling rhythm, then cools down, then erupts again in violence. Just when you think it is over, the lights in his transparent drum set activate one by one to create a brilliant 'lava flow' silhouetting Bonham on the backdrop." Likewise, Robert Eckert in Indianapolis noted, "'Moby Dick,' featuring John Bonham's legendary half-hour drum solo, followed. In the opening minutes of the solo, Bonham had competition from a minor skirmish in the front of the stage between police and an overzealous fan. But the show remained onstage throughout the standard sound of the beginning of the solo, to his bare-handed exhibition, to his timpani solo that darted from speaker to speaker in and out of the rest of the arena." A review in Greensboro noted that "drummer John Bonham thundered away until the very foundation of the Coliseum shook to the rhythm" and that Led Zeppelin itself was "a powerhouse of heavy metal."

After opening the review with the notice that thirty-four people had been arrested during the show, the *Greensboro Daily News*'s Jerry Kenion nonetheless noted, "John Bonham, called Bonzo, is a one-man percussion ensemble, a fact which he demonstrated during a 20-minute solo" at the show. "First, the drumsticks flew over drums, gongs and cymbals; then, he played with the palms of his hands, the sides of his hands. From that he went into percussion with a synthesizer, which in quadraphonic sound seemed to drown the audience in marvelous, rumbling sounds. . . . The audience cheered and clapped with hands held high at the conclusion of Bonham's 20-minute exhibition."

Despite mixed reviews, the shows were a smash hit, proving that American audiences had been starved for Zeppelin. Mick Bonham recalled, "Tickets had been in such demand that rioting had occurred at many venues, the worst of which was at the Boston Garden, resulting in the band being banned from appearing there."

Regardless of their efforts to turn their image around this time, their reputations preceded them when it came to lodging as well. When the band checked into the Plaza Hotel in Manhattan weeks later, the posh hotel demanded a $10,000 security deposit before accepting the reservation.

✳ ✳ ✳

TO EASE THE GROUP BACK INTO THE SWING OF THINGS, GRANT planned a short break for them during March, in between the East Coast and West Coast dates, culminating with a three-night residency at the LA Forum. Straight from the airport, the band's first order of business was to check into their unofficial LA "home"—the Rainbow Bar & Grill on the Sunset Strip, where they immediately held court in the club's VIP area. To pass the time, John added another expensive automobile to his collection while in LA: a Ford sedan built to hot-rod specifications, which he promptly took out and raced on the Sunset Strip.

"[John] had just bought this new motor and was doing about 90 mph up and down the Strip," John Paul Jones later recalled. "He was going mad, and you know what the police are like over there about speeding. . . . Anyway, it wasn't long before the highway patrol pulled him over, and they jump out of the car, with guns already out. At this, John jumps out of his car shouting, 'Hold on, hold on!' One of the officers briskly asked John, 'What the fuck do you think you're doing?' to which he replied, 'Well, look, I've just come back from the Forum where we just played a blinding gig, and I've got this brand-new car.' And then he says, 'Come and have a look at it. . . . Have a look at the bloody size of the engine!'"

According to Jones, who was watching from the window of his room inside the Riot House, the police officers were so surprised by John's cavalier attitude, they humored him and took a peek under the hot rod's hood. "It's gone from an emergency situation to them all looking under the hood discussing brake horsepower," Jones remembered. "The next thing, the police are leaving, telling Bonzo to go steady next time and him offering them tickets for the next show. It was amazing, but he got away with it again."

It was far from the first time that John had been able to smoothly turn on the charm when he needed to, using his down-to-earth earnestness to talk his way out of sticky situations. Jones also recalled a situation in Texas when he and John made the error of going to a local bar filled with good ol' boys none too impressed with the hippie looks of the two musicians. "Bonzo was in high spirits, so I was trying to keep a low profile on him," Jones recalled. "As we made our way through the bar, the place went quiet, and everybody's interest seemed focused on us. . . . I wanted to get out of the place, but Bonzo ordered more drinks. The atmosphere was turning nasty, and it looked like we might end up in trouble, but as only Bonzo could, he turned and asked, 'Okay, what sort of cattle do you boys raise around here?' The whole atmosphere changed, and within minutes everyone had gathered 'round and were talking about longhorns and steers! And there in the middle was Bonzo, talking about his Herefords and what feeds were the best. . . . He had this amazing knack of getting out of sticky situations and could talk his way out of anything."

※ ※ ※

IN NEW YORK, ZEPPELIN BROKE DOWN AND PAID THE PLAZA THE $10,000 to let them stay—but the hotel was going to work for it: the band's roadies carted up massive amounts of their "necessities," including tons of luggage, instruments, Jimmy's film equipment in order to work on Kenneth Anger's soundtrack, and John Paul Jones's piano. Since John had been the chief reason for the hotel's steep security deposit, he made a few demands of his own, including a billiard table to practice his favorite game, snooker.

The group would be playing Madison Square Garden on February 3, 7, and 12, with gigs on Long Island and in Philadelphia, Maryland,

and Montreal in between; as such, New York City became base camp. Once settled in, they were immediately bored.

Richard Cole later recalled, "One night in New York, Mick Jagger called to see if any of us wanted to accompany him and Ronnie Wood to a club in Harlem. . . . Jimmy, Bonzo, and I decided that it sounded better than spending the night in the hotel, [and] I phoned for a couple of limos and we went downstairs to meet Mick and Ronnie in front of the Plaza."

Jimmy joined Jagger and Wood in the first limo, making John ride with Cole in the second. Feeling snubbed, John became boorish and started grumbling under his breath. As the limo driver communicated with his partner in the other car via the vehicle's radio unit, John overheard the two discussing the potential danger of riding into Harlem at such a late hour. Cole could almost see the lightbulb over John's head flicker.

"Matty," John called to the driver, "I know you've got some guns up there—give me one of them after you check to make sure it's unloaded."

Matty, the driver, did as he was told and handed an unloaded Beretta to John over the seat.

"Okay," John said. "Now, pull alongside their limo."

The driver veered into the next lane and sidled as coordinated with Jimmy and the Stones' limo as he could muster. In the backseat, John signaled to the men in the other car, mouthing to Jagger to lower his limo's window. Jagger flashed his million-dollar smile and played along—just as John drew the Beretta out and aimed it right at him. He shouted, "I'll teach you fuckers to leave me behind!"

Cole recalled, "In the other limo, they went absolutely berserk. There were screams from the backseat as Mick, Ronnie, and Jimmy simultaneously hit the floor. . . . Their driver slammed down on the accelerator and sped through two red lights, convinced that Bonham's insanity had turned him into a killer."

Arriving at the Harlem club, John climbed out of the limo and apologized. It was only a joke, he said.

✳ ✳ ✳

Later that week, Danny Goldberg arranged a dual interview between Jimmy and renowned beat-generation writer William S. Burroughs for publication in the countercultural magazine *Crawdaddy!* Jimmy later claimed that the meeting was "one of the great experiences" of his life. The following night, Burroughs attended Led Zeppelin's first show at Madison Square Garden and embraced the fully immersive experience, forgoing the recommended cotton balls for his older ears in the face of Zeppelin's 70-watt sonic powerhouse. Conducting the interview over dinner, Burroughs spoke to Jimmy of Morocco's ritualistic approach to music, to which Jimmy sheepishly admitted he hadn't yet visited the country.

In his published essay, the older author likened the hypnotic nature of the group's rock 'n' roll to the trance music of the Master Musicians of Jajouka in Morocco, a more primitive band of sonic magicians known for loud horns and drums like a thunderstorm. Much to Jimmy's delight, Burroughs suggested that the band's music inspired a form of astral projection of a spiritual nature among its audience.

Of the Madison Square Garden performance, *Disc* magazine wrote, "The new songs, from *Physical Graffiti*, are among the best Zeppelin have yet undertaken, with 'Kashmir,' an Arabian night fantasy, among the stunning highlights."

Local student reviewer Brian "Rat" Ganin noted, "Drummer John Bonham stole the show with a 20-minute drum solo during 'Moby Dick,' a cut from *Led Zeppelin II*, for which he received the only standing ovation of the night, except for the encores. It was a powerful and melodic creation which made [jazz-fusion player] Bill Cobham look fast but uninteresting."

✳ ✳ ✳

After the appalling scene John had caused en route to Los Angeles the previous month, the Zeppelin crew was apprehensive about inviting guests aboard *The Starship*—particularly journalists. On their return trip to the East Coast, Jimmy and Peter Grant stayed in their bedrooms, while John Paul Jones challenged other passengers to his favorite game, backgammon. Robert remained jovial, chatting with visitors and flight crew or lounging in the common area watching videos. At first, Grant was certain that a private jet would give the band a sense of "home" even on the road, but soon enough John's abhorrence of flying reemerged and his drinking subsequently escalated. With fewer outsiders onboard, there also seemed to be less chance for incident. On the flight to Detroit, however, that assumption proved false.

"There was a hideous moment when Bonzo had taken the thick glasses off the face of a midwestern promo guy named Danny Markus and stomped on them," recalled Danny Goldberg. "All of us, including Markus, froze into the pretense that nothing of consequence had happened." For no apparent reason, John approached the Atlantic Records regional manager midflight, grabbed the eyeglasses right off the man's face, and crushed them with his bare hand, grinding the glass into the carpet. Grunting, John then continued to the back of the plane without a word. As usual, Richard Cole rushed over to keep Markus calm. Goldberg later reasoned, "It was a particularly ugly example of the way some performers lost common civility when intoxicated with extended periods of adulation."

During the stops along the East Coast, the band's concert reviews remained strong. "Critics have come to borrowing phrases from each other to complain about the world's most popular hard rock band, the top of the pops," observed Hugh Cutler following the February 8 show at the Philadelphia Spectrum. "Perhaps it's a natural penchant of critics to take potshots at the big shots. . . . Led Zeppelin manager Peter Grant credits two factors for his gang's success: 'Number 1—Jimmy is an absolutely unparalleled guitar player, and the boys have a fanatical devotion to perfection. Number 2—they aren't overexposed. They take their time doing their records and they aren't overbooked.'"

Of John's moment in the spotlight, Cutler wrote, "An extended drum solo, augmented by a synthesizer which phases the pounding to arc and echo among the speakers like a jet takeoff, is probably the highpoint by common consensus. The crowd roars, too, when smoke billows around the players' feet as multicolored spotlights, footlights and strobe-lights blink frantically. Overload."

More with this tour than ever before, John and John Paul Jones had both garnered more critical praise—perhaps due to Robert's ongoing vocal struggles and Jimmy's short solo turns. Before long, the two rhythm musicians pulled Danny Goldberg aside and asked that they be given more prominence in the spotlight—perhaps more publicity thrown their way or more serious interviews regarding their creative contributions. As promised, Goldberg mentioned this to Jimmy and was referred to Showco's lighting director, who claimed he had strict orders from Jimmy that neither Jonesy nor Bonzo should be spotlit. The subject ended there.

On February 10, the band flew to Washington for a show at the massive Capital Centre in nearby Maryland. Columnist George F. Will covered the band's performance for the *Baltimore Sun*, writing, "When Led Zeppelin descended on Washington recently, 18,700 concert tickets were snapped up in three hours. Some people who could not get tickets vented their disappointment just as, perhaps, disappointed Viennese did when they could not get into a Mozart recital. They threw bottles at police."

Following two more shows in New York, Zeppelin took a ten-day break. Jimmy and Robert flew to the Caribbean island of Dominica, while the rest of the group went home to their families.

Eager to return home, John appeared happier than he'd been in weeks. He could finally spend some time with his pregnant wife.

Chapter Nineteen

FEBRUARY 1975–MAY 1975

Physical Graffiti was finally released on February 25, 1975—arriving to much fanfare and more than a year late. Advance sales alone amounted to $15 million, and, much to the band's delight, the album debuted on the *Billboard* chart at a very respectable number three. Notably, with the release of *Physical Graffiti*, Led Zeppelin accomplished a feat unheard of in the history of rock bands owning their own vanity labels: a whopping nine albums on the American charts—their own six releases, plus the Swan Song debuts of Bad Company, the Pretty Things, and Maggie Bell. Completing the band's incredible business coup, *Physical Graffiti* was soon *Billboard*'s number-one album.

✳ ✳ ✳

AFTER TWO WEEKS OF REST, JIMMY AND ROBERT RETURNED FROM Dominica and resumed the seemingly never-ending tour. Both John's bandmates and Zeppelin's work crew were growing concerned with his behavior; each time back on the road, his moods had become more morose and depressed, almost always manifesting as violent rages and drunken escapades. Passing through Texas, Richard Cole had a feeling that John was apt to get himself arrested for bad behavior and assigned a former FBI agent named Jack Kelly to work a specific detail to keep a watch on John for the rest of the trip. As John often drank during the day, this also forced upon Kelly the additional job of acting as occasional chauffeur for the unpredictable drummer.

One afternoon in between Zeppelin shows in Dallas, Kelly drove as John watched the city pass by out the window. A beautiful, customized 1959 Corvette parked on the street caught John's attention, and he ordered the security agent to pull over for a closer look. "Jack," John said to Kelly, "I want you to wait by this car until the owner comes for it, and I want you to tell him that Mr. Bonham would like to buy him a drink. And if he won't come, see if you can have him arrested."

Kelly was unsure if such a request was part of his job description, but, nonetheless, he did as he was told. A few hours later, John paid the Corvette's owner $18,000 in cash for the car, about $5,000 more than its true street value. However, John's British license had recently been suspended for drinking and driving through Birmingham, meaning he had no valid US driver's license, either. Under strict orders from Peter Grant, John had the Corvette trucked to Los Angeles, where it was stored in the basement garage of the Hyatt House while Zeppelin's legal department spent the rest of the week at the California Department of Motor Vehicles attempting to get the drummer insurance and temporary plates.

According to Danny Goldberg, "Everyone was terrified that Bonzo would get into an accident while on tour. So, [attorney] Steve Weiss solemnly convinced him that he was unable to get insurance on short notice that would cover a British driver of a Texas car being driven in the United States."

The whole time, John sat in the parked sports car with Mick Ralphs of Bad Company, revving the engine and pouting. Quickly bored, John sold it two days later.

Two weeks later, John made another impulse buy, acquiring a restored Model T Ford, which he shipped back to Old Hyde Farm in Worcestershire. "TWA Airlines staff could hardly believe their eyes when they came to unload a recent shipment from America," one local hot-rod trade weekly announced. "One described the curious thing as a 'cartoon on wheels,' and another comment was 'a local delivery vehicle designed by Monty Python for Mary Poppins!!'

"In fact, it was a Model-T hot-rod bought by John Bonham of Led Zeppelin!" the article went on. "Weighing approximately 4,000 lbs. and valued at $9,000, the hot-rod was shipped by a freighter from San Francisco to London's Heathrow. . . . Only hope it goes!!"

※ ※ ※

DURING THEIR STAY IN LA, THE BAND WAS BOTH THOROUGHLY EXhausted from the Texas concerts as well as disappointed to learn that a huge concert in Florida (with a half-million-dollar payday) had been canceled; Peter Grant had leaned on the promoters a little too hard, and the venue couldn't come up with the excessive amount in time. With a brief amount of time to kill, the band laid low at the Riot House, and Danny Goldberg courted the British press. Flown in from London, the journalists were put up in their own rooms at the hotel, unfortunately near John's suite. Still brooding over his Corvette disappointment, and as dissatisfied with his media coverage as ever, John took to keeping the reporters awake all night by blasting Alphonse Mouzon drum LPs at full volume.

This time around at the Riot House, things were decidedly calmer than they had been in the past; no more motorcycles in the hallways and far fewer ribald shenanigans with the groupies. Later, Richard Cole confessed that it was during the 1975 North American tour that the drugs circulating around the band and its entourage were harsher, with Page and Bonham the likely culprits. Many of their peers within the rock 'n' roll community had begun shooting up, and it was only a matter of time before smack was made available.

"I can't speak for the others, but for me, drugs were an integral part of the whole thing, right from the beginning, right to the end," Jimmy later told a reporter, although he omitted which drugs. "And part of the condition of drug taking is that you start thinking you're invincible."

During various recording sessions at Headley Grange, so many substances flowed that Zeppelin's roadies would get up early and pile their own cocaine mounts from the crumbs the band had left behind. Now, however, the members of Led Zeppelin were in their late twenties and far from invincible. John, in particular, was beginning to feel the burden of years of hard living. On the way to the airport to the San Diego concert, the caravan of rented limousines had to pull over several times at different gas stations due to John's stomach ailments. Embarrassingly, he was soon keeping Pepto-Bismol in his jacket pocket like a flask.

Despite the physical toll, John's performances onstage and new innovations were garnering the appropriate praise. A San Diego reviewer wrote of the night's performance, "People don't wait 24 hours in the rain to see other groups, but for Zeppelin, they do," adding of John's solo turn, "Drummer John Bonham gets into the act with a 20 minute solo which made the arena boom. One segment of the concert scene which deserves more credit are those who work the sound mixers, and who, on the kettle drum solo, changed the sound from merely a booming beat to a quadraphonic rock out," unaware that John had largely designed those synthesized elements.

※ ※ ※

"On our last full day at the Riot House, the tedium of touring finally caught up with Bonzo," Richard Cole later recalled. "To fight off the boredom, he decided to shoot jump shots out the window of his suite—not with basketballs, but with television sets. One by one, half a dozen RCA color sets sailed out toward Sunset Boulevard, shattering into slivers of plastic and glass that carpeted the driveway leading up to the hotel entrance."

"I'm not going to get into any trouble this time," John told the road manager before taking the first shot. Being cheeky, the drummer had confiscated the television sets from roadies' rooms, rather than use his own. "When the hotel's assistant manager raced up to try to catch the troublemaker in the act," Cole remembered, "he found everything in place in Bonham's suite, including the TV tuned to an early-afternoon soap opera."

Having pulled the wool over management's eyes, John attempted to drag his suite's grand piano to the window as his next ammunition—but it proved too bulky to move.

Meanwhile, the band was taking a huge risk by continuing to invite press to Zeppelin events, especially including the tour travel itself. Even with increasingly positive reviews from mainstream media, the individual members of the band remained more than skeptical; in John's case, it was continued aggression. One of his least favorite music journalists who had become a fixed staple of the band's American tours was Nick Kent, an English rock writer whom John loved to tease with the derogatory nickname "Nick Bent." Kent made the grave error of giving *Physical Graffiti* a mixed review in *NME* magazine, and when John encountered the writer soon after, he and Richard Cole doused the scribe in Bloody Marys. "Your life isn't worth piss," the two reportedly told the writer. Kent, for his part, was understanding about the group's reaction. Like many others who had been in the eye of the Led Zeppelin storm, he chalked it up to drugs. "Taking cocaine just enabled Bonham to drink more," Kent later claimed. "The combination of cocaine and alcohol is almost as dangerous as heroin, because you end up with two separate addictions. . . . Plus, people were worried about him getting into heroin. It was like, 'Whatever you do, don't let him do smack. He'll snort the whole gram and overdose.'"

Kent added, "I've never seen anyone behave worse in my life than Bonham and Cole. I once saw them beat a guy senseless for no reason and then drop money on his face." Old friend Glenn Hughes later recounted a similar incident from the time. "I remember we were having a bit of a party at the Rainbow," Hughes said. "John takes an eight-ball of coke out of his pocket and throws it into his cupped hands and cups the whole eight-ball up to his face—and we're watching the crumbs as they fall down. I mean, you've heard of excess, and this is one of those moments when you can't believe what you're seeing."

Swan Song's later publicist Janine Safer recalled her own feelings on seeing John's spiral following the 1975 tour. "Personally, I was never in fear of Bonzo. I thought he was really a doll, one of the sweetest people. Miserably unhappy whenever Pat wasn't with him. Not very bright and not intellectually inclined. . . . He liked playing the drums, and he loved his wife. He would be completely unhinged when she wasn't around."

❊ ❊ ❊

AFTER LA, *THE STARSHIP* HEADED NORTH TO VANCOUVER AND SEATTLE.

In Seattle the *Oregonian's* John Wendeborn wrote of the March 13 show, "The Zep is different in one way because it plays three-hour nonstop concerts with no opening act. It gives the fans value for money spent. . . . This foursome can work together like a well-lubricated set of gears, but each one can also be made to honor his own commitment to sound. . . . Bonham is a dynamic drummer who moves around his kit easily while setting up booming rhythms. As a soloist, he had one long period to demonstrate his ability. For the first few moments, he did little more than show he can play a few paradiddles and ratamacues. But he got into the spirit eventually by building, emotional layer upon layer, a powerful solo. It lasted some 20 minutes and finished with Bonham playing several of his drums through a synthesizer that added to the occasionally bizarre sound effects."

When the tour ended in Los Angeles at the end of March, Led Zeppelin stayed in California. With the tax exile in full effect, they weren't able to go home, much to their frustration. John knew that Pat was due in only a few months, and he desperately wanted to be there for the birth of his second child.

"[John] was very emotional," Richard Cole remembered. "He was extremely close to his wife and son, and he didn't want to be away from them, but he had to because of the tax thing. So, he'd get depressed, and if anyone said anything to him, Bonzo would whack them."

On March 26, the group hosted a party at the Hyatt Regency in honor of the Pretty Things, a group signed to their Swan Song label whose debut album had stagnated. After years of internal strife, the band regrouped yet again, and Zeppelin hoped a lavish public endorsement would inspire the band to pull it together. The guest list for the event included the members of Bad Company, the most successful of Swan Song's bands whose first album had sold a million and a half copies in the United States. Unfortunately, the party also welcomed dozens of journalists from various media outlets, and the members of Zeppelin still were not entirely capable of playing host at swanky soirees. John was thoroughly smashed by the time the first reporter made the grave error of approaching him.

John was alone at the bar when Andy McConnell, a quiet and mild-mannered British journalist for *Sounds*, sat down next to him. Apparently, John was one of McConnell's musical heroes—but that wasn't to last much longer. "Mr. Bonham," the young man said, "I would just like to tell you that I think you're the greatest drummer in the world, and I've always wanted to shake your hand."

Accounts of the next few moments differ, but what was agreed was how John grasped the writer by his lapels, bringing them eye to eye. "I've had enough from you cunts in the press!" John was reported to have shouted, his voice level high enough to immediately summon onlookers and security men, all prying the drummer from the shocked journalist. Initially, young Cameron Crowe wrote of the altercation with a slightly more understanding take on John's behavior. "At a party hosted by Zeppelin in honor of the Pretty Things, Bonham threw several stomach punches at *Sounds* correspondent Andy McConnell. McConnell, who'd had an amicable meeting with the drummer earlier in the afternoon, shined a flashlight in Bonham's face and cracked, 'You're an ugly fucker, aren't you?' Bonzo responded by knocking McConnell across the room."

Regardless of what had started the altercation, one unnamed roadie told Crowe that the result was inevitable. "You just don't do things like that to Bonzo, especially when he's had a few drinks. . . . After a certain point, the Beast goes on the prowl, and the only thing that amuses him is pillage."

Danny Goldberg later recalled, "Like many rock musicians, Bonham was unable to internalize the fact that just because one particular writer for a publication had once written something unfriendly about him, all other writers for the magazine were not complicit or even aware of such insults. . . . I spent a lot of the evening calming McConnell down and promising future access and cooperation from the band if he would refrain from referring to the embarrassing outburst in his column."

Later that night, Goldberg was fast asleep in his room at the Hyatt House when he heard a loud pounding at his door. He looked over to see that it was three o'clock. "I know you're in there, Goldilocks!" It was John.

"I know you're in there, and I want you to call that fucking little geezer from *Sounds*," the drummer raged. "Tell him I want to do another fucking interview! I'll give that horrible little fucker an interview he'll never forget!"

Confused as to the proper protocol in such a situation, Goldberg ignored the yelling until he heard a frustrated John lumber back down the hall and go back to his room. Goldberg recalled, "The next day, I nervously explained to Peter my rationale for ignoring the drummer. Peter waved it off. 'If you think you get woken up, imagine what I get. You're just the fucking publicist; I'm the manager. If it gets too bad, you can do what I do—get two rooms, tell the band you're in one, and actually sleep in another.'"

"*Exuberant* is a good term for Bonzo," Robert Plant later said. "He was full of life and vim and vigor and didn't give a fuck what anyone thought."

✳ ✳ ✳

In May Led Zeppelin was overjoyed to be able to return home to England. They brought with them their state-of-the-art special effects and laser-light show, which the United Kingdom had not yet seen. Advertisements for the Earls Court concerts immediately went up on April 19. Tickets to the three Earls Court shows on May 23, 24, and 25 were sold out within five hours, convincing the band to add two more concerts for the preceding weekend, May 17 and 18. Those thirty-four thousand tickets were quickly gone, as well.

Under the conditions of their tax exile, they were allowed only a few days at home at a time, and John really wanted to make his time at home with his family count. His younger brother, Mick, had recently gotten engaged to his longtime girlfriend, Linda Turner, and was planning a wedding for September. The Zeppelin dates at Earls Court were the first time the brothers had seen each other in months. "Since finishing work at Old Hyde, I had hardly seen John, so on Jacko's birthday, John and Matthew [Maloney] came over, and we took Jacko out on a pub crawl," Mick later mentioned. "As the night wore on, John told us about the gigs they were due to do at Earls Court in London. . . . John gave us some tickets for the show on May 23 before Matt took him home, and Jacko and I wobbled back to the flat."

Mick remembered, "It seem[s] crazy that in some of the previous years, Led Zeppelin could hardly get any media coverage in this country, and yet now, with the buildup to the Earls Court dates, every paper was carrying articles about them."

The template followed the stage shows from the US tour, and the band opened with "Rock and Roll," driving the British audience crazy. "This is a journey through some of our experiences," Robert told the massive crowd, "the positive ones and the negative ones, over the last six years." The band then proceeded to perform a three-hour retrospective, playing fan favorites from every one of their albums. Jimmy switched guitars for "In My Time of Dying," which Robert sarcastically dedicated to Denis Healey, the chancellor of the exchequer, the British figurehead directly responsible for the tax codes that had sent the rock 'n' roll community into exile.

Following "Trampled Under Foot," Robert introduced "Moby Dick." After John's solo, Robert announced, "John Bonham—master of the skins! The only man that can play drums and sing 'The Last Waltz.' John comes from a circus family—my God, how can such a heavy group be so silly! So, this is a song that goes right back to the beginning of our time. Bonzo refused to join us because he was getting forty pounds with Tim Rose. I had eight telegrams sent to the Three Men in a Boat in Walsall. . . . Nobody would believe in the New Yardbirds!"

Behind the drums, John smiled and called to Robert, "Nothing's changed!"

"While John was in full flight during 'Moby Dick,' Jacko was up and dancing in the aisles with the best of them," Mick Bonham recalled. "And as everyone looked on quizzically at this older person in a suit, he just kept telling everyone, 'That's my boy!' As I watched Jacko watching John, I realized that there's nothing more contented than the face of a father watching a son or daughter achieve their ambitions."

During the Earls Court series, John wanted to dedicate one of his epic "Moby Dick" performances to the most special member in the crowd—his son, Jason. "Tonight, there's a lad watching his dad," Robert informed the crowd, "who is a remarkable drummer even though he's eight years old. . . . He's a better drummer than 80 percent of rock-group drummers today, and he's eight years old! So, Jason Bonham, this is your dad—John Bonham! 'Moby Dick'!"

Despite Zeppelin's already lengthy career as a touring band, the Earls Court concerts were quickly recognized as major events for devoted fans and a form of milestone for the musicians. In the *Observer*, critic Tony Palmer wrote of the shows, "There is no theater like it, no action painting which approaches the constantly fluctuating patterns of light and sound which this lethal combination of talent has managed to unleash. If the Beatles dragged popular music from the inanities of middle-class, middle-aged business-oriented rap, then Led Zeppelin have propelled rock and roll into the forefront of artistic achievement in the mid-1970s."

For the Earls Court shows, *NME* sent Zeppelin press veteran Charles Shaar Murray to pen a lengthy two-page feature story. "It really was an occasion," the reporter wrote. "The tension and anticipation were as pervasive as it can only get when something that has been awaited with genuinely massive intensity is only a few seconds away. See, it's been one hell of a time since any of these people had a chance to see Led Zeppelin, who, after all, are one of the world's great rock and roll bands."

Murray continued, "Like Jimmy Page's guitar playing, John Bonham's drumming represents an enormous amount of raging energy rigorously channeled into specific areas. He never ventures into the areas of bombastic lunacy staked out by the likes of Keith Moon, preferring to be a rock and not to roll. His timing is flawless, his playing at once elegant, muscular and functional, if a trifle humorless. Where Moon's face is contorted into a demonic leer, Bonham's features betray little when he plays, except a stolid, careful pride in his work.

"Like Page, he never lets up," Murray continued, "never misses, used his control to modify and shape the inputs from his instincts. He plays clean, brisk and businesslike, supplying exactly the requisite amount of pressure to create that patented Zeppelin bulldozer effect. . . . Bonham's solo on 'Moby Dick' is one of the main Zep revelations. I've heard him do it several times, and each time I'm surprised to find myself enjoying it, because I've got a total loathing for drum solos."

Mick Bonham later remembered meeting up with John and the rest of the band following the May 23 performance. "After the show, we were to meet up with John and the other members of the band backstage for a drink. A large caravan had been towed in to act as a dressing room and drinks dispensary. As we arrived, John came over and hugged everybody, asking us what we wanted to drink. A crew member disappeared into the van for the drinks. Beers for us, of course, but only Coke for little Debbie. I had to laugh when I heard a voice in the van shout, 'Not *that*, you fucking idiot! It's for John's little sister! Coca-Cola, stupid!'"

Chapter Twenty

JUNE 1975–OCTOBER 1975

O n June 10, 1975, John and Pat welcomed their new daughter, Zoë Bonham.
Pat stayed in the hospital with the baby, surrounded by her sisters and other family members, while John kept watch on Old Hyde. Not much for being alone, he invited his one trusted reporter friend, Chris Welch, to visit the farm the following day.

"I went up to the farm to interview John in the summer," Welch later wrote. "I drove from London to Bonham's Worcestershire farmhouse. Driving up to the farm with its long white fencing, the spread reminded me of the Ponderosa ranch in the TV series *Bonanza*. It even had a ranch-style nameboard swinging in the breeze at the head of a long, straight, tree-lined drive. . . . Pat was in the hospital, having just had Zoë. . . . [N]aturally, there was much cause for some celebration." Even so, the journalist couldn't help but notice John's physical condition, the weight he had put on and the slowness to his movements. "He was hale and hearty. There were no sides to him."

John was uncharacteristically pensive during Welch's visit, the one and only time a reporter was invited into the sanctity of Old Hyde. Throughout the day, John escorted the writer around the hundred-acre property, talking music, life, his new daughter—and the future of Led

Zeppelin. Welch claimed, "Although John had received yet another six-month driving ban, he seemed content, relaxed, and satisfied with life."

Before setting off on the day's adventure among the farm, John and Welch enjoyed the drummer's refurbished den, a quaint lounge area complete with a drum kit, pool table, and "his jukebox stuffed with favorite records," which surprisingly included Cat Stevens, Joni Mitchell, Supertramp, and Abba (who would later allow Led Zeppelin to use their personal recording studio in Stockholm). Over a quiet drink, John made a surprising confession to Welch. "He confided in me that he was suffering from panic attacks before every concert. . . . John confessed to me that he found it harder and harder to do the long solos."

The casual interview took a lighter turn as John led Welch to his personal favorite area of the grounds—one of the old cattle barns that had been rebuilt into the drummer's lavish, private garage. "This is the hot-car shop," John chuckled as he opened the doors, first showing Welch "a trio of highly improbable vehicles"—one an elaborately painted taxicab, mounted on oversize racing tires. As John explained, the novelty taxi was "a show car," adding, "I bought her in LA, [and] she can do 150 mph." Next up was a 1967 Corvette with a seven-liter engine. Finally, they reached a 1954 two-door Ford, also with an eight-liter engine. Of the Ford, John told Welch, "It's an amazing car—look at all the chrome inside. She'd only done ten thousand miles when I bought her."

Last, but certainly not least, was the two-door 1923 Ford Model T John had impulsively purchased earlier in the year to replace his beloved, uninsurable Corvette from Dallas. As John proudly recalled, the hot rod had been customized with a tremendous seven-liter Chevrolet engine in San Francisco by Andy "the Rodfather" Brizio, a racer and mechanic who won the 1970 award for America's Most Beautiful Roadster with his creation Andy's Instant T, a Model T kit hot rod. John's could easily do 0 to 60 mph in 3.2 seconds.

In April 1971, John also bought a hot rod from Jeff Beck. Known as the "Boston Strangler," it was a Model T built in the 1960s by

Massachusetts mechanic Rick Heinrick, with a metal-flake green body powered by a huge engine and lacking silencers, making it roar like a jungle animal on the road. At one point, Beck smashed it up and reconstructed it with a full-height screen and gave the body a paint job in purple flake.

John would often take the faster cars in his collection up Hagley Road to the nearby Bromsgrove dual carriageway, a perfect track for testing high speeds.

Old pal Bev Bevan was one of the friends who experienced the terror of riding shotgun with John at the wheel of the Model T. "It was absolutely frightening. He said, 'I'll show you how quick it is.' He drove it down to the dual carriageway, and on a bend in the road, he actually parked it in the fast lane. . . . We just sat there waiting for a car to come screaming 'round the bend straight towards us at 70 miles per hour. He could see it in his rear mirror. And then he just floored the thing. . . . It went from naught to 100 in about four seconds, or something ridiculous. It was absolutely terrifying—but very typical of John!"

Early drum mentor and friend Garry Allcock recalled a similar terrifying experience with John. "[John] also owned an FF Jensen Interceptor four-wheel drive. He took me for a drive. He put his foot down and nearly frightened me to death."

Chris Welch was amused to learn that John's love of fast cars extended to his generosity toward his loved ones. According to John, after he'd made the terrible mistake of forgetting to buy Pat a birthday gift one year, he escorted her to a Birmingham showroom and purchased her a brand-new Aston Martin right on the spot. Adamant about demonstrating the luxury sports car's capabilities to his wife, John got the car up to more than 100 mph, making poor Pat swear she'd never set foot in the car again. "He always had six cars at a time," Bev Bevan recalled, "and he changed one of these cars every month. . . . He was a car salesman's dream. He'd come in and buy a Ferrari, a red AC Cobra, and an Aston Martin."

John's love of purchasing expensive automobiles had become a budding addiction; in the first eighteen months of Led Zeppelin's early success, he bought twenty-eight. From 1971 and on, John stopped counting. As Chris Welch noted, John didn't seem to keep the cars for long. To him, they weren't investments—rather, they were fun diversions that his riches now afforded.

Years later, a grown Jason Bonham shared a humorous memory of just how prevalent his father's impulse for automobile purchases could be. "One time at the end of one of Zeppelin's tours, Jimmy Page called the house and asked for John. My mom was confused and said, 'He's not back from the tour yet. How are you home?' And before Jimmy could answer, we all heard the roar of a sports-car engine, and sure enough, here comes Dad. He had gone straight from the airport to the dealership and picked up a Lamborghini."

And as strange and obscure as some of John's models were, they were nothing compared with the customized "Model T bread van" he'd purchased, mainly for the strange novelty of it. The bread van had been of John's personal favorites among his vast collection. One time during a recording session at Shepperton Studios in London, John had innocently parked the bizarre vehicle in front of the studio's main entrance. A local priest from the church down the street paused as he walked by the van. "This is a very dangerous-looking automobile," the priest said to John, making a stab at some light humor. "I better bless this car and this boy." John smiled politely while the priest walked back to the church to fetch some holy water, then proceeded to bless the car—and John.

Returning to the house from the large garage, John and Welch settled back in the lounge. As Welch continued the interview, nine-year-old Jason arrived home in his cub uniform and immediately began bashing away on his miniature drum kit, which was set up in front of John's jukebox. The journalist later recalled that even at that age, the young Bonham was very good and had obviously inherited his father's passion for the instrument. According to John, however, that wasn't all young Jason had gotten from his dad. "You can't teach him anything," John quietly told the reporter. "He's got a terrible temper."

The two men ended the day with a quiet drink at John's favorite local pub, Chequers, downtown. Over a few pints of ale, John elaborated on his mixed emotions about being on tour so frequently and his own insecurities as a musician. According to Welch, "Just the thought of having to power up Led Zeppelin for two to three hours every night on the road sometimes induced a sort of panic attack [in John]. It wasn't to do with stage fright while performing; it was the waiting beforehand. Indeed, I had seen him being sick before a show or remain tight-lipped and morose, unable to speak."

Finishing his pint, John told him, "I've got worse. . . . I have terribly bad nerves all the time. Once we start into 'Rock and Roll,' I'm fine. I just can't stand sitting around, and I worry about playing badly—and if I do, then I'm really pissed off. If I play well, I feel fine."

Night fell, and Welch prepared for his return drive to London. Before John let him go, however, he insisted on giving the reporter a special item for all his years of fair and accurate reporting. "While I was still mumbling faintly that he really shouldn't, John and Matthew loaded up my car with a huge, great black-and-white Ludwig Vistalite drum kit," Welch remarked, forever astounded at John's generosity. "The trunk lid was jammed open and tied up with string to accommodate a huge box on wheels full of hardware. . . . It was gone midnight as I bid farewell to John and drove home through country roads and motorways to London, unable to see anything out of the rear mirror and expecting to be stopped by police at any instant."

John knew it would be a good long while until the two men saw one another again. Led Zeppelin was nearing their deadline to leave the country due to their tax status. He'd given the writer the drum kit as a fitting farewell.

※ ※ ※

As overjoyed as John was with the birth of Zoë, he faced unwavering depression over his situation. Led Zeppelin's time as tax gypsies wasn't even remotely over; moreover, if they wanted to keep earning vast fortunes, there was no actual end in sight. He had a beautiful home and a beautiful family but could enjoy them only through a self-imposed time-share with his own success. In giving Chris Welch unprecedented access into the things he held most dear in his life, John had inadvertently given himself a sad tour of everything he was about to leave behind.

That knowledge in itself was an even further push into John's depression and frustration, which in turn was often redirected toward the wrong people. When Welch visited on June 11, John failed to mention he'd had a horrible fight the night before with, of all people, his closest friend—his own younger brother, Mick.

"John phones us to tell us the news [of Zoë's birth] and arranged to come over to the Conservative Club to celebrate that night," Mick Bonham later remembered. "Jacko and I arrived at eight and waited for John. . . . By nine, there was still no sign of him, so we carried on with our own celebration. At ten thirty, the stewardess came over to say that John was on the phone. It appeared that he had popped in at the New Inn for a quick one, but it had ended up a party and he wanted Jacko and me to pop over. There was no way we could go, as neither of us were in a fit state to drive." As all three men—John, Mick, and Jacko—had been drinking, a misunderstanding was inevitable. John became furious at what he deemed a slight against the birth of his new daughter. "At eleven fifteen, John rang again, this time in a terrible temper, and gave me a real *bollocking* for not going over, but as I tried to explain what the problem was, the phone went dead."

Not fully aware of the full extent of John's resentment, Mick innocently headed home with their father. Just after midnight, both men were jolted awake by a pounding on the front door of their apartment—John, in a drunken, angry rage. "As I opened the door, [John] burst in and tried to knock the crap out of me, with Jacko trying to get between us and stop the pandemonium. In the ensuing tussle, Jacko took a knock, which cut his lip. At this, John stopped, hugged his dad, and apologized. He then turned to me and said, 'Look what you've done now,' aiming a few more blows in my direction. . . . John looked around in disbelief, which gave me a breather, then, again focused on the job at hand, shouted at me again and disappeared out the door."

As it happened, John and the members of Led Zeppelin were due to leave for the next round of their tax exile. Mick Bonham didn't speak to his brother for another year.

※ ※ ※

A FEW WEEKS AFTER THE BAND'S TRIUMPHANT EARLS COURT concerts, Peter Grant pulled Richard Cole aside and explained to him precisely why he valued those shows so much. "In a sense, [Grant] saw them as 'good-bye gifts' to the country," Cole later admitted. "'We're moving out,' he said. 'The taxman is driving us out of England. These will be the last concerts here for quite a while.'"

The last go-round of their exile had been bad enough, as none of Zeppelin's members had been particularly enamored with the 1975 tour. Sure, they had made a ton of money—but that very fortune was the cause of their forced exile abroad. "This is home," John insisted. "I'm not going anywhere." However, the band's financial records dictated a change of heart. To stubbornly stay in the United Kingdom would be to turn over the majority of their earnings to the government. Instead, while each member of the band kept a home in England, they were limited in terms of the number of days they could spend in the country before being flagged by the taxman, forcing them to relocate elsewhere for the time in between.

John held out longer than the other three; he had been determined to stay by Pat's side as much as possible during her pregnancy. "Fuck the money," he told Richard Cole at the time. "I'm gonna spend time with my wife right here where she needs me."

After Zoë's birth, John was urged by the band to come to his senses. He joined them in Jersey, the largest of the Channel Islands. Baked in tourism and sunshine, John immediately longed for the warmth and familiarity of Old Hyde. Asked what he thought of the island, John remarked, "The natives here don't seem to do much but drink and wife swap."

Robert, however, opted to take his family on holiday to Morocco. Weeks later, he was reunited with Jimmy, who wanted to make good on his promise to William S. Burroughs to see this ancient part of the world and learn its musical history. Afterward, they joined the other Zeppelin members in Montreux, where touring plans were discussed for the coming year.

Although estranged at the time, John would later tell his brother, Mick, the one true highlight of this period: meeting the members of the Count Basie Orchestra during the Montreux Jazz Festival in July, all thanks to John Paul Jones and esteemed jazz drummer Butch Miles, who was a big fan of John's Zeppelin work. "John became apprehensive, asking why Basie's drummer would want to meet him," Mick Bonham recalled, "but backstage, the roles were reversed—it turned out that the drummer was one of *John's* biggest fans and had studied his style and copied a lot of this techniques. . . . That meant a lot to a drummer in a rock 'n' roll band."

John Paul Jones later echoed how much that meeting had meant to John. "I said, 'Butch Miles, this is John Bonham.' Bonzo went to shake his hand, and Butch went, 'John Bonham! Wow, man. I grew up listening to your music. I learned to play drums listening to your records.' So, they got on really well."

Following the jazz festival, Jimmy, Charlotte, and their daughter, Scarlet, joined Robert, Maureen, and their two children on the Greek island of Rhodes. On August 3, Jimmy took a brief trip to Sicily to get a firsthand look at Aleister Crowley's old farmhouse and abbey, which had recently been put on the real estate market, and then planned to meet Robert's family in Paris. The next day, however, disaster hit. Maureen Plant had been driving the rental car with Robert in the passenger's seat, and both their children and Jimmy's daughter were in the back. Suddenly, Maureen lost control of the vehicle, swerved off the narrow island road, and ended up with the car smashed against a tree. At first, Robert looked at his unmoving wife and thought she was dead. Richard Cole received a panicked phone call from Jimmy's assistant the following day, and he quickly sprang into action, using every available resource at Led Zeppelin's disposal to get the Plants the best possible medical care. Maureen's skull and pelvis were fractured, and Robert's ankle and elbow were shattered; the children were okay. On the quaint Greek island, there was no way to get to the closest hospital without flagging down a farmer's fruit truck.

John and Peter Grant were in Jersey when the frantic phone calls began. Richard Cole successfully got Robert and Maureen back to England, where they were told she would be in the hospital in intensive care for weeks and that Robert wouldn't walk for at least six months. Again, the miseries attached to the tax exile quickly presented themselves: Robert would have to leave his wife as she recuperated, since, under the legal guidelines, his allotted time at home in England was already almost up. Begrudgingly, he allowed Richard Cole to arrange a flight for him to meet John and Peter Grant in Jersey. Richard packed up and went, too, as did Benji LeFevre, who acted as Robert's chief caretaker for the next half year.

When Robert arrived on the island, John was able to temporarily check his own depression at the door. He was just relieved his old friend was alive.

✳ ✳ ✳

Longing for the comfort of friends and family, John extended an invitation to old Midlands mate David Handley to join both him and the slowly recuperating Robert Plant on the tropical island a few weeks later. "Jersey was the nearest they could get to Britain while they were tax exiles, so they camped at the Atlantic Hotel for a few weeks," Hadley recalled. "They said they'd do a gig for a small club owner, who had been very friendly and helpful to them. . . . They just asked that he didn't tell anyone about it beforehand."

While Hadley was there for another "long weekend" with John, he was privy to one of Zeppelin's surprise appearances at Behan's nightclub. Robert performed in his wheelchair, his leg still in a cast. "So, these guys shuffle onstage, and the club owner says, 'Ladies and gentlemen, a special treat tonight—Led Zeppelin!'" David Hadley laughed. "They all thought he was kidding, of course, but once the band actually started to play, people ran out into the street to round up all their friends. And there was Robert singing in a wheelchair in this little club. . . . It was a wild few days."

Listless again, John used his exile on Jersey to further indulge himself with luxury cars. "Bonzo put on a fancy-dress outfit later and drove a Bentley 'round the island with the police chasing him," David Hadley later remembered. "I think he did three laps of the island, but they couldn't catch him. He'd learned all these moves to outwit the police."

John's favorite car for careening around Jersey, however, was his Rolls-Royce. One afternoon, he parked the Rolls outside a local pub and began washing it with a bucket and sponge he'd brought along. With John dressed in cutoff jeans and a T-shirt, no passing bystander would have guessed him as the vehicle's owner. Soon, a well-dressed elderly man happened by and paused to look over the car, as well as John's handiwork with the soap and sponge. "Well, well, well," the man smirked. "This is the first time I've ever seen a man have to wash his own Rolls-Royce!"

Quite simply, John was in no mood. As if on the turn of a dime, he inexplicably lost his cool. "Is that right?" he shouted through gritted teeth, thoroughly startling the old man. John then put on a memorable performance, slamming one of the Rolls's doors shut and kicking the car's side panels—thoroughly beating the shit out of the vehicle. The temper tantrum continued for several minutes, and the old man watched aghast. When John was finally finished and out of breath, there were dozens of dents all along the Rolls's exterior.

"I suspect that's the first time you've ever seen a man smash his own fucking Rolls-Royce as well?" John asked rhetorically, catching his breath. "Why don't you fuck off and mind your own business?" John then walked into the pub and ordered himself a Pimm's.

✳ ✳ ✳

NO ONE IN LED ZEPPELIN WAS IN A PARTICULARLY GOOD MOOD. Although grateful for Robert and Maureen's survival, the episode had, nonetheless, quashed any plans for a profitable tour, rendering them exiled with nothing to do. The band also worried that such a lengthy hiatus could affect not only their collective wallet but also their credibility; with Robert out of commission, how were they to stay relevant? It might be ages before the group could tour again. Peter Grant came up with a possible solution: resurrect the long-dead Led Zeppelin concert film. While the band debated releasing the footage, Jimmy and Robert quietly brainstormed how possible recording sessions might be arranged.

The band agreed to leave Jersey once and for all and meet again in September in LA. There, the familiar surroundings of California—debauchery and all—could bring a sense of normalcy and routine to early rehearsals. Initially, Richard Cole booked the band, as usual, into the Riot House, but with all the changes that had occurred—and since the band was getting older—the hotel just didn't seem to hold the old charm. As a change of scenery, the group rented individual beach houses in swanky Malibu Colony, where Robert began his intensive routine of songwriting and physical therapy. He soon asked Danny Goldberg if he believed in karma.

In his own house on Malibu Colony Drive, Jimmy set about crafting the music for the next album, while also overseeing the day-to-day operations of Swan Song, which had recently signed a new band called Detective, fronted by Jimmy's friend Michael Des Barres, to replace the now-defunct the Pretty Things. Although Detective was given an extravagant million-dollar deal—plus the bonus prestige of affiliation with Led Zeppelin itself—Des Barres soon grew disillusioned with what he perceived as a lack of general participation on Zeppelin's part. "When Bonzo owns a fifth of you," the singer later claimed, "you know the situation is out of the ordinary. Once we signed with them, we never even saw any of Led Zeppelin for two years. We dealt with Danny [Goldberg]. We were produced to sound as much like Led Zeppelin as possible."

"The vibe around Led Zeppelin became druggier than I had previously seen," Goldberg later noted. "I became close friends with Detective's Michael Des Barres and his wife, Pamela. . . . When it came time to take a Swan Song signing photo, I got a limo to pick up Jimmy at the Malibu Colony. I brought him to my room at the Beverly Hills Hotel, where the members of Detective and Neal Preston were to meet us. Jimmy was nodding out the whole time we were in the car, and when we got to my room, he lay down on the couch and immediately fell asleep. When the band got there, Michael and I tried repeatedly to wake him, but it was to no avail. . . . After around a half hour, I had Neal photograph Detective sitting next to the sleeping Page and then sent him and the band members home."

When Jimmy awoke hours later, he was incensed that Goldberg had sanctioned photos of him sleeping beside Swan Song's latest signed band. "There had been rumors that Jimmy was doing heroin, and this behavior made me believe them," Goldberg recalled. "Not surprisingly, Page had a different explanation—he said he had taken a Valium and must have overreacted to it. . . . He let me circulate the photo but later complained that in doing so I had 'made him out to be a twit.' In retrospect, he was absolutely right. The photo never should have seen the light of day."

Jimmy's former lover Lori Maddox later claimed the guitarist had done heroin for seven years straight and then went to Switzerland and had his blood changed like Keith Richards. Page, a notoriously private person, has never publicly acknowledged or discussed the use of the drug.

"The house Robert and I stayed in was right in the middle of the Colony," Benji LeFevre said, "and when El Niño raged for days and days, it took all the sand away from the beach, and a couple of houses collapsed. . . . There was lots of Charlie [cocaine], and I said to him, 'You've got to slow down, man, because otherwise you're not going to get better.' . . . At the same time, in Jimmy's house up the road, it was closed doors and closed curtains. We used to refer to [heroin] as 'Henry Hall.' Robert started to get very disillusioned about the whole thing. It was a time of real reflection for him."

After Jimmy and Robert's monthlong writing retreat, John and John Paul Jones flew out to Malibu in late October and rehearsals began. At first, the four used the beach houses as rehearsal space, but the band soon relocated to the Hollywood-based SIR Studios. During this tumultuous time, however, LA proved the worst possible influence on John's frame of mind—and his behavior. As Richard Cole later put it, "Bonzo was really out of control in Malibu."

Disgusted with the living arrangement in Malibu, John made the odd decision to move into the Riot House all by himself, much to the chagrin and disapproval of everyone, including Peter Grant. "John moved out to the Hyatt House," Grant later recalled. "There was a lot of tension about that period, [with all of us] all holed up in houses we didn't really want to be in."

With Robert in poor condition due to his leg, Jimmy holed up with his own vices and self-doubt, and John Paul Jones becoming ever more disillusioned with the entire enterprise, John let loose on the Sunset Strip and was left to his own devices: in Beverly Hills, he got pulled over for driving recklessly on the way to Safeway; he hung out at the Rainbow, as usual, and at Trader Vic's; he saw Little Feat in Venice; he went to the Roxy to see Bob Marley with Ringo Starr and Keith Moon. When staying at the Beverly Wilshire, he lay around and watched the Marx Brothers and Monty Python. "Bonzo was a huge adult with the emotions of a six-year-old child and an artistic license to indulge in any sort of infantile or destructive behavior that amused him," recalled Danny Goldberg.

"Bonzo was a sweet, cuddly, goofy fella until he got drunk, and then you wanted to avoid him," Michael Des Barres's wife, Pamela, later recalled. "I saw him slug my friend right in the jaw just for being in the doorway with him at the Rainbow."

On a particularly eventful evening, John walked alone into the Rainbow Bar & Grill and took his normal stool at the bar, ordering up twenty black Russians. After knocking back half of them, he turned to scour the room for familiar faces. Pamela Des Barres's friend, an assistant to Sunset Strip promoter Kim Fowley, made the mistake of smiling at him. According to some accounts, John invited himself over to the assistant's table and bellowed in her face, "What the fuck did you say?" and as the young woman began to answer, John punched her in the face, sending her to the floor. According to Kim Fowley, however, the altercation was more of a balanced wrestling match. "She was a fighter," Fowley said. "A sensitive girl, but she could battle—and she and Bonzo had a bout of Greco-Roman wrestling on the floor."

On another night in the Rainbow, John was planning to meet up with Bad Company drummer Simon Kirke, and while waiting for his friend's arrival, picked a fight with the wrong person—one of the venue's martial arts–trained bouncers, named Bear. "After the gigs . . . John was pretty much a loose cannon," remembered Kirke. "John had been restrained after drinking fifteen brandy Alexanders and taken to jail. . . . Bear was quite apologetic because he'd had to apply a choke hold on a very drunk and combative Bonzo and had actually rendered him unconscious." Bear had the option of pressing charges—he had numerous witnesses to John's instigative behavior—but let it go.

Even John's friends who had no problems with taking part in the rock 'n' roll party lifestyle began to see the danger in his behavior, as well as the potential for an alcohol- and drug-infused downward spiral. "John and I spent many nights doing coke, and it got to a point where he'd tip a pile onto a plate and just throw it at his face," Tony Iommi later claimed. "You'd think about saying something, but John was hard to talk to when he was like that."

As Danny Goldberg remembered, "Bonzo figured in many of Led Zeppelin's dramas because, while affable when sober and transcendent when playing the drums, he was an angry and mean drunk, referred to at such times by the other band members as 'the Beast.'"

To publicist B. P. Fallon, the band's occasional misbehavior—particularly John's—was a logical extension of the creative hedonistic ideal. "If you freak out every now and then and misbehave, does that mean you're a monster? Not necessarily." To Fallon, it went with the territory. "Bonzo was the guy who drove the train, night after night, not for a few minutes but sometimes for four hours. . . . If he'd painted or sculpted, everyone would have said, 'How great.' But he didn't— he drummed, like nobody in the world."

"Notwithstanding . . . occasionally sweet moments, the general atmosphere was one of tension, exacerbated by the huge quantities of cocaine," Goldberg recalled of the later tours. "Although I was never to personally witness any violence, the threat of it always seemed to be just one bad mood away."

❊ ❊ ❊

NOTHING SEEMED TO FILL THE VOID IN JOHN'S HEART WHEN HE WAS separated from his family. As soon as the smallest wiggle room was allowed in their tax status, John hopped the next flight home.

In September of that year, John's brother, Mick, married his fiancée, Lin. Moving out of his apartment with Jacko, Mick and his new wife soon had a two-bedroom flat of their own in Winyates. "Along with the birth of my two children, it would be one of the three happiest days of my life," Mick later recalled. "Sadly, I had always believed that on my own wedding day, my big brother would have been by my side." Although the two brothers had spoken since their falling-out the night of Zoë's birth, a second misunderstanding forced John to attend the wedding of Pat's brother, Jeff, on the same day as Mick's. "It wouldn't be for many years that I would find out just how much it had actually hurt John not to be at our wedding," Mick remembered, "something I would never have wanted to happen."

One afternoon many months later, Mick was sitting in the lounge of their flat, watching the street from the balcony. In the distance, he heard the unmistakable rumble of a speeding sports car drawing near.

"That's John!" Lin Bonham exclaimed to her husband, smiling.

"It couldn't be," Mick said. "The music papers had said he'd had to go and live abroad."

Mick later recalled, "Without waiting to find out, I was up and running down the three flights of stairs and out into the car park to find John walking toward me with that heartwarming smile across his face. . . . No words were exchanged; we just hugged each other until Lin arrived and joined in."

John breathlessly filled his brother in on the past half year's worth of triumphs and tragedies—from Robert and Maureen's car crash to the optimism surrounding his recovery, from the now-resurrected concert film to the band's progress for the next album's rehearsals. "John had spent his year of nonresidency in hotel rooms in New York, Jersey, and the South of France, fighting off boredom and other people," Mick recalled. "And with no gigs, the year dragged on for what seemed like an eternity. John also told us about his hatred of having to live away from his family—and was only allowed so many days back in the country and that he would have to leave again tomorrow."

True to his word, John left for Coventry the next morning.

✳ ✳ ✳

REHEARSALS FOR THE NEW ALBUM, NEWLY TITLED *PRESENCE*, CONTINUED at SIR Studios in Hollywood. Despite his rumored weakened condition, Jimmy's playing was as hot as ever, and the new album reflected his reignited passion for heavy, guitar-driven hard rock. And although he would have been happiest surround by Pat, Jason, and little Zoë, being let loose on the drum kit unabashed was John's solace. He and Jimmy wanted to make *Presence* the band's heaviest album yet.

Another facet to the band's newfound focus was the pent-up energy felt by all four. Even relegated to a wheelchair, Robert was bursting with a form of stamina that would normally have found its place onstage. With the plans for a fall tour out the window, the band fueled their road adrenaline into the music.

Then new tax-law regulations came into effect and ruined everything, only this time it was from the States. The band couldn't be in England for too long or risk financial hardship; likewise, if they remained stagnant in America over a given allotment of time, they'd be screwed as well. A rolling stone gathers no moss; in this case, it was the members of Zeppelin.

With the rehearsals finished, the group decided to record *Presence* at Musicland Studios in Munich, Germany.

Chapter Twenty-One

NOVEMBER 1975–JANUARY 1977

John, Jimmy, and Robert took a brief detour through New York City on their way to Europe and then flew separately the rest of the way. Jimmy arrived in Munich first.

Despising air travel, John insisted on flying with personal assistant Mick Hinton, who now acted as not only his drum tech but also his valet and—as observed by Richard Cole—"indentured servant." For the Munich trip, John was booked in the first-class section of the British Airways airliner, while Hinton took a spot in coach. Unable to cope with another trek around the globe, John knocked back two full bottles of champagne and fell asleep. At the insistence of the other passengers, the steward didn't wake him when dinner was served. Two hours later, John roused on his own and discovered he'd pissed himself in the seat. He craned his neck and bellowed for the ever-loyal Hinton's attention. The assistant had been reading *Sports Illustrated* and nodding off as well, but at John's command he raced to first class and reported for duty.

"Quick—walk in front of me!" John whispered and then used Hinton as a human shield to stroll to the men's room. As yielding to John Bonham's every whim usually called for even the most unexpected circumstances, Hinton had packed an extra pair of pants in his carry-on bag, which he now handed to his boss. Freshened up, John made Hinton switch seats with him while the drummer took his place in coach and went back to an alcohol-induced slumber.

✳ ✳ ✳

THE BAND BEGAN THEIR INITIAL RECORDINGS FOR THE ALBUM ON November 12, kicking off with a jazzy number for which John and John Paul Jones had contributed the most preliminary songwriting input, "Royal Orleans." On the earliest takes, Robert rose to the occasion of the genre, singing in a deep Dr. John impression. At the one-minute mark of the final cut, John brought on a groovy rhythm, playing sixteenth notes hand-to-hand on his hi-hat—seamlessly interweaving his syncopated four-way dexterity, all the while emphasizing his left hand and left foot, shuttering the cymbals like a well-oiled machine.

The band agreed the sessions were off to a good start.

The Munich studios were located directly under the Arabella Hotel, and Richard Cole had booked the band there out of convenience. Both the hotel and the studios were in recent demand, as many British tax exiles had been using the facilities; the Rolling Stones, in fact, were booked immediately following Zeppelin's sessions. Under severe pressure to lay down tracks while the band was the most energetic—and with another band coming in right afterward—Jimmy loosened his usually ironfisted perfectionism and let the tracks for *Presence* hit naturally hard and heavy. Unlike in the past, there would be no acoustic shadings or John Paul Jones's signature keyboard—just wailing, all-out guitars, and overdubs.

The album's opening number would not only amount to Led Zeppelin's longest studio cut but also become one of John's most revered rhythm tracks. "Achilles Last Stand" stood as the ultimate example of Jimmy's multilayered guitar harmonies, coupled with Robert's usual love of myth and fantasy—in this instance, images of warfare and the strength of Atlas, accentuated by the singer's primal, painful cries.

As the album's true epic, it took more than a full minute for John's theatrical introduction, his roaring beat at lightning speed and sneaked between rapid backbeats. On fire, John tossed off a heavy triplet roll inspired by Buddy Rich, almost three minutes in, an introduction to yet another new fill from his bag of tricks, playing consecutive hand-to-hand sixteenth notes, the first three beats on the snare and the fourth and fifth on the left and right crash cymbals, underpinned by the bass drum—a staple of heavier, grungy rock that would take shape in the coming decades.

"I played a sparse riff on 'Achilles Last Stand,' which allowed [John] to work quite quickly," John Paul Jones later said. "We changed tempo on that one—and most rock bands can't do that. . . . It's not easy to stop in the middle of a number at exactly the right place. We could do anything with tempos."

Presence was an album truly pieced together under dire circumstances; Jimmy's playing and Robert's lyrics directly reflected their desperation. Nowhere is that more evident than in two key tracks, "For Your Life" and "Nobody's Fault but Mine," the first of which amounted to a sad ballad about the Los Angeles cocaine scene from which the men had just escaped. Kicking off with Jimmy's guitar and John Paul's bass locked in unified soul riffs, John glued the moody piece together with little more than hi-hat and tambourine. Two minutes into the song, however, he slyly slipped a couple of high-speed triplets into the mix with his foot, incorporating a new riff into the lengthy composition.

The most playful of the album's songs, "Candy Store Rock" was the band's callback to their beloved golden-age rockabilly, cut straight from Elvis's cloth. With the song light on substance but heavy on musicianship, Robert came alive during the rollicking recording. Likewise on "Hots on for Nowhere," a genre bender that allowed John to keep playing with the rockabilly shuffle.

"Nobody's Fault but Mine" was Robert and Jimmy's moody reworking of an old Robert Johnson song, "Hellhound on My Trail"; it was the group's first major foray into heavy blues in years. The lyrics, a confession of sins sinned and repentance unattainable, paint images of lost love and addiction in the guise of a dirty jam. Later, critics would call the song Led Zeppelin's exorcism, but not stipulate which demon they'd actually been casting out.

✵ ✵ ✵

THE SEVEN SONGS WERE RECORDED AT BREAKNECK SPEED. ONCE THE band wrapped, however, Jimmy still needed to add his overdubs and finalize a working mix. He estimated three days would be enough extra time and called Mick Jagger directly, explaining the situation. Jagger agreed to wait a few days before the Stones came in to begin their sessions for *Black and Blue*.

In order to record the initial seven tracks, Jimmy had already been pulling eighteen-hour days for two weeks; now, he stayed up nights too in order to complete all the work. "After we finished recording all of our parts, the engineer, Keith Harwood, and me just started mixing until we would fall asleep," Jimmy explained. "Then, whoever would wake up first would call the other, and we'd continue to work until we passed out again." Jimmy considered the completion of *Presence* a test of sheer will, and he had no intention of failing. Within eighteen days, the entire album was finished. He told one reporter, "The day we finished, the Stones came in and asked how we'd gotten on. I said, 'All right. I've finished thanks to the two extra days you gave us.' They said, 'The tracks?' And I said, 'No, the whole thing.' And they couldn't believe it."

✵ ✵ ✵

AFTER UNBELIEVABLY KNOCKING OUT AN ENTIRE ALBUM IN UNDER A month, the band returned to the island of Jersey the first week of December. In decidedly better spirits than during their previous stay on the island, Led Zeppelin had—for all intents and purposes—regained its creative mojo. On December 10, they surprised the patrons of Behan's West Park and Anne Port Bay Folk Club in St. Helier yet again, delivering a surprise set. "Led Zeppelin, who had not played together in public since their spring U.S. tour, made a surprise comeback last week when they gave an impromptu 45-minute performance in Jersey's largest niterie," *NME* reported. "John Paul Jones and John Bonham had, the previous week, sat in with resident rock pianist Norman Hale [formerly with the Tornados] and they promised to return with other members of the band. They duly kept this promise and played a set which included some of their own material, as well as 'Blue Suede Shoes' and several other rock classics."

The day before Christmas, Jimmy flew off to New York to mix the soundtrack for the band's long-gestating concert film, finally titled *The Song Remains the Same*.

And with that, the year 1975 was at an end, and the band was officially off duty. Blissfully, John flew home to Old Hyde.

✳ ✳ ✳

AS PER THE REGULATIONS OF THEIR EXILE, THE BAND WAS ALLOWED only a few days before hopping aboard a flight for New York City the first week of 1976. As they settled into the lush Park Lane Hotel near Central Park South, the members of Led Zeppelin began to vocally express their discontent. Robert, having been forced to leave his bedridden wife's side the year before, was particularly disgusted, complaining bitterly how all the talent in England was being punished for their success. To John and John Paul, he noted that even Mick Jagger had taken up residence only four blocks away on the West Side.

More to pass the time than anything else, the group congregated at Swan Song's Manhattan office and went over the details of *The Song Remains the Same*. Peter Grant had long since fired the original director, Joe Massot, whom he accused of making "the most expensive home movie ever made," and replaced him with a filmmaker named Peter Clifton. The new director's chief function was to assemble the three-year-old concert footage and band vignettes—the "dream sequences"—and create a coherent film out of the pieces. Nothing could be done to improve the quality of the footage—or the mediocre soundtrack, for that matter—but with no tours planned, the film was the best asset Led Zeppelin had for the new year.

Meeting adjourned, the group was unleashed upon New York. John, quickly restless, made an unannounced—and decidedly unwelcome—visit backstage at a Deep Purple concert at the Nassau Coliseum on Long Island. The Purple players later mentioned that John was extremely drunk from the moment he arrived, staggering his way through the wings off the stage and then lunging at an empty microphone during the show. The audience cheered his drunken cameo appearance before the band's roadies could stop him. "My name is John Bonham of Led Zeppelin," John bellowed in the mic, "and I just wanna tell ya that we got a new album comin' out called *Presence* and that it's fucking great!"

The audience was more forgiving than the band—but John wasn't done yet. Turning on his heels to leave the stage, he grabbed the microphone one more time. He gave Deep Purple's lead guitarist a wry grin. "And as far as Tommy Bolin is concerned, he can't play for shit!"

Whether John's faith in *Presence*'s creative worth was true or not, the cheers he received foreshadowed the album's record-breaking advance orders; it became the first Led Zeppelin release to reach platinum status before even hitting store shelves on March 31.

Jimmy told the press, "[The album] was recorded while the group was on the move, technological gypsies, no base, no home. All you could relate to was a new horizon and a suitcase. . . . So, there's a lot of movement and aggression."

For the cover, the band again retained the services of Hipgnosis, the London-based art-design firm. Overtly conceptual, the album's cover prominently depicted a Norman Rockwell–esque traditional nuclear family at the dinner table, joyfully staring at a mysterious black obelisk sculpture at the table's center. Danny Goldberg later added that journalists kept the American Swan Song phones off the hook inquiring about the meaning of the mystical object; in England, Richard Cole informed reporters that the musicians didn't even know what it was. As depicted, the small statue seemed to resemble a normal household object, perhaps used for healing or spiritual guidance. As Robert later told Cameron Crowe, the cover of *Presence* was meant to be left up to interpretation, another element of the Led Zeppelin mystique. "Whatever you want it to say, it says," Plant explained. "'The Object' can be taken in many ways. Let's just say that we love plucking these little niceties out there. We used symbols [sort of cosmic hieroglyphics] on the *Four* album, too. They're fun, and they only add to the music. . . . But there's not much fun in knowing everything, is there?"

※ ※ ※

THAT SPRING, IT APPEARED THAT BIRMINGHAM WAS AS HAPPY FOR John's return as he was to be back. "Arriving back home in May 1976, we all met up at the Conservative Club in Studley," Mick Bonham explained. "Although it had been a year since our last night out, I was glad to see that silliness was still the order of the day. . . . Playing a frame of snooker, John hit the cue ball so hard that it left the table and demolished one of the wall lights. His punishment? Cries of 'Good shot, John' from the other members watching the game."

Jason Bonham was now ten years old. He hadn't inherited merely his father's natural abilities on the drums—the boy now shared John's passion for fast cars and racing, too. While John was away, Pat's brother-in-law Allan sponsored young Jason at the Schoolboy Moto Cross club, taking him to local meetings and age-appropriate races. Enthralled to see his son taking up his shared interest, anytime John could attend Jason's races and help in sponsoring the children's club, he made himself readily available. Mick Bonham recalled, "Lin and I finally saw [Jason] race in June 1976, and although I thought that cowboys and Indians would be a safer bet, Jason wasn't scared and became a very competent rider. . . . Soon, the whole 'Schoolboy' thing would become a big part of John's life, too."

That month, John had to attend to some shake-ups at Swan Song, although he had long lost interest in the record-label company. To everyone's shock, Danny Goldberg announced he was leaving the company—although the details regarding his departure were vague.

Richard Cole claimed that Goldberg had been fired when he dared question Peter Grant's ethics surrounding Bad Company's promotion. "Danny was fired because nobody could be permitted to quit Led Zeppelin," Cole said. "But Peter Grant started to cry anyway: 'I never thought I'd live to see the day,' he sobbed, 'when I'd hear myself say, "Danny Goldberg is fired."'"

Goldberg later insisted that he actually left because of another artist he personally championed for Swan Song, a singer-songwriter simply named Mirabai. "Peter had agreed to let me manage [her] and sign her to Swan Song," Goldberg clarified. "I was besotted with her spiritual songs, but the recording was not exciting to any of the members of Zeppelin. Peter got Atlantic to release it, and I drove them crazy, vainly hoping that their PR or promotion departments would somehow make the record happen. . . . In May of 1976, Peter gave me the choice of giving up Mirabai's management or leaving. . . . I was filled with the irrational confidence and self-righteousness of youth."

Goldberg added, "On the other hand, I left at exactly the right time. The drug abuse in the band had gotten out of control and created a more sour, negative vibe than they'd had when I first started working for them. . . . [But Peter] had transformed me from a PR guy to a rock executive." As late as 2019, Goldberg dutifully continued to refer to Grant as his "mentor."

With a huge void left behind, Robert and Jimmy focused their energies on the one tried-and-true success for the label, Bad Company, whose second album, *Straight Shooter*, had performed almost as well as their debut. Before flying back to England at the end of May, Jimmy and Robert surprised Bad Company's audiences by making a guest appearance onstage; every little bit helped.

Still the band had to keep moving, and England wasn't an option. On June 21, John was among the many A-list celebrities—including Ringo Starr, Diana Ross, Robbie Robertson, and Elton John—who attended Paul McCartney's sold-out Wings concert at the LA Forum.

John was grateful to spend the rest of the summer with Pat, Jason, and Zoë in the South of France; then, in September, the entire

Bonham family flew to Montreux, where John agreed to meet up with Jimmy. The two men were rarely alone together and used the meeting to briefly unwind and then experiment. "I had recently acquired an innovative piece of equipment, the Eventide Clock Works Harmonizer," Jimmy later remembered. "I discovered one setting where you could arrive at a steel-drum sound. . . . I wanted to employ this color, if possible, in the palette of John Bonham's drum-orchestra project."

The project in question was a lengthy new drum-solo composition John was itching to finish, something that could act as a long-overdue follow-up and replacement to "Moby Dick." Alone in the Montreux studio, Jimmy recorded John's solo track with the intention of synthetically distorting it in layers—something John had been playing around with in live performance for years. When journalist Lisa Robinson once asked him how he made those strange electronic noises using the timpani drums during "Moby Dick," John had smirked, "It's all magic. . . . Didn't you see me playing with me little black wand?" With the new Harmonizer, Jimmy believed he'd found the perfect gear to flesh out John's piece even more with the sonic effect.

Simply titled "Bonzo's Montreux," the song was based in a straightforward groove, without flourishes or fills; John and Jimmy agreed to experiment together with overdubs and the Harmonizer's other offerings. "When it came to be mixed, I used the keyboard of the Harmonizer to construct the final *gliss-phrases*. . . . The percussion employed on this track with John Bonham's kit were overdubbed bass drums, snare drums, tom-toms, timpani, timbale, congas, backwards echo, and Harmonizer. . . . I'm sure John's inspiration came from the Brazilian samba schools." Happy with the finished product, Jimmy shelved the mixed track for future use, then flew back to England to be with Charlotte.

Surprisingly, John sent Pat and the kids back to England, while he, Mick Hinton, and Matthew headed off to Monte Carlo. Soon, Richard Cole joined them, since "someone had to look out for . . . the old Beast." John's dueling sides, the loving family man and the drunken, mischievous Beast, were more at odds than ever.

"The thing is," Cole continued, "that Bonzo really loved his wife and family and didn't want to be separated from them. And he would get drunk and do things and then be very emotional and so sorry the next day."

One such night, John and his entourage headed off to an expensive nightclub in downtown Monte Carlo called Jimmy'z. He had been drinking throughout the day and soon started using Mick Hinton as his verbal whipping boy. Against better judgment, John packed a gas gun into a shoulder holster beneath his flashy white suit. While in the casino, John began to tease Hinton a little too much, finally deciding to scare the living daylights out of him by pulling out the gun.

"Now, if you know Jimmyz," Cole later explained, "you got Onassis and Saudis and all them down there. You got these rich fucking Turks and the Mafia and the fucking heavy Corsicans, and all of these wealthy guys have got guys with guns with them! Now, you imagine some longhair in a white suit standing up and pulling a gun out, the whole place is gonna fucking go bananas and someone's gonna get shot to death for no reason."

To the scared amusement of the group, John began waving the gas gun in Hinton's face, finally hitting him with it and enraging Cole. "I said, 'Fucking leave him alone,'" Cole recalled. "He says, 'Shut up, you cunt, or I'll do you as well.'"

It was then that, for the second time in their relationship, Cole punched John in the face, again breaking the drummer's nose. The gun fell to the casino floor. Cole quickly grabbed it, instructing Hinton's girlfriend to run off and hide it before the police arrived. As the Monte Carlo police entered the room, John, holding his bleeding nose, began arguing with Cole about where to hide all the cocaine they had on them.

The whole group was arrested.

Fortunately, they were held for only three hours. Examining himself in the mirror, John laughed. He thanked Cole for the second broken nose. "I needed that," John told him, smiling. "Now, it's fucking straight again."

✳ ✳ ✳

AT THE END OF OCTOBER, THE BAND RETURNED TO NEW YORK CITY for the first of two US premieres for *The Song Remains the Same*. As the film was being released only to satisfy the fans after a year off the road, Peter Grant pushed for as much publicity as possible, arranging identical events later in Los Angeles and then in multiple locations in the United Kingdom. In conjunction with the film's release, Swan Song put out the full soundtrack as Led Zeppelin's second double album.

Critical reaction to both was mediocre, at best. Reviewers quickly jumped on the outdated footage and confounding dream sequences, citing the film as both self-indulgent and overly violent in the same breath. "Far from being a monument to Zeppelin's stardom, *The Song Remains the Same* is a tribute to their rapaciousness and inconsideration," Dave Marsh scathed in *Rolling Stone*. "While Led Zeppelin's music remains worthy of respect (even if their best songs are behind them), their sense of themselves merits only contempt."

Despite the negative reviews, the movie ultimately grossed an estimated $10 million at the box office during its theatrical run—and theater audiences of the midnight viewings were seen giving John's "Moby Dick" segment a standing ovation. As expected, the film's soundtrack album also went platinum, ensuring another hit for Swan Song records as 1976 neared its end.

Following the New York trip, John was happy for an excuse to return home: the UK film premiere. And while he hadn't been present for his brother Mick's wedding, he was able to celebrate the birth of his niece, Emma Michelle Bonham, in person on October 26. "After making several phone calls informing the new grandparents, I went over to tell John and Pat the good news," Mick Bonham later noted. "Celebrations were held in the best possible taste, with the consumption of a couple of bottles of the old Dom Perignon. . . . The party got under way and grew louder as the night wore on, terminating with John and I passing out at the same time and being driven home."

The first of multiple UK premieres for *The Song Remains the Same* was set for November 4, running concurrently at the Warner West End cinema and the ABC on Shaftsbury Avenue. Although John and the band were obligated to attend as many as possible, it was the premiere at the Futurist Cinema in his hometown of Birmingham on November 21 that held special significance to the drummer. For the special occasion, John invited all his friends and family down to Old Hyde, serving prescreening refreshments in his beloved lounge before escorting the group to the theater in a coach he'd rented for the evening. Following the film, John invited his guests to an after-party reception at the Opposite Lock, a nightclub at the side of the canal by Gas Street.

At first, John was nervous to screen the film for his family; after all, none of the members of Led Zeppelin was particularly enthralled with the result. At the reception, however, he let his guard down and enjoyed his family's company, even bringing along Jason's miniature drum set so the boy could entertain the adults. As Mick Bonham later recounted, a scuffle with the club's DJ soon turned ugly. "[Jason] was only a young lad, and he got up on a drum set and was playing away to records. The DJ was set up in a box. . . . While Jason was playing, the DJ suddenly says, 'If you think yer so good, let's hear you play this,' and puts on Sandy Nelson's 'Let There Be Drums.' Now, no one drummer can copy another drummer, so of course Jason was totally befuddled by this, and it upset him—he looked really embarrassed."

Seeing his ten-year-old son's flustered reaction to the insensitive DJ's behavior was all John needed to summon the Beast. "Our John was not very happy about this at all," Mick remembered. "The DJ was kind of smirking to himself, when all of a sudden, there was a loud smack! John had hit him, and he was quickly disposed of by a couple of heavy-looking blokes and thrown into the canal."

John's guests were properly amused. "Whoops!" he said, feigning surprise. "Somebody must have fallen off the 'bonk'!"

John was always protective of his family and even more so when it came to his young son. Aside from the principal issue of the incident, John was genuinely proud and encouraging of Jason's budding drum talents. When the boy had been no less than two years old, John bought him a miniature Japanese drum kit made to scale with a fourteen-inch bass drum. He later remarked, "Jason has got his mother's looks, but in character he's just like me—he's always drumming. Even when we go out in the car, he takes his sticks to bash out on the seats. . . . Before the end of Zeppelin, I'm going to have him onstage with us at the Royal Albert Hall."

Friend Dave Pegg remembered getting his first taste of the next generation of Bonham skill during a memorable visit to Old Hyde. "When I joined the Fairports, we made an album called *Full House*, and I took the album over to show Bonzo because he'd given me the Zeppelin one, and I thought, 'I've made it. I'm in a proper band now.' He phoned me up a few weeks later and said, 'It's great, mate. I really like it.' I took Dave Swarbrick over, and we got there, and Bonham said, 'Listen to this, Peggy.' He'd got his son, Jason, a miniature drum kit, and he put *Full House* on—and Jason played along with it, and he got it all."

The fallout with the DJ was only the start of bad things at the Birmingham film premiere, as, unfortunately, another friendship would be severed before the night was over. After his abhorrent misbehavior at the Deep Purple concert earlier in the year, John attempted to make amends with friend Glenn Hughes, Purple's bassist. "It all ended up badly with me and John," Hughes recalled. "When *The Song Remains the Same* premiered in LA, he called me and said he wanted to meet me at the Rainbow. . . . Then Robert invites me to the premiere in Birmingham. I get to the party, and I see little Jason playing drums. I go to the bar, and out of the corner of my eye, I see—fifteen or twenty feet away—the unmistakable figure of Bonzo in full 'Bonzo' mode."

Although innocent, Hughes had initially been interrogated by John regarding a malicious rumor of the bassist having an eye on Pat Bonham. "Lo and behold, [John] springs up like a bear and clocks me right on the chin," Hughes recounted. "Hurts me pretty bad, chips a big tooth out of the bottom of my mouth—and the same security team that we did Deep Purple with only months before now escorts me out of that venue."

Even after having Hughes ejected from the club, John wasn't quite finished. "There were six Rolls-Royces lined up, and John threw a house brick through the front window of one of them, thinking it was mine," the bassist claimed. "That was the last time I saw him, and it still saddens me. I had so much love for him that it broke my fucking heart."

✳ ✳ ✳

IT HAD BEEN NEARLY TWO YEARS SINCE ROBERT'S NEAR-FATAL CAR accident and now, finally, Led Zeppelin considered a return to touring. In conjunction with the release of *Presence*, the band began rehearsals in late 1976 in Fulham, Manticore, opting for a converted theater owned by Emerson, Lake & Palmer to refine a live version of "Achilles Last Stand." "I think Zeppelin rehearsed there twice," Benji LeFevre later estimated. "Robert and Jonesy would turn up at midday, and we'd go to the Golden Lion. . . . Jimmy and Bonzo would show up later, and we'd all get fucked up. Someone would say, 'Shall we go and rehearse, then?' And they'd say, 'Ah, not today.'"

The proposed tour would be Led Zeppelin's eleventh—and, with fifty-one shows across the United States, their most ambitious yet. But after all, they'd been gone a long time. So long, in fact, that tastes in rock 'n' roll had apparently shifted without the band really noticing.

In England, a new form of anger-ridden, deliberately sloppy rock called "punk" had ignited the young counterculture. It was assumed that the so-called punk scene had been a direct response to two elements—rage against the pre-Thatcher British government and the perceived overindulgence of bloated, excessive "arena rock," of which Led Zeppelin led the pack. Viewed as dinosaurs by the younger rock crowd, Zeppelin would have to remind an entire generation why their signature heavy blues-rock had been so popular and influential earlier in the decade, now rivaling rebellious, grumbly proponents such as the Sex Pistols, the Clash, the Damned, and Generation X.

In an effort to face their competition head-on, John, Jimmy, and Robert instead chose to see just what they were up against firsthand, attending hole-in-the-wall punk shows in London. In January they made a surprise appearance to see the Damned live at the Roxy—a tiny underground venue on Neal Street in Covent Garden that had become the lion's den of the punk scene. Robert and Jimmy attended the first night's show, then coerced John to tag along two nights later, on January 17. They were instantly out of their element, arriving at the club with publicist B. P. Fallon and a small crew of Zeppelin roadies in limousines; John, however, was thoroughly amused by the name of the Damned's drummer: Rat Scabies.

"Suddenly, the place went quiet, and I noticed the whole Led Zeppelin entourage had walked in the door to the welcome of 'What are those old hippies doing here?'" recalled Glen Matlock, the original bassist for the Sex Pistols. "After a while, we thought, 'Wait a minute. These are one of the biggest bands in the world, and they've bothered to take the time to come and see what we're about,' so we went over and introduced ourselves."

During the Damned's first set, Matlock sidled up to the Zeppelin group at the bar and started up a conversation about their adventures on the road. "I was chatting away to Jimmy and Robert when a loud crashing sound was coming from the stage, so I went to see what was happening," Matlock recalled. "I was amazed to find John at the back of the drum kit with an angry snarl on his face, and, standing bolt upright, he let out a tirade of abuse at the band. He was shouting, 'Where's the fucking band gone? They've only been playing for fifteen minutes! We play for three fucking hours because we're real men and not a bunch of wimps! Where's that Mouse Scabies? I'll show him how to play. Bollocks, leave him where he is. I'll play with the band!' and he carried on calling for the band to come back on."

Jimmy and Robert rushed to the stage and, with the help of a few of their roadies, lifted John from behind the drum kit and carried him outside. According to Matlock, "The funniest thing was that as they lifted John off the floor and started to carry him out to take him up the stairs, he was still bolt upright shouting for Mouse Scabies to come out. By this time, the audience had returned to their original mood and were shouting, 'Piss off, you old hippie!'"

Chapter Twenty-Two

MARCH 1977–JULY 1977

LED ZEPPELIN "TOUR '77"

"Rules of Engagement"

1. Never talk to anyone in the band unless they first talk to you.
    1a. Do not make any sort of eye contact with John Bonham. This is for your own safety.
2. Do not talk to Peter Grant or Richard Cole for any reason.
3. Keep your cassette player turned off at all times, unless conducting an interview.
4. Never ask questions about anything other than music.
5. Most importantly, understand this—the band will read what is written about them. The band does not like the press, nor do they trust them.

Led Zeppelin's eleventh campaign across the United States was slated to begin in March. The group spent the bulk of the preceding month in vigorous rehearsals. It had been years since their epic series at Earls Court, and these new concerts had to rival their memory—all while incorporating the new heavy material they were pushing off *Presence*.

The group soon learned that things would be different this time around. For one, their beloved *Starship* was officially grounded. Not to be outdone, Peter Grant made a few phone calls and booked the lavish *Caesar's Chariot* directly from the owners of the Las Vegas casino. Once again, Showco was responsible for the band's stage spectacular. Adrenaline was running high as Led Zeppelin prepared to wow Dallas for the tour's opening gig.

And then Robert came down with tonsillitis. The tour was postponed a month, and the band sat on their hands, unable to even properly rehearse as their gear had already been shipped to America. And to John, there could be no compromise when it came to the rehearsal stage; the new kit that he would unveil for the 1977 tour was state of the art and dramatic on all fronts. With full-length tension lugs, his recently acquired Ludwig setup sounded different from all his kits before it—this one was even louder.

After the stop-and-go of the first few months of the year, Zeppelin's tour finally began on April 1 in Dallas. Using the Earls Court concerts as their new template, the band's stage show ran a minimum of three hours per night—fifteen songs and two encores. Although the reviews were strong and the ticket sales even stronger, morale among the group and its crew was at an all-time low. Peter Grant's wife had just left him, and, unable to deal with the embarrassment and emotions, the huge manager was doing more cocaine than ever before. Jimmy's physical condition was still weak compared with that of previous years, and Robert had to monitor his vocal cords as a precaution. Unbeknownst to the public, Led Zeppelin was slowly coming apart at the seams.

"I think that's what was really the fucking end of everything," Richard Cole later said of the 1977 tour. "It's funny, but I hated that last tour. You could feel it . . . something very bad. It was all the drugs, I suppose. . . . I dunno, but there was something wrong—it wasn't the same."

It was during this tour that John introduced his final definitive drum setup: a Ludwig stainless-steel model, featuring a fifteen-by-twelve-inch tom-tom.

John first met California drum maker Jeff Ocheltree in 1975. Ocheltree had previously worked for one of John's personal favorite drummers, Billy Cobham, and John hired him on as a drum-tech consultant for the 1977 tour. According to the drum tech, an important factor in how John achieved his incredible, lush sound using the stainless-steel kit came from his tuning practices, paying particular attention to tuning the bottom head, a technique used more often in jazz than rock. He claimed, "With the toms, [John] tuned the bottom head tighter than the top head. . . . [I]f you have a loose bottom head, you get a real mid- to low-end sound. He didn't want that—he wanted the drum to speak, like Cobham." John's old friend drummer Dave Mattacks also remembered that John kept the stainless-steel kit's bass drum "tuned like his top tom."

The other most noticeable change in the band's routine came in the form of the questionable new members of their entourage and road crew, led by one of Grant's new security enforcers, a thirty-four-year-old brawler and character actor named John Bindon. Bindon had appeared in a few classic British gangster films, including *Performance*, wherein he played a henchman, and *Get Carter*, as a mob boss—roles that echoed the one Bindon played in real life. Paranoid for the band's safety, as well as snow-blind by increasing drug use, Bindon was precisely what Peter Grant was looking for in a right-hand man. Often, the double-team negative influence of Bindon and Richard Cole brought out John's most volatile behavior during this tour—and it was just getting started.

Also on board now was Peter Grant's new assistant, another rough-and-tumble type named Rex King. "Bonzo was not particularly responsible for himself now and needed someone to pack his bags and get him out of bed and into the limo," recalled Benji LeFevre. "Rex was considered a good candidate because they thought he would be neat and tidy. One day a carpet fitter, the next day on tour in America on Zeppelin's private plane."

Zeppelin's future road manager Phil Carlo described King's job as "basically like a playmate for Bonzo on the road."

※ ※ ※

"FOR THOSE OF YOU WHO SAW THE DALLAS SHOW AND WERE AFRAID you might have been gypped because of the fire marshal's limitations on Zeppelin's pyrotechnics, don't worry," wrote Pete Oppel of the *News*. "The only special effect in the Fort Worth show, absent from the Dallas performance, was a flash pot that flared during John Bonham's drum solo.

"Then there was Bonham's drum solo," Oppel continued. "Wars have been fought in less time than it takes Bonham to get through a drum solo."

The first week of April, Zeppelin played four shows at Chicago Stadium, a twin pair of consecutive nights followed by a gap of days off in between. "For their last two tours, spaced at two-hour intervals, their concerts have become events," wrote Lynn Van Matre in the *Chicago Tribune*, "a phenomenon which no doubt strikes some as incomprehensible. . . . This is a band, for instance, that plays for three hours straight with few dull moments once it gets rolling. Wednesday, it took a couple of songs; the band tends to build to a cumulative effect, rather than launching all of its firepower at once."

Van Matre continued, "The special effects fared equally well, though they're nothing particularly new—lasers and smoke, firepots and flashes. The firepots got a real workout during Bonham's drum solo; so did Bonham, turning in a performance that was actually entertaining as opposed to the usual merely endurable solo stuff by too many drummers."

It was only a week into the tour, but John was already homesick and bored. Alone in his suite at Chicago's Ambassador East Hotel, he picked up the phone and dialed Richard Cole's room. "What's there to do, Cole?" he said. "I can't sit still here. Isn't there anything exciting to do in this fucking city?"

Cole had already done all he could to keep John entertained. "I had reserved Bonzo a two-bedroom suite just as he wanted it," Cole explained, "with one of the bedrooms furnished with only a pool table, no furniture. But, after hours of billiards, the novelty of the pool table had worn off. 'We're checking out later today,' I told him. 'Calm down, and we'll be out of here before you know it.'"

According to Cole, John often "had difficulty relaxing in the aftermath of a concert" and would "become super hyper and fidgety and sometimes feel the need to bang away at something long after he had left his drum kit." On this stay at the Ambassador, after Cole returned to his room, John had "decided to unwind by methodically demolishing his hotel suite." Chairs had been smashed to pieces against the walls of the suite, couches were overturned or thrown out onto the balcony, and lamps and end tables were in shards.

Hearing the demolition down the hall, Cole raced to John's room. John gave the road manager a sheepish grin as he entered the war zone. "Well, don't just stand there!" John said, holding up one end of the pool table. "This table is as heavy as an elephant—give me a hand!"

The tour roared on through the American Midwest. "The 19,000 or more sweltering fans shouted and applauded in agreement with Plant's remark, 'Welcome to the sauna,' and some of the men took off their shirts while girls wrapped up their hair," wrote Alexandra Trozzolo, youth-scene writer for the *St. Louis Press*. "Lasers of different colors surrounded the stage forming a 3-dimensional green pyramid with yellow lasers shooting up through it. . . . John Bonham, 'Bonzo' to Zep fans, played a fantastic solo, then turned to kettle drums hooked to a synthesizer, creating a new sound never heard on any of the group's albums. 'Yea, Bonzo!' fans near us kept yelling as the man some say is the best drummer in the world did his thing." Later that week, Angie Czelusniak wrote of the band's Cincinnati show, "Five limousines escorted by police slowly drive past hundreds of cars packed with eager fans waiting to see the ultimate heavy metal group perform. . . .

The limo carries the world's top guitarist, Jimmy Page. Fans gather around taking pictures. He smiles and waves to them. Next comes the stunning drummer John Bonham and bassist John Paul Jones." Of the show, Czelusniak went on, "Bonham did a stunning drum solo that lasted slightly long. The platform he was on suddenly came forward near the end as lights flashed."

At the show in Detroit, reporter Stephen Ford noted, "Led Zeppelin, the volatile English rock group, drew 80,400 peaceful fans to the Pontiac Silverdome Saturday, April 30—believed to be the largest audience ever to watch a concert indoors in the U.S. . . . Police reported more than 40 arrests, mostly for drug possession, [and] two spectators were treated for burns received from fireworks thrown at the stage and about six persons were treated for apparent drug overdoses. . . . Four nights earlier, a fan was killed at Led Zeppelin's appearance at Cincinnati's Coliseum, when an unruly crowd pushed him from the stadium's third level. He plummeted into the street and was struck by a car."

Richard Cole told Ford, "This is one of the smoothest show's we've ever had. . . . For the amount of people, I'm pleasantly surprised. Frankly, we expected trouble."

As Richard Cole and John Bindon took turns threatening hotel and restaurant staff in order to keep them quiet regarding the band's behavior and destruction—sometimes paying off the more agreeable ones with wads of cash—the band was forced to turn a blind eye to their own downward spiral. With the exception of John Paul Jones, Led Zeppelin's members were in bad physical shape. "When they did the acoustic set at the front of the stage, Bonzo would sometimes nod out while he was playing the tambourine," Benji LeFevre later said. "I think there must have been an enormous amount of personal frustration for him and Jimmy, because they couldn't understand why they couldn't play properly anymore."

⁂

THE BAND HAD THE FIRST TWO WEEKS OF MAY TO THEMSELVES. EVEN in his weakened condition, Jimmy considered following in the later shadow of Aleister Crowley and traveling to Cairo. Alone in his suite one night, he'd caught a documentary on television about the mysteries of the pyramids. In one shot of archival footage, a Zeppelin could be seen looming high over the massive, ancient shapes, which Jimmy took as a sign. He hopped a flight to Egypt for a week, then returned to his family in England.

Surprisingly, Jimmy had invited John's assistant, Mick Hinton, to accompany him on the trip—a first for both the guitarist and the drum technician. Richard Cole found it strange that it had been Hinton and not him who had been extended the invitation—much to John's amusement. During their return flight to England, John needled Cole about his insecurity. "On the flight home, Bonzo said to me, 'Do you know the reason Jimmy is taking Mick and not you to Egypt?'" Cole recalled. "'He knows that if he decides to sacrifice someone, he'd find it a lot harder to do away with you than Mick!'" Funny enough, John's joke made Cole feel a little better.

A few hours into the flight, John, who'd been quiet for a while, stared out the window at the world below. Finally, he nudged Cole again. "The longer you tour," John said, "and the more successful and the bigger you get, the more touring just becomes a fucking chore. . . . It's work. We make a lot of money, but we don't have a life. With the bodyguards, we're imprisoned by our own success."

Cole gave John a quizzical look. John said, "Sometimes, it's like a fucking nightmare."

※ ※ ※

"WITH THE RESPONSIBILITY OF A YOUNG FAMILY, I HAD FINALLY GOT myself a proper job as a salesman at Viscount Furniture," Mick Bonham later recalled. "So, it came as a big surprise when, in May, during the halt to Zeppelin's attack on the States, John and Pat arrived at the shop to give my career a little boost."

John had wanted to surprise his younger brother. The two embraced in the middle of the furniture store—and then John and Pat bought a fortune's worth of items from Mick, fattening his commission. "The manager was so impressed, he said I ought to lunch with them," Mick laughed, "and off we went in John's latest purchase—a Mercedes six-door limousine. John drove, while Pat and I sat in the back, watching TV, sipping champagne."

John wasn't about to let his little brother go back to work, not when he was allowed back home in the United Kingdom for only a small amount of time. Instead, the Bonham boys and Pat surprised Robert at his farm nearby, and the four spent the afternoon sipping good wine and brandy and telling stories about the tour. Soon, the men were reminiscing about their younger days around Birmingham and the old Brum scene.

As Mick remembered it, "John was also in a state of excitement because, at long last, he had been voted number-one drummer in both the *NME* and *Sounds*."

The Zeppelin tour would have one more extended break later in July. John promised Mick that he would fly home then, too.

✳ ✳ ✳

ON MAY 12, THE MEMBERS OF ZEPPELIN MET UP IN LONDON AT THE Grosvenor House Hotel to receive an honorary award for their "colourful and energetic contribution to British music," an appropriate recognition from the establishment to a heavy-rock group whose behavior, onstage and off, now seemed almost acceptable in the face of the obnoxious and irreverent punk scene. A week later, the band was back in the States.

The second wing of the long tour began again in Alabama on May 18 as the band trampled through the American South. The first week of June, they returned to New York for nearly a week's worth of sold-out shows.

Trusted media ally Lisa Robinson covered the series extensively, writing, "When Led Zeppelin performed six sold-out shows at Madison Square Garden, Mick Jagger, Faye Dunaway, and Keith Richards were backstage and Carol Channing was in the audience. . . . When Zeppelin comes to the United States, they storm across the country with a relatively small entourage (20 people), do three hours of non-stop, ear-splitting rock several nights a week and still manage to throw in some musical surprises. . . . [M]anager Peter Grant once told me that rock 'n' roll remains vital by not playing too long at one hall, and by the end of the week at Madison Square Garden, Led Zep was itching to move on. . . . So, as 20,000 fans were still cheering for another encore, at the sixth, final Garden show, Zep sped away in four cars to JFK airport where their private 707 jet waited to take them to Los Angeles."

Having arrived in LA, the group had no regrets about forsaking their old stomping ground, the Riot House. The scene was getting progressively sleazier—the groupies younger, the drugs harder. Instead, Richard Cole checked them into the more upscale Beverly Hilton, where John had stayed off and on during the *Presence* rehearsals. In a show of good faith, Jimmy agreed to a handful of interviews, as did Robert, whose leg was almost fully healed.

However, the band remained selective regarding which media outlets they'd be open to speaking with. Insisting that the questions pertain primarily to his musicianship, Jimmy told *Guitar Player* magazine: "My vocation is more in composition really than in anything else. . . . Building up harmonies, using the guitar, orchestrating the guitar like an army—a guitar army. I'm talking about actual orchestration in the same way you'd orchestrate a classical piece of music." He then riffed on Stravinsky, his beloved Everly Brothers model Gibson, and a 1959 Les Paul given to him by Eagles guitarist Joe Walsh. After the journalist left, Jimmy admitted to Zeppelin photographer Neal Preston that he resented his aging and weakened appearance in pictures.

John couldn't keep himself away from the Sunset Strip, most of all the Rainbow. As John was a fixture of the renowned dive for the better part of the past decade, even regulars saw a change in the aging drummer this time around. "I loved Bonzo," said Jimmy's ex-flame Lori Maddox. "When he was straight, he was the nicest guy in the world, but when he was drunk, he was a maniac. The Beast, for sure, but he still cared about people, and he used to lecture me when they were in town then. One night at the Rainbow in '77, he goes, 'Lori, I've been coming here for seven years. . . . For seven years, I've seen the same faces.' He goes, 'I don't want to come back here in seven years and find you here.' And that was a good piece of advice, you know? That night, Bonzo changed my life in a lot of ways."

Mirroring their successful series in New York City, Zeppelin played a show in San Diego at the end of June, then six shows at the LA Forum. "An amber galaxy of match flames cast a dim glow over the crammed Sports Arena as Led Zeppelin took possession of the stage last night," Robert P. Laurence wrote of the June 19 performance at the San Diego Sports Arena. "At its best, the show captured what is best about rock 'n' roll, its power to stir the human juices and inspire feelings of joyous abandon."

With two and a half weeks off, John flew home straight from LA and threw a lavish double-birthday party for his brother and son. John also treated himself to a new toy—an AC Cobra COB 1, formerly owned by racing champion Duncan Hamilton, a previous winner at Le Mans. Celebrating his return home to Birmingham, John assembled a pit crew outside his favorite pub, Chequers, and put on a show for the adoring local patrons.

Mick Bonham later commented, "John flew back to America, still a happy man, not knowing that trouble and heartache were just around the corner."

✳ ✳ ✳

ON JULY 17, THE THIRD AND FINAL LEG OF ZEPPELIN'S 1977 TOUR commenced at the Seattle Kingdome. There, John performed his now-legendary half-hour "Moby Dick" solo, unaware that it would be his last performance of the signature song in America.

"From almost any vantage point in a room big enough to hold 67,000 people, any performers are inevitably going to look pretty ridiculous," wrote Jeani Read of the Seattle show, "like tiny toy replicas of themselves, unable to compete with their own giant split-screen instant-replay images. With a band like Led Zeppelin, that kind of visual discrepancy between truth and illusion points up to a parallel discrepancy in artistic truth and illusion. . . . Zeppelin's performance was mainly striking for being a massive triumph of superficial effect over routine musical content."

A week later, the band was booked for two nights at the Oakland Coliseum, once again organized by Bill Graham, one of the group's most irksome promoters. As had been the case at the Kezar Stadium shows in 1973, the band's private security team and road crew clashed with Graham's people almost immediately. This time, however, Zeppelin had their pit bull, John Bindon, running their army. Tensions were high. To make matters worse, Graham—who always resented the amount of money Peter Grant commanded to book Zeppelin—found out that the mandated $25,000 advance he'd had to scrounge up had been used to replenish the band's supply of narcotics.

On the night of the first of two concerts, July 23, war was declared.

It had started innocently enough during the concert when Peter Grant's teenage son, Warren, began removing "Led Zeppelin" signs from the doors of the band's trailers, hoping to keep them as souvenirs of the trip. Not knowing it was the manager's son, one of Graham's security men named Jim Matzorkis ran over and took them away, reprimanding the boy for the theft. In the end, Matzorkis was merely in the wrong place at the wrong time: John had run outside to grab a cigarette break and saw the altercation taking place. As young Warren was close friends with Jason Bonham—the two teens often hung out together at Swan Song's London office—John was livid. First, he unleashed a tirade of insults at the security man, before finally kicking him squarely in the groin. As Matzorkis tumbled to the ground, John turned on his heels and returned inside to his drum kit.

The incident quickly aroused attention; Graham was furious at his employee's treatment, and Peter Grant was even more infuriated that his son had been manhandled by a stranger. A standoff ensued, and Grant demanded that the promoter hand over Matzorkis for a proper apology. Although he would later regret it, Graham pointed Grant—

now joined by Richard Cole and John Bindon—in the direction of the trailer where Matzorkis was recuperating from John's vicious crotch kick. "In one move—I was behind Grant—[Grant] just grabbed Jim's hand, pulled [Jim] toward him," Bill Graham later said, "took his fist with the fingers all covered with rings, and smashed [Jim] in the face. I lunged at Grant, [and] he picked me up like I was a fly and handed me to the guys by the steps, who just shoved me out, threw me down the steps, and shut the door. I was now outside the camper. . . . I couldn't open the door; there was no way to get in."

Grant punched Matzorkis first—then, it was Bindon's turn. Locked out of the trailer, Bill Graham began screaming for help, only to summon more of his security detail, whom Richard Cole began smashing with a metal pole. After Bindon attempted to rip Matzorkis's eyes out of his head, Grant called him off, and the group retreated. But it was too late: the trailer was covered in blood, and Matzorkis was rushed to the hospital.

Miraculously, Led Zeppelin showed up the next night for their second show—but only after Graham was presented with a waiver absolving the band's crew from any wrongdoing. Being under duress, Graham knew the document would never hold water and agreed to sign. He spent the rest of the night avoiding the band and dodging Robert Plant's shocked and sincere apologies. The following morning, as the band and its entourage were preparing to check out and fly to New Orleans, Richard Cole looked out the window of his suite only to see a SWAT team descending upon their hotel. Instinctively springing into action, Cole warned the entire group and went from room to room flushing cocaine down the various toilets. Within minutes, however, he was apprehended—along with John, Grant, and Bindon. Adding insult to injury, Bill Graham had deliberately notified the local news media of the pending arrests, ensuring that TV cameras would capture the four rock 'n' roll hooligans being brought out in handcuffs.

In lockup, Grant was outraged. "What bullshit," Grant said of the arrests. "What is Graham trying to prove?"

John shook his head. "Did you notice that he waited until the second concert was over to turn the police loose? He didn't want to lose any money by arresting us too early."

All four men were charged with assault, and a civil suit of $2 million was filed on Jim Matzorkis's behalf. John and the others were released on $250 bond apiece and, eventually, given suspended sentences and placed on probation.

And with that, John was through with America.

※ ※ ※

AFTER THE MEN'S RELEASE, THE ENTIRE GROUP OPTED TO GO THEIR separate ways for a while. Disgusted, John Paul Jones loaded up his family and headed for the hills, literally—an extended camping vacation was in order. Jimmy stayed behind in San Francisco, thinking over the band's next moves, while Robert, Grant, Cole, and John finally flew out to New Orleans. Richard Cole recalled, "Once we got let out of jail, we had our pilots on standby and got the fuck out of there to another state." The men were quiet on the plane.

Checking into the Maison Dupuy in the French Quarter at dawn, it soon became tragically evident that Zeppelin couldn't leave their troubles behind. "I remember we walked into the lobby," Cole later recalled, "and as I was checking the group in, there was a call for Robert from his wife. I said, 'Your old lady's on the phone,' and he said, 'All right, I'll take it.'"

The men adjourned to their suites, and no one heard from Robert for hours. When he finally rang Cole in his room, he explained that he'd been sitting alone in shock. His five-year-old son, Karac, was dead.

The details of young Karac's shocking death came in vague snippets. On July 24, Karac had become ill with a violent stomach virus. When his condition worsened the following day, Maureen summoned an ambulance—but the child died before even reaching the Kidderminster hospital. It was already all over the news, and, coupled with the headlines regarding John's and Peter Grant's arrests, insensitive rumors regarding a "Led Zeppelin curse" and Jimmy's interests in black magic made the rounds.

Robert was inconsolable. He asked John and Cole to return to England with him immediately, along with his assistant, Dennis Sheehan. *Caesar's Chariot* wasn't certified to leave the country, so the men flew commercial; from Heathrow, Cole was able to charter a private plane to get Robert back to his family.

A small funeral was held for Karac Pendragon Plant in Birmingham a few days later. After the services, Robert sat on the lawn of the crematorium with John and Cole, and no one said a word. During the funeral, however, Robert wrapped John in a bear hug and spoke into his ear. "You're my oldest mate, Bonzo," he said. "I can count on you to always be there for me, can't I?"

Robert would remember that moment years later. "Bonzo saved me," he would say. "And while he was saving me, he was losing himself."

Bad Company drummer Simon Kirke later remembered another line overheard at the funeral. "When Karac died, I heard a strange thing from Bonzo, 'Fucking Jimmy and his magic shit.'"

Chapter Twenty-Three

JULY 1977–MAY 1979

The members of Led Zeppelin shared an unspoken suspicion that the death of Karac Plant might signify the demise of the band. Robert, sullen and pensive, abandoned his rock 'n' roll star persona completely. According to friend Roy Harper, "Those were very dark times. He actually blamed Zeppelin for that. Not a particular person, just Zeppelin as an entity. . . . I think he probably came to an end with the band long before the others did."

John Paul Jones had not returned to the United Kingdom for the funeral, instead remaining with his family in the States. "I was in Oregon, and I called to New Orleans," Jones recalled. "Anyway, Robert had gone home with Bonzo, and I went on to Seattle. It was a very strange time. . . . We just knew we had to give him time." Likewise, Jimmy kept his distance, and Peter Grant, recently divorced, took his children on an extended vacation to New York.

John disappeared to Old Hyde, lost. In September he had been drinking heavily at Chequers when, on the way home at midnight, he lost control of his Jensen and plunged into a tree. When the smoke cleared, John felt pains around his midsection and was having difficulty breathing. He was able to pull himself out of the wreck and walk to the nearest phone booth. Instead of calling for an ambulance, he summoned a chauffeur, leaving the wrecked sports car to be towed the following day. John sustained two broken ribs—and a reminder of his own mortality.

"Arriving back on the farm, John immersed himself in family life," Mick Bonham said. With no plans for Led Zeppelin anytime in the near future—or possibly ever again—John threw himself back into the quiet, humble farming life he'd so often daydreamed about during the band's tumultuous tours. He spent all his free time with his family and began taking a hands-on place in young Jason's racing competitions.

One day working at the furniture shop, Mick Bonham was utterly dumbfounded when his older brother called him regarding a strange new passion project he had in mind.

"Mick, I've got this idea," John said over the phone. "How about getting all the lads who worked on Old Hyde and getting back into the building business?"

"What we gonna do?" Mick asked, not quite sure if John was being entirely serious.

"Renovate old farms."

"Whose?"

"Mine," John said. "I just bought one."

Mick thought for a moment. "What's the wages?"

And just like that, J. H. Bonham and Son had returned to life. John hired his brother and his father, Jacko, for carpentry, Stan and Peter Blick for bricklaying, and the rest of the old construction crew. On September 5, the company began scouting projects.

More than a decade after he'd made his promise to put music over the safety of a stable career in construction and masonry, John was coming full circle.

For their first project, John and his crew chose a decrepit house adjacent to Old Hyde known as Beech Elm Farm. Arriving on the scene, Mick immediately questioned John's seriousness regarding this second career. "What we saw left us wondering whether John really knew what he was doing," Mick remembered. "The word *derelict* doesn't come near to what state the house was in—this place had fallen down. . . . Closer inspection revealed that the barns and outbuildings were in better condition, so that's where we started, firstly securing a shanty for us and a nice office for the gaffer [foreman]."

Mick added, "Over the next three years, we would renovate three farms altogether, incorporating a lot of hard work and several excursions into silliness."

✳ ✳ ✳

In February 1978, the legal team for John, Peter Grant, Richard Cole, and John Bindon pleaded nolo contendere to the assault charges from the Oakland Coliseum. All four were found guilty but were handed lenient fines and suspended sentences. Upon hearing the news, the long-suffering Graham remarked, "So, they'll never learn."

Grateful for the entire debacle to be over and done with, John invested his newfound time and energy into charitable causes. That same month, the local Birmingham newspaper reported, "Drummer John Bonham, 29, of Led Zeppelin rock band, is putting up 4,000 [pounds] for a 'super kids' series of motor races, the first of which will be at the Hawkstone Park circuit in Salop. The aim is to raise 10,000 [pounds] for a national children's hospital."

"With all the breaks in John's music career," Mick Bonham remembered, "he would spend a great deal of his time working with Jason and the Kawasaki Schoolboy Team at many of the meetings arranged by the West Mercia Schoolboy Scrambling Club. He also helped sponsor some of the meetings to help raise money for the many different causes."

John also helped launch the Superkids charity, an organization to raise money for disabled children during racing events. At one such fundraiser, John raffled off his motorcycle from *The Song Remains the Same*, with all the proceeds going to charity, and on November 24 he got up behind the drums and played with a local band at the

Annual Presentation Dinner for the Scrambling Club. Before leaving, he offered the awestruck younger musicians advice on their craft and encouraged them to keep playing no matter what.

"He was very supportive of all sorts of local events and charities," Robert Plant later said. "You know, he comes from Worcestershire, the countryside. It created a different mentality, so that one's reaction to one's own things was a lot different than if you were living in New York, London, or San Francisco. You go back to a country town . . . "

Many in John's life noted that for the first time, he seemed to truly be at peace with himself. "Dad never played drums at home, really," Jason Bonham later recalled. "My drums were the only drums set up at the house. . . . If he did [play], it was because there was a party and he was drinking and people would coax him into playing mine. But that was rather rare.'"

"With all his involvement in the building and Jason's [racing], John seemed more relaxed than he'd been for some time," Mick Bonham confirmed. "Yet there were still a couple of issues that worried him. What would become of the band? And if they didn't play for some time, would they be forgotten?"

✳ ✳ ✳

THROUGHOUT THE WINTER, NO ONE HEARD MUCH FROM ROBERT. HE and Maureen had been through two consecutive tragedies with her car crash and their son's death, and although it hadn't yet taken a drastic toll upon their marriage, Robert had been absent for her long recovery due to life on the road. By all accounts, he was in no rush to resume a music career. But still, his friends decided not to give up. John and Pat would surprise him at home, bringing a bottle of wine and sincere attempts to bring him out of his desperate funk. When Maureen Plant became pregnant that spring, Robert's spirits were boosted, and the members of Led Zeppelin thought the time might be right to remind him of his other passion—his love of music and performance. More as therapy than anything else, John pushed Robert to at least consider meeting up with the group to jam, perhaps rehearse some new material as a catharsis. Eventually, it worked. In March the full group met up for three days at Swan Song's offices in London. After much pushing and pulling, the four men finally reached an agreement: for the first time in ten months, Led Zeppelin banded together at the rented Clearwell Castle in the Forest of Dean on the Welsh border on May 2, 1978.

During the summer, Robert slowly inched his way back into the spotlight: jamming with a local Worcestershire R&B group in July, then sitting in with Dr. Feelgood at a club on the chic island of Ibiza a month later. As spirits and morale lifted, John got a second flicker of his own mortality in September—Keith Moon had died suddenly from an overdose of Heminevrin, a drug prescribed to wean alcoholics from their addiction. John was shocked and heartbroken—his young friend was only thirty-two.

In October, John was surrounded by musician friends, a positive reminder to him that, like Robert, making music was more than a job—it was a vocation. He and John Paul Jones had been invited by Paul McCartney to take part in a massive all-star recording session for his latest Wings album at Abbey Road Studios. The two tracks recorded that day, "Glad to See You Here" and "The Rockestra Theme," featured the two Zeppelin veterans, as well as Pete Townshend of the Who and Pink Floyd's David Gilmour.

Reinvigorated from the Wings jam, John and Jones soon teamed back up with Robert and Jimmy in November for their first official Zeppelin rehearsals in years. After Robert's grieving period, Jimmy felt the time was right to begin considering a "comeback" album of sorts—and, possibly, a tour.

✳ ✳ ✳

THE NEXT ALBUM WAS RECORDED IN STOCKHOLM, SWEDEN. DISCO-pop superstars—and one of John's guilty-pleasure favorites—Abba were allowing Zeppelin use of their personal recording base, Polar Studios.

As had been the case with the band's previous go-round, this new project came with significant changes to workflow and approach. With Robert being a hard sell and Jimmy and John still battling their under-the-table addictions, the bulk of the composing and production work was handled by John Paul Jones. Thoroughly rested from the past year, Jones rose to the challenge, presenting the group with a number of keyboard-based pieces that he hoped to flesh out. Although Jimmy wasn't nearly as keen on the idea of a Led Zeppelin album downplaying its previous guitar-driven sound, he wasn't in any condition to fight; ultimately, more than anything else, the band was relieved to even be functioning again as one unit.

"Robert and I were getting a bit closer—and probably splitting from the other two, in a way," John Paul Jones later recalled. "We were always to be found over a pint somewhere, thinking, 'What are we doing?' And that went into *In Through the Out Door*. Basically, we wrote the album, just the two of us. . . . I'd got a brand-new instrument as well, the Yamaha GX1—'the Dream Machine'—which was inspiring me. And suddenly, there was no one else to play with. Bonzo turned up next, and we had it all worked out by the time Jim showed up."

With Jones at the primary helm this time out, the music was especially elaborate and sophisticated, something that quickly invigorated John's own competitive edge. He too had been out of the loop at the drums, spending most of the past year working construction with his company and donating his remaining energy to Jason's racing-related charity events. But he had never completely put down his sticks, and, during the November rehearsals, it was quickly apparent that all four members were antsy to play.

"On the fourth floor of the Sheraton, we had four suites, one in each corner for each member of the group," Benji LeFevre explained. "Then, there was me, Rex King, and Andy Leadbetter, who looked after 'the Dream Machine.' At the end, we had to account for tens of thousands of pounds! I went to Robert and said, 'Look, we've been scoring for Jimmy and Bonzo and this and that. [Swan Song] is going to be saying, "Where's all the money gone?"' He said, 'Oh, don't worry, just write up something for fish and chips.' So, I got a piece of paper and wrote, 'Giggle and Spend, Ltd.: Fish and Chips, $25,000.' And Robert signed it."

But reforming Led Zeppelin came with an addendum, a stipulation that the group's three "family men"—John, Robert, and John Paul Jones—unwaveringly insisted upon the following: never again would the band come before family on their lists of priorities. With that in mind, it was decided that throughout the recording sessions, the members could commute between Sweden and their homes in England; for the next two months, Zeppelin's members flew out to Stockholm from Heathrow every Monday morning and returned to their families every Thursday.

During one such long weekend break, John stopped by to see old friends, brothers Reg and Chris Jones, who had launched a new band of their own called Grit. John had never forgotten all the help and friendship the brothers had bestowed on him when he was only seventeen years old; aside from being given the plum role as drummer in A Way of Life back in 1966, he had often crashed on the floor of their house on the nights when an angered Jacko tossed him out. Now, the Jones brothers' new band also featured an old friend, Ace Kefford, on bass, and John jumped at the chance to catch their gig at Shenstone College. By coincidence, another former Way of Life member, Johnny Hill, was in attendance, and, giving the audience a thrill, the full group took to the stage and jammed. For one night only, A Way of Life returned.

Under the strict eye of John Paul Jones, Led Zeppelin cranked out new music like a machine throughout the month of December. In the next rehearsal hall, a punk band called Generation X was preparing for a tour. One night, as Zeppelin was heading out, the punkers' spike-haired lead singer caught their gaze and, in true insolent fashion, hurled insults at the aging "dinosaurs." John found himself somewhere between amusement and aggravation and asked a roadie for the kid's name. "That's Billy Idol," he was told.

✳ ✳ ✳

DURING THE RECORDING SESSIONS, ZEPPELIN KNOCKED BACK GAL-
lons of Sweden's incredibly potent chemical beer for warmth against
the blistery winter chill, determined to have a rough mix completed
within weeks. More than anything, Robert wanted to be with Maureen for her January due date.

"The control room was in the middle of a semicircle of glass with
all the separation rooms around it," recalled Benji LeFevre, "so everybody could see each other. . . . The engineer had warned us that
sometimes the fire alarm would go off for no reason. The first room on
the left from the control room was where Bonzo sat. One night, he was
in there, nodding off but still keeping the groove. The fire alarm went
off, and all these firemen came bursting in with extinguishers. Bonzo
just looked up and carried on playing."

Although most of the material was based on Jones's keyboard
sketches, Jimmy added his own uneasy and turbulent guitar over-
tures and themes into the overall sound. After Jimmy had been unable to complete his promised soundtrack for filmmaker Kenneth
Anger, producing only a half hour of material that Anger publicly
bashed, the guitarist was left with some atmospheric music without a
home. With "In the Evening," one of Zeppelin's most chilling themes,
Jimmy took some of the subsequent *Lucifer Rising* material and combined it with Jones's own lengthy composition and Robert's words.
Here, John's use of restraint and minimalism is masterful, and the
advanced technology of Abba's recording equipment replicated every one of his subtle sounds perfectly—making even the most minute
utterance of his kit, such as the sticks cracking upon the drum heads,
burst like a shotgun blast.

With the playful "South Bound Saurez," Jones and Robert returned
to one of the band's favorite experimental tones—New Orleans rock
'n' roll—and John's Bo Diddley–influenced pattern shows it. A tightly
rehearsed simple rhythm track completed, Jimmy merely laid one of
his experimental solos into the mix, and the track came right together.
Likewise, so did the comical "Hot Dog," the band's parody of country

hoedown music, which was, surprisingly, destined to be released as a US single.

If there was a bona fide "hit" to emerge from the Stockholm sessions, it would most likely be the deceptively complex "Fool in the Rain," one of Zeppelin's most atypical and unusual songs, inspired by Jones after he'd heard a similar percussion riff during the televised Football World Cup in Argentina earlier that year. Within the song, John was allowed to switch styles and time signatures, giving him free rein to play a half-time feel with the backbeat on three. During his tricky groove, his right hand shuffles at a standard pace, while with his left John gives softer "ghost" notes in between. And during the bridge, John really shone, shifting the entire rhythm to an Afro-Cuban 6/4 vibe with the cymbal bell pattern crossing the groove. Then, with John Paul Jones's love of complexity winning out, the composition again transformed halfway through the track, forcing the band to double the tempo and morph into a samba. John used a frenzied, yet controlled, timbale-like triplet snare-drum roll, landing precisely on beat one of the returning original groove and tempo. Even more surprising, despite all the sophisticated dexterity to play it through, the song was decidedly radio-friendly.

Divisive among Led Zeppelin's fans, "Carouselambra" was John Paul Jones at his most elaborate; an episodic ten-minute sprawl with all the bells, whistles, and twists of a Tilt-a-Whirl, the synth-heavy track was originally titled "The Epic." With the song broken down into three distinct sections, Jimmy changed guitars for the second, taking up his double-necked Gibson EDS-1275 normally saved for live performance and filtering his lead through a Gizmotron, finally capturing that elusive string "orchestra" feel. Robert's reflective lyrics, mixed with the nightmarish suggestions of riding a carousel on LSD, made the song an experiment unto itself. Knowing it would be incredibly difficult to replicate onstage, the band nonetheless set as their goal using the lengthy song as a showstopping centerpiece in the future.

Despite Jimmy's protests, Robert's maudlin ode to his deceased son, "All My Love," originally titled simply as "The Hook," became the most widely recognized song from the finished album. Within the ballad's lyrics, Robert tied together the themes that been haunting him since July 1977—death and dying, rebirth and resurrection, and the eternal nature of love itself. For the album's close, the band revisited one of their greatest strengths with a down-and-dirty blues howl, "I'm Gonna Crawl."

With Led Zeppelin recording solid material at breakneck speed, when the sessions wrapped weeks later they even had three songs left over, none of them particularly weak. "Darlene" was a simple boogie-woogie bursting with Robert's playful, classic rock 'n' roll Elvis persona intact, while allowing John Paul Jones and John to have some fun vamping up their stride styles. The other two tracks, "Ozone Baby" and "Wearing and Tearing," rocked so hard, finding Zeppelin as close to breaching into punk-rock territory as they'd ever get, that the songs were immediately considered for stand-alone releases as singles, or perhaps an EP outside of the finished album. Of course, John attacked his kit on both tracks, reassuring the group that, if performed live, both songs would bring down the house.

The sessions for the album soon to be entitled *In Through the Out Door* were finished by the beginning of December, and mixing began a few days before Christmas; the bandmates all agreed to complete the final mix by February. Satisfied and exhausted, the band immediately flew home to their families. Just before leaving Sweden, they received news that didn't really seem to shock anyone all that much: John Bindon had been arrested for stabbing a man to death inside a nightclub. He would eventually be acquitted of the manslaughter charges, but as a form of New Year's resolution, the group finally washed their hands of him.

Robert, for one, had better things to think about as 1979 began. On January 21, Maureen Plant gave birth to their new son, Logan Romero Plant.

✳ ✳ ✳

JOHN STARTED OFF THE NEW YEAR AT A RELAXED PACE, AS WELL. Having pumped out another Zeppelin album in about a month—the third such feat in their entire history—the drummer was satisfied that the group hadn't lost a step. Now, with the mixing for *In Through the Out Door* under way, he could enjoy his home and family unfettered, spending his days, as Mick Bonham recalled, "working on farms, going to [races], and drinking at the Chequers pub." On January 4, John scored tickets for him, Jacko, and Mick to attend the State Express Snooker Tournament, being particularly happy to introduce his father to six-time world champion Ray Reardon, British comedy legend Arthur Askey, and TV personality Leslie Crowther—all of whom Jacko adored.

With his career and personal life almost always in a state of commotion, John hadn't been able to spend nearly as much time with his young sister, Debbie, as he had hoped. While he and Mick were closer in age, Debbie was often left out of the Bonham boys' shenanigans. It was a shame, as she worshipped her big brother and, on more than one occasion, had stopped into the London Swan Song office hoping he would be around. He never was, and having been reached by the office by phone, he'd end up having to send her back home to Joan in one of Led Zeppelin's luxury company cars. But Debbie was sixteen now, and finally with some time on his hands, John planned to do something special for her.

He knew that she loved horseback riding, and at Old Hyde he owned a trailer that could accommodate horses—although it was usually used for Jason's motorbikes. On her weekends with Jacko, Debbie often wanted to attend local horse shows, giving John the big idea for her surprise. As Mick Bonham recalled, "John had asked her to come with us to have a look at a horse he wanted to buy. After an inspection, Debbie advised John that it was a perfect beast, so we brought it back home."

During their drive back to Old Hyde, John flipped on the radio and caught the latest hit by British rockers the Police, "Roxanne." He,

Mick, and Debbie all sang along, and John commented that he loved their drummer, Stewart Copeland, and that the group would be "the next big band—the ones to knock Zep off the top spot." As a loyal sister, Debbie assured John no band was going to do that to Led Zeppelin, and, as he smiled, he told her the big news: the horse he had just purchased was for her. Tears of joy ran down the girl's face as she leaned over and hugged her big brother. "I'm going to call him Achilles!" Debbie announced.

"Although John loved this period of his life, he was a drummer through to the bone," Mick Bonham later said. "When he heard that Zep was booked to do a major gig at Knebworth, his face beamed. . . . [But] as the date of August 4 drew near, though, doubts began to creep into his mind. After two years away from playing live, could Led Zeppelin still pull the big crowd?"

❋ ❋ ❋

Jimmy had been hoping for a Led Zeppelin tour for more than a year, regarding their aborted 1977 US campaign as unfinished business. He spoke with Peter Grant first, who was obviously overjoyed upon hearing the band would even consider another tour; then he confirmed with Robert and Jones. John was the last to be asked, but he was as enthusiastic as the rest, and in May the formal announcement came down that Led Zeppelin would re-form to play two massive outdoor shows in the amphitheater at Knebworth Park, north of London. *In Through the Out Door*, elaborately packaged with six different variant covers, was to be released in conjunction with a potential tour.

It had been a long time, but Led Zeppelin was back.

Chapter Twenty-Four

MAY 1979–MARCH 1980

On May 28, John hung up his workman's clothes and bricklaying gear and headed back to his day job—rehearsing with Led Zeppelin. His nerves regarding the group's first major concert in years were as strong as ever, but all four men were confident in the album they'd completed, and the fact that *Circus* magazine had voted them top band proved Americans still craved their sound.

On July 1, John was present for the birth of his nephew, James Colin Bonham. Mick claimed he'd intentionally picked a name with those initials in honor of his older brother, ensuring there would forever be another "J. B." in the family. A few weeks later, Mick drove John and Robert to Birmingham Airport, watching as they boarded a private jet bound for Copenhagen, Denmark, where Zeppelin would be performing at the Falkoner Theater for the first time in a decade.

❋ ❋ ❋

IN COPENHAGEN THE BAND QUICKLY MET UP WITH A GRATEFUL RICHard Cole. Since the band hadn't toured in what felt like an eternity, Cole had been relegated to manning the Swan Song office in Chelsea—a dungeon of inactivity since the disbanding of both the Pretty

Things and Detective. With Peter Grant in a world of his own, Cole spent the better part of the year doing drugs and drinking alone in his office. He jumped at the chance to fly to Denmark for the Knebworth warm-up shows, once again suiting up for a new Zeppelin tour. His first order of business was procuring the needed cash for narcotics and the inevitable trashed hotel rooms—although this time around, Robert and John Paul Jones wanted nothing to do with the usual excesses. "I had their money for drugs, because Jimmy and Bonzo and I needed the fucking gear," Cole later admitted. "My dealer was in the next room in the hotel, and when I was polled about it in this big meeting that Robert called, Jimmy said he knew nothing about it. Bonzo said, 'Don't be so fucking stupid. If there's no gear, there's no show.' . . . Peter knew what was going on. He sort of winked at me as if to say, 'Don't worry about it.'"

The two nights in Copenhagen worked as live rehearsals for the band's English comeback. In an attempt to keep things relatively simple, they decided to use their 1977 concert set list as the working template with two additions, "In the Evening" and "Hot Dog" off the upcoming *In Through the Out Door* album, and one deletion, "Dazed and Confused." In the case of the latter song, Jimmy incorporated his signature bowing routine into the prelude for "In the Evening." For his part, John stuck with his Ludwig stainless-steel kit from the previous tour.

The band had approached the two concerts as cautiously optimistic, and when both performances went off without a hitch, all four musicians were sure Knebworth would put them back on top. They had eleven days left to prepare. Upon their return to London, they rented out the nearby Bray film studio in order to perfect the intricate laser-light show in complete secrecy. Satisfied with the full show, Zeppelin parted ways, not to meet again until the Knebworth sound check.

On the morning of August 2, each member of the band arrived separately. They agreed to run through four songs in preparation for the upcoming weekend—their tried-and-true "Rock and Roll," new songs "Hot Dog" and "In the Evening," and a fan favorite from the cataclysmic 1975 tour, *Physical Graffiti*'s "Trampled Under Foot." John also brought along Jason, now thirteen years old and as dedicated to both racing and the drums as his dear old dad. When the time came for Zeppelin to run through "Trampled Under Foot," John made his bandmates chuckle, saying that he was going to run out to the middle of the field to hear how they sounded from a distance. As a playful bait and switch, he stuck Jason behind the drums and handed him his signature oversize Ludwig hickory sticks—then instructed the four to play. To everyone's amazement, the younger Bonham became the spitting image of his father—and nailed it.

Later, the proud father beamed as he approached Jason and the band. "That was the first time *I* ever saw Led Zeppelin," he laughed.

✳ ✳ ✳

Two days later, John was up early for the day's big event. As was his routine, he wanted to get to the stage early for a final sound check. Even a decade on, no one realized Jimmy Page wasn't the only perfectionist in Led Zeppelin. Earlier, Danny Goldberg observed much of the group's individual insistence on quality regarding their own performances. "The band was ruthlessly critical of their own performances. Bonham was the most obsessive. He would show up for sound checks an hour before the other guys to customize his drum sound to each venue."

Unbeknownst to each other, they were all terrified about getting back on that stage. "For me personally, it took half the first night to get over the fact that I was there and over everything that was going on," Robert later admitted. "My voice was all clammed up with nerves."

Mick Bonham offered to pick up John's part-time assistant, Matthew, that day, and there was no way he was going to miss his brother's big comeback. On the way to Old Hyde that afternoon, just as he had done every time Led Zeppelin was playing locally since 1968, Mick stopped by a newsstand and bought the day's paper, combing the headlines for announcements about the band. He found a full-page piece in the *Birmingham Record Mirror*: "The Sun Shines Again," with a group photo of Zeppelin. "When I showed it to John, it made his day." Around lunchtime, Mick and Matthew headed to the fairgrounds in one car, John, Pat, and Jason following right behind. Upon their arrival, the band was moved by the support of their countrymen; the crowd was tremendous, banners displaying the band's name and the musicians' individual symbols from the fourth album held high above a sea of upturned faces.

The Bonham clan convened at a caravan set up for Zeppelin and their families, and John headed off to meet his bandmates. Before leaving that day, John had disappointed Debbie by forbidding her from attending the event; in the past, John had seen too many riots and acts of violence, injuries, and drug pushing at Zeppelin shows to trust a teenage girl among the crowd. He promised her that there were plenty more concerts in the future, indoor events where security would be tight and she would be safe—and urged her to wait it out. But John had forgotten that Debbie, too, was a Bonham and, as Mick recalled, "not one to be fobbed off." He added, "With iron-will determination, and much to the alarm of our mum, Debbie bought a ticket and traveled down with friends—and was somewhere in the crowd."

Notified that Debbie had disobeyed his wishes, John became frantic. It was only moments before the band was set to begin, so he instructed Mick and Matthew to take a pair of binoculars and scour the crowd for any sight of her. As the minutes ticked by, it was obvious that looking for one teenage girl in a Led Zeppelin audience was like searching for a needle in a haystack. John found a good spot for Mick on the side of the stage to take photographs of the performance and then, against his better instincts, tried to focus on the upcoming show.

At eight o'clock sharp, Mick got his camera ready and stood off to the side. "After a lengthy wait," Mick recalled, "Led Zeppelin appeared onstage to a tumultuous roar."

The group opened with "The Song Remains the Same" and "Celebration Day," two songs chosen to symbolize their joy on returning to the stage. From there, they ran through an entire history of their greatest hits, selecting favorites from fans as well as some of their own—"Out on the Tiles" gave John a moment to shine, making up for "Moby Dick" being excluded; "Nobody's Fault but Mine" and "Achilles Last Stand" were picked to represent *Presence*; John's stand-out moments from *Physical Graffiti*, "Kashmir" and "Trampled Under Foot," were played consecutively; and Jimmy presented his bow routine as the band launched into the sinister symphony that was "In the Evening." They closed with "Stairway to Heaven," and their encores were a throwback to the earliest albums—"Rock and Roll," "Whole Lotta Love," "Heartbreaker," and "Communication Breakdown."

After three hours, Led Zeppelin left the stage drenched in sweat and bathed in the cheers of the ocean. Valhalla! All four looked overjoyed to be back.

John's relief was quashed the moment he got backstage. "While everyone sat around cooling off, it was reported that there was a commotion outside with a young girl," Mick Bonham said. "Apparently, one of the security guards had thrown her against the fence after she had repeatedly pestered him to let her into the compound, claiming she was Bonzo's sister."

"I got there, and I tried to get in backstage," Deborah Bonham later explained. "I told the guy I was John Bonham's sister, and he said, 'Oh, yeah? Where's your pass?' And then it got to be quite frantic because I didn't let it go, and he threw me against the fence."

Worried sick about Debbie being lost in the crowd, John had barely been able to focus at the start of the show. Now, he immediately grabbed Mick and Richard Cole and raced to find her, prepared once again to punish a security guard if he had, indeed, raised his hands to the girl.

"At that point, Richard Cole came out and said, 'It's Bonzo's sister! Let her in!'" Deborah Bonham recalled. "John came 'round the corner, and he just saw me and he ran and picked me up in the air, and I burst into tears. And he hugged me and held me for ages, and then he put me down and said, 'What did I say to you about not coming?'"

According to Mick, "She told me years later that she would never have gone against his wishes, but for the fact she had some strange feeling that if she didn't see him then, she never would again."

John, for his part, was relieved on two fronts: his sister was all right, and the show had been a tremendous success, meaning their second show the following week would go all right, too. Years earlier, he would have happily gone out and celebrated like the old days— drank and smoked and snorted. But not tonight.

Instead, John and Pat headed back to Old Hyde and went right to bed. They had to get up early for Jason's racing competition in the morning.

✳   ✳   ✳

IN THROUGH THE OUT DOOR WAS INITIALLY SLATED FOR A WIDE RE-lease coinciding with the Knebworth shows, but, as usual, a number of factors delayed the album's street-date, primarily the sophisticated packaging. Each individual LP came wrapped in a brown-paper sleeve, hiding which of the six variant covers that buyer would be getting. Delayed by this promotional ploy, the album came out in mid-August, about a week after the second Knebworth show.

British critics largely dismissed the band's ninth album, again cit-ing the advanced age of the members and the self-indulgence of the lengthy, synth-heavy songs as pretentious or, worse, boring. It briefly topped the UK charts, but soon dropped off. America, however, was a different story. A decade earlier, it had been the States that embraced Led Zeppelin before any other country; now, American audiences flocked to pick up the group's latest offering. In that country alone, *In Through the Out Door* sold a whopping four million copies in only three months and inspired a renewed interest in the band's earlier works; by October all nine Zeppelin albums were in the *Billboard* Top 200.

Although the album and the concerts had been largely success-ful, there were no immediate plans for launching a major world tour or a follow-up album. In many ways, the one-two punch of the *In*

Through the Out Door marathon recording sessions and the Knebworth concerts had been to prove a point: Led Zeppelin *could* fly again, if it wanted to. Yet the spark had visibly dimmed for all four musicians, and a lack of drive stifled rumors of an immediate US tour.

Later, Richard Cole claimed that the greatest enemy Led Zeppelin ever faced was the rampant drug use that had slowly escalated over time. "[Knebworth] was the last thing I did with them. I was smacked out of my mind on heroin. I couldn't even handle the money or anything." After a nineteen-year-old "friend of the band" died mysteriously of an unspecified drug overdose in Jimmy's home in Sussex, he not only looked for a new place to live, but also disappeared for a holiday to Barbados with no word on his return.

That left the other three members to act as the public face of Zeppelin. During the rest of the year, John, Robert, and John Paul Jones donated their time and energy into UNICEF charity events and, on November 29, attended the *Melody Maker* winners' reception to receive Led Zeppelin's numerous awards. John indulged in more than his fair share of drinks at the event, ending the night by proclaiming that the Police should have won more awards that year. As Robert and John Paul Jones led John out of the reception, he began to sing "Message in a Bottle" loudly throughout the hall.

John was well known to be critical of bands he disliked but was equally passionate about those that impressed him. Approaching the decade's end, John stated more than once that the Police was his favorite among emerging younger bands—being particularly fond of the group's drummer, Stewart Copeland. Only months before, he treated Jason and Debbie—both huge Police fans—to see the band at the Birmingham Odeon on September 13. "I remember thinking how great it was that John still wanted to see up-and-coming bands, even though Zeppelin was so huge and the Police certainly weren't," Deborah Bonham later said. "The band was totally fantastic, and, as they came off, John congratulated all of them. We were then asked backstage to meet them. . . . John was so complimentary! He met with Stewart Copeland, who was slightly in awe of him, and also with

Andy Summers—both lovely chaps. They seemed overwhelmed that John Bonham of Led Zeppelin had come to watch them and, more importantly, thought they were great."

The only musician apparently unimpressed with the superstar drummer was lead singer Sting. Deborah recalled, "John mentioned to them that he was playing the Albert Hall in London for 'Rock for Kampucha' [sic] with Paul McCartney and a bunch of guests, and would they like to come down and get up for a jam? To this, Sting said, 'Paul who?' and as John walked over to him, Sting said, 'Hey, don't step on my blue suede shoes.'"

Years later, Jason Bonham remembered the evening taking a slightly more aggressive turn, telling an interviewer, "[Dad] managed to get me backstage, and he threatened to punch Sting—it was hilarious. Dad stepped on his foot, and [Sting] was very cocky back then. . . . I remember [Sting] saying, 'Hey, man, don't step on my blue suede shoes.' My dad said, 'I'll step on your head in a minute.'"

Defensive of John, Debbie spent the entire ride home ranting about Sting's insolent behavior—much to her brother's amusement. "In the car on the way home, I mouthed off about how disgusting I thought it was, and who the hell did he think he was in front of such greatness. John turned 'round and said, 'You know what, we were like that when we first made it. It's only natural. . . . [T]he guy is going to go a hell of a long way. He's got an incredible talent.'"

All the same, once home, Debbie removed the Sting poster from her bedroom wall.

※ ※ ※

As John had mentioned to the Police, early rehearsals had already started for McCartney's Rock for Kampuchea charity concerts. Aside from performing with Wings, the former Beatle was a chief organizer of the event, helping gather a roster of high-profile acts at London's grand Hammersmith Odeon during Christmas week. The performers were donating their time to raise funds for war-torn Cambodia. The December 26 kickoff featured Queen, and the rest of the week saw the Clash, the Pretenders, the Who, Elvis Costello, and Robert Plant take the stage. Robert performed on December 29 along with McCartney and John, although in different acts; Wings was the concert series' penultimate act, while McCartney's all-star "Rockestra" performed the finale.

John was close with three of the former Beatles: he counted George Harrison and Ringo Starr among his closest friends, and he and McCartney had gotten on well since "Beware My Love," a collaboration for *Wings at the Speed of Sound* in 1976. They worked together again two years later for the band's follow-up, *Back to the Egg*. "Bonham was always on my top-five drummer list and a great friend and ballsy drummer," McCartney later said.

The London rehearsals for December 29's Rockestra performance had gone well. In gratitude, McCartney invited John and his family to Wings' December 12 concert at the Birmingham Odeon. Face-to-face with one of his childhood heroes, Mick was at a loss for words. "I felt well and truly out of my depth," he later remembered. "I had grown up with the Beatles and was a great admirer of Paul's work, [and] after John introduced me to the members of Wings, I shrank back into the corner." Mick shyly attempted to compose himself when McCartney's wife, Linda, came over and checked on him.

The day before the concert, John, Robert, and John Paul Jones had stayed in London at the Blake Hotel. On December 29, Mick drove Pat and Matthew from Old Hyde to the posh theater, where the group was surrounded by the likes of Elvis Costello, Pete Townshend, and Chrissie Hynde, along with comedian host Billy Connolly. Unbeknownst to the crowd, the night would also be Wings' "farewell" concert. Following their final bow, the Rockestra took center stage; with the other musicians, John could be seen sporting a silver top hat from his spot behind the kit. He masterfully bashed his way through a short set that included 1978's "The Rockestra Theme," the Beatles' "Let It Be," and a rollicking cover of Little Richard's "Lucille."

Although sharing the spotlight, the night saw three members from Led Zeppelin together onstage for the first time in months.

Knebworth was a half year ago. What were they waiting for? While together at the Blake Hotel, it was inevitable that the topic would be discussed. Jimmy and Peter Grant soon returned from their respective holidays and were summoned to the Swan Song headquarters. None of their families were much surprised when the news was shared: Led Zeppelin was set to tour Europe the summer of 1980.

John and comedian Billy Connolly shared many laughs at the Rock for Kampuchea rehearsals. Soon after the concert, Connolly asked John to make an appearance on his variety show, *Alright Now*, but John was never particularly comfortable during on-camera interviews. When he sat down with Connolly on March 4 without the buffer of another Zeppelin mate, he appeared visibly awkward—even surrounded by adoring fans. B. P. Fallon once observed, "Bonzo was a very warmhearted man. He wasn't necessarily at all times best equipped for being regarded as a deity."

Perhaps out of humor, but more likely because he was out of his comfort zone, John nodded at Connolly and offered one-word answers. All the answers seemed vague. Everything seemed up in the air. And it would be John's last television appearance.

PART FOUR

ASH

1980

Bungelosenstrasse: "The Street Without Drums"

Chapter Twenty-Five

APRIL 1980–SEPTEMBER 1980

R ehearsals for Led Zeppelin's "Cut the Waffle" tour of Europe began at the Rainbow in Finsbury Park, London, during April, then continued at the New Victoria Theatre the following week. The tour itself would be short—a single leg through Germany, Belgium, the Netherlands, Austria, and Switzerland. And depending how those gigs went, the band would consider a similar tour of the United States later in the year.

Not only were the bookings kept to a comfortable minimum, but the laser-light shows, dry ice, smoke, mirrors, excessive wattage, and extended solos were all among the "waffles" being cut. More strikingly cut was Richard Cole, whose excessive drug use, in Peter Grant's eyes, had rendered him largely nonfunctional. To Cole, drugs had been part of the Zeppelin experience all along, but he acknowledged his full-blown addictions had compromised his ability to run a comeback tour. "Drugs for the band were often given to me by fans, by friends," Cole claimed, "who would knock on my hotel room door [and] say something like, 'We have a present for you.' The band rarely turned anything down."

Grant replaced Cole as road manager first with Rex King, then later Phil Carlo.

Cole saw John for the last time at a pub on King's Road during a break in rehearsals. Due to Grant's generosity—and insistence—Cole was reporting to an expensive rehab clinic later that week. "While John and I drank brandy Alexanders, I grumbled about Peter Grant," Cole recalled.

"Don't worry," John told his former road manager, "you'll get off that shit and be back with us before the summer's over." After taking Cole for a quick spin in his new Ferrari Daytona Spider convertible, John dropped him off back at the pub. "I hope you bastards miss me," Cole said as he closed the door.

Cole later claimed, "I began seeing a very nasty side of [John] at times, an anger built on frustration [that] grew out of his own mixed feelings about Led Zeppelin itself. . . . Like the rest of the band, Bonham no longer needed to play for the money." According to Cole, John admitted, "It's becoming harder to be somewhere where I don't want to be," and was planning on giving it up sometime soon. A few days later, Cole checked into the Excelsior Hotel in Rome, where, the following morning, counterterrorism officials broke down his door and found enough cocaine to send him to maximum-security prison for six months.

※ ※ ※

IN MAY JOHN WAS BACKSTAGE AT BLACK SABBATH'S HAMMERSMITH Odeon show, where, according to Tony Iommi, John became really upset with the new lead singer, Ronnie James Dio. "John was on the side of the stage having a good time and drinking Guinness, getting more and more sloshed as the show went on. We came offstage, and he said, 'That guy's got a great voice for a fucking midget!' . . . Of course, Ronnie heard him. Bonham meant it as a compliment, really, but it didn't come out as one. Ronnie turned to John and said, 'You fucking cunt!'"

Iommi continued, "It nearly came to blows. That would have been a lopsided fight because John was a bit of a hooligan. So, I said to him,

'Look, please don't.' . . . He went away then, but, blimey, it could have been quite nasty."

"When he had too much to drink, he did get quite aggressive and started picking fights," Bev Bevan admitted. "He wasn't a friendly drunk—he went the opposite way, which was a shame."

One of the last times Bevan saw John was during a week when both Zeppelin and Bevan's Electric Light Orchestra were in LA. Zeppelin had not yet abandoned their normal place in the Riot House at that point, and Bevan had gotten onstage with a house band for an impromptu jam. "They were very kind and said, 'You're a great player,'" Bevan recalled. "I said, 'Well, thanks very much, but you should see my pal John if you want to see a drummer.' So, he turned up and was being very generous, buying us all drinks. . . . But for every drink he bought the band and me, he had six. I would have a brandy and Coke, and he would have six brandy Alexanders. He had a little tray of them, and he'd knock them back like Schnapps."

In Bevan's estimation, John had consumed about twenty-four drinks in the space of an hour. "[John] was all over the place, and he couldn't keep time," said Bevan. "That was the last time I saw him."

According to Bevan, "He was a bit similar to Keith Moon. . . . They both felt they had to live up to their reputations."

✳ ✳ ✳

DURING THE SECOND WEEK OF JUNE, ZEPPELIN CONTINUED THEIR rehearsals on the "L" stage of Shepperton Studios in London, finally ready for their first show in Dortmund on June 16. Everyone immediately noticed how much weight John had gained, having let himself go over the past few months. Sporting a full beard and perpetually hidden behind dark aviator glasses, he looked a decade older than a man who had just turned thirty-two.

The European tour hosted a few new variations, small changes made primarily out of convenience. The band now opened with an homage to the very first song they'd ever jammed to in 1968, "Train

Kept a-Rollin'"; more than a decade later, it sounded more sophisticated and united than ever. As the concerts ventured through Cologne, Brussels, and Rotterdam, Zeppelin alternated "Rock and Roll," "Communication Breakdown," and "Whole Lotta Love" as their encores. Both John and Jimmy forfeited their extended solo routines.

On June 27, John looked ill before heading out onto the stage for the band's eighth show. As they played into the third song, John collapsed off his drum and had to be carried backstage. The group told the press the cause had been "exhaustion." Nevertheless, as concerned as the band was over John's health, he continued through the final dates of the tour, which ended on July 7 in Berlin.

Afterward, Jimmy canceled a series of concerts planned in France. As John reassured a reporter, "Overall, everyone has been dead chuffed with the way this tour's gone. . . . There were so many things that could have gone wrong. We want to keep working, and of course we want to do England."

Still, John was very relieved to get back to Old Hyde on July 9. The whole concept of disappearing from his family for such long durations made very little sense to him at that point, but he nonetheless agreed to go with the band to Montreal, Canada, on October 17 as the kickoff for their first American tour of the new decade. Rehearsals would take place at Jimmy's house in Windsor, as well as Bray Studios, during the month of September. At the end of July, John surprised his father by offering him one of the cottages on the farm's property, ensuring someone would always be taking care of him. While his father moved in that August, John took Pat and the kids to the South of France for a long-overdue holiday. Mick picked them up at Birmingham Airport on September 9, later noting that the holiday, it seemed, had been just what the doctor ordered for John, who was in a buoyant mood and looking forward to the next tour of the States.

That week John and Mick continued helping Jacko move into his new cottage. On Wednesday, September 24, he arrived to meet them for some additional decorating. Mick recalled, "John arrived on site early and in a very cheerful mood and thought it would be a good idea to get all the cars washed and polished. . . . At lunchtime, John's personal assistant, Rex King, arrived at the farm to take him down to London. As they disappeared down the long driveway, I waved."

In the car, John insisted that King pull over and stop at the nearest pub before heading to Jimmy's for the rehearsal. There, John ordered and drank four quadruple vodkas, amounting to approximately forty individual shots, with orange juice, and ate a few ham rolls for lunch.

At Bray Studios in Berkshire, John continued to drink throughout the rehearsal, until, by the end, he was too intoxicated to continue. "We set up in Bray," Mick Hinton explained. "Come first rehearsal, Bonzo arrived looking, well, worse for wear. . . . He got on the drum stool, fell off it two or three times, and I think Robert said, 'Let's call it a day and sort it out tomorrow.' In fact, I don't think any rehearsing was done."

From there, they all went to Jimmy's house on Old Mill Lane in Windsor, where John polished off three more double vodkas. Reportedly, John's behavior during the get-together had "become erratic, loud, and abrasive," and he spent most of the evening venting his unhappiness about having to be away from home for the upcoming US tour. Just before midnight, he fell asleep on the living room sofa, and Jimmy's assistant Rick Hobbs, carried him up the spiral staircase. He found an empty bed in one of the many bedrooms that overlooked Queen Elizabeth's castle and laid the drummer on his side against some pillows. Then Hobbs turned out the light and closed the door behind him as he left.

The next morning, Benji LeFevre drove Robert and John Paul Jones to the Bray sessions from their suites at the Blake in London. Knowing that John and Jimmy had, mostly likely, been up very late, Robert and Jones decided to swing by the Windsor house to ensure everyone was awake and ready to report for duty. When they got to the waterfront home, Jimmy was up and walking around the ground floor, but there was no sign of John.

"Is Bonzo up?" LeFevre asked.

Jimmy hadn't seen him.

"Where's he sleeping?"

"Top of the spiral staircase."

LeFevre nudged John Paul Jones. "All right, I'll go tip him out of bed," he said heading up. Jones followed steps behind.

The two tiptoed into the bedroom where John lay. LeFevre called John's name and began to gently shake him. When there was no response, he shook him a little harder. Nothing was working. LeFevre turned the drummer over to find his face pale and blue. Panicked, the two men checked John's vitals: he wasn't breathing—and he had no sign of a pulse. John's body was cold to the touch. LeFevre and Jones looked at each other, unable to speak.

John Paul Jones later recalled, "I remember after we found him, I came out, and Jimmy and Robert were laughing about something. . . . I had to go in and say, 'Hold it,' and tell them what happened."

An ambulance was called, but it was obvious that John had died sometime that morning.

LeFevre followed down a moment later. "When I came down, Jonesy had gone out to the garden, and Robert was standing there. He made as if to go upstairs, and I said, 'Please don't.' I got hold of [Peter Grant's assistant] Ray Washburn and said I had to speak with G."

Grant was at his Sussex manor when Washburn entered the bedroom and handed the large man a few tablets of Valium and told him to sit down on the edge of the bed.

"Someone is on the phone for you," Ray said.

"Who is it?" Peter said. "What's wrong?"

"It's about John Bonham."

Grant knew something was wrong. "Well, what about him?"

"He's dead."

Led Zeppelin's head of security, Don Murfet, was quickly called and instructed to report to Jimmy's house right away. "It was down to me to contain the situation, limit the damage," Murfet later claimed. "Professionals to the end, Benji and Rex King and Rick Hobbs had already cleaned up, by which they meant that they'd got rid of anything potentially incriminating or embarrassing to the band or John's family. By the time Peter and Ray arrived . . . the three of us discussed all the angles. That resolved, Peter and Ray went off to console the boys in the band."

The group decided Robert would be immediately dispatched to Old Hyde to tell Pat of John's death before it leaked to the press. Benji LeFevre remembered that Robert didn't want her "to hear it second-hand." Just as John had been there for Robert following Karac's death, Robert "wanted to be there to hold her hand." Now fourteen years old, Jason Bonham was the one to answer the door upon Robert and Maureen's arrival, surprised to find his father's friends there, but not his father. "He says, 'Is your mom here?'" Jason later remembered. "And I went, 'Yeah. Hold on.' 'Robert's here? What's he doing here? Where's your dad?' I remember seeing family arrive out of the corner of my eye and getting upset, and I didn't know why I was upset, but I knew something was up."

Moments later, a grief-stricken Pat Bonham walked back out and pulled Jason aside. "My mom came in and said, 'Your father's passed away.' . . . I remember not knowing really what the hell was going on. When you don't know anything about death, and no one close to you has died . . . I can play that day back perfectly clean in my head."

Mick Bonham was home watching Diana Ross on *Top of the Pops* when he got the call from Jacko. "The only words I heard were, 'Come over to the farm straight away,'" Mick later said. "My father was speaking them, and he could barely get the words out for crying. . . . I'll never forget that moment. It became frozen in time, like a scene from a film, and is as clear today as it was back then. In all my years, I had never heard or seen Dad cry, and I knew it meant that something had happened to a very close member of the family."

Mick composed himself and immediately headed over to Old Hyde to be with his sister-in-law and Jason and Zoë. He arrived to find guards posted on either side of the farm's gate and Robert waiting for him. "[Robert] told me to leave my car and walk up the drive with him. As he did so, he gently broke the news to me that John had died sometime during the previous night. I don't know how to explain the impact his words had on me in that split second and how I felt afterwards. But as I sat with my family, the only thing I knew was that the brother I loved so much, my lifelong hero, was gone. . . . My only respite from the nightmare came, as ever, from Lin, who held me tight for the rest of the night while I tried to make sense of it all."

John Paul Jones returned home to his wife and children. "It made me feel very angry," he said later of John's death. "The waste of him."

Jimmy stayed behind in Windsor. John's shocking death had made headlines across the world, and Led Zeppelin was blasted round-the-clock on British and American radio. That night from his bedroom window, Jimmy could see a gathering of grieving fans outside his home.

Friends speculated that John's behavior was a combination of nervousness regarding the upcoming tour and his genuine disdain for being away from home once again. "We had just started rehearsing for a tour of America when Bonzo died," John Paul Jones claimed, "[and] it was just at the point where we had all come back together again. . . . Bonzo had been getting a bit erratic, and I can't say he was in good shape, because he wasn't. There were some good moments during the last rehearsals . . . but then he started on the vodka."

Later, Robert remembered John's demeanor had been dark and self-deprecating as they drove to Zeppelin's final jam together. "On the very last day of his life . . . he was not quite as happy as he could be," Robert recalled. "He said, 'I've had it with playing drums. Everybody plays better than me.' . . . He said, 'I'll tell you what, when we get to rehearsal, you play the drums and I'll sing.' That was our last rehearsal."

By 1980 John had stopped dabbling with heroin but had begun drinking much more heavily and frequently. At the time, he'd begun self-medicating with an antianxiety drug called Motival for his frazzled nerves, as well as the deep depression he'd battled since the criminal charges and ensuing lawsuits in Oakland.

At the Regina Coeli maximum security prison in Rome, Richard Cole learned of John's death by a fellow inmate who'd read a newspaper obituary. Hearing that a member of Led Zeppelin had been found dead, Cole first assumed it was Jimmy. Then he was told no—John Bonham drank himself to death. "I barely remember walking back to my cell," he later remembered. "I crawled onto my bunk and stared silently at the sixteen-foot-high ceilings."

"Are you all right?" his cellmate asked.

"I'm not sure," Cole said. "One of my friends has died."

※ ※ ※

ON OCTOBER 8, A FORMAL INQUEST WAS HELD IN EAST BERKSHIRE. Coroner Robert Wilson determined that John had died of inhalation of vomit in his sleep, suffering a pulmonary edema—the swelling of blood vessels due to excess fluid being present. In effect, Wilson said, it was an accident.

One article reported Jimmy was "too weak to stand in the witness box" as he offered his testimony. The guitarist claimed John had been "pretty tipsy" when he arrived at the September 25 rehearsal, adding that it was hard to tell how drunk the drummer had been that particular day, as he drank all the time. Road manager Rex King spoke of John's binge on the way to Windsor from Old Hyde and his condition throughout that day—as did Jimmy's assistant, Rick Hobbs, and Benji LeFevre. Coroner Wilson noted that the police visited Jimmy's house after the ambulance arrived and found nothing suspicious at the scene.

The cause of death was officially noted as due to "consumption of alcohol" and, under the dubious banner, "death by misadventure"— an accidental, senseless death, a victim of rock 'n' roll: success, excess, gloom, and doom. The blessing and the curse.

When his body was discovered, its most identifying marks were his perpetually calloused hands: years of drumming, years of laying brick, years of roping bulls. One way or the other, it seemed as if by predestination that John should die with calloused hands. A worker's hands.

Every element of his being spoke of hard labor.

John Henry Bonham III, who had died at birth and been reborn.

Dead again at thirty-two.

✳ ✳ ✳

ALL PLANS FOR LED ZEPPELIN'S TOUR OF THE UNITED STATES WERE immediately canceled.

As news around the world kept up with further details of John's death and funeral arrangements, tributes poured in from the music establishment. At the service on October 10, more than 250 fellow musicians and fans gathered a few miles from Old Hyde alongside the Bonham family at St. Michael's Church, in Rushock, Worcestershire. Onlookers stood in the rain outside the cemetery, watching in silence. Flowers and notes of condolence arrived from Carmine Appice, Phil Collins, Cozy Powell, and nearly every musician who had either worked with John or revered him from afar. An oversize wreath came from Paul and Linda McCartney. Following the services, the funeral procession made its way to the Worcester Crematorium.

"I went to the funeral," said Bev Bevan, who attended with ELO bandmates Jeff Lynne and Roy Wood. "It was the worst I have ever been to because [John] was so young. His wife and family and relatives were utterly distraught. . . . There was much weeping. The church was jammed, and there were so many people outside."

Media speculation regarding Led Zeppelin's future began to make the rounds, along with rumors that Carmine Appice, Phil Collins, or Bevan himself were among the drummers being considered as John's replacement. A brief statement from Swan Song, published in *Melody Maker* on December 4, abruptly ended the discussion:

> *We wish it to be known that the loss of our dear friend and the deep sense of undivided harmony felt by ourselves and our manager have led us to decide that we could not continue as we were.*

> —LED ZEPPELIN

BEYOND

Before the Swan Song letter was published, Robert, Jimmy, and John Paul had joined a grief-stricken Peter Grant, along with a few of the closest crew members, for a final band meeting at the Savoy Hotel in Jersey. There, it was quietly and unanimously agreed that Led Zeppelin, the band, was through. Grant, who soon retired from the music business completely, said of the group's decision, "There was no question of it . . . never any thought."

Robert later added, "I knew how much Bonzo loved what he did. . . . I thought it would be terrible to just fob the whole thing off and say, 'Well, that's it. We'd better get someone else now so that we can carry on this sort of amoebic carnage game.'"

"The realization was that they weren't going to do Led Zeppelin anymore," Deborah Bonham remembered, "which I think we all felt great relief about." Deborah was only eighteen at the time of her brother's death but already had it in mind to continue in the family's musical tradition. The previous year, Robert produced some demos for her, culminating in Deborah's first record deal in 1985. Over the years, she toured extensively in Europe and the United Kingdom, opening for such performers as Van Halen, Donovan, and even John's old friends Tim Rose and Paul Rodgers. In the 1990s, her band would open for nephew Jason at the very club that had launched his father's US success—Whisky a Go Go in LA—and during a 2016 performance on the left bank in Hereford in England, Robert joined her for a duet of "When the Levee Breaks." As Robert had remained close with the Bonham family, he even appeared on Deborah's 2014 album, *Spirit*.

In Deborah's words, "[John] had a big heart, he was a people's man, a family man. . . . It's been very emotional . . . but remembering John is always like that."

✳ ✳ ✳

At the Twenty-Third Annual Grammy Awards in February 1981, John Bonham became the first member of Led Zeppelin to score a win. Presented for Paul McCartney's "Rockestra" recording, John was among the esteemed musicians recognized for the song's Best Rock Instrumental Performance. Decades later, his fellow Zeppelin mates would be granted honorary Grammy Awards for lifetime achievements in music, but John's win made him the sole beneficiary of such an honor while the band was still active—he just hadn't lived long enough to accept it.

Although neither Phil Collins nor Cozy Powell ended up taking over for John in Led Zeppelin, both drummers contributed to Robert's first solo album, *Pictures at Eleven*, in June of the following year. It proved to be Robert's only album for Swan Song before the label was dissolved in 1983.

Before the company's last gasp, Jimmy assembled *Coda*, the final Zeppelin album in the group's official canon. Released in November 1982, the compilation brought together years of Zeppelin outtakes and leftovers, some of which were among John's greatest drumming highlights. As a cohesive album, critics considered it weak. Taken individually, however, such tracks as "Bonzo's Montreux," "Ozone Baby," and "Wearing and Tearing" received praise for spotlighting John's later technical wizardry. Jimmy himself spent the first half of the decade with hits and misses as a solo artist, first scoring the action film *Death Wish II* in 1982 while concurrently finishing *Coda*, then working with old friend Paul Rodgers from Bad Company in a new supergroup called the Firm two years later. The band released two consecutive albums, one of which included a variation of Jimmy's long-gestating masterpiece, "Swan Song," now reconstructed as "Midnight Moonlight." With a sleek 1980s gloss featuring Rodgers's newly added lyrics and Tony Franklin's overtly contemporary fretless bass, the nine-minute track was a mere ghost of the epic it had been during the Headley Grange sessions in 1973. After one tour of Europe and the States, the Firm mysteriously disbanded after the first of three Led Zeppelin "reunions" kick-started rumors that the heaviest of all rock bands might fly once more.

Initially, Robert Plant and John Paul Jones had distanced themselves from their hard-rock personae. Robert, in particular, had reinvented himself with his solo debut—then even more so with an EP of reimagined R&B classics under the "Honeydrippers" moniker. His new music was far removed from Zeppelin's hard-driven rock. Likewise, by 1985, John Paul Jones had all but retreated back into the quiet, pre-Zeppelin life of John Baldwin, happy at home in the English countryside, deliberately keeping a low profile with smaller solo projects or producing other acts.

But then came Live Aid.

On July 13, 1985, organizers Bob Geldof and Midge Ure put together the largest benefit concert in modern music history, booking two enormous shows simultaneously at Wembley Stadium in London and John F. Kennedy Stadium in Philadelphia, both to raise funds for Ethiopian famine relief. Combined, the two shows had a record-breaking 160,000 people in attendance—not counting the millions of home viewers who tuned in for the twenty-minute acts from dozens of best-selling superstars like Queen, U2, Dire Straits, the Who, David Bowie, Elton John, and Paul McCartney. When Robert Plant was contacted to perform, it was suggested that he jam with Eric Clapton, who was also booked—but Robert advised the organizers that Jimmy Page and the Firm were available, so why not have them together instead?

Ecstatic that half of Led Zeppelin would even consider such a reunion, the two were asked to invite John Paul Jones. "Well, if you're gonna do a Zeppelin number," Jones joked to his former bandmates, "I know a Zeppelin bass player." Ironically, Jones ended up playing keyboard, while Robert's touring bassist, Paul Martinez, took Jones's old spot. With Phil Collins and Tony Thompson doubling up as dual drummers—no one man could fill in for John Bonham—Led Zeppelin made their return before the whole world. At eight o'clock, the group went live, performing "Rock and Roll," "Whole Lotta Love," and "Stairway to Heaven," driving the audiences wild and providing a younger generation with their first glimpse of the legendary originators of heavy metal.

The rumors of a tour or a new album were quickly cast aside. Robert insisted that the show was a onetime event meant for a charitable cause, and John Paul Jones could go either way. Jimmy, however, missed the energy and excitement that the brief return to the spotlight had provided. Although the world was hungry for Zeppelin's return, it would be another three years before the men would gather publicly to make music again.

On May 14, 1988, the men regrouped for the fortieth anniversary of Atlantic Records, closing a marathon concert—with Jason Bonham filling in for his father for the first time. As a show of family unity and recognition for the younger man's own brilliance, Jimmy asked Jason to play drums for both his 1988 solo album, *Outrider*, as well as its subsequent promotional tour. More than a half decade later, on January 12, 1995, Jimmy, Robert, and John Paul met in the Grand Ballroom of New York's Waldorf Astoria Hotel for the black-tie induction of Led Zeppelin into the Rock and Roll Hall of Fame. Although the musicians were in great company—the Allman Brothers, Martha and the Vandellas, the Orioles, Neil Young, Frank Zappa, and, posthumously, Janis Joplin—it was the reemergence of Led Zeppelin that gave the exclusive audience their $1,500-per-plate money's worth.

In a dark twist of fate, Peter Grant had died of a heart attack two months earlier at the age of sixty, missing the chance to see his three living protégés back on top.

Although Robert and Jimmy would collaborate on an acoustic special for MTV and release two duet rock albums—1994's *No Quarter: Jimmy Page and Robert Plant Unledded* and 1998's *Walking into Clarksdale*, neither of which included Jones—the re-formed Led Zeppelin didn't set foot on a stage together for another decade. On December 10, 2007, a massive concert was held at the O2 Arena in London as a memorial for Atlantic executive Ahmet Ertegun, who, at the age of eighty-three, had died tragically after falling backstage at a Rolling Stones concert in New York. The benefit concert hosted numerous acts, but it was the announcement of Led Zeppelin's first full-length concert performance in almost three decades that set the news media ablaze. As had been the case in 1995, there was only one man truly accepted as John Bonham's fill-in—his son, Jason, who by now had decades under his belt with numerous rock bands.

As early as 1982, when Robert Plant first began the initial recordings for *Pictures at Eleven*, Jason, then fifteen years old, would hop on the back of his friend's scooter and ride to Robert's home studio. Sharing the pain of their mutual loss, Robert asked Jason to help out on drums for a few tracks; the album's song "Fat Lip" had even been written as a dedication to John. It was apparent to the singer that the teenager was already performing well beyond his years; after all, the boy was now the same age his father had been when scouted for the Blue Star Trio in the early 1960s. After Jason filled in for his dad at 1988's Atlantic Records tribute concert and with Jimmy Page's tour that year, Jason's own talents—along with his famous last name—assured him a string of high-profile gigs: as a guest at the Moscow Music Peace Festival in 1989 and starting his own eponymous rock band that same year, playing in Paul Rodgers's band for a Muddy Waters tribute album, and finally joining Guns N' Roses guitarist Slash at the 1994 Woodstock festival in the States. In 2010 Jason started his own ongoing touring group, re-creating his father's greatest hits with the show Led Zeppelin Evening, as well as joining Sammy Hagar's super-group the Circle in 2014 and, in 2016, became an ongoing member of the rock group Black Country Communion. Many times, Jason would be joined onstage by younger sister Zoë, who followed the family lineage as a singer-songwriter in her own right.

Like his father before him, Jason Bonham had become the consummate in-demand rock 'n' roll drummer.

* * *

FOREVER PROUD OF HIS SONS, JACKO BONHAM DIED OF NATURAL causes at Old Hyde in 1989, his funeral held in the same church that hosted his oldest son's service only nine years earlier. Years later, Mick Bonham recalled that his father "had never gotten over" John's premature death and that their mother, Joan, never did either. After a long career as a popular DJ in the United Kingdom, Michael "Mick" Bonham suffered a fatal heart attack on January 14, 2000. He was only forty-nine years old. At the time, Mick had been working on a memoir focusing on his memories of John, which his wife, Lin, published posthumously.

As the last member of the Bonham family standing, Joan Isobel did her sons and former husband proud in her twilight years, becoming a singer in a novelty rock 'n' roll band of her own, the Zimmers, a group formed of senior citizens by the BBC for a documentary about the United Kingdom's treatment of the elderly. Popular as the band was, Joan was part of their album, *Lust for Life*, which was released in 2008. She died in 2011 at the age of eighty-one.

* * *

OF ALL THE MEMBERS OF LED ZEPPELIN, ROBERT PLANT'S SOLO CA-reer was arguably the most successful, leading to years of critically acclaimed albums with numerous new bands. Jimmy, as the band's original producer and retainer of the master tracks, oversaw the releases of the later compilation *Led Zeppelin: BBC Sessions* in 1997, the live album *How the West Was Won* and the home-video release *Led Zeppelin DVD* both in 2003, and years' worth of remasters and rereleases; however, his personal career peaked with Zeppelin's heyday.

John Paul Jones's highest-profile post-Zeppelin project came along in 2009 with a one-shot supergroup of his design: Them Crooked Vultures. As the band's elder statesman of rock, Jones oversaw a lineup of younger bandmates, all admitted Zeppelin acolytes: Dave Grohl of Nirvana and Foo Fighters fame and Queens of the Stone Age's Josh Homme. After nearly three decades, the band became Jones's biggest hit outside of Led Zeppelin.

As for the memory of John Henry Bonham—with the passage of time, the posthumous accolades only mounted.

It began with a heartfelt and cerebral percussion-ensemble piece of classical music by American composer Christopher Rouse in 1988. *Bonham*, as it was titled, was written to champion the drummer's "orchestral approach" to the instrument and opened with a drum ostinato, referencing such Zeppelin classics as "When the Levee Breaks," "Custard Pie," and "Royal Orleans" within its instrumental composition. Rouse, who would later go on to win the Grammy Award for Best Classical Composition and the Pulitzer Prize for Music, as well as eventually become the composer in residence for the New York Philharmonic in 2012, saw *Bonham* debut in Boston before national recognition upon its 1989 performance by the New England Conservatory of Music. When performing the piece, Rouse had advised his musicians to always use the fattest sticks possible.

In 2005 John came in first on *Classic Rock*'s list of the "50 Greatest Drummers in Rock," narrowly squeezing out friends Keith Moon and Ringo Starr, as well as early influences Ginger Baker and Mitch Mitchell. In 2007 *Stylus* magazine also ranked John as the number-one drummer in the same category. He was described by *Modern Drummer* magazine as "the greatest drummer in rock 'n' roll history," and the following year *Blabbermouth* named John as the rock musician that "rock fans want brought back to life," beating even Elvis Presley and

Jimi Hendrix in the hypothetical competition. John again topped the reader poll as greatest drummer in rock 'n' roll history in 2009, according to *Rhythm* magazine.

In 2016 Led Zeppelin's oldest media nemesis, *Rolling Stone*, named John as the greatest drummer of all time out of a list of one hundred candidates.

And while rock 'n' roll fans may have voted John as the artist they would most want to see rise from the grave and return to the world of music, his legacy and discography nonetheless continued well into the decades that followed his death. As music changed drastically following Led Zeppelin's demise, the hip-hop genre found John's lush, booming, bass-driven patterns sampled in new songs more than any other musician; the Beastie Boys used John's drums on three songs on their 1986 debut, *Licensed to Ill*, alone; German group Enigma likewise used "When the Levee Breaks" within their global hit "Return to Innocence"; in 1988 artist Schoolly D used "Kashmir" in the song "Signifying Rapper," incurring the legal wrath of Jimmy Page and Robert Plant; and Jimmy even joined rapper Sean "P. Diddy" Combs in a duet titled "Come with Me," which also drew heavily from "Kashmir."

Over the past half century, the sound of John Bonham's syncopated thunder and patterns of his reign have been inescapable.

"The diehards just didn't get it and, to a certain extent, never did," recalled Jon Hiseman, who had replaced Ginger Baker in the Graham Bond Organisation and later joined John Mayall's Bluesbreakers. "But the blues-rock musos I knew were all great fans of Led Zeppelin and John's big, open sound."

"Behind his almost brutish and chaotic appearance, he was an endearing man," remembered Black Sabbath's Bill Ward. "Studious and a hopelessly caught-up-in-drums-and-drummers man. . . . His knowledge of drumming was overflowing, [and] this was the Bonham I knew."

"You heard monstrous things that Bonzo had done, just abusing people and stuff like that," Dave Pegg later recalled. "Personally, when I knew John, I never saw that side of him. He was always a real gentleman and would go out of his way to help people."

Lifelong friend and partner in crime Carmine Appice would continue to sing John's praises for decades. "John was new and fresh, with plenty of aggression and energy. . . . He had great hands, feet, and feel."

In a contemporary setting, generations of rock drummers continue to cite John Bonham as their ultimate inspiration and, in effect, a force responsible for the changing sounds of rock 'n' roll itself. "Bonzo's sound came from a combination of brute power, subtle finesse, and impeccable groove," stated Dream Theater's Mike Portnoy. "John Bonham is the only one who could ever truly sound like John Bonham. That sound was him—not necessarily his drums."

Devoted John Bonham disciple Dave Grohl spent his decades-spanning career as the drummer of Nirvana and mastermind of the Foo Fighters being, perhaps, the most vocal of all high-profile fans. "John Bonham is the greatest rock drummer of all time," Grohl declared. "Bonham played directly from the heart. . . . When he hit a groove, it was so deep it was like a heartbeat [and] had the ultimate feel. He could swing, he could get on top, or he could pull back."

Grohl added, "I don't know anyone who thinks there's a better rock drummer than John Bonham—it's undeniable!"

The Police's Stewart Copeland also weighed in on John's influence, stating, "John Bonham—the mountain! [He] had one tom-tom in front of him that shattered the earth when it spoke, one tom-tom to his right that thundered to the cosmos, and he would absolutely move the earth off its axis with one snare-drum hit! . . . He was the holy grail of drummers."

⁂ ⁂ ⁂

To forever mark the place when the thunder and lightning first struck, John's birthplace at 84 Birchfield Road, in Headless Cross, Redditch, was bestowed with a blue plaque, signifying its cultural and historical significance. On what would have been John Bonham's seventieth birthday, May 31, 2018, a statue was unveiled in Mercian Square in Redditch. It was a consummate likeness of John at his drum kit: an image of John knocking at his timpani drums on his birthday at the LA Forum in 1973, meticulously replicated by sculptor Mark Richards, immortalizing the drummer in his most famous pose—now in nearly three tons of bronze. The memorial is emblazoned with these words: "The most outstanding and original drummer of his time, John Bonham's popularity and influence continue to resonate with the world of music and beyond." Every year in Birmingham, fans gather at the statue during the week of John's birth for a music festival in his honor.

※ ※ ※

IT ISN'T EASY FOR AN OUTSIDER TO FIND THE GRAVE, AND THAT'S THE way the insiders have willed it.

A headstone rises out of the earth. It is perpetually adorned with oversize hickory sticks stabbed into the soil around it, and miniature drawings of three interlocking rings pepper the stone. These are the symbols left behind by the few pilgrims, the most devoted outsiders, who found their way to the small Rushock Parish graveyard of St. Michael's Church.

"Cherished memories of a loving husband and father, John
Henry Bonham, who died Sept. 25th, 1980, aged 32 . . .
He will always be remembered in our hearts.
Goodnight my Love, God Bless."

Under the trees, under the sky—there is silence there.

The thunder has passed and smoke has cleared. There, the harbinger of the storm and earthly elements is now at rest—a golem molded of primal rhythm and of sound itself, now returned to clay.

A god of fire has smoldered, and his fire has turned to ash.

ACKNOWLEDGMENTS

While John Bonham may be remembered interchangeably as one of the greatest drummers, if not the greatest, in rock 'n' roll history, as well as what at least one 1980 obituary labeled him, "the ultimate room destroyer," it was the stories of his love of his family, his Birmingham roots—demonstrated in his overtly generous acts of charity—and lifelong devotion to his craft that gave my research and personal revelations true weight.

And so it is with the deepest and greatest respect that I offer the final product to the family John so deeply cherished—his wife, Pat; children, Jason and Zoë; and siblings, Deborah and the late Michael "Mick" Bonham—all of whom have spent the decades since John's untimely death ensuring that his legacy remains endless.

I owe a massive debt of gratitude to the following people for their invaluable time and efforts, crucial advice and leads, and shared anecdotes and personal memories: Garry Allcock, Stephen Averill, Bev Bevan, Chris Charlesworth, Stewart Copeland, Cameron Crowe, Danny Goldberg, Anthony Green, David Hadley, Mark Kiel, Dave Pegg, Neal Preston, Dina Regine, Ellen Sander, Jim Simpson, and Chris Welch. A very special note of thanks to four Led Zeppelin biographers who have, individually, been sources of inspiration, as they are among the very best music journalists working today and all of whom provided context and consultation while I went about my own efforts: Mark Blake, Barney Hoskyns, Paul Rees, and Chris Salewicz—gentlemen and rock stars all.

As with my previous book, I would like to thank my late mother, Linda Kushins, who instilled a love of reading, art, and spirituality, and to my father, Eric Kushins, for encouragement and a lifetime of music; also, my brothers, Sean and Brandon, and sister, Leyla; my nieces, Sera and Kylah; and my second families, Aunt Deedee and Uncle Bill, Megan, Michael and Stephanie, and their little Ava Jo Maggi; and Aunt Robin and Uncle Joe, Joseph, Molly, and Edward. This book could not have been written without the love and patience of Kristine and canine son, Jackson Browne Villa, as well as her parents, George and Marilene Villa, and siblings, Kevin, Chynna, and Pio. In my life, there have been two rock stars who have acted as my greatest defenders and champions, and it is my distinct honor always to present completed work to my agent and friend, the irreplaceable William Clark, and editor of my dreams, Ben Schafer. I can't thank Hachette Book Group and Da Capo Press enough for their faith and belief in my projects as well. A very major thanks to Carrie Napolitano, who was amazing to work with, as well as Amber Morris, John Pelosi, and Annette Wenda for all their hard work and advocacy.

To my closest friends and bandmates—Allen Boulos, Ben Owens, Dan Leo, Derek Muro, James Heinz, Ric Chavez, Joshua Diolosa, Ricky Cardoza, Robert Edwin Currie, Tom Rizzuto—and to so many in my personal village who have inspired, aided, and abetted: Kevin Avery, Scott M. Burnstein, Rick Canny, Rich Clark, Doug Collette, Anita Gevinson, Arlene Marie Giudice, Max Greenspan, George Gruel, Jeff Guinn, Raymond Harrington, Eugene Hunt, Gabino Iglesias, Gregg Jakobson, Malcolm Jones, Jon Langmead, Tommy Lee, Tom Lehmann, Art Lyzak, Brian MacDonald, Lou Mavroudis, Jay McInerney, Parrish McKittrick, Mauricio Meleiro, Neil Nathan, Russell Papia, Ryan Rayston, Barry Richards, John Silva, Charlie Silvestri,

Gary Snyder, Gregg Sutter, Carrie Thornton, Neil VanEerde, Cathy Vu, Ross Warner, Mark Watts, Mikhal Weiner, Patrick Zaw, and Jordan Zevon.

Much of this book was written during a period of personal reflection and study at the historic Nyingma Institute in Berkeley, California, and I am indebted to many there who inspired me through their friendship and ideas: Michelle Groy, Cas Verde, Pauline Yu, Deans Pema Gellek and Lama Palzang, Sangjin Park, Clay Smith, Angelo, Chase, Sophia, Eddie, Tony, and Rhonda. At the University of South Carolina, particularly the Irvin Department of Rare Books and Special Collections, I owe a debt of gratitude to Tom McNally, Robert P. Smith, and Elizabeth Sudduth—all of whom spend their days and nights curating the works of America's greatest writers for the posterity of history; they are heroes to me as much as the authors whose works they protect.

Two of the most influential artists of my youth passed during the writing of this book, both supernovas within their own orbits, and to whom I've often looked as reminders of innovation and excellence: Nick Tosches and Edward Van Halen—thank you both for bringing the ever-needed light and shade. And to the departed heroes who instilled in me a love of words and a continued endurance for personal best: Elmore "Dutch" Leonard and Warren Zevon. To crib from the latter, they invented my job.

It is with distinct honor that one of my own personal heroes offered his time and energy to contribute, quite selflessly, as a most esteemed "opening act" within this volume of John Bonham's life story: the incredible Dave Grohl, whose Foreword to this work demonstrates not only his own profound love of John Bonham, but the far-reaching influence that Bonham's life and legacy continue to have on each new generation of rock 'n' roll—and that the inspiration of music never dies . . .

I am eternally grateful to all.

THE BANDS OF JOHN BONHAM

The Blue Star Trio

Terry Webb and the Spiders

The Senators (recorded "She's a Mod")

The Nicky James Movement

Locomotive

Pat Wayne and the Beachcombers

Steve Brett and the Mavericks

Danny King and the Mayfair Set

A Way of Life

The Crawling King Snakes (with Robert Plant)

A Way of Life (again)

Band of Joy (with Robert Plant)

Tim Rose

The New Yardbirds / Led Zeppelin

SELECTED DISCOGRAPHY

12" ALBUMS

Various Artists, *Brum Beat*, Dial, 1964.

Recorded at Hollick & Taylor Studios, Birmingham, UK, 1964; released February 1, 1964.

Led Zeppelin, *Led Zeppelin*, Atlantic, 1969.

Recorded at Olympic Studios, London, September–October 1968; released January 12, 1969.

Led Zeppelin, *Led Zeppelin II*, Atlantic, 1969.

Recorded at A&M Studios, Quantum Studios, Mirror Sound, and Mystic Studios, Los Angeles; A&R Studios, Juggy Sound, Groove, and Mayfair Studios, New York City; Ardent Studios, Memphis; and Olympic and Morgan Studios, London; additional recordings in Vancouver, 1969; released October 22, 1969.

The Family Dogg, *A Way of Life*, Bell Records, 1969.

Recorded at Chappell Studios, IBC Studios, and Landsdowne Studios, London, April–May 1969; released November 1, 1969.

Screaming Lord Sutch, *Lord Sutch and Heavy Friends*, Cotillion Records, 1970.

Recorded at Mystic Studios, Hollywood, May–September 1969; released May 25, 1970.

Led Zeppelin, *Led Zeppelin III*, Atlantic, 1970.

Recorded at Island Studios, Olympic Studios, London; Rolling Stones Mobile Studio, Headley Grange, Hampshire; November 1969– August 1970; released October 5, 1970.

Led Zeppelin, *Untitled (Led Zeppelin IV)*, Atlantic, 1971.

Recorded at Island Studios, London; Rolling Stones Mobile Studio, Headley Grange, Hampshire; December 1970–February 1971, July 1971; mixed July 1971; released November 8, 1971.

Led Zeppelin, *Houses of the Holy*, Atlantic, 1973.

Recorded at Island Studios, London; Rolling Stones Mobile Studio, Stargroves and Headley Grange, Hampshire; December 1971– August 1972; released March 28, 1973.

Led Zeppelin, *Physical Graffiti*, Swan Song, 1975.

Recorded at multiple studios, UK, July and December 1970, January– March 1971, May 1972, January–February 1974; released February 24, 1975.

Maggie Bell, *Suicide Sal*, Swan Song, 1975.

Recorded at Startling Studios, Ascot, UK, 1974; released March 15, 1975.

Led Zeppelin, *Presence*, Swan Song, 1976.

Recorded at Musicland Studios, Munich, West Germany, November– December 1975; released March 31, 1976.

Led Zeppelin, *The Song Remains the Same*, Swan Song, 1976.

Recorded live at Madison Square Garden, New York City, July 27–29, 1973; released October 22, 1976.

Wings, *Back to the Egg*, Parlophone, 1979.

Recorded at Abbey Road Studios and Replica Studio, London; Lympne Castle, Kent; and Spirit of Ranachan Studios, Campbeltown, June 1978–February 1979; released June 8, 1979.

Roy Wood, *On the Road Again*, Warner Bros. Records, 1979.

Recorded at AIR Studios and DJM Studios, London; Lea Sound Studios, Pelsall; Music Centre, Wembley; and Rockfield Studios, Monmouthshire, 1978; released August 1979.

Led Zeppelin, *In Through the Out Door*, Swan Song, 1979.

Recorded at Polar Studios, Stockholm, Sweden, November–December, 1978; released August 15, 1979.

Led Zeppelin, *Coda*, Swan Song, 1982.

Recorded at Sol Studios, Cookham, Berkshire, England, January 9, 1970–November 21, 1978; overdubs recorded 1982; released November 19, 1982.

Led Zeppelin, *BBC Sessions*, Atlantic, 1997.

Recorded live at various venues, London, March and June 1969, April 1, 1971; released November 11, 1997.

Led Zeppelin, *How the West Was Won*, Atlantic, 2003.

Recorded live at the LA Forum, Los Angeles, June 25, 1972, and the Long Beach Arena, Los Angeles, June 27, 1972; released May 27, 2003.

45 RPM SINGLES

(NOTE: Led Zeppelin singles are for US releases only)

"She's a Mod" / "Lot About You" (The Senators) (1964)

DSP 7001

"Good Times Bad Times" / "Communication Breakdown" (Led Zeppelin) (1969)

Atlantic 45-2613

"A Way of Life" / "Throw It Away" (The Family Dogg) (1969)

BLL 1055

"Arizona" / "The House in the Heather" (The Family Dogg) (1969)

BLL 1077

"Whole Lotta Love" / "Living Loving Maid (She's Just a Woman)" (Led Zeppelin) (1969)

Atlantic 45-2690

"Immigrant Song" / "Hey, Hey, What Can I Do" (Led Zeppelin) (1970)

Atlantic 45-2777

"Everybody Clap" / "After the Feeling Is Gone" (Lulu) (1971)

Atlantic/Polydor 2091-083

"Black Dog" / "Misty Mountain Hop" (Led Zeppelin) (1971)

Atlantic 45-2849

"Rock and Roll" / "Four Sticks" (Led Zeppelin) (1972)

Atlantic 45-2865

"Over the Hills and Far Away" / "Dancing Days" (Led Zeppelin) (1973)

Atlantic 45-2970

"D'yer Mak'er" / "The Crunge" (Led Zeppelin) (1973)

Atlantic 45-2986

"Trampled Under Foot" / "Black Country Woman" (Led Zeppelin) (1975)

Swan Song

SS70102

"Candy Store Rock" / "Royal Orleans" (Led Zeppelin) (1976)

Swan Song

SS70110

"Keep Your Hands on the Wheel (Said Marie to the Driver)" / "Giant Footsteps" (Roy Wood) (1978)

Warner Bros. K17248

"Rockestra Theme" / "Old Siam, Sir" (Wings) (1979)

Parlophone 1A 006-63366

"Fool in the Rain" / "Hot Dog" (Led Zeppelin) (1979)

Swan Song

SS71003

SOURCES

ARTICLES

Alterman, Loraine. "Led Zeppelin: Swan Song Is a Beginning." *Rolling Stone*, June 20, 1974.

Arenschield, Steve. "Led Zeppelin in Concert—Novelty, Poignancy, and Holocaust." *Greensboro (NC) Chronicle*, February 5, 1975.

Armstrong, Don. "The Roots of Rock Music Instrumentation in Jazz." *Music Journalism History*, March 22, 2019.

Atkinson, Rick. "Zeppelin Still Tops." *New York Times*, August 1, 1973.

Beech, Mark. "When Led Zep Met the Damned: Punk's Roxy Celebrated After 40 Years." *DanteMag.com*, June 23, 2017.

Black, Johnny. "Screaming Lord Sutch: Loony Institution." *MOJO*, August 1999.

Blanchard, Wayne. "Bonham: From the Perspective of His Peers." *Drum! Magazine*, May 23, 2012.

Brack, Ray. "Led Zeppelin Fans Sour Out of Sight . . . Together." *Charleston (SC) News*, April 3, 1970.

Brown, Mick. "Led Zeppelin: Zeppelin Drummer Found Dead." *Guardian*, September 26, 1980.

Calta, Louis. "Led Zeppelin Ticket Sales Stir Crowds and Disorder." *New York Times*, January 8, 1975.

Charlesworth, Chris. "Bad Company: Led Zep Join the Company." *Melody Maker*, May 29, 1976.

———. "Led Zeppelin: Whole Lotta Zeppelin!" *Melody Maker*, February 1, 1975.

———. "Review: Led Zeppelin." *Melody Maker*, January 1, 1973.

Chong, Florence. "The Likeable Boys." *Hong Kong Standard*, October 8, 1972.

"Confident, but Oh So Brash and Brutal." *Hong Kong Standard*, October 8, 1972.

"Cops Move in—and Zeppelin Walk Off to Stop a 'Police Riot.'" *Disc and Music Echo*, April 18, 1970.

"Coroner Rules Bonham Death an Accident." United Press International, October 7, 1980.

Crites, Michael. "The Apex of Rock and Roll Attendance." *Watcher*, May 21–27, 1973.

Crouse, Timothy. "First There Was the Hindenburg . . ." *Boston Herald*, September 15, 1970.

Crowe, Cameron. "The Durable Led Zeppelin: A Conversation with Jimmy Page and Robert Plant." *Rolling Stone*, March 13, 1975.

———. "Led Zep Conquers States, 'Beast' Prowls to the Din of Hordes." *Rolling Stone*, May 22, 1975.

———. "Led Zep Won't Stop Touring." *Circus*, November 1973.

———. "Zeppelin Alchemy: Transmuting." *Los Angeles Times*, October 7, 1973.

———. "Zeppelin Rising . . . Slowly." *Rolling Stone*, August 12, 1976.

———. "Zeppelin's *Presence*: Secrets of the Object Concealed." *Rolling Stone*, June 3, 1976.

Demorest, Stephen. "Maggie Bell, Led Zeppelin: Led Zeppelin Erect a Kingdom." *Circus*, March 1974.

Dennis, Felix. "Led Zeppelin: *Led Zeppelin*." *Oz*, March 1969.

Dunkin, Zach. "Led Zeppelin Gives 10,000 a Big Night." *Indianapolis Times*, April 5, 1970.

Elwood, Philip. "Led Zeppelin Zooms High at Kezar." *San Francisco Examiner*, June 3, 1973.

Ganin, Brian "Rat." "Zeppelin at the Garden." *Load*, February 7, 1975.

"Giving Out That Old Group Therapy." *Birmingham Observer*, January 8, 1970.

Gray, Bill. "Zeppelin Soars with 'Neon' Rock." *Detroit News*, February 1, 1975.

Grow, Kory. "The Damned Talk 40 Years of Shapeshifting Punk." *Rolling Stone*, April 14, 2017.

Hafferkamp, Jack. "Led Zeppelin a Downer." *Chicago Daily Herald*, September 6, 1971.

———. "Zeppelin: Nobility of British Kink." *Chicago Daily News*, July 9, 1973.

Hall, James. "Led Zeppelin's 'Wounded Pit Bull': The Terrifying, Tragic Talent of John Bonham." *Telegraph*, July 7, 2020.

Hall, Russell. "John Bonham Once Threatened to Beat Up Sting." *Gibson.com*, January 24, 2011.

Henderson, B., and C. Yarbrough. "Stadium Rocks: Led Zeppelin Plays to 50,000." *Atlanta Constitution*, May 5, 1973.

Herbst, Peter. "Zeppelin Fans the Real Show." *Boston Herald American*, July 23, 1973.

Hilburn, Robert. "Case For and Against Led Zeppelin." *Los Angeles Times*, June 1, 1973.

Hill, R. J. "Crowd Doesn't Hamper Zeppelin's Good Sounds." *Spectrum*, June 11, 1972.

Hollingworth, Roy. "Peter Grant Shuns MSG." *Melody Maker*, June 15, 1972.

Holloway, Danny. "Zeppelin." *NME*, June 26, 1972.

Hoskyns, Barney. "Let's Get Physical: The Story of Led Zeppelin's *Physical Graffiti*." *Classic Rock*, September 2010.

Houghton, Mike. "Led Zeppelin: Interview with Jimmy Page." *Sounds*, July 10, 1976.

Hughes, Mike. "The Led Zeppelin: My! My!—Groovy." *Memphis Press-Scimitar*, April 18, 1970.

Ingham, John. "Led Zeppelin: *The Song Remains the Same*." *Sounds*, October 16, 1976.

Jahn, Mike. "Led Zeppelin: Madison Square Garden, New York." *New York Times*, September 21, 1970.

———. "Led Zeppelin Brings Driving Style Here." *New York Times*, September 21, 1970.

Kent, Nick. "Jeff Beck: Beck Looks Back." *NME*, October 28, 1972.

———. "Jimmy Page: Shy Rock Star Almost Unburdens Himself." *Creem*, April 1977.

Klein, John. "Led Zeppelin Concert Wows Cleveland Crowd." *Chronicle Telegram*, August 27, 1970.

Kubernick, Harvey, and Justin Pierce. "Stairway to Heaven." *Melody Maker*, March 28, 1975.

La Rose, Phil. "Zeppelin Decibel Rate Deafening." *Advocate*, February 29, 1975.

Laurence, Robert P. "Led Zeppelin Puts Extra Roll in Its Rock." *San Diego Union*, June 20, 1977.

Laycock, John. "Zeppelin Are Sexy." *Windsor Star*, February 1, 1975.

"Led Zeppelin: Led Zeppelin." *Melody Maker*, March 29, 1969.

"Led Zeppelin: Led Zeppelin." *Record Mirror*, April 12, 1969.

"Led Zeppelin: Review." *Record Mirror*, January 10, 1970.

"Led Zeppelin: Review." *Variety*, September 4, 1971.

"Led Zeppelin at the Odeon." *Birmingham Post*, December 17, 1972.

"Led Zeppelin Breaks Attendance Record as Well as an Old Barrier of Silence." Associated Press, May 6, 1973.

"Led Zeppelin Drummer John Bonham Found Dead at London Home." Associated Press, September 26, 1980.

"Led Zeppelin Shows Distinctive Style." *Baltimore Sun*, June 12, 1972.

"Led Zeppelin Tour: Great Expectations." *Rolling Stone*, May 24, 1973.

"Led Zeppelin Wraps Up U.S. Tour with Record Gates and $4-Million Gross." *Variety*, August 1, 1973.

Lloyd, Jack. "Good, Bad Mixed by Led Zeppelin." *Philadelphia Inquirer*, June 14, 1972.

Loder, Kurt. "John Bonham, Ultimate Room Destroyer: 1948–1980." *Rolling Stone*, October 30, 1980.

MacCluskey, Thomas. "Led Zeppelin Has Arrived." *Rocky Mountain News*, March 26, 1970.

———. "'Rock' Concert Is Real Groovy." *Rocky Mountain News*, December 28, 1968.

MacDonald, Patrick. "Led Zeppelin—Rock as Extravaganza." *Seattle Times*, July 18, 1973.

Makowski, Pete. "Led Zeppelin: Earls Court, London." *Sounds*, May 24, 1975.

"Massive Tour for Zeppelin." *Record Mirror*, January 3, 1973.

McKee, Margaret. "A Zeppelin That Didn't Go Down." *Memphis Press-Scimitar*, April 17, 1970.

Melichar, Jill. "Heavy Hung over Led Zeppelin Show." *Houston Chronicle*, March 30, 1970.

Mendelsohn, John. "Led Zeppelin: *Led Zeppelin*." *Rolling Stone*, March 15, 1969.

———. "Led Zeppelin: *Led Zeppelin II*." *Rolling Stone*, December 13, 1969.

———. "Led Zeppelin Plays for Forum Audience." *Los Angeles Times*, September 7, 1970.

"*MM* Pollwinners Rock the Party of 1970." *Melody Maker*, September 26, 1970.

Morley, Paul. "Ghosts of Progressive Rock Past: Led Zeppelin at Knebworth." *NME*, August 11, 1979.

Morton, James. "John Bonham in Retrospect." *Modern Drummer*, February–March 1981.

Murray, Charles Shaar. "But Can They Kiss You Goodnight?" *NME*, May 24, 1975.

———. "Led Zeppelin: Zeppin' Out." *NME*, June 16, 1973.

Nash, Robert. "Led Zeppelin Breaks One Record Too Many." *Record World*, August 11, 1973.

Natelli, John. "10 Ways to Sound Like John Bonham." *Drum! Magazine*, January 9, 2013.

Nicholson, M. "Zeps Slap Hub with Plenty of Inertia." *Boston Globe*, July 23, 1973.

Norcross, Rick. "Led Zeppelin No Lead Balloon in Tampa." *Tampa Bay Times*, May 6, 1973.

Oppel, Pete. "Led Zeppelin Exceeds Limits of Endurance." *Dallas News*, April 2, 1977.

Osgood, Charles. "The Grateful Led: A Tale of a Lark." *Chicago Tribune*, April 11, 1977.

Peacock, Steve. "John Bonham in the Talkin'." *Sounds*, July 27, 1974.

Power, N. "Zeppelin Fever." *Dublin New Spotlight*, March 7, 1971.

Raba, Tony. "Led Zeppelin and the Lovely Strangled Cat Sound." *Express and Star*, January 8, 1970.

Radel, Cliff. "Zeppelin Justifies 29-Hour Wait." *Cincinnati Enquirer*, April 22, 1977.

Read, Bill. "Review: Led Zeppelin." *River City Review*, May 5, 1973.

Reschke, Andrew. "Britain Rock Music Kings Heralded." *Syracuse Journal*, September 11, 1971.

Richmond, Dick. "Unusual, Maddening Performance by the Led Zeppelin at Arena." *St. Louis Post-Dispatch*, May 12, 1973.

Robbins, Dennis. "Led Zeppelin: Review." *University of Southampton-Wessex Scene*, March 12, 1971.

Robinson, Lisa. "Stairway to Excess." *Vanity Fair*, February 18, 2014.

———. "Stairway to Excess." *Vanity Fair*, May 13, 2017.

"Rock Drummer Died After Drinking 40 Measures of Vodka." *Guardian*, October 8, 1980.

Rose, Cynthia. "Led Zeppelin: Bonzo's Last Bash—Is It the End for Zeppelin Too?" *NME*, October 4, 1980.

Rosen, Steven. "Jimmy Page." *Guitar Player*, July 1977.

———. "Led Zeppelin: Chris Huston, Eddie Kramer's Co-engineer on *Led Zeppelin II*." *Guitar World*, July 1986.

———. "Led Zeppelin: Danny Goldberg's Hideaway." *Guitar World*, July 1986.

———. "Steel Driven Led." *Phonograph*, June 1, 1973.

Rudis, Al. "Everything You Always Wanted to Know About Led Zeppelin." *Chicago Sunday Sun-Times*, June 1, 1973.

Rukeyser, Louis. "A Night with Led Zeppelin." *Delta Times*, June 14, 1977.

Salewicz, Chris. "Led Zeppelin." *Let It Rock*, May 1975.

———. "Led Zeppelin: Smiling Men with Bad Reputations." *NME*, August 4, 1979.

Saunders, Metal Mike. "Led Zeppelin: *Houses of the Holy*." *Phonograph Record*, May 1973.

Schulps, Dave. "Jimmy Page: The Trouser Press Interview." *Trouser Press*, October 1977.

Scott, Robert. "Led Zeppelin Metal Destroys Indianapolis." *Indianapolis Star*, January 26, 1975.

"Screaming Lord Sutch." *Beat Instrumental*, June 1970.

Sherman, Bill. "Rock Band Led Zeppelin Is Fire of Supergroups." *Times-Picayune/New Orleans Advocate*, May 15, 1973.

Siefring, Ana. "Led Zeppelin 'Turns On' for Crowd at Coliseum." *Newport News (VA) Daily Press*, August 16, 1970.

Simson, Maxine. "Led Zeppelin Plays at Boston Garden." *Boston Herald*, September 8, 1971.

Sloan, Jordan Taylor. "Science Shows How Drummers' Brains Are Actually Different Than Everyone Else's." *Mic Magazine*, May 14, 2014.

Starr, Michelle. "Acoustic Levitation Is Science Wizardry at Its Best." *cNet*, September 16, 2012.

Strong, Keith. "Zeppelin Descends on the City Hall." *Sheffield Star*, January 3, 1973.

Sullivan, Colleen. "Coliseum Plays This One Safe." *Newsday*, June 15, 1972.

Sutcliffe, Phil. "Getting It Together at Bron-Yr-Aur: The Story of *Led Zeppelin III*." *MOJO*, April 2000.

Taylor, Peter Joseph. "A Redditch Childhood, 1937–46." *WW2 People's War*, BBC, September 5, 2005.

Telford, Raymond. "Led Zeppelin: Review." *Melody Maker*, January 10, 1970.

Terebelo, Sheri. "The Big Time Rock of Led Zeppelin." *Fifth Estate*, February 12–19, 1975.

Tobler, John. "Jimmy Page: The Life and Times of a Guitar Prophet." *Musician*, January 1984.

Upton, Pat. "Hit-Packed Zeppelin Throbs at Myriad." *Daily Oklahoman*, April 4, 1977.

Van Matre, Lynn, and William S. Welt. "The Band That Beat the Beatles." *Miami Herald*, July 29, 1973.

Wang, K. S. "A VelociRaptor, Ferrari, and Range Rover Share Jason Bonham's Incredible Garage." *Motor Trend*, August 16, 2019.

Wasserman, John. "Before and After with Led Zeppelin." *San Francisco Chronicle*, September 14, 1971.

Welch, Chris. "Beck, Bogert and Appice: Heavyweight Champions of the World." *Melody Maker*, September 29, 1973.

———. "Hard and Fast: John Bonham's Dark Road Down." *Louder*, September 25, 2005.

———. "Ireland Unites Under Zeppelin." *Melody Maker*, March 6, 1971.

———. "Led Zeppelin: Carnegie Hall, New York." *Melody Maker*, October 25, 1969.

———. "Led Zeppelin: John Bonham, Over the Hills and Far Away." *Melody Maker*, June 21, 1975.

———. "Led Zeppelin: *Led Zeppelin III*." *Melody Maker*, October 10, 1970.

———. "Led Zeppelin: Page on *Zeppelin III*." *Melody Maker*, October 24, 1970.

———. "Led Zeppelin: *Presence*." *Melody Maker*, April 10, 1976.

———. "Led Zeppelin: Sounds Like Another Platinum!" *Melody Maker*, June 6, 1970.

———. "The Yardbirds: Only Jimmy Left to Form the New Yardbirds." *Melody Maker*, October 12, 1968.

Welch, Chris, with Andy Doerschuk, Jon Cohan, Jared Cobb, and Karen Stackpole. "City Man, Country Boy: The John Bonham Story." *Traps*, Autumn 2007.

Wendeborn, John. "Zeppelin Spews Musical Energy." *Oregonian*, March 18, 1975.

Whitall, Susan. "Led Zeppelin: A Psychobiograph." *Creem*, February 1979.

Williams, Mark. "Plant." *International Times*, April 11, 1969.

Williams, Richard. "Robert Plant: Down to the Roots." *Melody Maker*, September 12, 1970.

Wittet, T. Bruce. "John Bonham." *Modern Drummer*, July 1984.

Worthington, J. "Zeppelin Concert a Golden Memory for All." *Greensboro (NC) News and Record*, February 1, 1975.

Wright, Ian. "The Cars of Led Zeppelin Legend John Bonham." *6Speed online.com*, March 26, 2018.

Wuntch, Philip. "Led Zeppelin Hasn't Bombed Yet." *Dallas After Dark*, August 25, 1971.

"Yardbirds to Make Changes." *Billboard*, June 29, 1968.

"A Zeppelin Hits the City Hall." *Sheffield Star*, January 17, 1970.

"Zuper Zeppelin." *Edinburgh Press*, January 10, 1970.

BOOKS

Appice, Carmine. *Stick It! My Life of Sex, Drums, and Rock 'n' Roll*. Chicago Review Press, 2018.

Bonham, Mick. *John Bonham: The Powerhouse Behind Led Zeppelin*. Southbank, 2005.

Bradford, Anne. *The Haunted Midlands*. Hunt End Books, 2006.

———. *Old Redditch Voices*. Hunt End Books, 2005.

Bradford, Anne, and Barrie Roberts. *Midland Ghosts and Hauntings*. Quercus, 1994.

———. *Midland Spirits and Spectres*. Walkways/Quercus, 1998.

Childress, David Hatcher. *Anti-gravity and the World Grid*. Adventures Unlimited Press, 1987.

Cole, Richard. *Stairway to Heaven: Led Zeppelin Uncensored*. It Books, 2002.

Davis, Stephen. *Hammer of the Gods: The Led Zeppelin Saga*. It Books, 2008.

Evans-Wentz, W. Y. *The Tibetan Book of the Dead; or, The After-Death Experiences on the Bardo Plane, According to Lama Kazi Dawa-Samdup's English Rendering*. Oxford University Press, 2000.

Fremantle, Francesca, and Chögyam Trungpa. *The Tibetan Book of the Dead: The Great Liberation Through Hearing in the Bardo by Guru Rinpoche According to Karma Lingpa*. Shambhala, 1975.

Hoskyns, Barney. *Led Zeppelin: The Oral History of the World's Greatest Rock Band*. Wiley Books, 2012.

Minahan, John. *The Torment of Buddy Rich*. iUniverse, 2000.

Popoff, Martin. *Led Zeppelin: All the Albums, All the Songs*. Voyageur Press, 2017.

———. *No Quarter: The Three Lives of Jimmy Page*. Omnibus Press, 2016.

Rees, Paul. *Robert Plant: A Life*. Dey Street Books, 2014.

Salewicz, Chris. *Jimmy Page: The Definitive Biography*. HarperCollins, 2018.

Shadwick, Keith. *Led Zeppelin: 1968–1980*. Backbeat Books, 2005.

Thompson, Dave. *Robert Plant: The Voice That Sailed the Zeppelin*. Backbeat Books, 2014.

Tolinski, Brad. *Light and Shade: Conversations with Jimmy Page*. Broadway Books, 2013.

Tormé, Mel. *Traps, the Drum Wonder: The Life of Buddy Rich*. Oxford University Press, 1991.

Wall, Mick. *When Giants Walked the Earth: A Biography of Led Zeppelin*. St. Martin's Griffin, 2010.

Welch, Chris. *Led Zeppelin: The Stories Behind Every Led Zeppelin Song*. Carlton Books, 2016.

Welch, Chris, and Geoff Nicholls. *John Bonham: A Thunder of Drums*. Backbeat Books, 2001.

MISCELLANEOUS

www.exploreredditch.org.uk
www.johnbonham.co.uk
www.johnbonhammemorial.com
www.ledzeppelin.com
www.redditchhistory.org.uk

INDEX